Breadlines Knee-Deep in Wheat

Breadlines Knee-Deep in Wheat

Food Assistance in the Great Depression

JANET POPPENDIECK

RUTGERS UNIVERSITY PRESS

New Brunswick, New Jersey

Manufactured in the United States of America

Library of Congress Cataloging in Publication Data

Poppendieck, Janet, 1945–
  Breadlines knee–deep in wheat.

  Bibliography: p.
  Includes index.
    1. Food relief—United States—History. 2. Depressions
—1929—United States. 3. Agriculture and state—United
States—History. I. Title.
HV696.F6P66   1986   363.8′83′0973   85–2175
ISBN 0–8135–1121–6

For my parents

Men who can graft the trees and make the seed fertile and big can find no way to let the hungry people eat their produce. Men who have created new fruits in the world cannot create a system whereby their fruits may be eaten. . . . The works of the roots of the vines, of the trees must be destroyed to keep up the price, and this is the saddest, bitterest thing of all. . . . A million people hungry, needing the fruit—and kerosene sprayed over the golden mountains.

There is a crime here that goes beyond denunciation. There is a sorrow here that weeping cannot symbolize. There is a failure here that topples all our success. The fertile earth, the straight tree rows, the sturdy trunks, and the ripe fruit. And children dying of pellagra must die because a profit cannot be taken from an orange. And coroners must fill in the certificate—died of malnutrition—because the food must rot, must be forced to rot.

John Steinbeck
The Grapes of Wrath

CONTENTS

ACKNOWLEDGMENTS

A great many people have contributed in one way and another to the creation of this book. I want to thank the members of my dissertation committee at the Florence Heller School, Brandeis University, especially my chairman, David Gil, for encouraging me to turn my dissertation into a book and for wise counsel and critical insights from the earliest phase of this project. Financial support and time for research and writing have been provided by the Professional Staff Congress–City University of New York Research Award Program and by a Scholar Incentive Award for which I am grateful to the City University, the Union, Hunter College, and to my colleagues in the Department of Sociology at Hunter College, particularly Alphonso Pinkney.

Like any student of history, I am grateful to the many patient librarians and archivists who helped me locate material for this study. In particular, librarians at the following institutions have proven unfailingly helpful and resourceful: the New York Public Library, the Columbia University Library, particularly the Oral History Collection, the Duke University Library, the Hunter College Library, the College of Staten Island Library, the Wagner College Library, the Yale University Library, the Franklin D. Roosevelt National Library, the Herbert Hoover Presidential Library, the University of Minnesota Social Welfare History Archive, the Library of Congress, and especially the National Archives and Records Service, an institution that is doing a remarkably fine job in the face of enormous constraints. I am particularly grateful to Richard Crawford and Jimmy Rush at the National Archives, to Dale C. Mayer at the Herbert Hoover

Presidential Library, and to Dave Klassen and the staff of the Social Welfare History Archive. I would like to express special thanks to Vivian Wiser and Gladys Baker of the Agricultural History Branch of the Economic Research Service, United States Department of Agriculture.

Several Hunter colleagues have read parts of the manuscript and commented helpfully; thanks to Ruth Sidel, Tobey Klass, Arlene McCord, and Carole Burstein. Jeremy Brecher and Jill Cutler read an early draft of this book and helped me to set my priorities in order; their questions were crucial in shaping the final product, and I am grateful. Similarly, I want to thank the anonymous readers supplied by Rutgers University Press at various stages of this process; their comments and questions and the obvious care and insight with which they read the manuscript proved remarkably useful. My editor, Kenneth Arnold, has been patient, flexible, and insightful throughout the process. I have tried to follow much of the advice I have been given; nevertheless, the errors that may remain in the book are my responsibility.

Many friends and members of my family have provided both moral support and more tangible aid. Thanks to Sara Evans, Harry Boyte, Vivian Nally, Carol Poppendieck, Trudie Prevatt, Dee and Arnold Unterbach, Susan Hanson, Kathy Goldman, and the staff and board of the Community Food Resource Center for consistent encouragement. Thanks to Cynthia Herbert Ramirez for careful and thoughtful assistance with the hard work of producing the manuscript. Thanks to Judy Sexton, Angie Aquino, and Caroline and Frank Sandull for providing the loving child care that made it possible for me to concentrate on this work. I am especially grateful to my parents, Robert and Gertrude Poppendieck, not only for their considerable inspiration and encouragement but also for their logistical support through the many episodes of research at the National Archives. Finally, I thank my husband, Woody Goldberg, for his unwavering support and his willingness to help in innumerable ways, his careful reading of the manuscript, and the perspective provided by his unfailing sense of humor, and our daughter Amanda who will, I hope, help to create a world in which there are no longer breadlines knee-deep in wheat.

INTRODUCTION

The Paradox of Want amid Plenty

"For the American farmer, 1932 was a year of singular misfortune," reported the *New York Times* on New Year's Day, 1933. Between January and mid December, average farm prices had fallen by more than 18 percent, following a drop of nearly 50 percent in the two previous years. Two days later, a more detailed report on farm prices predicted a continuation of the rock bottom levels: "The huge surpluses of leading agricultural products that have been accumulated during the last few years are expected generally to preclude more than a moderate recovery in prices in 1933, even if there should be a decided falling off in production." On the same day, according to another *Times* report, a leading New York social worker told a Senate committee that relief agencies were losing their battle to prevent starvation. "Deaths due to insufficient food have been reported in several cities," declared H. L. Lurie on behalf of the American Association of Social Workers, and he warned of possible violence by the unemployed if adequate relief measures were not taken.[1]

For many Americans, this juxtaposition of hunger and abundance had become a central symbol of the irrationality of the economic system. "A breadline knee-deep in wheat," noted commentator James Crowther, "is obviously the handiwork of foolish men."[2] While oranges were being soaked with kerosene to prevent their consumption in California, whole communities in Appalachia were living on dandelions and wild greens. Corn was so cheap that it was being burned for fuel in county courthouses in Iowa, but large numbers of cows, sheep, and horses were starving to death in the drought-stricken Northwest. Dairies were pouring unsaleable milk down the sewers, while unemployed parents longed to provide even a pint a week for their growing children. In February 1932, Oklahoma union activist and editor Oscar Ameringer painted a vivid picture of this troubling contrast for a congressional committee. He joined a parade of witnesses to describe what he had seen in an investigation of the condition of the unemployed that had taken him to more than twenty states in four months. He described miners in the Mississippi Valley "suffering from the lack of decent necessities of life, [while] food and raw materials were rotting or were destroyed by the millions of tons." He told of women searching for edible scraps in the refuse piles of the markets in Seattle and of wheatfields unharvested in Montana. He described apples rotting by the orchardful while "millions of children . . . , on account of the poverty of their parents, will not eat one apple this winter." He told of sheep raisers cutting the throats of their animals and leaving them for the buzzards because they could not afford to feed them and the freight to market was more than the animals would bring. "The farmers are being pauperized by the poverty of industrial populations and the industrial populations are being pauperized by the poverty of the farmers," he summarized. "Neither has the money to buy the product of the other, hence we have overproduction and underconsumption at the same time and in the same country."[3]

As the Depression matured, this contrast of overproduction and underconsumption was given a name. It was called "the paradox of want amid plenty" or "the paradox of scarcity and abundance" or simply "the paradox." "I shall speak," said Walter Lippmann in an address to the 1932 meeting of the National Conference of Social Work, "of the paradox at the heart of all this suffering—the sensational and the intolerable paradox of want in the midst of abundance, of poverty in the midst of plenty."[4] By the time the New Dealers began their efforts to address the anomalies of production and consumption, the term was in fairly common use. "The paradox of want in the midst of plenty was constantly on our minds as we proceeded with schemes like the emergency hog slaughter," wrote Secretary of Agriculture Henry Wallace in 1934.[5] "The Surplus Relief Corporation helped us in the Department of Agriculture to solve the paradox of want in the midst of plenty," Undersecretary of Agriculture Rexford Tugwell told the assembled social workers of the National Conference of Social Work two years after Lippmann addressed them.[6]

The paradox embraced other needs besides food and other abundance besides agriculture, but no manifestation was more troubling than the "breadline knee-deep in wheat." In any hierarchy of human need, food is among the most basic. Everyone must eat to live, and sensational news-paper accounts of Depression-induced starvation regularly reminded the public of this fact, while more systematic studies documented the impact of unemployment on diet and reported the increase of hospital admissions attributed to malnutrition. Not only the central necessity of food but also the visibility, and in many instances the visible waste, of the food that could have met the pressing need made the paradox of want amid plenty particularly troubling in the agricultural sector. The farmers' surpluses, piled up on railroad sidings or spilling from elevators, were far more ob-vious than the unproduced potential of the industrial sector. The bicycles and radios that the unemployed could not afford did not rot before their eyes—food did. Finally, those dramatic instances in which food was de-liberately destroyed, oranges set afire or milk poured out on the high-ways, provided symbols upon which the anger and confusion felt by many could be focused.

The paradox played a crucial role in the development of food assistance programs in both the Hoover and the Roosevelt administrations, for, as we shall see, it was to the paradox, rather than to the simple hunger of the poor people or the nutritional inadequacy of their diets, that these pro-grams were addressed. Therefore, the term deserves a closer look. Tech-nically, a paradox is a statement that contains a contradiction or a state-ment that seems false but is in fact true. In common usage, it carries connotations of absurdity and abnormality. But the so-called paradox that evoked federal food assistance was not, in fact, a paradox; it was the nor-mal, predictable working of the economy rendered extreme by the De-pression. The American economy regularly has the capacity to produce goods and services that poor people cannot afford to buy but need or would like to own. Goods are distributed on the basis of purchasing power, not on the basis of need, and many human needs and desires go unfulfilled not because society is unable to produce the goods and ser-vices to satisfy them, but because the distribution of income does not permit those in need to purchase what they could use.

Similarly, the much-discussed surplus was clearly not a quantity be-yond what was needed. "The truth of the whole matter," exploded Repre-sentative Glover of drought-stricken Arkansas as Congress debated a food assistance measure in 1932, "is that if the hungry were properly fed and those needing clothes were properly clothed, there would be no great surplus of wheat, corn, cotton, rice or any other of our great staple crops but they would be consumed and the price for them would be far greater than it is now." [7] A few years later, a more systematic analysis came to a similar conclusion. In 1934, the Brookings Institution released a study of American income and consumption patterns based upon 1929 figures. The study concluded that to provide all families in the nation with a liberal diet in relatively prosperous 1929, the value of total food production would have to have been increased by approximately 40 percent.[8]

Throughout the Depression, however, the contradiction between rotting surpluses and empty stomachs was widely perceived as a paradox; this was the definition of the situation to which both the Hoover and Roosevelt administrations responded with the series of food assistance projects, programs, and policies that are the subject of this book. Neither the paradox itself nor the agricultural policies and politics that formed the context of food assistance measures under both the Hoover and Roosevelt administrations can be understood apart from the peculiar history of the American farmer in the twentieth century. Since this subject is one about which the urban reader is especially likely to be uninformed, Chapter 1 provides some background on the farmer and the agricultural economy in the decades before the Depression. Chapter 2 traces the impact of the Depression upon both farmers and unemployed workers and thus the mounting contradiction between waste and want. Chapter 3 describes the growing pressure for action to resolve this situation of want amid plenty and describes the fate of a measure for distribution of government-owned wheat that was introduced in the third session of the Seventy-first Congress in the fall of 1930. Chapter 4 follows a similar measure through the first session of the Seventy-second Congress a year later and analyzes the factors that finally led to its passage in March 1932 and to subsequent donations of additional wheat and government-held cotton. Despite their temporary character, these Hoover-era food assistance measures were significant, not only because of the relief they brought to those in need, but also because they resolved important questions about the impact of large-scale distribution of government-owned food and thus cleared the way for the ongoing food assistance measures created under the New Deal. The food assistance programs subsequently inaugurated by the New Deal cannot really be assessed apart from the extraordinary opportunity that confronted the Roosevelt administration when it came into office early in 1933. Chapter 5, therefore, focuses upon the closing months of the Hoover administration and the attitudes and events that shaped the particular "historical moment" occupied by the early New Deal.

The remainder of the book concerns the food assistance policies and programs of the New Deal. Chapters 6 through 9 are devoted to the initiation of federal surplus commodity distribution and its institutionalization in the Federal Surplus Relief Corporation. This section of the book contains chapters on the relief and agricultural policies of the New Deal, the particular series of events that culminated in the decision to purchase surplus agricultural products and distribute them to the poor, the institutionalization of this approach, the obstacles encountered, the results achieved, and the interest groups formed. The next several chapters concern the takeover of food assistance by the Department of Agriculture and its gradual adaptation for use as a tool in the maintenance of farm income. Together, these chapters explain how a program that was originally a relief measure for poor people became primarily a convenient outlet for products acquired in efforts to raise the incomes of commercial farmers. Food assistance was the first of the major federal programs of relief "in kind," and this story can tell us a great deal about the particular dynamics of noncash assistance programs. Furthermore, the New Deal years were formative for food assistance, as for so many other policies, and they explain a great deal about the performance of food programs over the subsequent decades. A concluding chapter discusses the long-range impact of New Deal food assistance policies and politics and their recurring legacy: want amid plenty.

This study has another subject as well, one that might be designated in broad terms as the fate of reform under capitalism, or more specifically, as the fate of the poor under the New Deal. Public discussion of the paradox, despite the inadequacies of that definition of the situation, represented a critical opportunity. People were angry about the juxtaposition of waste and want, and the paradox led many to question the wisdom of an economic system that could permit people to go hungry in the midst of such abundance. Such questioning was normal among left-leaning intellectuals, of course, but the spectacle of breadlines knee-deep in wheat brought such questions to the unsophisticated and to the traditionally conservative. Along with the enforced idleness of the unemployed, the contrast of hunger and abundance led to an unprecedented degree of skepticism about the desirability of capitalism, a degree of disaffection for the profit system uncommon if not unique in our national experience. In this sense, the contrast of hunger and abundance represented an opportunity for a substantial alteration of our basic approach to distribution. Indeed the Federal Surplus Relief Corporation was at first regarded by some of its creators as just such a major change in the system. "Not many people realized how radical it was—this idea of having the Government buy from those who had too much in order to give to those who had too little," wrote Secretary of Agriculture Henry Wallace in

1934. "So direct a method of resolving the paradox of want in the midst of plenty doubtless could never have got beyond the discussion stage before 1933." [9] But the FSRC did not realize its radical potential. In lieu of a major means of redistributing the nation's abundance to those in need, it became a sort of safety valve in a program designed to reduce the abundance to profitable levels, to restore scarcity.

The New Deal drew to Washington many who shared the skepticism about capitalism and were excited by the opportunities inherent in the crisis; they were high-minded, well-intentioned, clever, energetic men and women intent upon reform. But as the New Deal idled to a close in the late 1930s, the unique opportunities of 1933 had not led to a resolution of the contradiction of want amid plenty, nor even to a firm protection against starvation amid surplus. As Howard Zinn has written in one of the seminal critiques of the New Deal, "Yet, when it was over, the fundamental problem remained—and still remains—unsolved; how to bring the blessings of immense natural wealth and staggering productive potential to every person in the land." [10] The major answer to the questions raised by hunger amid waste had turned out to be reduction of the surpluses through production control. "If we do not have such obvious 'breadlines knee deep in wheat' as under the Hoover administration," wrote Norman Thomas," it is because we have done more to reduce the wheat and systematize the giving of crusts than to end hunger." [11] The long-term legacy of New Deal food assistance was inadequate indeed. As the nation mobilized for World War II, the poor inherited a set of food programs dependent upon rapidly-dwindling agricultural surpluses, funded by an appropriation regarded in Congress as "farmers' money," administered at the federal level by a bureaucracy devoted largely to raising and protecting the interests of commercial farmers, and operated at the local level by county relief authorities who had control of nearly every aspect of the program from eligibility and benefit levels to whether the county would participate in the program at all. Over the next several decades, the results of this situation were, again, hunger amid plenty.

What happened to the opportunities inherent in the widespread questioning of the early 1930s? Why was the nation left with a farm policy based on limiting production and raising the price of food instead of one based on finding the means to distribute the available abundance? How and why did the New Deal fail to achieve for the forgotten man and woman the sort of new deal that appeared possible in 1933? This study of Depression-era food programs is a case study of the process by which the reform energies and the unique opportunity of the early New Deal came to yield measures that, in historian Barton Bernstein's terms, "conserved and protected American corporate capitalism." [12] More specifically, it is an attempt to understand how high-minded, well-intentioned, and hard-working reformers produced so inadequate a set of programs in the face of so remarkable an opportunity.

Breadlines
Knee-Deep
in Wheat

CHAPTER ONE

The Plight of the Farmer

The huge surpluses of food and fiber that caused so much consternation among those aware of the hunger of the unemployed did not begin with the Depression. In fact, surpluses had plagued farmers sporadically for half a century and had crippled the agricultural sector for most of the decade before the Crash. The surpluses were both symptom and symbol of the deeply-rooted process of change in American agriculture. In the early decades of the American republic, when the vast majority of Americans were farmers and most farm products were consumed at home, the idea that an abundant harvest could be a problem would have seemed absurd and probably irreverent. But as subsistence farming and pioneer lifestyles gradually gave way to commercial agriculture and industrialization, and large, impersonal, aggregate markets replaced home consumption and neighborly trade, farmers faced the anomalies of overproduction. Increasingly, they found their well-being determined not by their own effort, thrift, and competence nor by the familiar hazards of weather, soil, and pests but by the mysterious fluctuation of prices. Looking back from the 1930s, a North Carolina textile mill worker recalled:

> We started off farmin' and stuck to it up to the fall of 1913 and '14. That year we planted cotton on a fourteen cent basis and got six cent for some and four and a half for the rest. Europe had got started in the war and the countries that had put in orders for cotton countermanded 'em and flooded our home market. Me and Sally made fourteen bales of

cotton, thirty-one barrels of corn and three hundred bushels of potatoes besides a sight of peas. It was one of the best crop years I ever knowed in Johnson County and we come out about the porest we ever done. We worked let me tell you, we worked to make that crop.[1]

Deeply schooled in agrarian values of hard work and individual responsibility for prosperity or poverty, farmers met these changes with confusion and resentment. With each successive drop in prices, new groups of agriculturalists were forced off the land or, as the economic literature labels the process, "released from agriculture." Since only fairly large farms could hope to make a living from the comparatively low prices of farm commodities, the maxim of the day became "get big or get out."[2] For those who did not have the resources to get big, the available choices were often painful ones. Getting out of agriculture is not as simple as switching from the manufacture of shoes to gloves; it involves the loss of a whole way of life, and as Harry Braverman has pointed out, a tremendous de-skilling of the worker.[3] Some of those "released," like the textile worker quoted above, found work in such rural small town industries as textiles. Some followed their sons and daughters to the big cities where industrial jobs were concentrated, adding the shock of a new environment to the misery of the loss of a farm. Some stayed behind, slipping down the agricultural ladder from owner to renter, from cash renter to sharecropper, eking out a meager living from a combination of subsistence farming and production of their region's cash crop. "He tried mill work," sociologist Margaret Hagood reports of one of the many southern tenant farmers she studied, "but after being outdoors all his life he could not endure being shut up inside, and so he soon went back to farming. He prefers farming to anything else and the first thing he would do if he had some money would be to buy a piece of land of his own."[4]

The percentage of farms operated by tenants increased steadily from the late 1880s through the relatively prosperous decades at the beginning of the twentieth century. By 1920, 38 percent of American farmers did not own the land they farmed. The rate of tenancy varied with region, and the term embraced a range of situations from relatively prosperous cash renters on good cropland in the Midwest who were accumulating money with which to make a down payment on a farm to the virtual debt peonage of the sharecroppers in the cotton or tobacco lands of the South who depended on the landlord for "furnish"—tools, feed, fertilizer, work animals, and rations—as well as land and living quarters.[5] Haphazard and inequitable tenancy laws gave tenants few rights and little security of tenure: leases generally were renegotiated each year and tenants frequently were evicted if the landlords thought they could do better with other renters.[6] As a result, both the land and the people suffered. "Renters don't take care of the land," said one tenant farm wife interviewed by Margaret Hagood, "because it ain't theirs and they don't know when they'll be leaving."[7] "The trouble is," said another tenant, "that just as sure as a tenant makes a farm more productive, the owner boosts his rent."[8]

The more prosperous farmers who did get big often did so by mortgaging the land they had in order to purchase additional acres or modern farm equipment. As the supply of free homestead lands dwindled, land values increased rapidly and so did the willingness of investors to lend money on farm mortgages. Meanwhile, the mechanization of agriculture, especially the substitution of the tractor for the horse- or mule-drawn plow, made larger holdings feasible and attractive.[9] With the pressure to expand operations on the one hand and readily available credit on the other, mortgage-financed farming rapidly became the norm in the first few decades of the twentieth century. The value of farm mortgages rose from $3.2 billion in 1910 to $10.2 billion in 1921.[10]

The First World War accelerated the process of change in agriculture. In response to war-generated demand and government urging, farmers expanded the acreage under cultivation and adopted such scientific techniques as increased use of chemical fertilizers to raise the productivity of their holdings. For most crops, however, the actual expansion of output did not occur until the war was nearly over, and with demand far exceeding supply, prices of agricultural commodities mounted rapidly. Inflated wartime prices sent cropland values soaring, creating a land boom in many farm areas and fueling an enormous expansion of credit at high wartime interest rates.[11] As described by an Iowa lawyer, the boom period initiated a land craze involving financial institutions and many segments of the population.

> The town barber and the small-town merchant bought and sold options until every town square was a real estate exchange. Bankers and lawyers, doctors and ministers left their offices and clients and drove pell mell over the country to procure options and contracts upon this farm and that, paying a few hundred dollars down and expecting to sell the rights before the following March brought settlement day. . . .
>
> During this period, insurance companies were bidding against one another for the privilege of making loans on Iowa farms. . . . Second, third and fourth mortgages were considered just as good as government bonds. Money was easy, and every bank was ready and anxious to loan

money to any Tom, Dick or Harry on the possibility that he would make enough in these trades to repay the loans almost before the day was over.[12]

The nationwide index of land prices rose from 129 in 1918 to 170 in 1920, with the rise of values much greater in the Cornbelt of the Midwest and in the south Atlantic states. "The bulk of this increase," according to economist Murray Benedict who made an extensive study of the problem, "was sheer inflation, an added dead weight of investment to be carried by American agriculture; a valuation supported by the input of large amounts of wartime savings and a greatly increased farm mortgage debt."[13]

Eventually and inevitably, a day of reckoning arrived. European relief measures organized under the leadership of President Hoover continued the abnormally high demand for American farm products for a brief period after the war, but as the European combatants reestablished their own agricultural systems, they reduced their purchases of costly imports. Croplands in Canada, Argentina, and other nations had also been dramatically expanded during the war to meet European demand, and farmers in these areas, with virgin soils and lower costs of production, were able to undersell American farmers in the European market. Congress made matters worse for the American farmer by adopting a strongly protectionist trade program and by terminating credits to European allies. The Federal Reserve system raised the discount rate sharply, putting tremendous pressure on member banks to reduce the volume of loans that had been permitted to expand during the war. And the Interstate Commerce Commission dealt another blow by granting the railroads sharp increases in freight rates.[14]

Farm prices began to decline rapidly midway through 1920, and by 1921 a full-scale farm depression was in progress. The overall index of farm prices fell from 228 in 1919 to 128 in 1921. The drop was even more precipitous in wheat, cotton, corn, and hogs. A typical variety of wheat brought $2.94 a bushel at the Minneapolis market in July 1920, but by December 1921, farmers were getting only $.92 for the same grade and type. Even at such prices, the world market could not absorb all that was produced, and huge surpluses of corn, cotton, and wheat began to accumulate, casting a pall over the Midwest, the South, and the nation's wheat-producing regions.[15] Perishable crops also were affected. As one commentator explained to a congressional committee, "The potato crop of the North was not worth at digging time the actual cost of the seed planted."[16] Others reported thousands of tons of cabbage and onions plowed back into the earth because growers could not find a market at any price.[17]

What the agricultural sector needed was an orderly means of adjustment to the reduced demand and a way of lessening the burden of debt contracted under inflated wartime conditions. The processes that led to increased output, however, were not easily reversed. When demand for a manufactured product decreases, industrialists can usually cut costs substantially by laying off workers and cutting back production. But the individual farmer, heavily committed to permanent capital investment in land and equipment, cannot significantly decrease costs by reducing output. Neither can the farmer exert much influence on the size of the total supply, since each is responsible for only a tiny share of a largely undifferentiated market. As prices fell, many farmers sought to increase their harvests and thus their share of the sagging markets, producing even greater surpluses and lower prices.

Nonfarm prices also underwent readjustment after the close of the war but not as sharply as agricultural prices. While farm prices fell, on the average, to little more than half their wartime levels, nonfarm prices fell by about 25 percent and then stabilized. The farmer was required to trade a substantially larger portion of his crop for a given nonfarm item than had been the case before the war. This change was drastic for some commodities. In 1919, a farmer could purchase five gallons of gasoline with the proceeds from a bushel of corn; in 1920, a bushel would buy only one gallon. In 1921, two bushels of corn were needed to obtain a gallon of gas, a particularly bitter blow for those who, in response to the lure of wartime price increases or the call of patriotism, had mortgaged land and livestock to replace horses or mules with a gasoline-powered tractor.[18]

This disparity between the levels of farm and nonfarm prices aggravated old agrarian resentments: the tariff, the cost of transporting produce to market, and a credit system and government more responsive to the needs of industry than of farmers. Farmers felt victimized and betrayed. A South Dakota lawyer, testifying before a congressional committee, captured the prevailing feeling:

> Our farmers, in response to the propaganda for "greater production," insistently urged by accredited representatives of the Government, did everything possible to raise a maximum crop. . . . If they had loafed upon their jobs, and had worked 8 hours a day instead of 16, and raised only one-half or two-thirds of a crop, it would have been worth a great deal more than the entire crop which they did produce.[19]

The farmers' frustration and the rural-urban rift were intensified as a wave of mortgage foreclosures and rural bank failures in the early 1920s placed the ownership of more and more farmland in the hands of city-based financial institutions, particularly insurance companies.

The worsening conditions generated an increase in political activity among farmers and a series of plans for dealing with their deteriorating economic condition. Marvin Jones, who began serving on the House Agriculture Committee in 1920, recalled:

> People in farming regions felt that the national policies were wrecking agriculture. The crisis of 1920 served to confirm the growing realization that widespread and cohesive organization among people in agriculture would be indispensable to insuring agricultural interests and a political voice powerful enough to influence national policy was needed.[20]

Organization among farmers was not new, but the postwar problems provided a spur to the existing farm organizations. Their increased activity was reflected not so much in rising membership rolls—numbers of paid-up members fell off as times got harder—as in militancy and visibility in Washington. Three national farm organizations competed to represent agriculture as the farmer's woes deepened: the National Grange, the Farmers' Union, and the American Farm Bureau Federation.

The oldest, and at the end of the war the largest, of these three was the National Grange or Order of the Patrons of Husbandry. Founded in the 1860s, the Grange was patterned on the Masonic Order. Secret rituals supplemented its social and educational program at the local level, and it had a state and national hierarchy of degrees, levels, and arcane titles. In the 1870s and 1880s, the Grange had been politically active and had won a number of important concessions from state legislatures and Congress, including railroad regulation, rural free delivery of mail, and various electoral reforms. But with the rise of the Farmers' Alliance, the militant farmers' movement of the late 1880s, the spirit of militant agrarianism had passed on to the Populists, and the Grange had retreated primarily to its fraternal and educational activities and some ill-fated ventures in cooperative business. It remained important in country life, however, providing an opportunity for social activities and the development of leadership skills. Regionally, it was especially strong in the older farming areas of the Northeast and in some parts of the Far West. During World

War I, it espoused peace and prohibition, and it did not establish a legislative office in Washington until after the war. Nevertheless, with a membership totaling well over half a million, the Grange was the largest farm organization at the end of the war.[21]

The Farmers' Educational and Cooperative Union of America, or the Farmers' Union, was the second oldest, the least conservative, and the smallest of the three national groups. Founded in Texas in 1902, its primary strength was in the cotton-producing areas of the South and the wheat-producing prairies. Its founder was an organizer for the Farmers' Alliance, and thus, the Farmers' Union was a direct heir of the populist tradition. Its program stressed the elimination of speculation in farm products, an end to the credit and mortgage basis of farming, the creation of farmer-controlled cooperatives, and the need for a more egalitarian society. In its first two decades, the Farmers' Union tried to achieve higher prices by holding crops off the market, but not until the 1920s, did it become active in a concerted effort for national legislation. After rapid growth in its first decade, membership of the Farmers' Union leveled off to about 140,000 at the end of World War I.[22]

The rising star among farm organizations was the American Farm Bureau Federation. The Farm Bureau was a peculiar creature, and since it became a dominant force in farm policy and politics, some background is in order. The introduction of new farming methods and technologies became something of a crusade in the early years of the twentieth century, as decades of research and technological innovation culminated in a rise in productivity for farms employing modern approaches. To disseminate these innovations, however, something more effective than lectures and exhibits at agricultural fairs or articles in the farm papers was needed. Demonstrations of new methods on the farmer's own land met this need, and the county agricultural demonstration agent, or county agent, became the channel through which the Department of Agriculture, with the assistance of the Rockefeller-funded General Education Board, and donations from Julius Rosenwald and several other philanthropic and business groups, encouraged farmers to experiment with and adopt new methods. At first, county agents were paid with private funds, but as the success of the approach gained recognition, both the Department of Agriculture and the states began allocating more and more public money to the system. By the time the Smith-Lever Act formalized federal participation by establishing the Extension Service in 1914, several hundred county agents were at work and more than $1.5 million dollars in state and federal public funds was being spent yearly. With special appropriations beginning in 1917 and pressure for increased agricultural production, both generated by the war, the system grew rapidly.

Since county agents could hardly work individually with each farmer, they were instructed to organize and work with local groups, called farm bureaus. Such groups were to be "nonpolitical, nonsectarian, nonsecret" and representative of "the whole farming population," but since the county agents' purpose was to inspire the adoption of new methods, they were directed to work with the most prosperous and the most respected farmers. These, it was assumed, would be most influential in the farming community. Once organized, the local bureaus were expected to contribute to the support of the agents' work, either directly from dues or indirectly by obtaining appropriations of county funds. Thus, the county agents became dependent upon the local farm bureaus, both as evidence of the effectiveness of their work and as a source of funds. Officially, the agents were employees of the federal, state, and county governments, and they were supervised by the director of the Extension Service attached to the state's land-grant college through which the federal share in the funds was channeled; but at the practical, day-to-day level, the agent was beholden to the local farmers who ran the farm bureau. "The farm advisers tended," Murray Benedict, has summarized," to be more responsive to the wishes of their constituents than to those of extension administrators." And as the local farm bureaus united into state organizations, and the state groups federated into a national unit, the county agent became, in political scientist Grant McConnell's words, "the publicly paid organizer of the American Farm Bureau Federation." Even after the Department of Agriculture belatedly realized the problems that might arise from the county agent's role as servant of the local farm bureau and tried, beginning in 1921, to proscribe the agent from such tasks as operating Farm Bureau membership campaigns and editing Farm Bureau publications, the Farm Bureau Federation had, in the county agent, a resource unparalleled in any other farm organization.

The national federation was organized in 1919 and 1920; by 1921, it claimed a membership of over four hundred thousand persons. Membership dropped off to around three hundred thousand where it remained for most of the Depression; many poorer farmers were deterred from membership by the relatively high dues set at the local level—typically ten or fifteen dollars. Although some initial disagreement arose between representatives of southern and eastern state federations who thought that the primary purpose of the national organization should be educational and those from the Midwest who advocated business operations and legislative action, the Cornbelt activism soon won out, and the Farm Bureau Federation opened a Washington office. "The Farm Bureau Federation," McConnell reports, "was a major political power from the first year of its formation." [23]

In the spring of 1921, the Farm Bureau Federation's Washington representative, Gray Silver, was instrumental in the formation of a bipartisan farm bloc in Congress. The bloc was composed of senators and representatives from the farm areas who committed themselves to work for legislation benefiting farmers without regard to party affiliation. Since the bloc quickly achieved control of the Senate Agriculture Committee, this challenge to traditional party discipline attracted considerable attention and excited some exaggerated fears. Although the farm bloc's existence as a formal organization was short, its members continued to work together to protect the interests of agriculture throughout the twenties, and its existence contributed to a growing recognition of farmers as an interest group among members of Congress, leaders of both parties, farmers themselves, and the general public. [24]

Despite the spate of organizational activity, farm leaders were confused about the causes of the farmers' plight and about possible remedies for it. During the early 1920s, most analyses of falling agricultural prices focused upon the peculiar conditions of farm marketing—the large number of farmers competing to sell in a limited market, the necessity of selling perishable crops immediately after harvest, the influence of storage facilities and freight routes on the sale of storable commodities, the long distances between the points of production and terminal markets—and other factors that induced farmers to take what they could get for their crops rather than holding out for more favorable prices. The proponents of market reform argued that the individual farmer had little control over market conditions but asserted that organized groups of farmers might emulate the monopolistic practices that kept industrial prices comparatively high.

The idea of cooperative marketing was not new. Most of the major farm organizations had advocated it, but producers' cooperatives, while providing many important services to farmers, had been generally unsuccessful in their attempts to secure higher prices for their members. Efforts to organize growers of such major crops as grains and cotton had failed to achieve control over a sufficient portion of the crop to have any substantial influence on prices. During the world war, however, producers of raisins, nuts, and other specialty crops in California had organized into highly successful marketing associations. The achievements of these organizations, some gaining control of more than 90 percent of their particular crop, led to renewed interest in marketing co-ops in the early 1920s. Efforts were made to organize large-scale, even nationwide, cooperatives for growers of the nation's major agricultural commodities using legally enforceable contracts to ensure the loyalty of participating producers. But this co-op movement, like its predecessors, ran aground on the traditional shoals of cooperative organization. As Murray Benedict has summarized, "Farmers were too numerous, too difficult to organize, and too hard to keep in line to make such an ambitious scheme work on a voluntary basis. It was the recognition of this fact that led eventually to a more general acceptance of the idea that government should be urged to help farmers carry out this program which they had found themselves unable to carry through without government aid." [25]

The most important theme in the demand for government intervention was the notion of altering the balance between farm and nonfarm prices to enhance the farmers' purchasing power of nonfarm goods. Looking back to the years before World War I as a kind of golden age, many farm leaders called for a restoration of the relationship between farm and nonfarm prices that had prevailed then. This relationship, statistically calculated on a crop-by-crop basis, was dubbed "parity" by *Wallace's Farmer*, an Iowa farm journal. It has been an important part of U.S. agricultural politics and policy ever since.

As farmers and farm organizations analyzed the agricultural price structure, their attention increasingly focused on the surplus as the villain. They concluded that the world price, at which any surplus that existed after domestic consumption would be sold, controlled the domestic price, even when the surplus constituted a relatively minor part of the total crop. One spokesman summarized this argument for a congressional committee:

> In other words, the 3.8% of these grain crops which we sent abroad to meet the general trade price level of the world in competition with the products of the Hindus and peons and the peasants of Europe, and the cheaper labor and the cheaper lands of other countries, that little dinkey surplus automatically fixes approximately the price of the 96.2% of that crop which we consume at home, and regardless of the cost of production. [26]

With this general analysis perceived as the root of the problem, farm leaders began looking for a plan to make the tariff effective for agriculture, to place American agriculture on an equal footing with American industry by segregating the surplus from the amounts sold for consumption at home.

In 1922, an agricultural implements manufacturer named George Peek and his associate at the Moline Plow Company, General Hugh Johnson, who had served together on the War Industries Board, published a pamphlet entitled *Equality for Agriculture* in which they proposed a government-sponsored, two-price system to aid American agriculture in achieving parity prices. One price would apply to goods in the American market; it would be protected by tariffs, thus enabling the farmer to regain a competitive footing with tariff-protected American industry. The surplus that could not be sold at home at the protected domestic price would be purchased by a government corporation and dumped abroad at whatever price could be secured on the world market. The losses incurred in this process were to be made up by assessing producers a small sum, an "equalization fee," for each unit of produce sold at the higher domestic price.[27]

George Peek was a tireless advocate for his plan, bringing it to the attention of Secretary of Agriculture Henry C. Wallace and various farm and rural business groups. In 1924, Secretary Wallace endorsed the plan and asked an Agriculture Department consultant to draft a bill embodying the Peek-Johnson proposal. Called the McNary-Haugen plan after the senator and representative who introduced it in legislative form, it became the central focus of efforts to obtain federal intervention on behalf of agriculture until the late 1920s. Support developed early in the wheat states where conditions closely approximated the problems that Peek's approach was designed to redress, but farm organizations in many parts of the nation opposed the plan at first or gave it only halfhearted support, viewing it as a sectional measure. As the plan was adjusted to include the interests of more and more producers, however, support for the McNary-Haugen legislation grew. The plan eventually gained the support of the three national farm organizations and of the congressional farm bloc, and by the late 1920s, opposition to McNary-Haugenism was equated with hostility to agriculture in many powerful circles. Congress passed the plan in 1927 and again in 1928, but a presidential veto was sustained in both instances, and it never became law.[28]

Critics of the McNary-Haugen approach argued that the higher, tariff-protected prices would stimulate greater production in those very crops requiring downward adjustment and that the limitation of McNary-Haugen protection to only a few basic commodities would make the plan an inducement to single-crop farming with its attendant evils. "The bill upholds as ideals of American farming the men who grow cotton, corn, rice, swine, tobacco, or wheat, and nothing else," said President Calvin Coolidge in his first McNary-Haugen veto. "These are to be given special favors at the expense of the farmer who has toiled for years to build up a constructive farming enterprise to include a variety of crops and livestock that shall, so far as possible, be safe, and keep the soil, the farmer's chief asset, fertile and productive." [29] The equalization fee was viewed by critics as an unfair and possibly unconstitutional use of taxing power since its purpose was not to raise revenue but rather to benefit selected groups of producers. The same criticism, proponents answered, might be made of the tariff protecting industrial products, but these tariffs had been deemed neither unwise nor unconstitutional by Congress. The probability that the measure would invite tariff reprisals by nations adversely affected by export dumping was another frequently heard criticism, as was the prediction that the program would be an administrative nightmare. [30]

The regressive nature of a tax on food received little attention in these discussions, and the fundamental issue of the wisdom of raising agricultural prices as a means of raising farm income was barely discussed. Direct supplementation of income, as opposed to manipulating prices, was probably too far beyond the scope of American experience and philosophy to receive much discussion, and the few free trade voices calling for adjustment of the disparity between farm and industrial prices by lowering or eliminating protective tariffs on industrial products were fighting a losing battle in a decade of increasing economic nationalism. [31]

Despite the measure's failure to become law and the probable validity of much of the criticism leveled against it, the McNary-Haugen fight had long-term implications for American agricultural policy. It called national attention to the needs of farmers and the problems of low farm prices and agricultural surpluses; it solidified the demand for government action to assist the farm economy; it popularized, among farmers at least, the demand for parity between agricultural and nonfarm prices and consolidated support for the idea that the prewar years of 1910–1914 had represented a fair price relationship between the two sectors. It served as a vast campaign of public education for farmers, their representatives in Congress, and many segments of the public, concerning the possibility of a fundamental shift in the role of the state in the direction of more active intervention in a whole sector of the economy. In doing so, it paved the way for even more drastic and far-reaching changes in agricultural policy that were to come in the 1930s. It provided a unifying focus for the efforts of the farm organizations, especially the American Farm Bureau Federation, and the McNary-Haugen plan's passage in Congress, despite the presidential vetoes, gave credibility to the organizations that had supported it. The duration of the McNary-Haugen crusade and its penetration of grass roots as well as state and national farm organizations left as a legacy a huge network of farm leaders, agricultural economists, and "dirt farmers" who knew each other, were used to working together, and were accustomed to thinking about and articulating the needs of farmers. This network was to prove important in agricultural politics and policy-making, and thus in the development of food assistance, for decades.

Enthusiasm for the McNary-Haugen plan began to decline after its second veto. Foreign countries had begun raising their own tariff walls against American farm products, making dumping abroad a less feasible approach to the disposal of surplus products, and concern about the tendency of higher prices to induce greater production increased as a general recovery of farm prices brought additional acres under cultivation. The farm organizations that had been briefly unified behind the McNary-Haugen plan went their separate ways. The Grange began advocating an export debenture plan that suffered from the same problems of reliance on international trade and inducement of increased output as the equalization fee approach. The Farmers' Union began calling for prices set by law to cover the cost of production. And the Farm Bureau Federation, which was so young as a national entity that much of its identity had been formed by the McNary-Haugen fight, began groping for an alternate approach. In the late 1920s, a number of agricultural economists, notably John D. Black at Harvard, W. J. Spillman at the U.S. Department of Agriculture, and M. L. Wilson at Montana State College, began to develop the idea of adjusting production to domestic need—or more accurately, to American buying power—through a program that would offer farmers a protected price for only a portion of their crop. This "domestic allotment" plan, as it came to be called, eventually became a cornerstone of New Deal agricultural policy.

With the election of Herbert Hoover in 1928, McNary-Haugenism retreated even further. Hoover, as Secretary of Commerce under Harding and Coolidge, had been one of the staunchest foes of the subsidized export plan. He saw it as a threat to international trade so important to the Commerce Department, an abuse of the taxing power, and most important, an unwarranted expansion of the role of the federal government. Farmers, he believed, should be helped to help themselves through aid to their cooperatives and other voluntary, rather than government and thus coercive, agencies. Hoover did see the need for some sort of assistance to farmers; in fact, in his speech accepting the Republican party's nomination, he referred to agriculture as "the most urgent economic problem in our nation today." [32]

Shortly after his inauguration in the spring of 1929, Hoover called a special session of Congress to deal with tariff revision and agricultural relief. The session took no action on the tariff but after much controversy, adopted a version of the president's recommendation for dealing with the agricultural situation embodied in the Agricultural Marketing Act of 1929. The act established a Federal Farm Board to encourage the organization of commodity-marketing cooperatives and promote effective marketing practices. A $500 million revolving fund was created from which the Farm Board was authorized to make loans to commodity cooperatives, primarily for organizational purposes, and to stabilization corporations created by the cooperatives to support prices by controlling surpluses. This latter provision eventually became much more important in Farm Board operations than the backers of the Marketing Act had foreseen. The Agricultural Marketing Act was a compromise measure that involved the government more heavily in agricultural affairs than the administration desired, but not so much as the farm organizations wanted; the government still could not reduce production or limit output to prevent the accumulation of surpluses, although the stabilization corporation provisions did allow the use of federal funds to assist in the removal of surpluses from the market. [33]

On the eve of the Great Depression then, American farmers were in a state of profound economic exhaustion. Prices had recovered somewhat from their disastrous postwar levels but not sufficiently to relieve most farmers of their debt burden; mortgage foreclosures, tax sales, and other debt-induced transfers had continued throughout the decade. Many farmers who held on to their land had been unable to make needed repairs or to replace aging equipment and livestock, and as the decade wore on, they had fallen further behind in the fierce competition for markets. Those who had savings or reserves generally used them; those who had none were in debt and over extended. Few were in any condition to weather the economic storm that lay just around the corner.

Politically, farmers were organized but defeated. The battle for equality for agriculture had been lost, and the outlines of new campaigns were hazy. Nearly a decade of political effort had produced a Federal Farm Board that inspired little hope or confidence, and disappointment created a sense of failure and confusion among farm leaders and rank-and-file dirt farmers. Farm organizations had been unable to solve the farm problem through the voluntary cooperation so prized by the new Hoover administration, nor through pressure for government action. Meanwhile, the apparent prosperity of the industrial sector and the visibly rising standard of living of nonfarm families heightened the farmers' sense of grievance. Carl Sandburg captured the spirit of the farmer in the late twenties when he recalled:

In the Sunflower State 1928 Anno Domini
a Jayhawker sunburnt and gaunt
drove to a loading platform
and took what he got for his hogs
and spoke before two other hog raisers:
       "Everything's lopsided.
"I raise hogs and the railroads and the banks take them away
   from me and I get hit in the hind end.
"The more hogs I raise the worse my mortgages look.
"I try to sleep and I hear those mortgages gnawing in the night
   like rats in a corn crib.
"I want to shoot somebody but I don't know who.
"We'll do something. You wait and see.
We don't have to stand for this skin game if we're free Americans." [34]

CHAPTER TWO

Depression: Deprivation and Despair

The stock market crash in the autumn of 1929 did not immediately cause grave apprehension among farm leaders. Some segments of the agricultural press, in fact, believed that the collapse of paper values might help to restore balance between the farm and nonfarm sectors. "The farmers of America are milking their cows and slopping their pigs as usual, while mother gets the breakfast and dresses the children for school," commented the *Prairie Farmer* in November. "Farm conditions are steadily improving, and the deflation of stock speculation will help to give farmers more adequate and cheaper credit, and to teach the nation that the stockyards are more important than the stock market." [1]

Like so many other optimistic predictions in the aftermath of the Crash, hope that the farmer was somehow immune to the impact of rapid deflation proved to be ill founded. The onset of the Depression intensified farm problems. When employment fell off, so did the nation's ability to buy farm products. As millions of unemployed workers and their families cut meat, milk, and fresh produce from their diets in an attempt to get by on savings or scanty relief, the food they could not afford piled up in warehouses or rotted in the fields, signaling deeper ruin in the countryside.

As the Depression deepened, industrialists were able to protect their price structure to some degree by curtailing output. In agriculture, price rather than output bore the brunt of adjustment to the Depression-induced decline in demand. Between 1929 and 1934, while industrial production declined 42 percent in volume and 15 percent in price, agricultural production declined only 15 percent in volume but 40 percent in price. The disparity between industrial and agricultural prices that had angered and mobilized farmers throughout the twenties grew worse. In comparison with the prewar years of 1910–1914, the ratio of the prices farmers received to the prices they paid for industrial goods fell from 109 in 1919 and 89 in 1929 to 64 in 1931. The proceeds from sixteen bushels of wheat, more than the average yield of an entire acre, were required to purchase a four dollar pair of shoes. In Iowa, some found it more economical to burn corn as fuel than to feed it to hogs that brought less than three dollars per hundredweight.[2]

The intensification of farm problems altered the focus of Federal Farm Board activities from the organization of cooperatives to price-supporting purchases. In the face of rapid accumulation of huge wheat and cotton surpluses and disastrous breaks in the prices of these two commodities, the Farm Board financed purchases of millions of bushels of wheat and bales of cotton through the Grain and Cotton Stabilization Corporations. The stabilization operations originally had been intended as a means of holding minor, temporary surpluses off the market for brief periods of time, not as a method for dealing with major overproduction, and they were not accompanied by any measures to reduce the quantities of wheat and cotton produced. As a result, the Farm Board's stocks of wheat and cotton grew steadily, and although the price declines were apparently slowed by the board's actions, prices remained so low that the organization could not sell its holdings without defeating its own purposes and adding to the difficulties of farmers. In fact, when the board announced its withdrawal from the wheat market in June 1931, stating that it could not justify further wheat purchases, the Kansas City price of wheat plunged approximately twenty-seven cents a bushel, undoing much of the price supporting effect of the board's purchases. As in any situation of sharp price fluctuation, those growers, cooperatives, and handlers who sold while the price was supported benefited from Farm Board operations while those who sold too early or too late did not, and the Farm Board made many enemies.[3]

Farmers might have withstood the sharp price declines brought about by the Depression had they not been so severely burdened by taxes and debts. Both had been calculated when prices were significantly higher, and much farm debt had been contracted at inflated wartime interest rates. New Deal historian Arthur Schlesinger has provided a cogent summary of the farmrs' plight: "A cotton farmer who borrowed $800 when cotton was 16 cents a pound borrowed the equivalent of 5000 pounds of cotton; now, with cotton moving towards 5 cents, he must pay back the debt with over 15,000 pounds of cotton."[4]

The result of the overwhelming debt burden was, in many cases, forced sale: mortgage foreclosure, bankruptcy, or delinquent tax sale—the heart-breaking loss of home, land, and years of investment. Agricultural economists estimate that in the years 1930–1935 as many as one-sixth of all farms in the nation were subject to forced sale of some type. The percentage would be even higher for farms producing significant commercial crops since many small subsistence farms lacked commercial value and thus were not mortgaged. Furthermore, the figure masks the additional thousands of supposedly voluntary sales that were actually debt-induced transfers to mortgagees.[5]

The figure also masks the human realities of debt-financed farming. The contemporary reader may have difficulty in appreciating the personal tragedies behind the statistics. One farmer, writing to the Rockefeller Foundation in search of help, articulated the poignant mixture of fears, hopes, and frustrations that told the story of thousands:

> we are going to have to give up our place the first Monday in January to the People's State Bank of Abbeville for $3500 mortgage. During normal times this property was worth from ten to fifteen thousand dollars. Work is very scarce in this county at the present time and we are very much in need of some assistance at this time. I am fifty years old, married and have two daughters fourteen and twelve years respectively. They are unusually bright and attractive children and I am so anxious to have them get as good an education as possible.[6]

Even the loss of a farm, and with it the hope for a comfortable old age or the plan for a child's education, did not necessarily free the farm family from the mesh of indebtedness. "The struggles people had to go through are almost unbelievable," recalls a farmer interviewed by Studs Terkel. "A man lived all his life on a given farm, it was taken away from him. One after the other. After the foreclosure, they got a deficiency judgment. Not only did he lose his farm, but it was impossible for him to get out of debt."[7] A farmer's wife remembers the bitterness of forced sale:

> This neighbor woman lost her husband, and of course he was owing in the bank. So the auctioneers come out there, and she served lunch, and she stood weeping in the windows. "There goes our last cow. . . ." And the horses. She called 'em by names. It just pretty near broke our

hearts. They didn't give her a chance to take care of her bills. They never gave her an offer. They just came and cleared it out. She just stood there crying.[8]

Some of the dispossessed became tenant farmers on the farms they had once owned. Some found work as hired hands or joined the swelling ranks of migrant laborers. Some remained near the land they had farmed, subsisting on charity and hoping for better days, a human reminder to their more fortunate neighbors of the consequences of the Depression. "To see these neighbors wiped out completely," another Iowa survivor recalls, "and they would just drift into towns and they would have to be fed."[9]

Dispossessed farmers constituted only a fraction of those who had to be fed. Unemployment had already begun to rise in 1928. In the months following the Crash, it spread across the nation like a killing frost, reaching at least 4 million wage earners, or nearly one out of every ten, by the spring of 1930. No one knew exactly how many people were out of work because the nation had no system for collecting such information, but most estimates agreed that the number of jobless workers had climbed to nearly 8 million by the spring of 1931 and grew steadily until the spring of 1933 when the most widely accepted figures indicated that approximately 15 million persons, or a third of the work force, were out of work.[10] There was no public unemployment insurance to cushioned the blow. Despite years of effort by Progressives, no state had an unemployment insurance law on the books when the Depression began. A few employers had experimented with plans voluntarily, and a few labor unions maintained unemployment funds or negotiated contracts including employer payments, but the proportion of the unemployed covered by such arrangements never reached even one percent of the labor force.[11] Being fired or laid off during the Depression meant the abrupt and complete termination of income, often without warning.

For the individual worker, the path from layoff to relief line was a bitter one. At first, the family lived on savings and the hope of finding another job. Occasionally, a wife or child was able to find part-time work. Then, as unemployment grew and factories posted permanent "no help wanted" signs, both the hopes and the savings ran out. Borrowing came next—against insurance policies until they lapsed, from more fortunate friends and relatives, and finally as credit from the grocer and sometimes the landlord. An extensive study of the impact of unemployment undertaken

by the National Federation of Settlements under the leadership of Helen
Hall found that after savings and insurance policies lapsed, most families
sold their furniture or lost it through failure to meet payments, then failed
to meet mortgage payments and lost their homes, and finally sold or
pawned wedding rings and other personal effects. Many doubled up with
other families in already crowded apartments to save on rent. Almost all
cut back substantially on food. They did not apply for relief until they had
piled up mountains of unpaid bills and all forms of credit had been exhausted.[12] "The human consequences of prolonged unemployment," social welfare historian Clarke Chambers tells us, "were unhappily easy to
summarize: malnutrition, sickness, comfortless homes, crowded housing, family discord, desertion, lowered morale and loss of self respect,
humiliation and pervading anxiety, hopes abandoned for talented young
children, bitterness and resentment for the parents."[13]

In his intensive case studies of families of unemployed workers,
E. Wight Bakke documented the impact of job loss on family consumption patterns. "Economy," he reported, "was chiefly exercised through
the curtailing of expenditures involved in the normal pattern of food supply." The families in his sample spent an average of eight cents per person
per meal and an average of 39 percent of their total expenditure on food.
Guests were no longer invited to dinner; some families cut the number of
meals per day from three to two. Fresh fruit disappeared, and eggs replaced meat; margarine or "drippings" replaced butter. "Dependence on
one staple almost exclusively under the impact of severe reduction in income was not uncommon," according to Bakke. "The staple tended to
vary with the national or racial group: macaroni for the Italians, corn
bread for the negroes [*sic*], beans supplemented by pancakes for the na-
tive White Americans. . . . Monotony is not the only vice of such limited
diets," he concluded. "In the words of one man whose family lived for
nearly a month on soup, beans and spaghetti, 'You know that stuff fills
you up, but you don't feel right; no pep or fight. You just want to sleep all
the time.'" For many families, Bakke found, giving up milk was the most
difficult adjustment. He reports the reaction of a former clock company
employee: "When you give up milk, as you finally do if you ain't on relief—they make an allowance for it—why then maybe for the first time
you think you might be better off on relief."[14] Eventually, millions of
families swallowed their pride and applied for aid from local governments
or voluntary (private) social agencies. And as they did so in increasing
numbers, the inadequacy of pre-Depression relief arrangements became
steadily more obvious.

CATALOGING IN PUBLICATION 10/99

Risks and outcomes in developmental psychopathology / edited
by H.-C. Steinhausen and Frank C. Verhulst. — New York ;
Oxford : Oxford University Press, 1999.

  p.   cm.

Includes bibliographical references and index.
Running title: Risks and outcomes in adolescent psychopathology

  ISBN 0-19-262799-6

  1. Child psychopathology. 2. Adolescent psychopathology. 3. Outcome
assessment (Medical care) I. Steinhausen, Hans-Christoph. II. Verhulst,
Frank C. III. Title: Risks and outcomes in adolescent psychopathology.

(Continued on next card)

98-52302
AACR 2 MARC CIP 10/99

The English Poor Law tradition of local responsibility for relief of destitution with heavy reliance on private charity had taken firm root in American soil. The isolation of the frontier settlements and plantations, the fierce independence of the incorporated towns, the religious and ethnic diversity that fostered mutual aid arrangements among successive waves of immigrants all contributed to the notion that the American way of relief was exemplified by self-reliant communities of neighbors taking care of their own. As industrialization and urbanization eroded the social and economic basis for this approach and the poor became strangers rather than neighbors, their incarceration in almshouses or county poor farms where they could be carefully supervised became the preferred method of assistance. The almshouses, however, were not able to keep up with the volume of misery produced in a largely unregulated industrializing economy, and each succeeding depression left more people receiving outdoor relief, that is, relief in their own or a relative's home rather than "indoors" in an institution. In the late nineteenth century, the Charity Organization Movement, strongly influenced by Social Darwinist ideology, attacked public relief, both as an inducement to indolence among the poor and as a hotbed of graft and corruption among urban political bosses. Although the Charity Organization societies that developed in most of the nation's large cities generally fell short of their goal of eliminating tax-funded outdoor relief altogether, they did succeed in imposing their own approach of careful investigation and supervision—the emerging methods of social casework—on many public and most voluntary relief agencies. The Progressive movement of the early twentieth century that emphasized the prevention of poverty by protecting workers from illness, industrial hazards, and exploitation gave some attention to relief and secured "mother's aid" or "widow's pension" legislation in some states, but only a few states actually contributed any state funds, and all made participation a local option. The development of professional social work in the postwar era and the growing fascination with psychological explanations for behavior increased the emphasis placed by both municipal and voluntary relief agencies on individual factors leading to poverty and dependency and thus on supervision and treatment of relief clients.[15]

Both ideologically and organizationally then, the nation was unprepared for the relief task imposed by massive unemployment. Many small towns or rural areas had no relief agencies at all or none except a county poorhouse that served as a dumping ground for the destitute aged, the retarded, the severely handicapped, and the mildly insane. Large cities generally had some form of "home relief" or public outdoor relief geared to helping a few thousand families; in addition, urban areas often had a haphazard patchwork of voluntary agencies, each with its own special focus, one serving a particular neighborhood, another serving a single religious or ethnic group, another devoted to a specific problem or task. Only in a few communities were these agencies organized into a local community chest or united fund. For disaster relief in case of flood, fire, or other acts of God, a chapter of the American National Red Cross provided aid, and rescue missions or shelters furnished bed and board for the homeless and transient. Inadequate even in good years, such relief arrangements were rapidly overwhelmed by the avalanche of need unleashed by the Depression.[16]

Despite the obvious inadequacies of this hodgepodge of voluntary and municipal relief efforts, belief in the superiority of the American way of neighborly concern was widely shared at the outset of the Depression. Mayors and social welfare leaders joined governors and members of Congress in pointing with dismay to the British dole, and asserting the value and capability of local institutions. No one was a more ardent champion of the American way than the president himself. Hoover believed strongly that "personal feeling and personal responsibility of men to their neighbors [were] the soul of genuine good will . . . the essential foundation of modern society," and he continued to assert the superiority of individual generosity throughout his term of office. "A cold and distant charity which puts out its sympathy only through the tax collector," he told a 1932 audience, "yields only a very meager dole of unloving and perfunctory relief."[17] Where voluntary giving was unable to meet the need and public funds were necessary, Hoover believed that responsibility rested firmly at the local level of government where he saw "the very basis of self government"[18] and "the bedrock principle of our liberties."[19]

Given these beliefs and his conviction that stressing unemployment would shake business confidence and retard recovery, it is not surprising that the president was slow to organize unemployment relief efforts nor that he adopted a policy of "official optimism" concerning the depth and duration of the nation's economic problems. Not until the fall of 1930 did the president appoint a presidential body to assist local communities in coping with unemployment, and even then, the President's Emergency Committee for Employment (PECE) was to provide only coordination, information exchange, and encouragement to local bodies.[20] Despite the appointment of the PECE, the flow of optimistic predictions by those in power continued. The president, echoed by many of the nation's governors and the heads of major corporations and financial institutions, maintained a steady barrage of hopeful pronouncements: the "business down-turn" would be short lived, it represented a healthy purge of inflated paper values, and prosperity awaited a strengthened nation "just around the corner." Hardly anyone talked about a depression, and no one knew how many people were in need of assistance.[21]

Such official optimism retarded the development of sound relief measures, and initial efforts to respond to the growing unemployment problem were pitifully inadequate. Local governments and community chests sponsored spruce-up and odd-job campaigns to persuade homeowners to create jobs for the unemployed; garden plots were allocated so that those out of work could grow their own vegetables; and the jobless were exhorted to use their initiative to devise such small enterprises as selling fruit or pencils. Even New York Congressman Fiorello La Guardia, soon to emerge as a champion of federal relief, proposed a scheme whereby every man with a job would buy a suit for an unemployed man, thus stimulating employment in the garment industry. Upon finding a job, presumably because he was so well dressed, the beneficiary would in turn purchase a suit for another jobless worker.[22] Very few voices were heard predicting a long depression or calling for major changes in the distribution of relief.

Nevertheless, the actual relief-giving agencies soon encountered a steady increase in applications for assistance. In major cities studied by social work administrator and historian Josephine Brown, for example, the number of families receiving assistance quadrupled between the first quarter of 1929 and early 1931. At first both private and municipal agencies, recognizing that the new poor were accustomed to working for a living, established work relief programs and attempted to create jobs that would not compete with private industry nor give hard-pressed local governments an excuse to cut payrolls. But local work relief, whether privately or publicly funded, could not keep up with the rising tide of unemployment. As the volume of need expanded, both municipal and private agencies modified their programs and sought ways of making the relief dollar go further. Community chest–supported agencies curtailed recreational and counseling activities to free funds for more tangible assistance. At first, the private family agencies continued the provision of cash grants for relief, a practice valued because it allowed some freedom of choice to recipients. As caseloads grew to staggering proportions, however, the time once available for supervising clients disappeared, and the portion of the family budget that the agency could supply dwindled. Many agencies adopted an emergency or disaster relief approach, replacing cash with grocery orders or direct provision of goods "in kind," that is, groceries, secondhand clothing, or household items.[23]

As the pressure on the relief dollar mounted relentlessly, many local agencies, both public and voluntary, attempted to take advantage of wholesale food prices by establishing commissaries where relief clients could receive food. As this system spread, it drew substantial criticism, because it caused embarrassment and discomfort for recipients and because it reduced the business of local food retailers. One social worker writing in *The Family* in the autumn of 1932 summarized the negative evaluation of the commissary approach: "At their worst, commissaries draw together crowds of disheartened people, who, in unattractive surroundings, have doled out to them a monotonous and inadequate diet, under circumstances that are bitterly humiliating."[24] By the end of 1932, studies of the commissary system had been conducted in New York, New Jersey, and other cities, and small, decentralized food outlets or direct arrangements between relief agencies and local merchants were recommended as alternatives to the large central commissary.[25]

Experience with the commissary system intensified the antipathy of social workers and relief administrators for relief in kind. Many saw such adaptations as a regression to an earlier and even more inadequate stage of relief provision. Writing in the early 1970s, Helen Hall, who spent the Depression years as director of New York's famous Henry Street Settlement, recalled, "Our depression had really brought us back to the breadbasket, the grocery order, the commissary, welfare cafeterias, and the script commissaries that had multiplied over the country, all humiliating forms of warding off starvation. One community after another grasped at something that seemed to offer economies to the community but not security to the unemployed."[26]

Cash grants, food orders, and commissary privileges, however inadequate, were generally given only to those who had homes and families. In many cities, unattached individuals and even couples with no children living at home were ineligible for all forms of relief in their own homes. Soup kitchens, breadlines, and flop houses were the only relief available to them. Many large cities established shelters or municipal lodging houses, but as the number of homeless people and transient job seekers grew, so did "Hoovervilles" of makeshift shacks erected in vacant lots or on the edges of cities from junk and salvage. Some cities created public kitchens to supplement the traditional rescue missions, but most free meal programs were funded by private charitable donations. In the early years of the Depression, especially in the winter of 1930–1931, breadlines proliferated; some eighty-two separate breadlines were operating in New York City alone. Like the commissaries, the breadlines drew the criticism of established social welfare leaders and agencies. Some were rackets, collecting more money in donations than they spent on providing food. Some, those run by the Hearst newspaper chain, for example, were viewed as publicity stunts for their sponsors. Even those that were altruistic and relatively well run were perceived as problems by organized charities; not only did they compete for charitable contributions, but their visibility gave the impression that a great deal of relief activity was in progress, and they were conducive to abuses that gave the unemployed a bad name and deterred much-needed giving.[27]

The relief arrangements of local governments and traditional social agencies were supplemented by the efforts of individuals and groups not normally philanthropic in purpose. Eating clubs at Princeton University began sending the leftovers from their tables to the unemployed, and a reporter for the *Brooklyn Eagle* suggested a central warehouse where families could send leftovers for distribution to those in need. A man calling himself "Mr. Glad" gave out coffee, sandwiches, gloves, and nickels in Times Square. Gangster Al Capone opened a breadline in Chicago. St. Louis society women distributed unsold food from restaurants. Someone placed baskets in New York City railway stations to enable commuters to donate vegetables from their gardens. Harlem radio personality Willie Jackson opened a penny restaurant where meals were sold for one cent per dish.[28]

In the long run, neither the economies reluctantly implemented by established relief agencies nor the spontaneous activities of the well-intentioned were able to squeeze enough out of available dollars to meet the need, and severe distress became evident. Numbers tell part of the story. When the major voluntary relief organizations began raising money for work relief in New York City in the fall of 1930, the standard wage rate for common labor in the city was approximately $5.50 per day. Thus, a fully-employed, low-wage worker could anticipate a wage of about $27.50 a week or $121.00 per month. In comparison, the emergency Work Bureau, established by the city's private charities, paid an average of $15.00 weekly to the jobless on work relief. In Philadelphia where the cost of living was similar, a work relief program initiated late in 1930 began by paying $4.00 per day. By the end of 1931, however, the average relief grant per family in that city had fallen to $4.39 *per week*.[29] In May 1932, the grant was cut again, reducing the weekly average to $4.23 per family. Of that amount, testified the executive secretary of the Community Council of Philadelphia, "about $3.93 is an allowance for food, . . . about two thirds the amount needed to provide a health maintaining diet." [30] At one time in New York, the average weekly grant fell to $2.39 with less than half of the unemployed heads of families receiving any relief at all.[31] Some cities made no pretense of supplying a reasonable budget. Baltimore gave its needy families an average of eighty cents worth of commodities each week, and Atlanta provided sixty cents per week for white recipients and less for blacks. Dallas excluded both blacks and Mexicans from relief. Some cities ran out of funds; Cincinnati paid each family the weekly grant every other week in hopes that some other means of support might be found during an off week. Most simply dropped families from the rolls and waited for them to reapply.[32]

What did people do in such circumstances? One study of four hundred families dropped from the rolls in Philadelphia found that they stayed alive principally by begging and foraging in garbage cans. Another Philadelphia study of an eleven-day hiatus in relief detailed the strategies employed by families to tide themselves over until help arrived in the form of an appropriation of dubious constitutionality by the state legislature. The study, summarized in *Fortune*, found that necessity provoked considerable ingenuity:

> One woman borrowed fifty cents, bought stale bread at three and one half cents a loaf, and the family lived on it for eleven days. Another put the last food order into soup stock and vegetables and made a soup. When a member of the family was hungry, he ate as little as he could. Another picked up spoiled vegetables along the docks, and except for three foodless days, the family ate them. Another made a stew with her last food order, which she cooked over and over daily to keep it from spoiling. Another family lived on dandelions. Another on potatoes. Another had no food for two and one half days. And one in ten of the women were pregnant and one in three of the children of nursing age. And they "got along." [33]

Scavenging in dumps and in the refuse piles of markets was a common strategy, not without its hazards. A committee of prominent Chicagoans visited one of that city's incinerators in 1932 to investigate reports of widespread scavenging. "A new truckload of 'soft' restaurant garbage, which consisted very largely of such food as watermelon, was dumped when the committee was present," noted the *Social Service Review*. "It was a warm day, the odors were bad, and there were clouds of flies everywhere. About a dozen people were waiting for this truckload and picked up vegetables and scraps of various kinds which they took away, some of them eating pieces of food they picked up." [34] On cooler days, the crowds were considerably larger; a Cicero man was arrested at one Chicago dump for striking a man who tried to cut in front of him in the line waiting for the truck. "Lines form every day at the garbage dump from eight in the morning to five in the afternoon," reported the Cicero *Herald*. "Men and women come there to see if they can't find food to carry back home with them. They get some, if they come early enough." [35]

Garbage dumps were not the only places from which people carried food home; jobs were another source. Not only household employees, but also those who worked for restaurants, hospitals, prisons, and other institutions serving meals supplemented their meager earnings by taking food home. A waitress interviewed by Studs Terkel remembered that her father, a railroad man laid off when the Depression struck, "always could get something to feed us kids." He got a part-time job in a Chinese restaurant. "We lived on those fried noodles. I can't stand 'em today." Next he got work delivering samples of breakfast cereals. "We lived on Corn Flake balls, Rice Krispies, they used to come out of our ears. Can't eat 'em today either." [36] School children hid tidbits from school lunches in pockets or book sacks to carry home to younger brothers and sisters. Another woman interviewed by Terkel recalled that she and other girls living in an orphanage routinely gave their brown bag lunches, packed by the dietitian at the home, to down-and-out men in the park. "We'd go through the park when we walked to school. . . . The men there waited for us to go through and hand them our lunches. . . . These were guys who didn't have work. . . . They weren't bums. These were hard luck guys." [37] Some of these hard luck guys probably turned around and took the lunches home to wives and children. "Father sleeping at Municipal Lodging House because he could get more to eat there than at home and frequently brought food home from there in pockets for children and wife," reads the report of an investigator for the Welfare Council of New York City who followed up on a neighbor's report that a woman and five children were starving in Brownsville. "Only other food they had for weeks came from under pushcarts." [38]

Sometimes, in desperation, mothers would send their children out to ring the doorbells of strangers. "Excuse me, Mister, but we have no eats in our house and my mother she said I should take my brother before we go to school and ring a doorbell in some house and ask you to give us something to eat," a little girl told writer Louis Adamic when he answered his mother-in-law's doorbell one winter morning. Adamic chatted with the children while his mother-in-law fed them breakfast and packed a lunch for them. The girl was polite and talkative while the boy was angrily silent. "He's always like this when he's hungry and we gotta ring doorbells," his sister explained. Adamic followed up by visiting the children's school where he was told that the number of children seeking meals on the way to school or from the school itself was on the rise.[39]

Not all of the strategies of the unemployed were as demeaning. Along the West Coast, mutual aid organizations formed by jobless workers arranged to exchange the services of members for the right to pick and distribute local farmers' unmarketable crops.[40] Relief gardens and canneries were popular. In some communities, relief recipients and others in need marched on welfare offices demanding expanded benefits, a tactic that was frequently successful.[41] Sometimes action to secure food was even more direct. Groups of men would enter a grocery store, gather up supplies, and ask for credit. When told that business was conducted on a cash basis only, the men would simply pack up the goods and leave. The stores generally refrained from calling the police, one observer reported, for fear that news coverage might lead to the spread of the practice.[42] "Such radicalism as existed," wrote historian Dixon Wecter from the vantage point of the early fifties, "was mainly the plain man's instinctive resentment of poverty surrounded by shops bursting with food and farms smothered under their own productive surplus."[43] In a less-organized fashion, people accosted customers leaving grocery stores and relieved them not of their money but of their food purchases, and families sent their children out to steal from wholesale markets and pushcarts and to snatch milk from the front stoops in affluent neighborhoods. As the Depression wore on, Baltimore and Ohio Railroad President Daniel Willard's famous comment, "I'd steal before I would starve," became a reality for many.[44]

Conditions in rural areas were worse than those in the cities. Many rural areas had no relief apparatus other than a county Red Cross chapter more oriented toward rescuing families trapped by floods or tornadoes than those stranded by economic upheavals.[45] The national Red Cross declined to undertake any unemployment relief until 1932, but many local chapters tried to respond to immediate need. "The situation locally is so overwhelming that no agency is standing on ceremony these days, but all are endeavoring to give relief as speedily as possible," reported one chapter to the national headquarters.[46] Nevertheless, Red Cross work at the local level suffered from the hazards of voluntarism. As critic and essayist Edmund Wilson observed of the organization's work in the hills of

Kentucky: "The people in the local chapters . . . get no pay for their work of raising money, investigating cases and distributing relief, and as they also have their own businesses and household duties to attend to, it is sometimes hard for them to get around to their work for the Red Cross."[47] Even where other agencies existed to supplement the Red Cross, fund-raising was difficult. The farm families who formed the backbone of the rural economy had exhausted any savings they might once have had in the long agricultural slump of the twenties, and rural banks, also weakened by a decade of low farm prices, failed earlier than the big city banks, further depleting rural resources.

Then, in the summer of 1930, a severe drought prostrated virtually all of the South and extended as far to the Northwest as Montana and as far to the Northeast as Pennsylvania. Although the Great Drought of 1930–31 has been historically eclipsed by the Dust Bowl drought of mid decade, for those directly affected, the first drought of the 1930s was catastrophic. Agricultural production in the drought area was sharply reduced to half of normal levels in some of the hardest-hit states. As harvest season approached, many small farmers had no crops at all. The crisis in animal feed was especially acute since normal pasturage and forage had dried up. In the debt-financed farm economy of much of the drought region, the prospect of no crops meant the inability of settling the year's indebtedness and thus, in most cases, no prospect of borrowing the seed and furnish that would get the farmer's family through the winter and permit them to plant a new crop in the spring. Bank failures were epidemic in the drought area, further reducing the availability of credit. The alternate sources of livelihood that farm families could turn to in good times— jobs in construction or in factories—were largely eliminated by the Depression, and the drought made the Depression worse by destroying what little purchasing power remained to farm families after years of low farm prices.[48]

Southern Illinois, many areas in Pennsylvania, southern Appalachian coal mining locales, and other regions were hit by both drought and the virtual collapse of the coal industry. When, in keeping with American relief ideology, desperate farm families turned to their coal mining neighbors for help, they found them equally desperate, wiped out by unemployment. Conditions in such areas became so severe as the winter of 1930–1931 wore on that the President's Emergency Committee for Employment (PECE) made an investigation. "The facts are," wrote Colonel Woods to Judge John Payne, the chairman of the American National Red Cross, upon the former's return from a trip to West Virginia, "that in many of the country districts in the state, and particularly in the coal mining camps, there exists at the present time desperate suffering.'' Woods attested to the fact that the local authorities had tried to alleviate the situation, but ''their funds now . . . are very thin, and they have little prospect of raising more, since the whole district has been hit so hard for several years by the plight of the bituminous coal industry. This leaves many families,'' Woods continued, ''in a condition where immediate help is needed if almost incredibly hard conditions, lack of food, lack of clothing, are to be mitigated.'' Woods concluded that it was already too late for prevention. ''The need now is for the promptest sort of relief to alleviate acute suffering.''[49]

Such privation in the countryside seemed incredible to some urbanites. How could a farmer be without food? ''I am in the fullest sympathy with the farmer,'' declared New York Senator Royal Copeland early in 1932. ''I was born on a farm. My relatives are farmers. . . . But there is never a day on the farm when they can not go out and kill an old rooster and parboil him long enough to make him edible . . . But in New York, or in Boston, or in any other of the cities, when hunger comes they have nothing to eat but sidewalks.'' Senator Norbeck of South Dakota replied, ''the Senator has been talking about that rooster for a year. Has it not occurred to him that the rooster may be gone by this time?'' ''Yes,'' replied Copeland, ''but my experience with farming farmers indicates that roosters are born every day''—the record notes laughter—''or every year; so I think perhaps there is a rooster still on the farm.''[50]

However, there had been no rooster in many of the most depressed rural areas for quite a while. In the cotton and tobacco regions of the South, the single cash crop system had gradually undermined the production of food for home use. The dual hardships of drought and depression found many sharecroppers and tenant farmers without livestock, poultry, or gardens to sustain them. In the areas where the drought hit hardest, many were forced to sacrifice livestock when pasturage and forage dried up because they could not obtain credit to bring in feed from outside the region.[51] In the mining camps that had been spared by the drought, different factors hampered self-provisioning. Since many of the miners had been born on farms, PECE urged the mine operators to permit farming on company land, and the Red Cross distributed packets of seed. Even where the skills needed for farming were still intact, however, the tools and livestock were long gone, as were jars and other equipment needed for large-scale canning.[52] The resources for a return to subsistence agriculture were simply not available to those who needed them most.

Rural families, like their urban counterparts, had strategies for surviving. "Just how did you manage?" Helen Hall asked a group of West Virginia coal miners' wives on a visit to the stricken region. In her autobiography, she recalls this response: "It 'pears like it 'ud be easy to say, honey, but our ways 'ud be hard fur you to understand. You see it was gravy soup lot o th' time—just gravy soup. . . . You puts flour in a pan an' browns it, an' then you stirs water inta it." "Is that what you gave your baby? . . . I must have sounded accusing," Ms. Hall recalls, "for the mother said apologetically, 'Oh, no, honey, not when I cud help it. A neighbor up th' way has a cow, an' she wuz mighty good to me. She sent up half a pint o' milk when she had it over. Sometimes it wuz ev'ry other day, an' sometimes none fur a week. But it helped a powerful sight.' " [53]

The miner's diet, Irving Bernstein asserts, "was a national disgrace," sometimes consisting of " 'miner's strawberries' (beans—for variety white beans one day and red the next), 'bulldog gravy' (flour, water, and a little grease), a 'water sandwich' for the miner's lunch pail (stale bread soaked in lard and water)." [54] Some subsisted on what they could gather in the woods. "We have been eating wild greens since January this year, such as Polk salad. Violet tops, wild onions. forget me not wild lettuce and such weeds as cows eat as a cow wont eat a poison weeds," wrote a Harlan County, Kentucky resident to the editor of *The Nation*. [55]

And like their fellow sufferers in the cities, rural citizens used direct action to obtain necessities. In England, Arkansas early in 1931, a group of about forty persons, denied aid by the local Red Cross agent because he had run out of application forms, headed for town determined to get food even if they had to take it by force. Shouting, "we are not going to let our children starve," a growing crowd persuaded local leaders to distribute provisions to several hundred people without charge. [56] Exaggerated by the press, the "food riot" at England became a symbol of the destitution of the drought sufferers, of the inadequacy of the Red Cross, and of the limits to the patience of the hungry. But it was by no means the only example of rural direct action. At Henryetta, Oklahoma, a crowd of several hundred marched on shops to obtain food. In the Ozarks, a crowd of backwoods people forcibly unloaded a carload of grain donated by Iowa farmers and shipped at the expense of editor and future Secretary of Agriculture Henry Wallace, rather than wait for the Red Cross agent who was supposed to oversee the distribution. Striking miners in Harlan County, Kentucky looted stores and raided gardens. [57]

Despite such actions, deprivation began to take its toll in both city and countryside. A study conducted in New York City found that 95 persons diagnosed as suffering from starvation were admitted to the city's four largest hospitals in 1931, 20 of whom died. Another 143 admissions were diagnosed as malnutrition, and 24 of these died. A survey of Pennsylvania's rural areas in 1931 found a rise of 25 percent in malnutrition among children and reported that the number of new patients at tuberculosis clinics had nearly doubled since 1929, a figure that the state's secretary of health attributed to growing malnutrition. A doctor reporting on the health of West Virginia miners' children in the fall of 1931 found their average weight 12 percent below standard and their diet conducive to infection and disease. A Columbia University professor of public health told a congressional committee that the records of the New York City Association for Improving the Condition of the Poor showed a deterioration in weight and growth among the children of the unemployed. And the Milbank Memorial Fund studied the health of seventy-five hundred families in eight cities, finding the rate of illness much higher among the poor and highest among those whose incomes had dropped sharply since 1929.[58]

The deprivation, even the malnutrition, might have been more acceptable if the food to relieve the need had not been so obviously available. As the breadlines lengthened, the huge surpluses of food and fiber that had troubled farmers for a decade took on new meaning. In the eyes of many, they became at once the means by which hunger might be relieved and the decisive element in the moral argument for its alleviation. "Starvation in a country which has been blessed with foodstuffs over and above the supply needed for itself and other countries where it finds markets is unthinkable," wrote a Tennessee judge who urged President Hoover to arrange for distribution of surplus grains.[59] "One of the tragedies of the present depression has been the fact that thousands of persons have been suffering acutely from hunger, or at least have been forced to do without nourishing food, during a year when the farms of the country were producing some of the largest crops ever grown upon them," declared an Ohio newspaper. "Elevators are bursting with grain for which there is no market, yet thousands have been suffering for want of bread," the editorial continued. "These two sides of the picture don't jibe. If Americans are hungry and there is food, they should be fed."[60] Commerce Secretary Lamont expressed the Hoover administration's concern in similar if more guarded terms: "In a country one of whose difficulties is to dispose of a surplus of many commodities, no person, seeking work in order to provide for himself and his dependents, should be permitted to suffer from lack of food or fuel."[61] Other conservatives used stronger language. "It is a disgrace and an outrage," declared Representative Hamilton Fish of

New York, "that this country of ours, with an overabundance of food stuffs, should permit millions of our own people to continue to be undernourished and hungry."[62]

For some observers, the juxtaposition of hunger and abundance symbolized the irrationality of the entire economic structure. It is "a sad indictment of our economic system that great masses of people can be hungry in a nation that is burdened with surplus food crops," wrote a California fruit grower who devised a plan to preserve ripe fruit and distribute it to charitable agencies on a nonprofit basis.[63] A system that permitted citizens to go hungry while storehouses were bursting with food "must be radically wrong in some particulars," Senator Robert Wagner told a Senate committee investigating unemployment.[64] Recalling what seemed to him the paralysis of the Hoover years, one New Dealer reflected: "If on an island the natives had piled all the food up on one side and drawn a line across it and then they'd all got back on the other side and said it was taboo and they couldn't get across to get the food, why we would have laughed at them, but somewhat the same damn thing was happening in this instance."[65] "We are able to produce so much," commented *The Nation*, "that a good share of us live in perpetual fear of having nothing, and all of us periodically, as at present, stop producing because we can find nobody who is able to buy the things everybody wants. Surely there was never a more insane situation outside of a madhouse."[66]

"Americans of the Hoover years of the Great Depression," historian Albert Romasco has written, "were a people perplexed by plenty. . . . America's poverty was not cut in the familiar pattern of the past; it was . . . the poverty of abundance."[67] Intellectual observers and social critics were fascinated by the novelty of the situation. "The writers of Ecclesiastes were wrong. There was some new thing under the sun, something the world had never seen before; want in the midst of plenty. Even stranger still, want begot by plenty," wrote radical editor Oscar Ameringer of what he called the "dying days of the Old Deal."[68] In past depressions, hopes would have centered on good crops, observed historian James Truslow Adams in an essay marking the advent of 1933. "Today, so far from there being any dread of famine or lack of commodities of any sort, we actually fear nature's bounty as exploited by our own too efficient methods."[69] Comparing these economic conditions to the depressions of 1837 and 1873, political commentator Walter Lippmann told the National Conference of Social Work that "in the mentality of the people there is a profound difference between this crisis and all its predecessors. This is the first time when it is altogether evident that man's power to produce wealth has reached a point where it is clearly unnecessary that millions in a country like the United States should be in want." [70]

The new era of abundance presented humanity, or Western civilization at least, with a new challenge to its ingenuity. "We have brought mass production to the highest level. We can produce goods for everybody. However, not one of us has given consideration to mass consumption," chided H. G. Wells in a radio broadcast in the fall of 1930. [71] Some observers were pessimistic: "What we dread," asserted James Truslow Adams, is "the ending of what I have elsewhere called 'the American Dream' from failure of mind and character to control and organize the vast forces at our disposal." [72] Others were more optimistic: "It is not a shortage of the good things of life that bothers us; it is a surplus," declared Henry Wallace. "Our fields and our factories produce more than the present economic system permits our people to consume. Human greed and human dumbness got us into this mess; it is up to human brains to get us out." [73] But in all the hopes and fears, a conviction prevailed that the juxtaposition of want and abundance was a new situation calling for new actions and new ideas. "We cannot regard . . . poverty as incurable," Congressman James Mead of Buffalo told the House of Representatives as it headed for adjournment in the summer of 1930, "in a land where the warehouses are bursting with a surplus of supplies." [74]

CHAPTER THREE

The Politics of Wheat and Drought

I n keeping with the American tradition of local responsibility for relief, initial responses to the troubling juxtaposition of hunger and surplus were local and direct. New York and Illinois dairy farmers distributed surplus milk to needy families on a regular basis. In the Far West and the Rocky Mountain states, farmers permitted the unemployed to pick surplus fruits and vegetables under the direction of self-help organizations, often bartering their surplus crops for services that they needed but could not afford. Fruit growers in California donated surplus citrus products to local chapters of the Unemployed Citizens League for distribution, and all across the nation, farmers arrived at welfare departments and charitable societies with truckloads of unsaleable produce for those in need.

Traditional social service agencies and municipal relief committees viewed the surplus as a means to stretch relief dollars. Columbus, Ohio conducted a campaign to "Save the Surplus" under the auspices of its Council of Social Agencies; "the gist of the plan," wrote the secretary of the local Community Fund, "is that surplus foods be canned by the surplus labor and placed in surplus jars, and that the canned products will be used by the regular relief agencies in the attempt to prevent suffering due to unemployment during the fall and winter."[1] In Independence, Missouri, the Community Welfare League established a cannery in a former jail, storing potatoes gleaned from surrounding fields in the cells and compensating the women who did the canning with sauerkraut.[2] In Houston, the Mayor's Employment Committee reported that beef, pork, chicken, and rabbit were being canned as well as fruits and vegetables.[3]

In many communities, civic and religious groups got involved in efforts to feed the hungry and prevent waste by distributing available surpluses. In Pittsburgh, a group of business and professional leaders formed a Surplus for the Needy Committee to procure and distribute surplus foods and other goods. Birmingham, Alabama Boy Scouts collected donations of produce that Girl Scout troops canned for consumption by the unemployed, and the Junior League arranged for distribution of surplus milk that local dairies had been dumping down sewers.[4] A Baptist clergyman in Chicago who solicited donations of surplus food for his three "singing breadlines" obtained sixty thousand bushels of peaches and pears from Michigan and trainloads of apples, cabbages, and potatoes—so much food that he was able to supply the city's church-related family relief agencies as well.[5] With the encouragement of the President's Emergency Committee for Employment (PECE), relief gardens were established in communities across the nation and canning the surplus from these plots became a popular activity for civic, religious, and fraternal organizations.[6]

A more ambitious approach developed by a group of California fruit growers involved canning surplus fruits in a commercial cannery and distributing them on a nonprofit basis to charitable agencies across the nation. The first project of the Economic Conservation Committee of America resulted in the distribution of nearly thirty-six thousand gallons of peach butter that reached every state and the territory of Alaska. The committee acknowledged that it had made only a small dent in the aggregate peach surplus but expressed hope that the idea would spread. "As long as there is want in the world," read the conservation committee's brochure, "waste of food crops is wrong both from an economic and a humanitarian standpoint." The brochure explained the logic of surplus distribution, anticipating almost all of the arguments eventually offered for New Deal surplus commodity donation and subsequent food assistance programs. Under the Economic Conservation Plan, the committee asserted, all would benefit:

> The farmer is paid a fair price for his surplus. The laborer gets a fair wage for his work. The canner receives a fair margin for the use of his plant and equipment. The Committee's cost of distribution has to be paid. But every expense is kept at a minimum—and not one penny is added to make a profit for anyone.
>
> As a result, food that otherwise would be wasted is supplied AT COST to charitable agencies and non-profit public institutions. Pro-

ducers and workers benefit. More people are fed per charity dollar. The public burden is lightened. Loss nowhere . . . gain everywhere.[7]

The idea had considerable appeal; by early November 1930, the committee's founder and director, J. R. McCleskey wrote to the PECE that foodstuffs aggregating nearly a million cases had been placed at his disposal on a nonprofit basis.[8] The success of the committee's project and the ubiquitous use of surpluses in local relief efforts suggest that many Americans agreed with the Economic Conservation Committee's condemnation of waste in the midst of want. The use of available surpluses to relieve need quickly became a public issue.

Probably nothing did more to focus public ire upon the paradox of hunger and abundance during the Hoover years than the acquisition of large supplies of wheat by the Federal Farm Board. The accumulation of a huge store of food in government hands moved the issue into the public arena. This ill-fated attempt by the Hoover administration to aid distressed farmers initiated demands for federal food assistance. With some 65 million bushels of wheat on hand by October 1930, enough to bake more than 4 billion loaves of bread, appeals for its distribution began to be heard with increasing frequency. The idea of feeding the hungry with the Farm Board's wheat occurred to many. The PECE files contain a number of letters suggesting distribution of the wheat, and both the Federal Farm Board and the National Drought Relief Committee indicated to the PECE that they had received similar proposals from a variety of sources.[9]

Suggestions from ordinary citizens to public officials, however, seldom garner much attention; PECE received thousands of earnest proposals, and very few found their way into law or public policy. Suggestions from celebrities, on the other hand, frequently capture the attention of the press, and this was the case when distribution of the wheat was proposed by former Secretary of the Treasury William Gibbs McAdoo, Woodrow Wilson's son-in-law who had been a major contender for the Democratic party's presidential nomination in 1924 and, in the autumn of 1930, was running for the U.S. Senate in California. In a statement released in October 1930, McAdoo noted "constant suggestions" that the wheat surplus be used as cattle feed to compensate for a drought-induced shortage in the corn crop and asked, "Why not feed this wheat to human beings?" Pointing out that the wheat had been purchased with the taxpayers' money, McAdoo declared, "It will be a travesty if deserving but unfortunate people are permitted to suffer hunger or starvation because the government hoards this wheat." [10]

As the opening session of Congress approached, distribution of the Farm Board wheat was discussed in a number of high places. McAdoo's proposal elicited sufficient attention that the Farm Board felt compelled to respond with a statement clarifying its own position: the law did not permit it to give the wheat away. Adding that the Farm Board would certainly follow the direction of Congress if that body should change the law, Chairman Alexander Legge pointed out that the Agricultural Marketing Act under which the board operated directed it to "exert every reasonable effort to avoid losses and to secure profits." [11] Agreeing that congressional action would be needed to free the wheat, McAdoo corresponded with several members of Congress, stressing the simplicity and economy of the plan, the nation's long history of appropriating aid for the victims of disaster both at home and abroad, the potential benefit to wheat producers, and the idea that the wheat rightfully belonged to the taxpayers who had paid for it. "Already it belongs to the people and should be used for the relief of those who are needy and suffering," he telegraphed Senator Charles McNary, chairman of the Senate Agriculture and Forestry Committee. [12] By mid November, he had a pledge from McNary that the idea would be presented to his committee at its first meeting, and by the end of the month, both the Democratic floor leader, Senator Joe T. Robinson of Arkansas, and popular Republican Senator Arthur Capper of Kansas had announced plans to introduce measures authorizing distribution of the wheat. [13]

Meanwhile, support for the wheat distribution proposal was expressed by a number of groups dealing with relief. Among those who took an interest in McAdoo's proposal was Economic Conservation Committee Director J. R. McCleskey. "It may interest you to know that . . . a great deal of sentiment in support of this wheat measure is coming into our office daily," he wrote to PECE Chairman Arthur Woods in late November, "from Governors, Mayors, Unemployment Committees, Community Chests and all sorts of relief agencies in every direction. . . . It is the people in the front line trenches who are struggling to meet the distressed conditions with vastly inadequate funds to feed even the destitute, who realize what it would mean to have Congress release this wheat." [14] McCleskey tried to enlist the support of President Hoover and several cabinet members as well as Colonel Woods, [15] but his efforts were dismissed by presidential advisors as self-serving. "McCleskey runs a mutual admiration society and is after publicity. I take it that McAdoo is trying to bother the Chief," wrote Alonzo E. Taylor of the Stanford University Food Research Institute to Secretary of the Interior Ray Lyman Wilbur. [16] The exchange of correspondence was passed along to the White House for the president's perusal. Woods wired McCleskey a noncommittal reply, stating that his committee was set up to "serve as a clearing house for the experience of communities and industries dealing successfully with unemployment problems" and to "carry out federal programs after decisions have been made by the President and Congress," and President Hoover made no public statement for or against the wheat distribution measure.[17]

With support from both sides of the aisle and no overt opposition from the administration, prospects looked fairly bright for the wheat distribution plan as Congress convened in early December. Republican Senator Capper introduced a joint resolution calling for the distribution of 40 million bushels to both the unemployed and the victims of drought through agencies to be designated by the president, and Senator Robinson proposed distribution of the wheat as a drought relief measure, calling it a proposal "about which there has been much said and nothing done."[18] McAdoo wrote to the director of the Economic Conservation Committee a few days after the session opened that he had received expressions of support from a number of his friends in Congress and hoped that something could be accomplished soon.[19]

Before hearings on the wheat proposal could begin, however, the hope for a productive meeting of Congress was shattered by the eruption of a battle over drought relief that was to dominate the entire session. When the severity of the crop loss and the extent of bank failure in the drought region had become clear the previous autumn, the Hoover administration had reluctantly agreed to support "seed and feed" loan legislation when Congress reconvened. Such loans, which had been granted on previous occasions, were intended to enable farmers who could not obtain commercial credit or furnish from a landlord to plant a crop in the coming year. Believing that they had the administration's support in what was to be a bipartisan drought relief effort, Representative James Aswell, a Democrat from Louisiana, and Republican Senator Charles McNary had agreed to cosponsor a bill authorizing $60 million for loans to farmers for seed, feed, food, fertilizer, tractor fuel, and other production needs. Significantly, this bill had the support of Democratic Floor Leader Robinson as well; Robinson was an outspoken leader of what would be called the "drought bloc" of senators and representatives from the drought area, many of them southern Democrats. The apparent accord between the president and leading Democrats led many to predict a harmonious session.

When the session actually opened, however, the administration, concerned about the budget and wary of inviting demands for loans to aid the unemployed, asked Gilbert Haugen, the chairman of the House Agriculture Committee, to introduce a bill appropriating only $25 million and excluding human food from the purposes for which the loan funds could be spent. The members of the drought bloc perceived this proposal as a betrayal, and they were furious.[20] To make matters worse, President Hoover responded to criticism of his State of the Union message with a pungent statement in which he estimated that the various relief measures already introduced in Congress would exceed prudent spending by $4.5 billion. Declaring that "prosperity can not be restored by raids upon the Public Treasury," he accused unspecified members of Congress of "playing politics at the expense of human misery."[21] The president's statement was widely interpreted as an attack on the Robinson and McNary-Aswell drought relief measures and was perceived by supporters of the wheat distribution plan as an indication of opposition to the Capper resolution as well.[22] The battle lines were quickly drawn with the drought bloc on one side and Hoover loyalists on the other, and a decidedly rancorous tone was established that prevailed throughout the session.

In the fight that ensued over competing drought relief plans, the Senate generally supported the more generous figures proposed by the drought bloc, and the House lined up behind the Hoover administration. Both the House and Senate agriculture committees sought clarification from agricultural economist Clyde Warburton, secretary of the National Drought Relief Committee convened by the president the previous summer and director of the Agricultural Extension Service that had administered all previous seed and feed loans. When Warburton testified that $25 million would be sufficient if food were excluded but inadequate if included, the inclusion of human food as a purpose for which the money could be borrowed became the central issue.[23]

The administration argued that providing food was relief, pure and simple, and a concern of local groups aided by the Red Cross; the loans, on the other hand, were a business proposition intended for production purposes and were to be secured by a lien upon the next year's crop. Production loan funds should not be used for "dispensing charity and disguising it by calling it a loan," and those unable to feed themselves should not be burdened with the obligation to repay nor the temptation to default; they were the appropriate beneficiaries of the nation's "great insurance company," the Red Cross. In the House, Majority Leader John Q. Tilson called the food item a provision of "revolutionary character" that would end the American tradition of reliance upon "community spirit and private generosity" and "establish the dole in the United States." The Red Cross, he insisted, could care for the needs of those rendered destitute "intelligently, thoroughly, and generously." [24]

The drought bloc, on the other hand, argued that the Red Cross was unable to cope with the enormity of the distress, that the relief that it had been providing was inadequate and was becoming more so daily. "The Red Cross is doing a good work," said Joe Robinson in explaining his bill, "but . . . it is not reaching and it will not reach thousands of cases where suffering is already occurring." By the time the fight reached its climax in February, the drought bloc could reinforce its claims with figures: the Red Cross was spending only 6⅔ cents per day per person, barely enough to keep body and soul together. Furthermore, the drought bloc argued, even if the Red Cross could assist all of those in need, many were "proud, formerly prosperous farmers" who did not want charity and would be able to pay back loans with interest if they could get through the immediate emergency. "A man who is honest, who is capable, who is diligent, who is proud, ought not to be humiliated," declared Senator Robinson; "he ought not to be degraded by being required to take charity for himself and have credit advanced for his mule or his horse." [25]

At the heart of the debate were arguments that would come to sound very familiar over the next two years on the severity of distress and the capacity of the nation's traditional relief apparatus to alleviate it without federal assistance. As David Hamilton has noted in his careful study of Hoover and the drought, "At a time when the nation's private relief agencies and its heritage of local relief work were being severely tested, the loan bill controversy was also a debate over the ability of the nation's traditional relief policies to cope with the large burdens they were facing." [26] The administration seemed to think that only those who were normally in a precarious economic position had been rendered destitute. Asked by Senator Thomas of Idaho if there were not a great many people "entirely destitute, without food, without groceries, and without clothing," Warburton's reply was revealing: "There are always poor people, but usually poor people are poorer under these conditions that exist this year than usual." Advocates of federal relief, on the other hand, assumed that the normally prosperous had also been wiped out: "It is not a ragtail outfit that is coming up here asking for this money," declared Senator Connally of Texas. "It is the good, substantial farmers and citizens of the state." [27] The debate, lacking reliable and complete information, permitted the substitution of opinions for facts. No one knew how many people were unemployed or devastated by drought, what resources they had available to live on, or how they were faring. Individuals, social workers, visiting nurses, Red Cross agents, even mayors, knew about their own communities, but they were absorbed in the tasks of obtaining and spending local relief dollars. No one had a national picture, and the Hoover administration, ideologically committed to local and voluntary relief and fearful that any national emphasis upon unemployment would shake confidence and worsen the Depression, was resisting efforts to acquire comprehensive national information.

The wheat distribution measure came up for consideration in this context of acrimony and ignorance. The Senate Agriculture Committee originally took up Capper's measure with several drought relief proposals, but when it became clear that Capper intended the wheat to go to the unemployed in the cities as well as to victims of drought and that technical information from the Farm Board would be necessary in order to assess the plan, a separate hearing was scheduled so that Farm Board Chairman Legge could be called to testify.[28] Legge appeared before the committee on December 11 and together the senators and the Farm Board chairman tried to determine what would be the impact of the donation of wheat upon the board's efforts to stabilize wheat prices at a level significantly above the world price. As Legge explained, the Farm Board was grappling with the total wheat supply, and the distribution of 40 million bushels of wheat to the needy would ease its task only to the extent that the total consumption of wheat might be increased, and "how much the consumption might be increased through such a procedure is anybody's estimate." Legge's own estimate was that the net added consumption would be limited, that the great majority of the 40 million bushels "would just replace so many bushels of wheat coming out of other sources of supply," and thus the Farm Board would have to make additional purchases in order to support the price.

In essence, the Farm Board chairman was arguing that the donation of wheat to relief agencies would encourage them to substitute government donations for what they otherwise would purchase. An increase in total consumption would occur, he believed, only to the extent that the wheat reached those "in need of bread and unable to obtain it from other sources," and although he would not hazard a guess, Legge implied that such extreme destitution was rare. Several senators took exception to Legge's estimate, among them Thaddeus Caraway of drought-stricken Arkansas. "Down in my state—I presume everybody dislikes to have to advertise the extreme destitution that confronts people living in his own commonwealth," he declared, "but I feel confident that one-third of the people living in the agricultural areas, if they consume any bread made of wheat this winter and next spring, will have to get it in that way." He added that he had no firsthand knowledge of the conditions in cities but that if "the depression is as great as it is reported to be in the industrial centers . . . the consumption would be very greatly increased if it were made available." He suggested that the committee seek information on the extent of need from the Red Cross, and having received a report on Red Cross applications later in the hearing, he estimated that "if this wheat were made available possibly five or six million people a day would eat bread that will not eat wheat bread this winter unless provision like this is made for them."

The severity of the deprivation, however, was not the only issue discussed. In response to Legge's contention that there would be "no difference" between donating the wheat and appropriating money to purchase wheat in the open market for the needy, the bill's sponsor discussed what he saw as a very important political difference: "There is a great deal of demand" for distribution of the Farm Board wheat, he argued, "from many sources. There is a feeling among a great many people that the Government, either directly or indirectly, owns a large quantity of wheat and at the same time there are more people in the country to-day who are really in need of food than we have had in this country for a great many years." In response to Legge's acknowledgement that these statements were true, Capper continued: "There is a sort of psychology in that situation which prompts or suggests to a great many people that the practical thing and the generous thing for this Government to do is to make available to these people in distress a part of the wheat which the Government owns." When Legge, apparently assuming that Congress would reimburse the Farm Board for any wheat that it chose to donate, continued to argue that a general appropriation for relief might be more helpful than a donation of a specific commodity, Capper clarified that his resolution did not provide for any money to change hands: "that is, there is a feeling that the Government can afford to give this wheat for this particular purpose at this time." Such an action, he believed, would be far easier to get through Congress than an outright appropriation for relief: "if we want to help these hungry people . . . it is going to be easier to get action in Congress on a proposition of this kind than it will be to get a direct appropriation. . . . You can get action in Congress when it is known that the Government has . . . 100,000,000 bushels or more of wheat and it is really a question of what is going to become of it." Senator Caraway agreed, pointing out that such action might improve the Farm Board's tarnished image as well: "I do not think anything could be done that would so popularize the Federal Farm Board. . . . There are a lot of people who would feel tremendously sympathetic about it."

Little opposition to the resolution was expressed by members of the committee, many of whom appear to have agreed with Capper and Caraway's interpretation of the situation. As one senator summarized in another hearing, "In view of the fact that every section of the country today is individually and collectively attempting to make provision for the needy people, do you know of any better way in the world to use this surplus wheat than to apply it in that way?" [29] Chairman McNary appointed a subcommittee of three, including Capper, to give the resolution further consideration, and this group proposed two amendments, one limiting the amount donated to 20 million bushels, and another providing that the Farm Board should receive a credit to its revolving fund for the market value of the wheat on the date of delivery to a relief organization. By the time the subcommittee reported back in mid January, the drought relief fight had escalated markedly with several members of the Senate Agriculture and Forestry Committee leading the drive for the more generous provision. The committee voted unanimously to report the wheat distribution bill favorably with the two amendments. It did so late in January, noting the "anomalous situation of having a surplus of wheat beyond the ability of the consumers of the Nation to purchase," while "there are thousands and hundreds of thousands of hungry persons sadly in need of bread" and "bread lines in all our big cities." [30] By the time the bill was reported, the Senate was thoroughly aroused over drought relief, and the full Senate promptly passed the resolution without opposition. [31]

The House of Representatives was a different story. House Agriculture Committee Chairman Gilbert Haugen had indicated his opposition to the wheat distribution plan before the session began, [32] and although several bills for distribution of the Farm Board stocks had been introduced in the House at the opening of the session, none had been taken up by the committee before the Christmas recess. Early in January, however, the "food riot" in England, Arkansas focused congressional attention upon the plight of rural families rendered destitute by the double burden of drought and depression. Although the incident ended without violence, it provoked considerable comment in Congress. A few days after it was reported in the papers, Representative Hamilton Fish of New York, a Republican and chairman of a Special Committee to investigate Communist Activities, introduced a bill calling for distribution of the Farm Board wheat through the Red Cross and another, presented as an alternative to the first, that appropriated $15 million to the Red Cross for the purchase and processing of grain. Fish linked his proposals to the work of his special committee, asserting that severe distress provided fertile soil for communist organizers whom he held responsible for the uprising at England.

Discussion on the floor of the House at the introduction of a bill was typically brief, but the central issues raised were the same ones that the Senate Agriculture Committee and the Farm Board chairman had struggled with a month earlier: what would be the effect of such a measure on the price of wheat and the correlative query, were people really going hungry? Asked by a colleague whether distribution of the wheat would weaken wheat prices, Fish put the matter simply: "I submit that if our people are literally starving and without money to buy anything, it would not affect seriously the price of wheat on the American market." He urged an immediate hearing on the proposal so that its potential impact could be assessed by the Secretary of Agriculture and the chairman of the Farm Board. Others voiced support for the wheat distribution idea as well, arguing that distributing the Farm Board's increasing supply would help, not hurt, wheat prices or asserting the moral issue: "it is a national disgrace that we have unparalleled destitution and hunger in America with this Government hoarding 125,000,000 bushels of wheat." [33]

Despite Fish's request for an immediate hearing, the House Agriculture Committee did not take up the measure until the end of the month, after the Capper resolution had cleared the Senate. By that time, the drought relief fight had come to a head. The House and Senate had agreed on a figure of $45 million, excluding human food, and the House had succeeded in defeating an amendment, proposed by Senator Caraway and passed by the Senate, providing an additional $15 million specifically for "food loans." The House also stopped an effort by Representative La Guardia to have funds for food loans made available to the urban unemployed. The fight was not over with the $45 million production loan bill, however; the day that it was passed, Senator Robinson introduced a bill appropriating $25 million to the Red Cross for use in relief in both rural and urban areas, appending it as a rider to the Interior Department appropriation bill then under consideration. This action started a whole new round of controversy, with proponents of the donation pointing to similar congressional appropriations to aid Red Cross work in famines abroad or natural disasters and administration stalwarts declaring that such a move would dry up the springs of private charity and ruin the Red Cross. The

Senate quickly passed the Robinson measure, and the House appeared to be weakening; in fact, when the Senate passed the Capper wheat distribution resolution in the midst of this squabble, some interpreted it as a possible trade for the $25 million donation. This atmosphere, complete with high emotions and short tempers, prevailed as the House committee began consideration of Fish's bill.[34]

The hearing was brief with Fish as the only witness.[35] He indicated his awareness of the chairman's opposition to the plan and his willingness to accept a cash gift to the Red Cross as an alternative if it seemed preferable to the committee. But he also explained his reasons for preferring the wheat distribution approach: "It is very difficult for me to reconcile the proposition that the Government of the United States holds in its own granaries or in other granaries 100,000,000 bushels of wheat at a time when American people are starving for the lack of food. It is hard to go out before the people and explain such a condition when there is abundant wheat owned and hoarded by the Federal Farm Board." In addition, a donation of wheat, as opposed to money, would avoid the constitutional difficulties that some members of Congress saw in making a relief appropriation directly from the federal treasury. Citing instances in which Congress had aided the victims of disasters abroad, Fish argued that "the first function of the Government is to take care of its own people in time of great emergency." Permitting people to starve, he declared, was "creating a hotbed for communism."

The representative from New York made a strong case, reporting that spokesmen for the Farm Bureau Federation and other farm groups favored the plan, but Chairman Haugen remained unconvinced. As he expressed it, "The farmer is now getting the benefit of the tariff for the first time in our history . . . simply because the Farm Board has purchased a quantity of wheat and forced the price up. If you put that wheat on the market, you are going to destroy whatever benefit the Farm Board has extended to the farmer." Fish and a member of the committee argued that the wheat would not be on the market, that it would be consumed by people who were not in the market for wheat, and thus would not depress wheat prices. But the chairman remained adamant that the proposal was unfair because it would mean relief "at the expense of the wheat growers."

Inevitably, his arguments led committee members to the question that much of the congressional session had been preoccupied with, and one to which no one seemed able to provide a definitive answer: were people really hungry? "Have we allowed anybody to starve in this country?" queried Representative Adkins of Illinois. "Of course," replied Fish, "what do people do when they are out of a job and have no money—what do they live on these days? . . . I would say, yes: there are a great many people starving in this country." "There are many indigent people," Adkins conceded, "but the question is, Does anybody starve?" Fish responded with some exasperation, "When you say 'starve' let me tell you that is what creates Bolshevism, when a family is undernourished and must exist on a few scraps of bread a day," but he admitted that he did not have facts and figures on the extent of the distress. "It is not up to me; I can not go out and ascertain how many people are unemployed or how many people are starving. I say it is up to the Committee to bring competent witnesses here who have investigated in different states to prove the facts. . . . If the people in Arkansas, Oklahoma, Tennessee and other States can not show how many people are starving and undernourished, I can not."

The committee called no additional witnesses, however, and Fish apparently did not succeed in convincing it that an emergency existed, since the House Agriculture Committee failed to report the bill. Why would a bill that had sailed through the Senate without opposition fail to clear the House committee or even to excite enough interest to induce the committee to call additional witnesses?

The primary reason was probably the chairman's opposition, which was neither ambivalent nor incidental to the measure. His opposition was consistent with an analysis of the farm problem that had shaped his work for a decade. The whole premise of McNary-Haugenism was that the price for which the surplus could be sold on the world market was debasing the domestic price and that segregation of the surplus would permit farmers to obtain an American price for the domestic portion of their crop, just as the tariff permitted industrialists to obtain a higher price on domestic sales. The Farm Board's stabilization purchases, Haugen believed, had finally given the farmer the benefit of the tariff. Haugen had expressed his opposition to the wheat distribution plan in early December in a letter to McCleskey who had written to solicit his support for the measure. "Of course our sympathy is with the destitute and jobless people," he wrote, "however, I doubt the advisability of distribution of the wheat bought and held to absorb the surplus production of wheat, to carry out the declared policy contained in the Agricultural Marketing Act . . . which would be of course at the expense of the producers." He suggested that the "dole system" would be a better approach to relief because it would be "done at the expense of all, rather than the expense of agriculture." [36] He repeatedly stated the same view in the hearing before his committee. Distribution of the wheat would "undo what the Farm Board has done for the farmer." Haugen's reluctance to do anything that he believed would undermine the Farm Board is understandable; the Farm Board was, after all, the only tangible achievement of the long McNary-Haugen crusade that had made his name synonymous with the demand for equality for agriculture. And the members of his committee, many representing relatively homogeneous districts where agriculture was the dominant, if not the only, source of income, were not likely to take a position that could be interpreted as unfriendly to the farmer.

That release of the wheat for consumption by the unemployed would harm the growers, however, was not obvious to all. At the other end of the Capitol, the Senate Agriculture Committee reached an entirely different conclusion. Like Haugen, Chairman McNary had a stake in any gains attributable to the Farm Board, a position that he expressed quite clearly: "I do not want to do anything that would injure the efforts or negate the efforts of the Farm Board to stabilize the price of wheat at a figure above the world's market. If return of this wheat to domestic consumption and the channels of trade would have that effect, I would want to meet the situation in some other way."[37] But in his committee, an alternative interpretation of the potential impact of the plan prevailed. Senator Capper argued that the Farm Board's stocks, because they were extraordinarily visible, were themselves damaging the farmers' interests. He read an excerpt from a letter from McAdoo making a similar point: "So long as this wheat surplus overhangs the market, it is inevitable that the price of wheat will be depressed to a greater extent than would otherwise be possible. It is obvious that a large consumption of wheat will benefit the economic situation . . . and, to that extent, the producer or the owner of wheat will be benefited."[38] The Senate committee appears to have accepted this line of reasoning, since it voted unanimously to report the bill favorably after it was amended.

Why did the Senate Agriculture Committee reach one conclusion, the House committee another? In part, the divergence may have reflected a difference in the political skills of the measures' sponsors. Senator Capper was a well-liked, well-respected man who was widely regarded as a spokesman for the farm bloc. He owned several farm newspapers, a fact that gave him considerable influence with other senators from farm states, and his loyalty to agriculture was unquestioned. Furthermore, he was a close friend of Senate Agriculture Committee Chairman Charles McNary. His friendships extended across the aisle, apparently, since Democrat Marvin Jones later described him not only as a "master politician" but also as "one of the most lovable men in the Senate . . . a great friend of mine." [39] Fish, on the other hand, who was chairman of the Committee to Investigate Communist Activities, appears to have alienated many of his colleagues in the House with his allegations of subversive activities in their districts. He was not a member of the House Agriculture Committee, and there is little evidence that he enjoyed friendly rapport with its members. Furthermore, while he presented powerful arguments in a philosophical vein to support his plan, he lacked facts and figures to prove his contention that "a great many people are starving." Pressed for numbers, he backed down and suggested that the committee call competent witnesses: "I would not want you to appropriate a dollar without investigation." [40]

At a more fundamental level, however, the divergent behavior of the two committees probably reflected their differing perceptions of the extent of need, a highly politicized issue in the third session of the seventy-first Congress. The Senate committee included a number of senators from states hit hard by the drought, and these men were able to speak convincingly, from firsthand observation and from accounts of trusted observers back home, of destitution and desperation. Neither committee had a comprehensive national picture, but Senator Caraway supplied his colleagues with figures on applications for Red Cross assistance in the rural areas of fifteen of the twenty-two drought states. Extrapolating from these figures, the senators estimated that 5 or 6 million people might be expected to consume the Farm Board wheat if it were released. By the time the hearing was held, the senators were probably predisposed to accept allegations of unmet need and suffering because of the rancor generated by what was perceived as the administration's betrayal of the drought bloc and the further animosity provoked by the president's intemperate words about playing politics with human misery. The Senate passed the wheat measure with considerably greater ease in 1931 than it did a year later when conditions were far worse, the surplus was much greater, and more Democrats were in the Senate. The strong emotions of the drought relief fight seem the only convincing explanation for the ease with which Capper's resolution passed the upper chamber in 1931.

The House committee was similarly predisposed to reject allegations of severe distress. Fish's assessment of the committee's unfavorable action, rendered a year later, is telling: "the Committee did not believe that there was enough hunger and malnutrition in the country to justify reporting the bill." [41] The drought relief fight had given the House committee a considerable stake in perceiving that the need was being adequately met by local and voluntary action, since the committee had sided with the Hoover administration throughout the long battle. Perhaps this stand simply reflected the fiscal conservatism of the members. It appears to have reflected the tighter Republican party control in the House as well, a control that was apparently strong in the agriculture committee. At the end of Fish's testimony before the House committee, ranking Democrat James Aswell asked the representative from New York if he had seen the majority leader, the Speaker, or Bertram Snell, the third member of the reigning GOP triumvirate, regarding his proposal. "You know," Aswell explained, "unless you have seen those gentlemen and got their approval, you cannot get action by this committee on anything they want."[42]

Finally, the Hoover loyalists on the House committee probably believed that the president opposed the wheat gift. The president had not taken a public stand against the measure, but both the press and members of the Congress assumed that his statements opposing federal appropriations for relief included the wheat scheme, and he made no move to contradict them. In fact, the administration seems to have tried hard to avoid saying anything of substance about the proposal. The secretary of agriculture, when his opinion was solicited by Senate Agriculture Committee Chairman McNary, simply referred the committee to the Farm Board, and the Farm Board in turn stated no opinion other than a belief that its revolving fund should receive credit if the wheat were donated.[43] At the hearing, the Farm Board chairman studiously avoided taking a position on the advisability of the project: "the question of what Congress may do is certainly nothing that is within the province of the Farm Board to suggest in the way of relief work."[44] PECE, pressed to take a position by McCleskey in his tireless letter and telegram campaign on behalf of the wheat donation, took a similar noncommittal stand; the president's committee, Woods wired McCleskey, was created to "carry out federal programs after decisions have been made by the President and Congress."[45] And letters to the White House suggesting release of the wheat were generally acknowledged with a polite thank you. Of course, such studied noncommittal might have been interpreted as permission to proceed with the matter. But in the context of the drought relief fight, with the administration's fervent denunciations of the dangers of the dole and the president's repeated assertions that there was no "actual suffering" because the nation's local and voluntary resources were sufficient, it is not surprising that his opposition was assumed nor that his supporters on the House committee would vote against reporting out the measure.

The fight was not finished, however, even with the House committee's adverse action. On the same day that the House Agriculture Committee considered the Fish wheat distribution measure, the chairman of the Red Cross announced that the organization declined to undertake unemployment relief and would not accept the money provided in the Robinson bill, even if Congress were to appropriate it. To some this announcement suggested that a donation of wheat might be the wiser course, and the next day the Senate, probably in an effort to bypass the House Agriculture Committee, attached the Capper resolution to a War Department supply bill. The next day the House voted down six versions of the Robinson Red Cross donation measure, and the angry drought bloc issued a statement, signed by forty-two Democratic senators, threatening to force an extra session of Congress unless the $25 million gift and five other bills including the wheat distribution measure were passed. The threat was not made lightly, since an extra session could be forced simply by Senate failure to approve pending appropriations that were required for the continuation of government activity.[46]

President Hoover, in response, issued a statement presenting the fundamentals of the issue of private versus public financing of relief. It was, as David Hamilton has noted, "perhaps the most important statement on relief issues during his term of office."[47] "This is not an issue," the president declared, "as to whether the people are going hungry or cold in the United States. It is solely a question of the best method by which hunger and cold can be prevented." Would the American people maintain their traditions of voluntary giving and local responsibility, or would they substitute appropriations from the federal treasury? "My own conviction," he asserted, "is strongly that if we break down this sense of responsibility, of individual generosity to individual, and mutual self-help in the country in times of national difficulty and if we start appropriations of this character we have not only impaired something infinitely valuable in the life of the American people but have struck at the roots of self-government." Local and voluntary efforts were "the American way of relieving distress among our own people," he contended, "and the country is successfully meeting its problem in the American way today." He reasserted his faith in the Red Cross and reported that because of its efforts, "no one is going hungry and no one need go hungry or cold." Finally, he pledged "that if the time should ever come that the voluntary agencies of the country, together with the local and State governments, are unable to find resources with which to prevent hunger and suffering in my country, I will ask the aid of every resource of the Federal Government because I would no more see starvation amongst our countrymen than would any

Senator or Congressman. I have faith in the American people," he added, "that such a day will not come."[48]

Despite the president's expressed opposition to the use of federal funds for food loans or anything else that might be interpreted as relief, the tone of the statement was conciliatory. Since neither party wanted an extra session of Congress, because neither had the votes to control it, both sides moved hesitantly toward a compromise. A second loan fund of $20 million was approved; half was to go for the establishment of agricultural credit corporations, and half could be used for agricultural rehabilitation loans to individuals for items including food, so long as the food was part of a larger package intended to reestablish the farmer in production. With the agreement of both sides to this belated compromise in mid February came the final demise of the wheat distribution plan in the seventy-first Congress. The drought bloc withdrew its threat of an extra session, the House rejected the Capper resolution rider to the War Department supply bill, and the Senate conferees did not insist upon it. Congress adjourned in early March without providing any tangible federal assistance for the unemployed.[49]

The wheat distribution resolution was not a major issue in the 1930–1931 congressional session, and it has been treated by historians, if at all, as a minor footnote to the drought relief battle or as one of many uncoordinated drought and unemployment relief proposals that poured into the congressional hopper at the opening of the lame duck. As the first congressional consideration of a federal food assistance measure, however, the discussions of distribution of the Farm Board wheat in the winter of 1930–1931 are enormously revealing. The major themes that emerged in these discussions—the impact upon farmers, the extent and severity of need, and the nature of public sentiment—have proven to be enduring ones in food assistance policy debates.

The dominant theme, in both the House and Senate committees, was the impact of the proposed donation on the growers of wheat. No apology for this preoccupation was made in either committee, and no one argued that the wheat should be released regardless of its effect upon prices. Both committees clearly defined their responsibility as that of protecting the interests of the commercial farmer; neither suggested that an agriculture committee might be charged with a broader responsibility for the way that the nation was fed nor that the committee's responsibility to commercial wheat farmers might be balanced by a responsibility to subsistence farmers and sharecroppers who were suffering from privation. Despite much nostalgia about farming as a way of life, it had become a business, and the agriculture committees of Congress saw their task as that of ensuring or enhancing the profitability of that business and protecting it in its interaction with other sectors of the economy. The impact of food assistance on producers has remained a preoccupation of congressional agriculture committees ever since, and support for program expansion always has been secured either as a trade for price support measures crucial to farmers or by convincing farm senators and representatives—as the Senate Agriculture Committee was convinced in 1931—that food assistance benefits producers rather than harming them. As a result, programs have often been shaped to insure such benefits to producers.

The second line of inquiry, which might be summarized as "how hungry are the poor," also has been an enduring question, one that has recurred in slightly revised form with each new variation of food assistance. Were the poor literally going without bread, so that the donation of wheat would result in an increase in total consumption; or would recipients simply shift to other needed items money that they already were spending on bread, thus providing relief "at the expense of the wheat growers"? How much of a given commodity can be distributed without disturbing the normal cash market for that commodity, either by reducing recipients' normal purchases or by inducing participants to sell or trade donated commodities for other items? Do food stamps actually increase the quantity and quality of food purchased by participants, or do they simply free funds for other uses? Or the question that has been raised by the Reagan administration's reductions in food assistance, can food assistance programs be cut without harming the nutritional status of participants? Is the recent increase in demand for the services of soup kitchens and emergency food pantries attributable to cutbacks in food assistance? It is impossible to read recent discussions and allegations of hunger task forces and emergency food providers or to study the efforts of the Senate Select Committee on Nutrition and Human Need to establish the extent of poverty-related malnutrition in the United States in the late 1960s without hearing the echoes of 1931: "No one is going hungry and no one need go hungry or cold." Adkins's comment to Fish, "There are many indigent people, but the question is, Does anybody starve?" has been voiced again and again in the years since the wheat distribution plan was rejected by the House.

Once people became convinced that starvation amid plenty was a reality, however, they refused to tolerate it. This intolerance is the third theme that dominated congressional committee consideration of the Farm Board wheat in the winter of 1930–1931 and has remained a major factor in the politics of food assistance. "Every consideration of humanity and justice," wrote McAdoo to the Senate Agriculture Committee, "demands that what belongs to the people should not be withheld from them in their hour of extremity. I am frank to say that if the Government should hoard this wheat, in the face of such a situation, and if men, women, and children should die in America this winter from want, it would be an exhibition of heartlessness and callousness that could not possibly be defended." [50] Taking a more conciliatory tone, McCleskey wrote PECE Chairman Arthur Woods asking him to urge the president to take the lead in securing the release of the wheat as a "Christmas gift to the nation." McCleskey averred that "it would afford as much satisfaction to the affluent class as it would relief to the destitute." [51] The ubiquity of local efforts to transfer the surplus to people in need, the widespread condemnation of waste that contributed to the success of such projects as the Economic Conservation Plan, and the strong moral tone of appeals for release of the wheat attest to what Capper called the "psychology" of the situation, proving it to be an enduring component of the food assistance policy-making process also. For the government to store large quantities of food while people go hungry has repeatedly proven an embarrassment necessitating action. The winter of 1930–1931 found the public initially somewhat indifferent, but subsequent events, as we shall see, forced even the recalcitrant House Agriculture Committee to support distribution of the wheat. That scenario has been repeated each time widespread want has disturbed the mask of American affluence, recurring most recently when the Reagan administration, in the face of vociferous criticism, began distributing cheese and dried milk held off the market to support dairy prices. Neither the Farm Board nor the New Deal solved the dilemma of agricultural surpluses, and each successive discovery of hunger in America has been a discovery of the particularly offensive and unnecessary spectacle of want amid waste, an aspect of our national life that repeatedly has proven its capacity to arouse indignation.

CHAPTER FOUR

Government Grain for the Needy

W hen Congress adjourned on March 4, 1931, the wheat distribution plan appeared dormant if not dead. In view of his public statements on relief, the president could not be expected to initiate any distribution of federally owned commodities, and the new Congress would not convene until the following December. The idea of distributing the Farm Board stocks to the needy, however, kept surfacing with each discussion of the board's enormous holdings, which had reached 250 million bushels by the close of the congressional session. At the end of March, the board announced that it would make no further stabilization purchases after May, that its resources were insufficient to permit the application of the price stabilization approach to the 1931 crop, and that it would concentrate on an orderly disposal of its holdings in a way that would not disturb the market. The price of wheat immediately fell to its lowest point in thirty-six years, and a row ensued over the board's refusal to set a minimum price for sales of its stocks. With farm leaders of both parties predicting that farm issues would dominate the next session of Congress unless the board changed its policies, the wheat distribution plan surfaced again. "No doubt it will establish a 'dangerous precedent' and 'rock the foundations of government,'" commented a retired Ohio agricultural official in a telegram to the Farm Board, "but it might prevent a special session of Congress, which would be cheaper in the long run." [1] Again in July, when grain analysts in Chicago released a report estimating that the carrying charges on the Farm Board's wheat were costing the government about $4 million a month, letters to the editor and pronouncements by public officials suggested distribution of the wheat for relief. As it had after McAdoo's appeal the previous year, the Farm Board released a statement acknowledging receipt of the suggestion from a variety of sources and repeating that it had no authority under existing law to give away the wheat. "Only Congressional action," reported the Associated Press at the end of July, "would enable the use of the wheat for relief purposes." [2]

Despite persistent appeals for a special session to deal with relief matters, the president had no intention of convening Congress before its scheduled opening in December. Nor had he altered his beliefs about the locus of responsibility for relief. Even when the National Association of Community Chests and Councils reported in July that a preliminary survey of member groups showed that relief requirements would probably be twice as great in the winter of 1931–1932 as they had been the previous winter, the president was not alarmed. He called Red Cross Chairman John Barton Payne to the White House for a chat, and Payne declared afterward that unemployment relief was "a local problem, pure and simple." Payne hastened to add that such local problems were not a concern of the National Red Cross; it had its own job to perform and "did not deal with unemployment as such." [3] Colonel Woods had resigned in April, with Hoover anticipating a decrease in unemployment that would make PECE unnecessary, but the committee was continued through the summer under the direction of staff member Fred Croxton and was replaced in August by the President's Organization on Unemployment Relief (POUR) headed by Walter S. Gifford, president of the American Telephone and Telegraph Company. The appointment of Gifford and an advisory committee of sixty-one prominent persons provided an opportunity for a reiteration of the principles of local and voluntary aid. The Gifford committee's purpose was to coordinate the activities of local groups and encourage them in their local fund raising activities, not to serve as a channel for tangible federal assistance.

Nevertheless, demands for federal participation in relief were heard with increasing frequency. At the beginning of the Depression, the president's preference for local and voluntary effort in relief had been widely shared, even by many who would eventually champion federal assistance for the unemployed. As the Depression wore on, however, the idea that unemployment was somehow a local problem crumbled before the mounting relief load and the exhaustion of local resources. Most municipal governments depended heavily on property taxes, and since few relief agencies gave grants sufficient to cover the payment of rents, property tax collections fell off markedly. Many cities were left with insufficient funds for services such as police and fire protection and nothing at all for relief. As unrest grew at the local level, Piven and Cloward have noted in their discussion of the impact of depression upon ideology, "mayors themselves became national lobbyists for the unemployed as they sought to cope with political discontent and shrinking revenues." [4]

The first line of defense, according to the prevailing ideology, was the state governments, and as towns and cities across the nation neared bankruptcy, the states began to act. Late in the summer of 1931, Governor Franklin D. Roosevelt presented the New York state legislature with the Wicks Bill providing for an appropriation of $20 million to assist the counties and municipalities in providing relief to be administered by the independent Temporary Emergency Relief Administration. When the legislature passed the bill in September, New York became the first state to make provision for the unemployed. New Jersey and Rhode Island followed suit before Congress convened in December, and five more states established relief administrations or similar bodies early in 1932; by early 1933, a majority of the states had done so.

Such state relief provisions, however, did not silence a growing demand for federal action. Some states faced constitutional provisions that prohibited borrowing funds or making appropriations for relief purposes. Some state legislatures convened every other year and would not be in session for many months. But more important, once the ideological commitment to local relief had given way, the vast resources and taxing power of the federal government seemed to many the obvious place to turn. And no resource of the federal government was as obvious as the Farm Board's burdensome supplies of wheat.

Late in August, Samuel McKelvie, a former governor of Nebraska who had served on the Federal Farm Board, suggested donating the wheat for relief and compensating the Farm Board. Predicting that "the Federal Government will be obliged to join with cities, counties, states and agencies of voluntary relief in feeding millions of people this winter," he identified donation of the wheat, which now exceeded 200 million bushels, as "the easiest way for the government to cooperate." He would wait for national reaction to his plan, he said, and if positive, he would take the matter to the president. A month later, announcing that he had received "nothing but favorable expressions" concerning the plan and that the predicted opposition of farmers had not materialized, McKelvie took his proposal to the Farm Board, relief leaders, and a representative of POUR. POUR found the plan "impractical," and the Farm Board announced its willingness to sell wheat and cotton to relief agencies on credit, but the free distribution idea would not go away. In November, Representative Hamilton Fish told a New York City audience that he would introduce a measure to release the wheat in the upcoming Congress. Affirming his opposition to a "financial dole," he declared that "feeding starving people . . . is another matter," drawing a distinction between money and commodities that was to prove quite important in the politics of wheat distribution.[5]

In other quarters, plans for more comprehensive federal assistance were under consideration. Senators Edward Costigan of Colorado and Robert La Follette of Wisconsin were both at work on relief bills embodying the suggestions of a group of social welfare leaders who had organized the Social Work Conference on Federal Action on Unemployment. When Congress opened in December, both Costigan and La Follette introduced measures that differed somewhat as to amount and method of administration but provided for federal grants in aid to the states for relief. The session opened on a far more harmonious note than had the previous year's, with the Democratic leadership determined to avoid any action that would appear obstructionist, but it was clear that the controversial matter of federal participation in relief would be among the dominant issues of the session. Both the Costigan and La Follette measures were referred to the Senate Committee on Manufactures, and in late December, a subcommittee chaired by La Follette began a series of hearings that provided, for the first time, a comprehensive picture of the suffering of the unemployed.

In the Agriculture and Forestry Committee, meanwhile, a variation on the previous year's wheat distribution discussions was underway. Senator Capper, joined this time by Burton K. Wheeler of Montana, introduced a resolution providing for distribution of the wheat. It was quickly approved in principle by the committee, and a subcommittee including both Capper and Wheeler redrafted the resolution, setting the amount to be donated at 40 million bushels. The committee reported the measure favorably on December 21. An effort to have the resolution considered immediately by the full Senate so that it could be passed before the Christmas recess was blocked, but the measure was placed on the calendar for early in the new year.[6]

Without the heat of the previous year's drought relief debate, the measure received closer scrutiny by the full Senate than it had a year earlier, but the protracted debate one might have expected on the first piece of relief legislation to reach the floor of the Senate did not occur. Some voices were heard addressing the fundamental issue of whether the federal government was to contribute to relief. Senator Gore of Oklahoma recounted the history of Roman "bread and circuses," declaring that this policy had "undermined and destroyed Roman character and in the end destroyed . . . Roman liberty itself." He argued that the Constitution did not permit the federal government to take money from one citizen and give it to another.[7] Senator King of Utah raised the issue of state and local responsibility, asking why the states and counties should not be required to borrow for relief first since the federal government was already anticipating a deficit, and Senator Tydings of Maryland suggested that a revolving fund to lend money to the states for relief would be a more prudent approach. From another perspective, advocates of more comprehensive federal relief criticized the wheat proposition as piecemeal, haphazard, and inadequate.

Even the measure's critics, however, seemed to assume that it would pass. In response to Idaho Senator Borah's suggestion that appropriating money to buy wheat directly from the farmers would be more helpful to wheat growers, a spokesman for the agriculture committee painted a disturbing picture: "The money has been appropriated; the money has been spent, and all we have to show for it is some cheap low-grade wheat in bins and elevators now being dissipated and destroyed by rats, mice, age, dampness, and weevils. What are we going to do with it?" The symbolism of such waste amid so much want simply overwhelmed opposition based on abstract principles. "This is the situation," declared George Norris of Nebraska, expressing surprise at the opposition that had been voiced, "the Government of the United States has 160,000,000 or more bushels of wheat stored in bursting elevators, while surrounding us on all hand are our citizens suffering for food. Should we quibble now as to whether we could get a better remedy, or should we oppose this measure because it does not go far enough?" Admitting that it would not relieve suffering completely, he summed up the spirit of the debate: "But it will be 40,000,000 bushels of wheat turned into food, donated to suffering people, and in this calamity that ought to be almost enough of an argument to cause us to pass the legislation."

Several senators created graphic images of the distress of their own constituents. "We are so sheltered here in Washington," declared Royal Copeland of New York in a moving statement, "we come so little in contact with the practical aspects of poverty that we have no appreciation . . . of what is going on in this country. I have been in New York for a couple of weeks, and frankly, I did not like to go near my office because of the appeals made to me there for jobs, appeals to which I could not respond, because I had no jobs to give. But I saw hundreds— yes, thousands—of men and women in the bread lines seeking food." Nor was the distress confined to the great cities. Senator Howell of Nebraska made an urgent appeal on behalf of farm families in the Great Plains where the drought had continued unabated, presenting a telegram that he had received that morning:

> These suffering people feel that some way ought to be provided so that they can get food for themselves and their animals. They can not understand why supply from Farm Board surplus wheat should not be sent to them, which would relieve the situation. The people are desperate. The need very great. If something is not done at once thousands of families will be forced to abandon farms, starved out, frozen out. Will come to towns, morale broken. Will not be restored in generation.[8]

Howell offered an amendment, which was quickly passed, making some of the wheat available for animal feed.

After Howell's amendment, two others were passed. One changed the rate at which the Farm Board was to be credited for the wheat from the average price that it had paid for its wheat to the market value on the date of delivery to a relief organization; the other provided that some of the wheat might be used by states for the relief of Indians. Senator Norris made the point that it cost the government money to store and insure the wheat, and then the joint resolution was passed without a roll call vote.[9]

Three days later, Senator Capper read a number of favorable editorials into the *Congressional Record*. These editorials, although they in no way constituted a random selection of press reaction, are interesting to note because they suggest the extent to which the concrete reality of the available wheat overpowered objections, even those based upon principle. "The man on the street, on Main Street and all the cross streets of the United States, can be depended upon to applaud. . . . It is difficult to convince the average person that anybody in the United States should be starving for bread when Uncle Sam has 160,000,000 bushels of wheat that he does not know how to sell, and for which he has already paid or become obligated to pay," said the *Philadelphia Bulletin*. "Such distribution of wheat may be in principle the equivalent of a distribution of Treasury funds, and be in denial of the principle properly established barring the use of Federal funds for direct relief. But the argument will have difficulty in overruling the sympathetic sentiment." Speculating on the president's attitude, the *Bulletin* continued, "The President has consistently opposed direct Federal relief, and with good and sound reason. The logic of his position may challenge this proposal. But logic may yield—ought to yield—if it can be shown that there is a way which this wheat can be converted into bread and furnish food for thousands of families that would go hungry without it." Other newspapers were less concerned with the principles involved. "It will be hard to drum up much opposition to the Capper resolution" said the Cumberland, Maryland *Times*. "Objections offered can hardly be based on anything more fundamental than red tape." "It would not be in the nature of a dole," declared the Waco, Texas *News Tribune*. "While the larger problem of general relief is tied up in long debate," said the *El Paso Post*, "there is no reason why this simple emergency measure should be delayed." The *Republican News* of Mount Vernon, Ohio agreed: "if there are hungry to be fed and the Government has wheat, feed them at all costs. There should be no hesitation about using this wheat for the relief of suffering humanity." [10]

The House Agriculture Committee, however, which took up the wheat measure on the same day the Senate passed the Capper resolution, found reason to hesitate and delay. Much had changed in the House committee since it had considered the Fish resolution a year earlier, and passage of a wheat distribution measure appeared more likely than it had the previous year. Gilbert Haugen, the most outspoken opponent of the wheat distribution plan, was no longer chairman of the committee. The Democrats had control of the House by a narrow margin, and the new chairman, Marvin Jones, was not only a Democrat but a supporter of the wheat distribution approach. In fact, the measure that the House Agriculture Committee took under consideration was one that he had introduced. Finally, the Democrats had a majority, though a narrow one, on the agriculture committee itself. Favorable action seemed imminent when the committee took up the measure in early January. [11]

The hearings, however, revealed that while much had changed in the committee, much had remained the same. It was still preoccupied with assessing the impact of the proposed gift upon the wheat farmer and the Farm Board, and that impact was still assumed to depend on whether the wheat distributed would represent a net addition to consumption or simply a substitution for wheat and wheat products already being purchased by relief agencies and clients. Like the drought relief fight of the previous year, the question quickly boiled down to the extent of unmet need in the country and the ability of the traditional relief agencies to alleviate it without federal assistance, and in echoes of the earlier discussions, no one seemed to know the answer. A spokesman for the Farm Board declared that if people were hungry, "anything anywhere ought to be taken and given to them," but added that he did not think that "anyone knows today how much would be used, or what effect it will have on the wheat market, because that will be determined by the amount used." [12] The committee turned to the Red Cross and the POUR for information, but neither could supply it. The Red Cross would accept responsibility for distributing the wheat if Congress passed the measure, but it would not state its position on the legislation. Asked by a committee member, "whether or not there is sufficient demand to warrant the use of this much wheat," Red Cross Chairman John Payne replied, "I have no such information. I do not know. . . . I do not believe such information is available." [13] Fred Croxton, assistant director of the POUR, agreed with Judge Payne that "no one can tell what the demand will be." Pressed by the committee to estimate the need, he replied, "We do not know. . . . We are not in a position to pass on whether or not this wheat will be used." A frustrated congressman asked, "Is there anybody in your organization, or is there any source of information from which we can get that information and get it quickly?" He answered, "None." [14]

Several members of the House appealed to the committee for release of the wheat, but no one offered the evidence of need—facts and figures on relief grant levels and the diets of the jobless—that was being presented by a well-orchestrated procession of experts in the Costigan–La Follette hearings at the other end of the Capitol. Some members of the committee suggested that the Salvation Army could supply the required evidence, but a representative who had been invited by the chairman failed to appear. Many of the relief experts who testified so effectively before the Costigan–La Follette hearings were representatives of social work and public welfare organizations based in large Eastern cities; the chairman's failure to invite them to appear before the agriculture committee is not surprising, given his rural background and relative inexperience in welfare matters. It is revealing, however, that no representative of the Social Work Conference on Federal Action on Unemployment volunteered to appear or sent so much as a letter commenting on the wheat distribution measure. Clearly the Costigan–La Follette hearings were the main show, and they absorbed the available energy, but the failure of leading social workers to take an interest in the wheat plan was also indicative of an attitude which would prove very important in the development of food assistance. Almost all social welfare leaders favored relief in cash and opposed such assistance in kind as the distribution of foodstuffs; they believed that the latter method was an antiquated form of relief, inconsistent with modern social work practice and the dignity of the client.[15] Throughout the Depression, social workers and relief experts would continue to demonstrate a kind of principled myopia about the possibilities of relief in commodity form.

If social welfare leaders displayed indifference to the wheat measure, the wheat processing industry did not. Letters and telegrams from grain dealers, millers, grain elevator operators, and others concerned with the wheat trade expressed strong opposition to the plan.[16] Although prompt action had been expected by many, the committee pigeonholed the bill for a month, and early in February, it voted not to report the measure. Interviewed by a reporter, Chairman Jones attributed rejection of the measure to a feeling among members of the committee that "if anything were done, the government should go out in the open market and purchase the wheat," and to the concern that the Farm Board had large loans outstanding against some of the wheat that would have to be paid off if the wheat were given away.[17] A Republican member of the committee, speaking for those who had voted against the resolution, later told the House that "the evidence as presented to our committee . . . was not sufficient to warrant a favorable vote."[18] The activities of lobbyists were also significant. The American Farm Bureau Federation's Washington representative told the organization's board of directors in March that the bureau's opposition to the Capper Resolution had been conveyed to the House Agriculture Committee before the committee voted not to report the measure.[19] Similarly, the Millers National Federation later told the White House that it had opposed the wheat distribution plan as vigorously as possible and felt this opposition had been instrumental in defeating it in the House committee.[20] After the committee's unfavorable action, the plan appeared dead, and the *New York Times* reported that, in the opinion of the House leadership, the committee had "fixed a definite policy against such legislation for at least the remainder of this session."[21]

The wheat distribution plan, however, was not the sort of idea that would quietly fade away. A few days after the House Agriculture Committee's vote, Representative Polk of Ohio, a member of the committee, denounced its Republican members for voting as a bloc to prevent the bill from coming before the House. He urged the preparation of a discharge petition to extract the bill from the committee. "This Congress only recently appropriated $2,000,000,000 to help the financial and business interests of the country through the Reconstruction Finance Corporation, but unless some extraordinary action is taken and this meritorious bill, which has been killed in committee, is called up by the Speaker at the request of petitions signed by a sufficient number of Members," he asserted, "you will have gone on record as unwilling to grant grain for food for the hungry." [22]

Meanwhile, the La Follette and Costigan bills, combined into a single measure providing for a fund of $375 million for grants in aid to the states for relief, had obtained the blessing of the Senate Committee on Manufactures. The relief measure reached the Senate floor at the beginning of February where it encountered fierce opposition from administration Republicans and conservative Democrats. In mid February, both the Costigan–La Follette measure and a substitute proposed by Democratic conservatives, which would have provided loans rather than grants to the states, were defeated in the Senate. The next day, Senator Wagner of New York introduced another bill that combined the administrative features of the Costigan–La Follette measure with the loan features of the conservative substitute, but it was promptly pigeonholed. Mid February found Congress still was unwilling to act on relief as the bread lines lengthened and the desperation grew.

A week later, however, desperation of another sort revived the wheat plan. In the northwestern Great Plains, where much of the nation's wheat surplus had been produced and stored, drought had been followed by grasshoppers and grasshoppers by a winter of exceptional severity. Neither the farmers nor the Red Cross could cope with the situation; feed was exhausted and cows and horses were starving. Late in February, the Senate Agriculture and Forestry Committee quickly approved a resolution introduced by Senator Norbeck calling for the release of 5 million bushels of wheat—less than 3 percent of the Farm Board's supply—to aid in feeding livestock and farm families in the drought area. The bill was promptly approved on the Senate floor without debate and sent to the House. [23]

The House committee just as promptly tabled the matter, but when Republican Representative Hamilton Fish initiated a discharge petition, partisanship intervened. The Democratic leadership did not want a Republican to extract relief legislation from a Democratic Party–controlled committee. The wheat issue was beginning to threaten the Democrats' image of a party concerned about the suffering. Although Republicans on the committee had voted against the Jones measure unanimously, while only a third of the Democratic members had done so, the vote had not been published, and news commentators were attributing the failure to report the earlier resolution to the Democrats who, after all, controlled the House. As the *Washington News* commented, "If Garner, the Democratic Boss, had exerted the power he has heretofore used, the relief measure would have been passed. Voters who are keeping a campaign score card will debit the Democrats with another costly error." [24] When the committee appeared ready to repeat the action by tabling the Norbeck resolution, the House Democratic leadership exerted pressure on the Democratic members. On the first of March, the House committee once again held hearings on the wheat plan.

These hearings were a marked contrast to the previous round. This time the witnesses, mostly members of Congress from the drought-stricken area, presented a factual and moving portrait of the situation, complete with numerous photographs of dead livestock and letters and telegrams from state officials and local notables. [25] The irony of the committee's willingness to release the wheat for starving cows and horses when it had been unwilling to do so for hungry workers was not lost on the committee itself. The House Agriculture Committee reversed its earlier stand and substituted what was essentially the Capper resolution, providing 40 million bushels for general relief purposes, including livestock feed in the drought area, for the Norbeck-Fish resolution providing 5 million bushels for crop failure areas only. With this change, the committee reported the bill favorably, and Chairman Marvin Jones asked for "right of way" so that the bill could be considered immediately. [26]

When the wheat measure reached the floor of the House on March 3, it was the first piece of relief legislation to do so in the Seventy-second Congress, and members expressed their frustration with that situation by alternately congratulating the agriculture committee for bringing the measure forward or castigating it for not having done so sooner. The debate that ensued was remarkable, both for the near unanimity of that usually discordant assemblage and for the rhetorical agility with which those who had publicly stated their opposition to federal relief explained their support for the wheat measure. The dominant tone was established by the first speaker in the preliminary debate on the special rule necessary for immediate consideration. "Under ordinary conditions I could not support such a measure," declared Representative Pou of North Carolina, majority spokesman for the rules committee, "but we are confronted, as everyone knows, by an unparalleled condition throughout the country. We have an abundance of food and yet there is widespread hunger." [27]

After Pou's remarks, many members rose to echo his sentiments. While they would not normally favor such a resolution, the extraordinary times demanded such action. Each presented an individualized interpretation of the paradox. "It is a disgrace and an outrage," pronounced Hamilton

Fish, "that this country of ours, with an overabundance of foodstuffs, should permit millions of our own people to continue to be undernourished and hungry." The chairman of the agriculture committee sounded the same theme: "We are living in rather strange times. We have a surplus of practically every commodity of any consequence, both industrial and agricultural, and yet we have a great deal of distress in America. I am an optimist in so far as our country is concerned," he added, "but it is certainly true that we have had a few kinks in our system of distribution." Representative Norton of Nebraska stressed the impact upon his own farm constituents: "It is a deplorable fact . . . that in the greatest agricultural Nation in the world the tillers of the soil are being driven from what once were their happy homes, because of the low prices of foodstuff, to the cities, where millions for lack of food are suffering from hunger and want." "We have an oversupply of the various necessities of life, and yet we find millions of people pleading for those necessities," declared Representative Lonergan of Connecticut; "we have underconsumption and not overproduction." "Can this, the richest nation on earth, turn a deaf ear to the hungry and starving?" asked Representative Crowe of Indiana. "Can this country, with too much foodstuff, turn away from the hungry mothers and helpless children of this land, and especially when the Federal Farm Board has its millions of bushels of wheat on hand with no apparent use for same?"

Nearly all of the several dozen representatives who spoke mentioned the carrying charges—insurance and storage fees—that were rapidly diminishing the value of the wheat at the rate of eighteen cents per bushel per year. "At the present price of wheat," House Agriculture Committee Chairman Jones estimated, "it will eat itself up, even if the weevils let it alone, in about two and a half years." Pointing out that the Farm Board had promised not to sell more than 5 million bushels per month, and that it would have at least another 115 million bushels to sell, he estimated that by the time the Farm Board had gotten around to the last 40 million bushels, its value would have been completely absorbed by the carrying charges. "This takes it out of the realm of the dole and makes it more like the situation of a man having an old suit of clothes or an old coat that he has no use for and that some one else needs very much." Others pointed out that the wheat might not withstand prolonged storage under prevailing conditions. Describing a "great fleet of ships" used to store Farm Board wheat in the harbor of the city of Buffalo, Representative Reed of New York pictured the steps necessary to prevent wheat from rotting under such conditions: "I happen to know that it is necesary for the Government, in order to prevent that wheat from spoiling, to have these great vessels towed over to the elevators and then go to the enormous expense of putting a cold blast through all these hundreds of thousands of bushels of wheat to keep it from spoiling. Far from being a dole," he argued," we will find ourselves, unless we take some action of this kind, in the position of letting hundreds of thousands of bushels of wheat rot, rapidly deteriorate in the holds of ships, with people begging for food."

Conservatives on both sides of the aisle took pains to distinguish the wheat gift from a dole. "I am as much opposed to a dole as any man in this Congress," declared Representative Glover of Arkansas. "But there is a difference between feeding a hungry man and a dole. There is no person that has a spark of feeling for humanity that would dare say that the Government, with all of this wheat in its hands and food that could be delivered to persons in distress, should stand by and let them suffer." "I am against all doles, but I think that during these perilous times when people are hungry that we ought to cut out all red tape and feed the people of America," echoed Representative De Priest of Illinois. "The resolution under consideration does not provide a dole," stated Representative Garber of Oklahoma in a careful exposition of the basis of conservative support for the measure. "It supplies a temporary need under a great emergency." Liberals and Progressives, however, grew impatient with the distinction. "The opposition to this legislation has raised the old worn-out cry of a 'dole,' and we have been reminded that the President . . . has voiced his opposition to legislation of this kind. I do not propose to quibble over what this measure may be called," said Johnson of Oklahoma, pointing out that no one had raised the specter of a dole when similar gifts had been made to feed the hungry in foreign lands. "Oh, the scarecrow in this bill seems to be the fear of some that it will be considered a dole. Their statesmanship will not permit them to vote for anything that smacks of a dole," taunted Representative Flannagan of Virginia in an emotional statement. "Well, I do not care what you call it; I am not interested in names, I am interested in feeding the hungry." When the applause subsided, he placed the issue squarely on a moral basis:

It is a sad spectacle to see men who have never felt the pangs of hunger, who do not know what it means to go without three good meals a day, who are living on the fat of the land, who have never experienced the despair unemployment brings, who are unacquainted with the misery and distress suffered by those who, through no fault of their own, are unable to provide for those God has committed to their keeping, and who must realize the immediate necessity for action, in the name of statesmanship, stand here and quibble over a name—over whether this is a dole or a relief measure—and let that be the critierion by which they will decided whether or not the hungry shall be fed. . . . Why if that is statesmanship all I have to say is—and I am a Presbyterian elder and believe my church will voice my sentiment—damn such statesmanship.

Only two statesmen spoke against the bill. As he had in the committee, Adkins of Illinois insisted that relief was the job of communities and states that could take care of their own if they wanted to, and that once established, a donation program would prove difficult if not impossible to stop. And Hope of Kansas, representing "a district which last year produced 14 per cent of all the wheat grown in the United States," argued, as he had in the committee, that the distribution of free wheat would weaken wheat prices and deprive wheat farmers of their rightful market. In addition, he asserted that the resolution would reduce funds that the Farm Board had available for loans to cooperatives since the board would have to use money from the revolving fund to pay off loans against the wheat donated. When the vote was taken, only Adkins and Hope voted against the measure. The vote was as close to unanimity as any that the House would have on relief legislation for a long while. The glaring contradiction of breadlines knee-deep in wheat had overwhelmed both partisanship and ideology.

The bill returned to the Senate where the process of approving several House amendments required only a few minutes, and then it went to the White House where the president's signature was far from certain. As several members of both houses had noted in the congressional debate, the bill violated the president's stated policy of no federal relief. The president's close ties to the Red Cross, however, the willingness of that organization to undertake distribution of the wheat, and the noncommittal stand of the POUR seemed to augur well for signature. The *New York Times* reported that the president would sign the measure: "Mr. Hoover's opposition to direct Federal relief is well known. In administration quarters, however, it has been represented that in view of the fact that a commodity rather than money is involved, he felt he should do his part in making the wheat available for food." The press taunted the president for drawing so fine a distinction between money and a commodity bought with public money, but for the most part, the reaction was favorable.[28] After conferences with the attorney general, the secretary of agriculture, the chairman of the Federal Farm Board who publicly lamented the unfairness of the resolution's failure to provide for reimbursement of the Farm Board, and the chairman of the Red Cross, the president signed the resolution into law. A few hours later, the first of the donated wheat left elevators in Nebraska for the drought-stricken section of South Dakota with the railroads providing free transportation.[29]

Given the near unanimity of the vote in the House, the criticism of the committee for not reporting the bill sooner, and the president's decision not to oppose the measure, the House probably would have passed the resolution had it been reported in early January, thus affording some assistance to the unemployed in the terrible winter of 1932. Despite the delay, Capper's prediction that getting Congress to release the wheat would be easier than getting it to appropriate cash had proven true. The wheat began feeding the hungry just three weeks after the Senate defeated the Costigan–La Follette measure and a full four-and-a-half months before Congress and the president finally agreed upon a program of relief loans to the states through the Reconstruction Finance Corporation. By the time the Emergency Relief and Construction Act of 1932 was nearing passage in mid July, the Red Cross had already distributed more than 25 million bushels of the wheat, and a second allocation was deemed necessary to meet needs that were expected before Congress reconvened in December. Early in July, Congress passed a measure authorizing donation of another 45 million bushels of wheat and 500,000 bales of cotton to the Red Cross, and a few weeks later, it passed an appropriation bill allocating money to the Farm Board to cover liens and obligations against the commodities donated. An additional 350,000 bales of cotton were approved in a measure passed in February 1933.[30]

Most historians of the Depression years have paid little if any attention to the Farm Board wheat donations, treating them as relatively insignificant, isolated actions with little connection to the emergence of federal relief. The relief loans to the states authorized by the Emergency Relief and Construction Act of 1932, on the other hand, are generally regarded as the culmination of the process by which opposition to federal relief was broken down, the entering wedge of the welfare state. The Farm Board wheat, however, deserves a larger place in the history of federal participation in relief for several reasons. As noted above, it was the first federal relief for the unemployed in the Great Depression, and as the first unemployment relief measure debated in both the House and the Senate in the Seventy-second Congress, it served as an opportunity for advocates of federal participation to marshal their arguments. More important, it was a sort of back door to federal relief since, as Senator Capper was fond of pointing out, the money for it had already been spent. Opponents of federal expenditure for relief thus were deprived of some of their most powerful arguments—the need for a balanced budget and the evils of higher taxation. By making it obvious that the government had the resources to relieve need, the wheat undermined the ideology and assumptions that prohibited federal aid to the jobless. With the money already spent and the wheat already in government hands, the symbolism of withholding it from the needy was too strong, even for President Hoover. Ironically, the president later claimed credit for the wheat and cotton donations, both in his reelection campaign and in his memoirs.[31]

The wheat episode was part of a broader process of ideological transition as well. Piven and Cloward have recently examined the historical process by which the myth of laissez-faire began to crumble.[32] They attribute to the early years of the Great Depression a major role in the debunking of the ideology that the state and the economy are wholly separate spheres. In depression remedies like the Reconstruction Finance Corporation, the state was massively intervening in the economy on behalf of business while refusing, for most of the Hoover presidency, to intervene on behalf of the jobless. The Farm Board's wheat stocks made obvious to many the willingness of the government to intervene on behalf of politically powerful entrepreneurs; the wheat was acquired, after all, in an effort to raise wheat prices. The visibility of the stocks escalated the demand for similar solicitude for jobless workers. "After what I have seen and heard in this Congress," declared Representative Gilchrist of Iowa in explaining his support for the wheat resolution, "I do not want anyone to tell me that the Government is not in business. . . . The Federal Farm Board is an example of this very thing. . . . Since we have come here this session, we have passed many bills whereby the Government is supporting this or that or the other business. . . . We have not yet given any direct aid to the man who is out of a job."[33] The process by which ideology changes is a complex one, but clearly the contradiction of grain rotting in government storage while the people went hungry helped to breach the ideological walls protecting the principle of local and voluntary responsibility for relief.

The Farm Board wheat and cotton donations also were important among the relief measures of the Hoover years in purely quantitative terms. By the end of 1932, for example, the value of the wheat and cotton distributed was estimated at approximately $36 million or a little over half of the total amount of Reconstruction Finance Corporation (RFC) relief loans dispensed at approximately the same time. That is, the wheat and cotton accounted for fully a third of the federal assistance that actually reached the states during 1932. In the long run, a total of about $40 million worth of wheat and $30 million worth of cotton was donated, although these commodities had cost the government a much greater amount when originally purchased, and Congress eventually allowed the Farm Board credits totaling nearly $200 million for bookkeeping purposes.[34]

Although various members of Congress stressed the abnormality of the situation, in succeeding decades, government price supporting purchases of agricultural commodities were to become the norm, and government warehouses stocked with edible commodities were to become a regular feature of the American landscape. Certainly the Congress that donated the wheat to the Red Cross had no inkling that it was embarking on the first of a long series of federal food assistance ventures. Indeed, a number of those who spoke in favor of the bill saw distribution of the wheat as a means of bringing the ill-fated Farm Board experiment to a close and assumed that the board's enormous losses, both financial and political, would be sufficient to deter any subsequent administration from attempting to support prices.

In retrospect, however, the Farm Board wheat donations may themselves be viewed as an experiment in food assistance. Even though the Red Cross was a voluntary agency and no administrative carryover crept into the public programs of the New Deal, the first wheat donation resolved, to the satisfaction of nearly all those involved, the basic questions that had surrounded the wheat distribution plan since it was first proposed. Were poor people hungry enough to consume the donated wheat without disturbing the market? What would be the effect of release of the wheat upon grain prices? The price of wheat did decline after the first wheat donation but no more rapidly than it had been declining and no more rapidly than the prices of other commodities. Almost everyone concerned concluded that indeed the wheat had reached people who would have gone without it. The rapidity with which the first donation was consumed and the generally favorable reports from the field did much to convince the skeptical. By May of 1932, just two-and-a-half months after distribution began, the wheat had reached three-quarters of the counties in the United States, and many communities, having underestimated the need or facing increasing unemployment, were applying for a second allotment. At the end of May, Judge Payne told President Hoover that the current supply would be insufficient and more would be needed to continue the program the following winter.[35] Legislation authorizing a second donation was introduced immediately in both houses of Congress, and in the debate on the matter, a number of members rose to report that the wheat had made a crucial difference to their constituents. The comments of Representative Clancy of Michigan were typical:

> The Government wheat which has been distributed in my city, a city of 2,000,000 people, with six or seven hundred thousand people in acute distress, has been a godsend. It has been distributed in the nature of bread and flour products to hungry children in the schools.
>
> Many families would be absolutely hungry and in danger of starvation if it were not for this flour, because our public and private welfare funds have been exhausted. Just last Monday it was estimated by John C. Cowan, chairman of the distribution committee, that the amount of these bread products distributed to starving people amounted to tens of thousands of dollars. We look for more acute distress this fall and winter. We need more flour and wheat products. I hope the bill will pass.[36]

Both the Farm Board and the Department of Agriculture endorsed the second wheat distribution measure, concluding that the first donation had been "helpful." At the end of 1932, Red Cross Chairman Payne told the House Agriculture Committee that he had received many favorable comments from the grain trade to the effect that the distribution had helped by providing employment in the mills and reducing the visible surplus without disturbing normal marketing operations.[37] Not everyone was persuaded, of course. Haugen of Iowa and Hope of Kansas remained convinced that commodity donation was "relief at the expense of agriculture," but Congress passed and the president signed the later donation bills with almost no debate on the fundamentals of surplus distribution. As House Agriculture Committee Chairman Marvin Jones commented, "at least no one can gainsay the advantage and advisability of this action."[38]

CHAPTER FIVE

The End of
the Hoover Era

The day before Herbert Hoover left office, he signed into law an act authorizing the Red Cross to exchange some of its Farm Board cotton surplus for articles containing wool, thus bringing down the curtain on his administration's response to the paradox of want amid agricultural surfeit. The winter of 1932–1933 was an exceptionally cold one, and the families of those who had been without wages for several years needed warm clothing, but typically, the wool-for-cotton exchange measure came too late to ward off the cold of what many observers have characterized as the worst winter of the Depression. But the winter's troubles were not confined to the weather. Unemployment figures reached new highs and agricultural prices new lows. Bankrupt municipalities cut meager relief grants still further as the cumulative effects of depression sent the number of recipients ever higher. Mortgage foreclosure, default, and bank failure reached epidemic proportions and so did disillusion and despair. Sparks of discontent flared here and there, and in the Cornbelt, the smoldering resentment burst briefly into prairie fire, igniting much discussion of the possibility of revolution. But the dominant attitudes were hopelessness and apathy—depression in a psychological as well as an economic sense. As the winter drew to a close, the vague unease took the firmer shape of panic when a banking crisis of unprecedented proportions swept the nation. On inauguration day, the banks in New York and Illinois were closed by the governors of those states, and the Stock Exchange and the Chicago Board of Trade suspended operations.

Springtime is all the more welcome after a hard winter, and the growing distress of the nation in the final months of the Hoover administration set the stage for the new president and the New Deal. Indeed, in the months between the adjournment of Congress in mid summer and the inauguration the following March, events seemed to conspire to present the incoming administration with a mandate for action and change. A full assessment of what the New Deal did, and failed to do, to resolve the great American paradox of want and plenty requires an understanding of the potentials and the limits of the opportunity that confronted the New Dealers, which, in turn, requires a close look at the final months of the Hoover presidency.

The obvious place to begin an exploration of the remarkable opportunity that eventually confronted the New Deal is with Herbert Hoover himself. The president's signature on the various relief measures that finally emerged from the seventy-second Congress came too late—and too grudgingly—to rescue his popularity, especially as the caution with which the RFC loans were to be dispensed became obvious. By the summer of 1932, satire of the president and his identification with symbols of the Depression had become rampant. Shantytowns had been Hoovervilles for years, but now empty pockets turned inside out were "Hoover Flags," jackrabbits shot for their stringy meat were "Hoover Hogs," and newspapers spread out to cushion the cement floor of the local relief shelter were "Hoover Mattresses." [1] In late July, the president decided to evict the remnants of the bonus army of World War I veterans that had come to Washington in June to plead for immediate payment of a bonus due in 1944. The armed rout that ensued from this decision widened the chasm between the president and the people, becoming for many both the conclusive evidence and the primary symbol of the incumbent's attitude toward those rendered destitute by the Depression. [2]

Clearly the national disaffection with Herbert Hoover's principles, style, and view of the world presented the Democratic party with a chance not only to gain the White House but also to implement new and decisively different policies. In recent years, much has been written of the continuities between the Republican policies of the twenties and the Democratic programs of the thirties, of the elements of the New Deal that were present in embryonic form within the Hoover program, and of the essentially conservative accomplishments of the liberal New Deal. Food assistance, as we shall see, is certainly a case in point of these arguments. Yet in the summer of 1932, Hoover's failures, rather than his achievements, were shaping the agenda of the next administration.

Nowhere was the president's failure to deal effectively with the realities of the Depression so widely acknowledged as in the area of relief. Even Hoover's friends and defenders generally have agreed that his inability to perceive the extent and depth of suffering among the unemployed and to adjust his principles to these realities was a crucial factor in the nation's rejection of his leadership. "If any one attitude lost the election in 1932," wrote Harris G. Warren in his friendly study of the president and the Depression, "it was Hoover's refusal to use federal resources in direct relief. . . . No matter how often he denied it, people were starving in the midst of plenty." [3]

Yet relief per se was not as great an issue in the presidential campaign of 1932 as might have been anticipated. Although Franklin Roosevelt, beginning with his "Forgotten Man" speech in April, had consistently identified himself with the needs of the impoverished and the unemployed and had declared in his acceptance speech that under the Democrats the federal government would "assume bold leadership in distress relief," he offered no specific plans or programs other than the idea of using the unemployed in conservation and reforestation work. Indeed the major statements of the two candidates on the relief issue sounded remarkably similar. They agreed that the primary responsibility for relief was local and voluntary, that the states should assist the localities in meeting this obligation, and that the resources of the federal government should be used only when states were unable to meet the need. Roosevelt stood on his record; he had called the New York state legislature into special session to enact the first statewide assistance to the unemployed when the inability of municipalities to meet the need had become evident. He had tried to secure an unemployment insurance measure in his own state and had convened the governors of other states for a conference on unemployment insurance plans. Hoover, in return, claimed credit for both the RFC relief loans and the distribution of the Farm Board wheat, though his claims must have sounded hollow to those who had followed the relief politics of the previous congressional session. Neither candidate moved beyond such claims and general principles to articulate specific programs. [4]

Their common emphasis on the importance of a balanced budget and the need for economy in government made the two sound even more alike. Each accused the other of advocating an expansion of the power and expenditures of the federal government; each pledged retrenchment. Even their attempts to balance the need for relief with the constraints of the budget had a similar ring. In a major address on the federal budget, Roosevelt qualified his commitment to avoid deficit spending: "If starvation and dire need on the part of any of our citizens make necessary the appropriation of additional funds which would keep the budget out of balance, I shall not hesitate to tell the American people the full truth and ask them to authorize the expenditure of that additional amount."[5] He sounded strikingly like the Herbert Hoover of 1931 who had pledged that "if the time should ever come that the voluntary agencies of the country, together with the local and State governments, are unable to find resources with which to prevent hunger and suffering in my country I will ask the aid of every resource of the Federal Government."[6]

The two candidates differed tremendously, however, in their ability to perceive that the time of starvation and dire need actually had come. While Roosevelt repeatedly referred to suffering, deprivation, and indeed starvation, Hoover argued with a persistence bordering on monotony that the American way of relief had worked effectively to "prevent hunger and cold" among the unemployed, offering as evidence his much-criticized surgeon general's reports showing a comparative reduction in mortality rates.[7] Two days before the election, he declared himself unable "to find a single locality . . . where people are being deprived of food or shelter" and predicted that the relief load of the coming winter would be lighter than that of 1931–1932. He continued to see prosperity around the corner; as he described the crowds who had gathered around the rear platform of his campaign train in the Midwest, Hoover was asked by a reporter, "Mr. President did any of them look like they have been forgotten?" "No," replied the president, "and I noticed many of them are able to come in automobiles."[8]

If the public's rejection of Hoover's approach to relief was generally silent like the crowd that lined the streets when the president spoke in Detroit, the farmers' growing impatience with the failure of his agricultural policy was increasingly visible and dramatic. After the second veto of the McNary-Haugen plan in 1928, each of the three major national farm organizations had moved in its own direction, eroding the unity generated by the long fight for agricultural equality. The Grange had espoused a scheme known as the export debenture plan that, like McNary-Haugen, relied on dumping surpluses abroad. The American Farm Bureau Federation had at first given considerable support to Hoover's Farm Board, urging it toward more decisive intervention in markets, and in 1931, the bureau's president, Sam Thompson, was appointed by Hoover to serve on the Farm Board. As the inadequacy of the Farm Board's effort became obvious, however, the Farm Bureau had begun agitating for monetary reforms and parity prices, although it was not specific as to how to achieve such prices. The Farmers' Union had demanded legislation to guarantee prices high enough to cover the cost of production. By 1932, the Farm Board had become a symbol of broken promises, and the farm organizations seemed united only by their disaffection with the administration.[9]

As conditions grew worse in rural areas, some farmers grew impatient with the ineffective leadership of the existing farm organizations and called for local direct action. Threats of a farm strike that would withhold farm products from the market were heard throughout the Cornbelt where corn and hogs, two of the hardest-hit commodities, were the basic source of income. In Iowa, a faction within the Farmers' Union, led by veteran organizer Milo Reno, inaugurated the Farmers' Holiday movement in February 1932 and began an organizing campaign with plans to withhold farm products the following summer if farm relief sufficient to guarantee the cost of production prices was not forthcoming. The term "holiday" that was, in Arthur Schlesinger's words, "a sardonic reference to the 'bank holiday' so affably proposed for the business community,"[10] caught on quickly, expressing the farmers' grievances against the city and its financial institutions. The following verse, printed in the *Iowa Union Farmer* in early March, captures the spirit of the term and the movement:

> Let's call a "Farmers Holiday"
> A Holiday let's hold
> We'll eat our wheat and ham and eggs
> And let them eat their gold.[11]

As the presidential campaign got underway in the spring of 1932, the growing holiday movement was injecting a new and strident note into the politics of the Midwest.

In May, the Farmers' Holiday Association was officially launched as a national movement by representatives of a number of corn, wheat, and dairy states. The Holiday Association grew rapidly as organizers traveled around the Midwest addressing groups of farmers and obtaining pledges to participate in the withholding action planned for the summer. In the quick expansion of the Holiday Association's membership, Reno's original idea of holding goods off the market to demonstrate the importance of farmers and force legislative action to guarantee the cost of production, gave way to the notion that the withholding of produce by itself would force prices up.[12]

When the farm strike finally began in August, it was almost universally interpreted as an effort to raise prices directly by creating shortages rather

than as a form of political pressure. The strike differed from the organizers' original plans in other ways as well. Angry farmers in the Sioux
City area began picketing the highways leading to that city, turning back
with spiked logs and threshing cables strung across the roads the trucks of
nonparticipating farmers trying to deliver produce. Eventually the strikers
succeeded in blockading the entire city. A strike, which was organized
independently of the Holiday Association but which included many of its
members who were dairy farmers associated with the Sioux City milk
shed, was called for early August. The striking milk producers not only
attempted to turn back trucks but also in some instances, opened the cans
and poured the milk onto the highways. This dramatic symbol of unprofitable abundance focused attention on the strike and on the difficulties and discontent of farmers.[13] It also provoked considerable criticism of the paradox. Overt acts of destruction are more dramatic and
easier to criticize than inaction, however prolonged, and because milk is
virtually synonymous with good nutrition and health, a symbol of moth-
erhood and a test of the ability to provide for one's family, its destruction
was particularly offensive.

After the Sioux City events, highway picketing and similar activities
spread to other parts of Iowa and to Nebraska, with sporadic incidents
occurring throughout the Midwest. As tempers wore thin, however, the
movement's leaders began to fear its potential for inducing violence.
Deputies escorting trucks to market were accosted by pickets; an interstate freight train was halted while produce cars were uncoupled. In late
August, arrests at Council Bluffs, Des Moines, and Omaha, and finally a
mass arrest of eighty-seven pickets at Sioux City, signaled that the movement had exceeded the tolerance of county authorities. After a shotgun
attack injured fourteen pickets at Cherokee, Reno declared a temporary
truce in the farm strike, using a planned conference of midwestern governors as the rationale.[14] The governors did hear testimony from some forty
witnesses and forwarded a series of mild resolutions to President Hoover.
Although Reno declared himself satisfied with the governors' response,
various state Holiday Association leaders disagreed and sporadic picketing persisted into the autumn.

This first summer of Farm Holiday Association actions did not produce
any specific accomplishments of higher prices or cost of production legislation. In fact, marketings were increased in the terminal markets nearest
Sioux City enough so that prices actually fell. But the actions were important in dramatizing the plight of farmers and signaling a hiatus in their
traditional conservatism. "The farmer is a pretty independent individ-

ual," reflected one Holiday Association sympathizer recalling the withholding actions. "He wants to be a conservative individual. . . . But it was hard. The rank-and-file people of this state—who were brought up as conservatives, which most of us were—would never act like this. Except in desperation." [15]

Franklin Roosevelt, by then the Democratic presidential candidate, needed little urging to consider the situation of the agricultural economy seriously. The discontented Midwest was fertile soil in which to nourish a Democratic victory, and the Farm Board debacle had made Hoover's farm policies especially vulnerable to attack. Roosevelt had needed support from the West and Midwest in order to secure the nomination. "The political premise of his campaign for the nomination," advisor Raymond Moley wrote later, "was that his delegate strength must be found in agricultural states. For the industrial and financial East had other candidates and regarded Roosevelt with misgivings." [16] But Roosevelt's interest in the farmers' cause was not merely a vote-getting ploy. The candidate and several of his principal advisors had argued repeatedly that no general recovery would be possible without the restoration of the purchasing power of farmers. "Our economic life today is a seamless web," Roosevelt stated in a major farm address in Topeka in mid September. "Whatever our vocation, we are forced to recognize that while we have enough factories and enough machines in the United States to supply all our needs, those factories will be closed part of the time and those machines lie idle part of the time if the buying power of fifty million people on the farms remains restricted or dead as it is today." [17] He gave urban workers the same message; "We need to give to fifty million people, who live directly or indirectly on agriculture, a price for their products in excess of the cost of production," he told a Boston audience a week before the election. "To give them an adequate price for their products means to give them the buying power necessary to start your mills and mines to work to supply their needs. Fifty million people cannot buy your goods. . . . You are poor because they are poor." [18]

In contrast to Hoover, who stated his opposition to any farm relief measure that would extend government bureaucracy into agriculture, Roosevelt urged "national planning in agriculture." Although he did not use the term "domestic allotment," Roosevelt gave the approach what many interpreted as an endorsement in his Topeka speech, announcing his intention to "give that portion of the crop consumed in the United States a benefit equivalent to a tariff sufficient to give you farmers an adequate price." [19] At the same time, however, he assured his listeners that any plan he adopted would be self-financing. The confusion was compounded by his stated commitment to the Democratic party platform that condemned "the unsound policy of restricting agricultural products to the demands of domestic markets," and his call for "such planning of . . . production as would reduce the surpluses and make it unnecessary in later years to depend upon dumping those surpluses abroad in order to support domestic prices." [20]

A certain amount of vagueness about the specifics of a plan for farm relief was an asset to candidate Roosevelt, since the major farm organizations had not agreed on a single approach, and many farm leaders were impatient with the domestic allotment proposition. The lack of unity among the major farm organizations furnished the candidate and his party with an exceptional opportunity to offer leadership in devising a farm policy. But neither the Democrats in general nor Roosevelt's advisors had a clear position other than their belief that farm price recovery was the *sine qua non* of general recovery, and Roosevelt appears to have opted instead for the establishment of friendly relationships with the leaders of farm organizations. What impressed these farm leaders most about the Democratic candidate was his interest in their views, evinced in preelection meetings with farm organization representatives, and his announced readiness to "be guided by whatever the responsible farm groups themselves agree on" in devising an actual farm bill. [21]

If Roosevelt's statements were vague and sometimes conflicting, his intention to act was clear. He proposed to "take a method and try it: if it fails, admit it frankly and try another." [22] "We must lay hold of the fact that economic laws are not made by nature," he declared in his acceptance speech. "They are made by human beings." [23] Thus, the economic laws could be changed by human action. Representing President Hoover's attitude as one of defeatism and despair, Roosevelt asserted, "I will not believe that in the face of a problem like this we must merely throw up our hands. I have unbounded faith in a restored and rehabilitated agriculture." [24]

President Hoover did seem to despair of finding a solution to the farm problem, short of general recovery, that was consistent with his principles; conceding that the Farm Board's stabilization operations had caused difficulties, he recommended repeal of the provision permitting the board to buy and sell commodities. For the most part, he confined his farm speeches to an attack on the Democratic proposal for negotiated reductions in tariffs and to nostalgic recollections of the joys of rural life experienced in his Iowa boyhood. "In any event, Iowa is a mystery to me," he told a group of newspaper editors just after his major farm address in Des Moines. Calling it "the most fertile piece of soil in the world," he praised its "wealth of productivity" and stated his own version of the paradox. "God gives to us every year a most magnificent return for human labor and yet a man made mess defies even the work of Providence in aid of mankind. Everything has been given to your State that could be given in natural resources and other possibilities, and yet we prove ourselves unable to capably administer it." He called it a problem "of more gravity to the American people than any we have met since the Civil War," [25] but he offered no solutions. It was an odd way to campaign for the farm vote.

In the autumn of 1932, the nation's voters overwhelmingly rejected the Hoover approach to the Depression. Roosevelt captured the entire South and West with a popular vote of 22.8 million compared to Hoover's 15.75 million. Roosevelt lost six states in the Northeast but carried most of the large metropolitan centers in that region. He received enormous numbers of votes from the foreign born, from areas where unemployment was especially high, from coal miners, and from farmers. In northwestern Iowa, the traditionally Republican center of the previous summer's farm strike, Roosevelt won by a majority of better than two to one. Harlem voted Democratic, deserting the party of Lincoln for the first time, as did large numbers of black voters in other cities. Roosevelt carried 282 counties that had never before voted Democratic. He brought with him a Democratic Congress with 59 Democrats, 36 Republicans, and one farmer-laborite in the Senate and 313 Democrats, 117 Republicans, and 5 farmer-labor representatives in the House. [26] The decisive victory, however, could bring no immediate change. Under the old lame duck system, an entire winter—and an entire session of the seventy-second Congress—had to pass before inauguration in March.

By the winter of 1932–1933, conditions in both city and countryside had become disastrous, and distress was turning into disorder. Farmers had learned a great deal about direct action through the agitation of the Farm Holiday movement of the previous summer. As the pressure of debts forced even greater tax and mortgage delinquency, farmers organized to resist foreclosure and tax sales. Sometimes they showed up in such large numbers and with such overt hostility that the sales were canceled or postponed. When sales were scheduled for the courthouse, an organized demonstration might occur, similar to the march in a northern Michigan town that one observer described as "inevitable, irresistible, overpowering . . . like an army with banners." [27] When a sale was to be held on the farm itself, Holiday Association sympathizers came by to "help pitch hay," carrying pitch forks, of course. Occasionally, overt violence occurred, but more often, the threat of action sufficed, and the mortgagee was induced to come to terms with the debtor. Local groups, called Debt Adjustment Committees in some areas and Councils of Defense in others, were established to assist in debtor-creditor negotiations, and as word of the dramatic and potentially violent foreclosure reactions spread, the creditors' willingness to negotiate increased.[28]

In strongly organized communities, "penny sales" that settled rather than postponed obligations were conducted. A debtor would declare bankruptcy, and the land, livestock, and implements would be put up for auction to satisfy outstanding debts. Neighbors and Holiday Association sympathizers would purchase the land for a few cents an acre and the cattle for a penny or two a head. When the sale was over, the creditor would receive only a few dollars toward the debt, the debt would be wiped out, and the land and property would be given back to the bankrupt farmer, now technically debt free. This innovative tactic made creditors almost as anxious as debtors to postpone the day of reckoning. In February, the large insurance companies that held about a fifth of all farm mortgages announced an informal moratorium on foreclosures, and several states passed legislation making such moratoria official and binding.[29]

Although direct action tactics were eloquent in themselves, farm leaders sought to make their meaning clear to all levels of government. In Nebraska, a leader of the Holiday Association movement threatened mass action if help were not forthcoming from the state legislature: "200,000 of us are coming to Lincoln and we'll tear that new State Capitol Building to pieces." [30] In Washington, Ed O'Neal, president of the normally conservative American Farm Bureau Federation, warned Congress that revolution could occur in the countryside within a year unless something was done to aid agriculture. Farmers were "losing their homes, their savings of a lifetime and all incentive for orderly living," he reported, and he demanded that the lame duck session take action on a domestic allotment plan and a farm mortgage relief measure.[31]

The cities, in comparison, remained relatively quiet, although scattered instances of forceful action occurred. In Seattle, thousands of members of barter groups took over the county-city building. In Detroit, groups of unemployed workers entered self-service grocery stores, stocked up on provisions, and left without paying. Unemployed miners in the coal towns of Pennsylvania dug coal at closed mines to heat their homes and then began to bootleg the fuel in substantial quantities while local law enforcers looked the other way. In Chicago, groups of unemployed citizens, usually unarmed, stopped bread and milk delivery trucks and walked away with the cargoes. Piven and Cloward report fairly widespread local actions by the unemployed to secure benefits at local relief agencies. In December, when Congress reconvened, its members found Capitol Hill surrounded by police armed with tear gas and riot guns; a second national hunger march sponsored by the Communist-led Unemployed Councils had arrived in the city chanting, "feed the hungry, tax the rich." [32]

Even without massive demonstrations, however, neither Congress nor the incoming administration could have been oblivious to the plight of unemployed workers and their families. The breakdown of local resources that finally had forced Congress and the administration to agree on the RFC relief loans the previous spring had accelerated, and the paltry sums dispensed by the RFC by the end of 1932 came nowhere near filling the need. La Follette, working on yet another relief bill, sent out a questionnaire to mayors all over the country, asking about the numbers of persons receiving municipal assistance, adequacy of the amounts provided, and the cities' financial situations. In their replies, which La Follette had read into the *Congressional Record*, mayors described unprecedented deprivation, the breakdown of local relief mechanisms, and the desperate need for federal aid. Social workers testifying on behalf of the new Costigan–La Follette Bill reported that in cities surveyed by the American Association of Social Workers, only about a quarter of the unemployed were receiving any relief at all and that the relief allotments were so small that they did little more than keep body and soul together. [33]

The ravages of depression were by no means confined to the working class. Although manufacturing employees had been among the first to feel the pinch, by the winter of 1932, the contagion of joblessness had reached many solidly middle class, normally affluent families and communities. Stuart Chase reported an inventory of the situation in Sunnyside Gardens, a Long Island community in which in 1929, "500 families were living happily and prosperously in a model suburban community" comprised largely of "professional people, writers, artists, architects, businessmen." By 1932 their combined income had been halved, and

two families out of five had one or more members unemployed. Half of all life insurance policies had been cancelled, while loans on remaining policies had cut the equity in half. Bank deposits had been depleted by 76 per cent. All assets had been depleted by 78 per cent compared with 1929. Half the group could no longer retain their homes in Sunnyside without financial help. Unpaid doctor and dentist bills had increased 150 per cent. Personal borrowing had increased 578 per cent.[34]

Even families who were otherwise untouched by the Depression began to suffer as bank failures multiplied. Stories of people forced to apply for relief because literally everything they had to live on was in a padlocked bank were not uncommon. And millions of otherwise prosperous depositors were unable to realize cherished plans because their savings were inaccessible.[35]

With the long arm of Depression reaching into so many households, with so much severe and obvious suffering among the long time jobless, and with overt rebellion cropping up in the countryside, discussion of the possibility of revolution was heard with increasing frequency. "Many people are discussing the possibility of a revolutionary crisis resulting from the rebellion now sweeping the farm States," commented the *Nation* early in 1933. Adding that while such a conclusion appeared "far fetched," the mortgage moratoria and other "radical measures to reduce the indebtedness and interest burden on farmers" then under consideration by state legislatures were themselves "revolutionary in that they would employ the power of the state to interfere with private contracts."[36] The revolutionary impulse was observed in other places. After spending months on the road with penniless transients, homeless men, women, boys, and girls, writer John Kazarian concluded that "the revolt, if it comes, will originate with the wandering unemployed, for of all the jobless, they are the most restless and adventurous. Wherever they congregate, in the jungles over a can of coffee, on freight trains, or in the parks, one hears rumblings of rebellion."[37]

With hindsight, these hopes and fears can be dismissed as gross exaggerations. The votes for the Communist and Socialist candidates in the 1932 elections were remarkably small. The rebellious farmers of the Midwest were fundamentally conservative; they were not interested in remaking the economic system but rather in securing their property rights within it. The actions of the organized unemployed—demonstrations, hunger marches, grocery store raids—that added to the fear of revolution, were generally local and immediate in character. No groups of any size or significance plotted to seize the revolutionary moment if it should occur. But in assessing the opportunity for change that confronted Franklin Roosevelt and the New Deal, the talk of revolution was probably more significant than the reality. "The word revolution is heard at every hand," wrote George Leighton in *Harpers* in March 1932.[38] In such an atmosphere, the tolerance for reform is often far greater than normal.

Among those who remained unimpressed with the revolutionary portents were many who had growing questions about the economic system and many who were being politicized by what they saw. "When I got out of law school in 1927, I was not a political person. I was an H. L. Menckenite character," recalled *Nation* editor Cary McWilliams, explaining how the thirties had changed him: "Going around the state in those years, you saw California as synonymous with abundance. It's so enormously rich, especially in agriculture. Yet you saw all kinds of crops being destroyed. . . . at a time when thousands of people were in real distress. So my Menckenisms began to fade."[39] "The persistence of the depression," historian William Leuchtenburg has written of the winter of 1932–1933, "raised questions not merely about business leadership but about capitalism itself. When so many knew want amid so much plenty, something seemed to be fundamentally wrong with the way the system distributed goods."[40]

Such widespread questioning of the prevailing order and of the extralegal means employed by rebellious citizens in both city and countryside signified a pervasive loss of the legitimacy by dominant institutions. In order for the defiance of established authority to arise at all, as Piven and Cloward have argued, "people have to perceive the deprivation and disorganization they experience as both wrong, and subject to redress."[41] The visible farm surpluses contributed to both of these perceptions. Hunger was obviously "subject to redress," while surpluses spilled from elevators or spoiled in fields and orchards. And the waste, especially amid want, was widely condemned as morally wrong in a society in which a long pioneer heritage had enshrined thrift. The juxtaposition of want and waste then, contributed to the delegitimation of the dominant order, and this delegitimation, which reached its peak in the winter of 1932–1933, in turn contributed to defining the scope of the opportunity for reform that confronted the incoming administration. Many of those who experienced this loss of legitimacy did not develop clear critiques of capitalism; they did not connect the contradictions that they condemned with the normal workings of the economy. Rather, as we have seen, they perceived the troubling juxtaposition as a paradox and a temporary aberration. But the feeling that something was very wrong and that extraordinary measures might be necessary to correct the situation was widespread and growing as inauguration day approached.

Roosevelt, in the period between his election and inauguration, made few commitments and his apparent lightheartedness left many observers questioning his readiness for office. But he and the experts who surrounded him were quietly studying reports and proposals, gathering ideas, and building a legislative program. Members of the brain trust that had been convened to advise him during the campaign continued to discuss ideas and proposals and assisted the president-elect in recruiting his cabinet, but much of the work was shrouded in secrecy. In part, this secrecy reflected the incompleteness of Roosevelt's plans. Normal procedure called for a brief special session of Congress to approve presidential appointments shortly after the inauguration, but no full session of the new Congress would be convened, and thus no major legislation passed, until the following December. Roosevelt was certainly aware that anything could happen in that period, and he had no intention of tying his hands by premature specification of a program. In addition, Roosevelt was determined to keep as much distance as possible between himself and the Hoover administration that was so contaminated with gloom and defeat.[42]

Whether by intent or accident, the president-elect's elusiveness contributed to the building of the dramatic opportunity that awaited him when he did take office. The mystery that surrounded his intentions—and for that matter, his capabilities—added to the mounting sense of suspense and anticipation. If any additional dramatic tension was needed, it was provided by an attempt upon the president-elect's life in Miami in mid February. The assassin's bullets missed Roosevelt but hit several bystanders and fatally wounded Mayor Cermak of Chicago.[43]

Finally, with inauguration less than three weeks away, the nation's banking system began a rapid toboggan ride downhill, gathering momentum as it slid and leaving behind a trail of closed banks and state bank holidays. Beginning with the closing of Michigan's banks on Valentine's Day, just a day before the assassination attempt, panic spread through the financial establishment. By the eve of the inauguration, thirty-eight states had declared official moratoria on bank withdrawals, and in the early morning hours of March 4, the governors of New York and Illinois followed suit, bringing to a halt transactions in the naton's financial citadels. Coming to a head on inauguration day, with a timing that Frederick Lewis Allen subsequently called "too cruelly precise," the banking crisis seemed to symbolize the end of an era.[44] It was not, of course, as sharp a demarcation as it appeared to many. The great continuities of American culture and its institutions—continuities of power, wealth, and ideology—remained to constrain the nature and direction of change. But within these constraints lay a significant margin of possibility; as the Roosevelt administration took office, a unique combination of events, personalities, and the difficult to measure but nevertheless very real national mood combined to offer the new administration a remarkable chance to make good its commitments to the forgotten people at the bottom of the economic pyramid.

CHAPTER SIX

The Promise of the New Deal

When Franklin D. Roosevelt took office on March 4, 1933, proclaiming that the nation had "nothing to fear but fear itself" and promising direct, vigorous action, the banking crisis had eclipsed both the relief and agricultural problems. Roosevelt responded immediately, declaring a national bank holiday, and calling Congress into special session to deal with the banking collapse. Originally, Roosevelt intended to convene Congress for only a few days to pass emergency banking legislation, but the cooperative mood of the incoming Congress and the pressure of the nation's needs made him receptive when Secretary of Agriculture Henry Wallace and Assistant Secretary Rexford Tugwell urged that the special session be held over to pass a farm measure.[1]

Thus began a whirlwind of activity in an atmosphere of crisis that came to be called the "hundred days." Congress remained in session for three months and produced an unprecedented volume of major legislation, reshaping parts of the nation's financial, agricultural, and industrial life. Like a thundershower after a long drought, the activity of the hundred days was almost too much to be absorbed; historians are still trying to sort it out. Food assistance was not established directly by any of the fifteen pieces of legislation in this first New Deal deluge, and the details of this period, which have been ably recounted elsewhere, need not concern us here.[2] But New Deal food assistance was intimately linked to both unemployment relief and agricultural adjustment, both of which were priorities for the new administration in the hundred days, and these two aspects of the early New Deal program, the policies established and the agencies created to administer them, require our attention. The farm program is especially important in this context, not only because food assistance was initiated as a by-product of agricultural adjustment, but also because one of the most significant functions of the food distribution program was, as we shall see, to enhance the acceptability of an agricultural program that was drawing tremendous criticism.

With the nationwide bank holiday buying time for relay teams of exhausted treasury officials to grapple with the banking crisis, the new administration turned its attention to the area of national life and economic distress that candidate Roosevelt and his advisors had identified, both privately and publicly, as the place where recovery must begin—agriculture. In keeping with his campaign promises, Roosevelt insisted that the bill submitted to Congress should be one that had the endorsement of the major national farm organizations. Accordingly, once the decision to hold over the special session was made, the new secretary of agriculture, Henry Wallace, called the various farm groups and leaders to Washington to work on a bill.[3]

Wallace preferred the domestic allotment approach, and support—or at least tolerance—for this approach had been nurtured in a series of pre-inauguration conferences between representatives of the incoming administration and farm leaders. But the secretary believed that the new administration would engender unnecessary opposition by committing itself to a single method. Therefore, he proposed an omnibus measure that would authorize a variety of approaches, leaving the choice among them to the secretary of agriculture. Wallace and Tugwell, along with attorneys F. P. Lee and Jerome Frank and USDA economist Mordecai Ezekial, prepared a basic rough draft while the farm leaders were on their way to Washington.[4] The farm spokesmen, meeting on the train from Chicago, came to similar conclusions. According to Tugwell, "when they arrived they presented us with a memorandum which asked us to do what we had already done." The Department of Agriculture presented its draft plan; the farm leaders passed a resolution endorsing it, and then Wallace and Tugwell took them to see the president. Tugwell's recollection of what ensued illustrates the style of New Deal politics in the cooperative atmosphere of the period immediately after inauguration. "We explained to him gravely that the farm leaders had demanded action, that we had responded with a bill which we thought was workable and suggested that since the situation was so acute that he send it to Congress immediately." Roosevelt congratulated the farm leaders for achieving consensus on a single program and urged them to use their influence to speed the passage of the measure through the legislature.[5]

In fact, little consensus existed. As recalled by Marvin Jones, chairman of the House Agriculture Committee, who had tried, at the urging of the president-elect, to secure passage of a domestic allotment measure in the lame duck session, the process was primarily one of appeasement: "They took these various measures that we had fashioned . . . and put in all the features that all of the groups wanted. . . . There wasn't any attunement at all."[6] But despite the lack of consensus and the rubber-stamp character of the farm leaders' participation, Roosevelt and Wallace apparently succeeded in making at least some of those involved feel that the bill was their own, as suggested by an account from Studs Terkel's *Hard Times*:

> It was Wallace who saved us, put us back on our feet. He understood our problems. When we went to visit him, after he was appointed Secretary, he made it clear to us he didn't want to write the law, he wanted farmers themselves to write it. "I will work with you," he said, "but you're the people who are suffering. It must be your program." He would always give his counsel, but he never directed us. The program came from the farmers themselves, you betcha.[7]

Even if the involvement of farm organizations in the preparation of the bill was largely for show, the show was an extraordinary one with significant implications. The call that Wallace sent out was not a general invitation to interested parties; no one was summoned to speak for labor, consumers, or the public interest. Similarly, the pre-inauguration meetings between Rexford Tugwell and Secretary of the Treasury Henry Morgenthau, for the incoming administration, and farm leaders were conducted within the framework of the idea that the farm organizations should design the plan for agriculture. In one sense, this was not new; as political scientist Theodore Lowi noted in 1969, the idea "that agricultural affairs should be handled strictly within the agricultural community is a basic principle, established before the turn of the century and maintained since then without serious reexamination."[8] But the very disarray of agriculture and the web of interdependence between city and countryside, factory and farm, to which Roosevelt had addressed himself with great vigor, might have called this traditional assumption of separate agricultural consideration of farm matters into question.

Immediate political realities, however, dictated otherwise. The administration needed the support of the farm organizations—to confer legitimacy upon its farm program, to aid in securing its passage though Congress, and to assist in getting the rank and file dirt farmers to cooperate with the plan. Farmers and farm organizations traditionally had been skeptical, even hostile, toward any plan involving reduction of output. "They said there was a deep revulsion among farmers," Tugwell recalled of the farm representatives who visited with Roosevelt after his nomination, "against reversing the first tenet of their occupation—making the land produce to its utmost." [9] If farmers were to be persuaded to try such a scheme, it would have to be presented to them as their own program, by their own leaders, and as an approach representing the best interests of agriculture. It could not appear diluted by concern about the national interest or the consumer. And if the ongoing support of agricultural organizations was to be secured, the prestige that the new administration was conferring upon their leaders by casting them publicly into the role of experts on farm issues and legitimate representatives of the nation's farmers could not be tempered by the inclusion of other sources of expertise and representation.

Farmers were consumers too, of course, and many of them, especially farm laborers and tenant farmers in the single crop regions, produced little if anything for home consumption and were compelled to purchase most of what they ate. A rise in the price of flour, cornmeal, and hog products would be as hard or harder on these farmers as it would be on impoverished city dwellers. But these farmers were not the ones represented in the farm organizations that helped to draft the New Deal farm bill. In fact, the leading role was played by the American Farm Bureau Federation, which represented the nation's most prosperous farmers—the larger landowners in the Midwest and South. Second place went to the Grange, which was particularly strong among the fairly prosperous truck farmers of New England and the middle Atlantic states. The Farmers' Union, within which the Farm Holiday Association had been nourished, was the least cooperative with the new administration and had the least influence on it. The exclusion of the Holiday Association itself was ironic since its members had risked so much to demonstrate the farmers' desperation. Roosevelt himself later credited the holiday movement with a major role in creating the situation in which far-reaching legislation could secure passage, but typically, the more established and conservative organizations were the ones to receive public recognition. [10]

Once extended such recognition is not easily withdrawn. As Christina Campbell observed in her careful study of the Farm Bureau and the New Deal, the farm legislation drafting conference "seemed to be an official recognition of the right of farm organization leaders to be consulted in the making of national agricultural policy. This meeting set the precedent," she continued, "for the practice of consultation which may have been looked upon by the Roosevelt administration as a grant of privilege only, but which became, in Farm Bureau thinking an inalienable right." [11] By the same logic, the exclusion of consumers and poor farmers from the process also set a precedent. In the neat reciprocity that developed, with farm leaders supporting the administration's controversial farm program and the administration enhancing the image of these leaders among their own constituents, there continued to be little room for consumers, sharecroppers, or impoverished farm tenants, and the measures devised and implemented reflected their exclusion.

Longer range historical forces influenced the administration's failure to consult consumers as well, or to give more than token consideration to their needs in the development of the farm program. As the nation had industrialized and urbanized, agriculture had increasingly come to be viewed as a distinct, somewhat mysterious area of national life. An agricultural press discussed farm issues, but the urban press gave them little attention. A separate system of agricultural colleges engendered an array of farm disciplines: soil chemistry, plant genetics, agricultural statistics, and most salient for this study, agricultural economics. By the time the need for government intervention in the economy on behalf of farmers was acknowledged, almost all of those thinking seriously about farm policy were farm reared, trained in an agricultural discipline, and employed in such farm-oriented institutions as state or federal agricultural agencies, farm-related businesses, or agricultural colleges. The USDA's Extension Service, with its county agents in every farm county in the nation and its close ties to local farm bureaus, experiment stations, and land-grant colleges, knit the system together into a vast network within which farm problems and agricultural policy could be considered without much intrusion from other sectors. [12]

Even in Washington, where the articulation of farm matters with other issues might have been expected, the farmers' hegemony over farm policy persisted. Although one might reasonably expect a department of agriculture to be primarily concerned with a nation's food supply, and thus with the needs of consumers, the U.S. Department of Agriculture had, from its inception, been concerned primarily with the welfare of farmers, and, as agriculture became commercialized, with the profitability of the larger farms producing for the commercial market. Consumers per se had little voice within the department, except as they represented demand. In

Congress, of course, the urban consumer had a voice. "Frequently, when legislation . . . was under discussion," recalled House Agriculture Committee Chairman Marvin Jones, "we'd have objection from people who represented primarily retail districts, city districts. Having no farmers in their districts, they couldn't justify supporting a bill that was aimed directly at increasing prices of farm products."[13] But the effectiveness of such city voices in agricultural matters was reduced, not only by the overrepresentation of rural voters and the power of the farm bloc, but also by the congressional committee system. Agricultural legislation received its primary consideration in the House and Senate agriculture committees, and seats on those committees generally went to senators and representatives from farm states and districts who were supposed to be knowledgeable about farming and who could benefit politically from the assignment.

In this context then, it is not difficult to see why consumers received little consideration in the formulation of farm policy proposals. The entire thrust of agricultural politics in the 1920s had been based on the notion that the farmer was treated unfairly by the economic system and that the prices farmers received were unjustly low. While some of the unfairness was attributed to greedy middlemen—processors and distributors—the idea that consumers had benefited, unfairly if inadvertently, from the economy's discrimination against agriculture was deeply imbedded. Virtually all of the proposals that dominated the farm policy in 1933—McNary-Haugenism and other two-price schemes dependent upon export dumping, price fixing, restriction of output, and even to a degree, currency inflation—sought or implied the achievement of higher farm income at the expense of the consumer. Direct subsidies derived from the general treasury and thus progressive taxation were not considered.

Of the various proposed approaches, the domestic allotment plan to which Roosevelt had gradually and quietly become committed in the course of his campaign and in postelection negotiations with farm leaders, showed the most flagrant disregard for the consumer. The plan called for inducing farmers to reduce output in return for benefit payments, with the idea that the lower output would bring higher prices and that cooperating farmers would receive more from the combination of benefit payments and higher prices than the noncooperating farmer would receive from selling his total, or even increased, output.[14] But consumers were not only to pay the higher prices, they were to provide the benefit payments as well. Looking for a means to finance the benefit payments and hoping to enhance the constitutionality of the measure by rooting it in the taxing power, the supporters of domestic allotment devised a scheme for

taxing each commodity included in the plan at the first point of processing: the flour mill, the slaughterhouse, or the cotton gin.[15] The processing
tax was essentially a sales tax on food and fiber that would ultimately be
paid by the consumer. Under a complex scheme, it would be calculated so
as to yield parity. The income received by cooperating farmers from
benefit payments plus improved prices on their crops would be roughly
equal to the income they would have received if farm prices had maintained the same ratio to nonfarm prices that had prevailed before the
World War I. The processing tax, therefore, securely linked the evolving
domestic allotment plan to the parity goal of McNary-Haugenism and
blithely proposed to hit the the consumer twice—once through the overall
commodity price rise and again through the processing tax.

The advocates of domestic allotment were aware of the impact of the
plan on consumers, but they gave little attention to its regressive effects.
As Tugwell later summarized their thinking: "The farmer ought to be satisfied . . . to get as much as he had had in good times, and consumers
could not object if prices, plus benefit payments, rose to such an equitable
level—that is, one at which everyone had been well off. Both farmers
and consumers ought to be glad for a return of such conditions." [16] Less
naively, Tugwell identified as the scheme's chief disadvantage the fact that
the revenue for the benefit payments was to come from consumers. "If,
however, it was accompanied by relief benefits and public work for the
unemployed," he reasoned, "it would be tolerable." [17]

In addition to the domestic allotment plan, the omnibus measure, entitled the Agricultural Adjustment Act, which the president sent to Congress on March 16, contained elements of most other major approaches
except currency inflation. It established parity prices as a goal, declaring
the policy of the nation to be the establishment and maintenance of a
"balance between the production and consumption of agricultural commodities, and such marketing conditions therefor, as will reestablish
prices to farmers at a level that will give agricultural commodities a purchasing power with respect to articles that farmers buy, equivalent to the
purchasing power of agricultural commodities in the base period." [18] The
act designated seven agricultural commodities as basic: wheat, cotton,
field corn, hogs, rice, tobacco, and milk and milk products. It also defined the base period as 1909–1914, the "golden age of agriculture" for
all commodities except tobacco, for which the base period was 1919–
1924. In dealing with these basic items, the secretary of agriculture was
empowered to reduce acreage or production for market; in order to do so,
he might make rental or benefit payments to producers. For any agricul-

tural commodity, basic or otherwise, the secretary was empowered to enter into marketing agreements with processors or associations of producers to control prices. The secretary was also empowered to license processors, associations of producers, or others engaged in handling agricultural commodities to eliminate unfair practices or charges that might prevent the accomplishment of the basic aims of the act. An appropriation of $100 million was made for administrative and startup costs, but the primary means of financing the program would be to levy taxes at the first point of processing. The act provided that the revenue from the processing taxes might be used "for expansion of markets and removal of surplus agricultural products" [19] as well as for the primary purposes of the act.

Roosevelt sent the bill to Congress accompanied by a straightforward message: "I tell you frankly that it is a new and untrod path, but I tell you with equal frankness that an unprecedented condition calls for the trial of new means to rescue agriculture." [20] The House Agriculture Committee, which had spent almost the entire lame duck session working on a domestic allotment bill, did not hold hearings on the omnibus measure. "We . . . decided that with the new crop coming on we had better go ahead," recalled Chairman Marvin Jones. "Conditions in the country were so extreme, we drove that bill." [21] Indeed, the House passed the bill less than a week after its introduction. "Critics of Both Parties Assail Farm Bill but Will Vote for It" read the headline in the *New York Times*. [22]

Predictably, opposition to the processing tax was vociferous and immediate. The processors objected to the entire crop reduction approach, since their profits were derived from handling large volume. They preferred solutions based on export dumping, which would maintain the high volume of commodities flowing through their facilities. They also feared that the processing tax would induce the consuming public to substitute other, untaxed commodities for the taxed items. In their public campaign against the bill, however, they focused almost solely upon the tax, and as historian Richard Kirkendall has noted, tried "to promote a sense of identity between their interests and those of wage earners and urban consumers by arguing that the processing tax would promote unemployment in the processing plants and increase the cost of living." [23] Such arguments were voiced by others, as well. "What will the great mass of consumers think of this form of sales tax, resting heavily on food?" asked the *New York Times* rhetorically, for its pages had been besieged by a stream of letters from angry consumers ever since the voluntary domestic allotment bill had been introduced in the lame duck session. [24] The processing tax was described as "soaking the poor," "class legislation," and

"special privilege for the few at the expense of the many." "We city-bred
people are in great sympathy with the farmers," one woman wrote, "and
are willing to sacrifice much to help them, but we are not able to bear the
burden of highly taxed food." [25] "I cannot see how the administration justifies this tax on necessaries," stated Representative Tinkham of Massachusetts while the measure was before the House. [26] The clearest explanation came from New Deal fellow traveler Ernest K. Lindly; labeling the
processing tax "one of the worst features of the plan," he wrote in 1936
that "it grew naturally, however, out of the idea, then prevalent, of self
liquidation, and was in a general way consistent with the popular thesis
that special groups should not receive bonuses out of general taxation." [27]

In the long run, the fundamental criticisms of the Agricultural Adjustment Act were directed more at the whole notion of reducing production
to drive up prices—creation of scarcity—than at the processing tax by
which crop control was to be financed. But criticism of the scarcity approach to balance became much more prevalent after the program was
actually implemented, and it will be examined in the next chapter. While
the bill was under congressional consideration, critics focused on two
other issues: "regimentation," and the absence of currency inflation
among the many techniques authorized by the omnibus measure. [28] Many
members of Congress were shocked by the degree of control that the bill
proposed to give the secretary of agriculture, and they forecast a vast invasion of field and farmyard to supervise the farmer. "When you send out
this army of tax gatherers to tell the farmer what he can plant and what he
can sell, you are well on the road to Moscow," declared Representative
Martin of Massachusetts in a statement that expressed the sentiments of
many. [29] Nevertheless, the House of Representatives voted overwhelmingly
and very promptly for the bill. Apparently, support for the president was
the explanation. "In ordinary times I wouldn't vote for a measure of this
kind," said Chairman Jones who had declined to introduce the bill. "But
. . . we are at war, and . . . while this war is on I'm going to follow the
man at the other end of the avenue who has the flag in his hand. I'm going
to support the Commander-in-Chief." Similar sentiment was expressed
by the ranking Republican on Jones's committee: "filled with horrors and
hellishness as it is," said Representative Clarke of New York, "I'm going
to support the President." [30]

The Senate, however, proved less tractable. At first, the delay was due
not so much to the opponents of regimentation as to the advocates of inflation. Since both the banking and economy bills that had been passed
were essentially deflationary, and since the most immediate problem fac-

ing many farmers was not the price they would receive for their crop the next fall but the method they would use to stave off creditors in the interim, inflationary sentiment ran high among inheritors of the populist tradition and others from the farm states. Several attempts were made to attach inflationary amendments to the act, and when one came close to passing despite strong administration opposition, the White House became convinced that the inflationary drive would soon succeed. In order to avoid having inflation forced on him, Roosevelt agreed to accept an amendment proposed by Elmer Thomas of Oklahoma if it were rewritten in permissive rather than mandatory language. The revised Thomas amendment authorized the president to print greenbacks, remonetize silver, and alter the gold content of the dollar. The next day, Roosevelt used his authority to take the nation off the gold standard, thus somewhat preempting the inflationary surge. Meanwhile, early in April, the president submitted emergency farm credit legislation that permitted the federal government to refinance farm mortgages.[31]

The Thomas amendment and the new farm credit legislation made the farm bill more acceptable to farm state senators but less so to conservatives. The Senate continued to wrangle over the bill while planting season came and went, and all across America, farmers watched their fields turn green with the abundant crops that would only deepen their financial disaster. As the weather turned warm, signs of overt rebellion cropped up again in the Cornbelt, and this time, the use of force escalated. In one famous incident that captured considerable national attention, a group of farmers at Le Mars, Iowa, nearly lynched a judge in an effort to stop mortgage foreclosures and deficiency judgments. "What I remember most of those times," said an Iowa farmer recalling the incident years later, "is that poverty creates desperation and desperation creates violence."[32] Finally, the Farmers' Holiday Association set May 13 as a date for a national farm strike if Congress had not taken some constructive action toward meeting their demand for cost of production prices by that date. Mindful, perhaps, of the previous summer's grim mobs and ditches running with milk, Congress passed the Agricultural Adjustment Act on May 12, 1933, just in time to avert the threatened strike.[33]

The Agricultural Adjustment Act was regarded by its creators as emergency legislation designed to deal with the enormous surpluses of staple crops that had accumulated and to permit an orderly readjustment of output. But like so many other New Deal emergency measures, the act established policies and created constituencies that endured for decades. The processing tax that drew so much fire at the outset proved to be short lived. The tax and the programs it financed were invalidated by the Supreme Court in January 1936. However, the basic idea of raising prices by limiting output, the parity goal, and the idea that consumers rather than taxpayers should support such price increases remained a fundamental part of American farm policy until the early 1970s. For upper and middle class households in which only a small proportion of income was spent on food and in which progressive taxation meant a relatively large tax bill, such an arrangement was advantageous. But in poor households in which food purchase was often the major form of expenditure, it was a real and continuing hardship. That is, even after the demise of the processing tax, the impact of the Agricultural Adjustment Act remained profoundly regressive for more than thirty years.[34]

The socially destructive effects of the act were by no means confined to its impact on low income consumers. The overall effect of the 1933 act and its successors on income distribution within agriculture was to increase inequality. As acreage under the control of large landlords was taken out of production in return for benefit payments, many tenant farmers and sharecroppers were reduced to the status of day laborers or forced off the land altogether. On the other hand, the benefit payments were based on the amount of land owned or the amount of a given commodity produced. Thus, the largest benefits went to the largest, wealthiest farmers, including not only those who actually worked the land, but also the insurance companies and farming corporations who owned so much of it. Writing in 1965, agricultural economist Varden Fuller summarized the outcome succinctly: "The bulk of the program benefits for more than thirty years have been distributed in disproportion to need and . . . have been rewarding to the owners of land and unrewarding to the owners of labor."[35] The worst inequities probably occurred in the first few years. In 1936, for example, Senator Vandenberg of Michigan forced the publication of a list of large individual payments; some were greater than a million dollars, a lot of money in the midst of a depression. The 1936 Soil Conservation Act substituted a graduated scale of benefits, but not until 1970 was a ceiling on payments established—$55,000 per farmer per commodity, reduced to $20,000 in the 1973 act.[36] Considering the upward redistribution of income within agriculture promoted by the act and the regressive impact of raising food prices, the overall impact of the Agricultural Adjustment Act was an income transfer from impoverished consumers and farm laborers to wealthy farmers and farmland-owning banks and insurance companies.

While some of the negative effects of the adjustment act were predicted by critics or dimly perceived by Wallace, Tugwell, and others, most were obscured by the sense of urgency or drowned out by the noisy conflict between the defenders of laissez-faire on the one hand and the proponents of "unworkable schemes" on the other. Roosevelt and his agricultural lieutenants were too busy trying to cope with an emergency and placating the various groups and power brokers within agriculture to give much thought to the long-range effects of the new legislation. Nor did the fray subside completely once the bill finally became law. As Leuchtenburg has stated, "the law simply postponed the quarrel over farm policy."[37] In the meantime, the immediate task was to create and staff an agency to administer the new law.

Given the political and economic importance of agricultural recovery, and the differences of opinion over farm policy, what Roosevelt and Wallace needed in the Agricultural Adjustment Administration was an efficient, unified, adaptable organization that could implement the various experiments provided for in the bill. What they got was a large, ungainly, confused organization ridden with conflicts over ideology and general political orientation. Divergent beliefs about the farm problem and its solution, disagreements over the organization's operating style, and conflicting personalities hampered the AAA from its inception.

As chief of the new agency, Roosevelt appointed George Peek. A hero among farm leaders because of his tireless work on behalf of the McNary-Haugen plan, Peek had many supporters on Capitol Hill. Furthermore, he had the backing of Bernard Baruch, under whom he had served on the War Industries Board in World War I, and thus of other powerful Democrats influenced by Baruch. Peek's appointment was seen both as a reward for long service to agriculture and a means of reassuring congressional conservatives alarmed at the power given to the new organization. Peek, however, proved a poor teammate for Wallace and Tugwell. In the first place, he did not really believe in the domestic allotment plan that Wallace saw as the heart of the Agricultural Adjustment Act. According to Peek, "the sole aim and object of this act is to raise farm prices,"[38] and he believed that could be done by negotiating agreements with producer associations and processors to control the prices paid to farmers without necessitating restriction of output. Subsidized export and dumping abroad, he believed, could absorb any surpluses, and he did not share the secretary's conviction that such dumping was neither desirable nor feasible. In the second place, Peek did not want to submit to the authority of Secretary

Wallace whom he saw as his junior in the fight for agricultural equality, and he insisted upon reporting directly to the president.[39]

Both the policy conflict and the confusion over authority were aggravated by the appointment of liberal attorney Jerome Frank as general counsel of the new AAA. Frank had originally been recruited by Tugwell at the recommendation of Felix Frankfurter to serve as solicitor of the Department of Agriculture, but the appointment had been blocked by Jim Farley, Roosevelt's campaign chief and newly appointed postmaster general. Frank, who had given up a lucrative law practice in New York to join the new administration, was offered the AAA position instead, and the appointment was made by Wallace before Peek was appointed and insisted upon direct access to Roosevelt. Thus, Peek found Frank already established at the AAA, a fact that he probably resented, especially since Frank had once been a member of the law firm that had liquidated Peek's Moline Plow Company.[40]

Peek and Frank disagreed on almost everything. Frank, who was friendly with Wallace and Tugwell and had shared an apartment with them when he first came to Washington, agreed with them that restriction of production would be necessary in the short run. Peek preferred the marketing agreement approach. Peek, as noted, saw a rise in farm prices as the sole aim of the act; Frank saw the AAA as a broad instrument for social planning and believed that it should be administered with concern not only for the well-being of agricultural producers but also for the needs of consumers and the nation as a whole. Peek believed that the processors were essential allies in the effort to restore prosperity. Frank regarded them as greedy middlemen who could be expected to cheat consumer, producer, and government alike unless carefully supervised. This last disagreement generated an ongoing conflict; while Peek sought means to induce the processors to participate in marketing agreements to raise prices paid to farmers, Frank insisted that such agreements would not be legal under the act unless they provided for government access to the books and records of participating firms so that the government could ensure that increased prices paid by consumers were indeed being passed along to farmers. The processors vigorously objected to the idea, and Peek regarded Frank's insistence on the books and records clause as obstruction, while Frank became increasingly distrustful of Peek's friendliness toward the processors.[41]

Neither combatant operated alone. Peek brought in his own people, colleagues from the McNary-Haugen struggle and men with years of experience in agriculture, processing, and farm-related businesses, to head the various commodity sections of the new agency, though Wallace intervened to secure the appointment of two advocates of domestic allotment. M. L. Wilson was appointed to head the wheat section and Al Black to guide the corn and hog section. Frank, convinced that good legal training was a more important qualification than expertise in agriculture, brought in faculty members and recent graduates from prestigious Eastern law schools. He gathered a remarkable array of legal talent, and a number of the members of his staff were subsequently to become famous, either for government service or as victims of the McCarthy purges. But as newcomers to Washington, Frank's bright young lawyers stepped on a lot of toes.[42]

Recalling the legal division in the early years of the AAA, M. L. Wilson summarized a widely held perception: "None of them came from the farm. I don't think any of them came from any realistic knowledge of agriculture. They didn't know farm psychology, the farm community, or either the technology or the social economy of agriculture."[43] Apparently, they did not know much about farm politics, either. "The first thing I knew, they had a great group of new faces in the Department of Agriculture, men with whom I was not acquainted," Marvin Jones recalled. "A great many of the new men had never heard of me and didn't know what the Agriculture Committee was all about. A great many of them apparently didn't realize what the relationship between the Department of Agriculture and Congress should be."[44] When the fact that many of the newcomers, as Jones put it, "were not skilled in agricultural matters," became obvious, Senator Smith of South Carolina introduced a resolution in the Senate specifying that no one should occupy a policy-making position in the Department of Agriculture who had not had a minimum of five years of actual farming experience. The resolution failed, but its serious consideration was testimony to the growing concern among farm bloc members over the invasion of their preserve.[45].

Lack of agricultural experience was not the only characteristic that singled out the Frank group for attention and concern among old time agriculturalists. "I think that there was a type of person that didn't know anything about farming and that came from the city, who thought that we were pretty much on the verge of a revolution and that the whole Roosevelt regime was going to be almost revolutionary in character," recalled M. L. Wilson. "They thought it was going to do a number of very radical and very drastic things, moving in the direction of socialism."[46] Needless to say, George Peek did not welcome such a group within his fold. "A plague of young lawyers," he called them, claiming that "in the legal division were formed the plans which eventually turned the AAA from a device to aid the farmers into a device to introduce the collectivist system of agriculture into this country." [47]

Frank was instrumental in securing the appointment of veteran liberal Frederick C. Howe to the Office of Consumers Counsel. Wallace had insisted on the creation of this office to implement a provision of the Agricultural Adjustment Act intended to protect consumers: the act provided that the readjustment of prices should not "increase the percentage of the consumers' retail expenditures for agricultural commodities or the products derived therefrom, which is returned to the farmer, above the percentage which was returned to the farmer in the prewar period, August 1901–July 1914." [48] To the Office of the Consumers Counsel came, in Dean Albertson's words, "still another group of nonagrarian economists and humanitarians," [49] led by Howe and Gardner Jackson who allied with the social reformers in the legal division to form what Peek perceived as a radical, antiprofit, antibusiness cabal. "I later found that no end of intense young men in these divisions were out gunning for the profit system as though it were some kind of rapacious wolf," wrote Peek. [50] He tried to have Frank fired or transferred, and when that failed, arranged to have his own salary paid to attorney F. P. Lee, former counsel for the American Farm Bureau Federation, so Lee could provide him with legal advice on an informal basis. Frank, meanwhile, remained friendly with Wallace and Tugwell and increasingly was regarded as Wallace's representative within the AAA. [51]

In contrast to the large and conflict-ridden AAA, the Federal Emergency Relief Administration (FERA), the other major agency involved in the creation of food assistance, was small and harmonious. Similarly, the passage of the Federal Emergency Relief Act had been a relatively smooth process. Although opposition to the relief program existed, the arguments on both sides were familiar from the long fight that had culminated in the passage of the RFC relief loans and the Farm Board wheat distribution measure. Thus, Congress was prepared to act quickly when relief legislation was presented.

In March, less than a week after he sent the Agricultural Adjustment Act to Congress, Roosevelt sent an unemployment relief message recommending a triple approach: a conservation program to put unemployed, young men to work in the national parks and forests, a broader public works program, and an appropriation for grants to the states for direct relief to be administered by the Federal Emergency Relief Administration. The "tree army" was Roosevelt's preferred approach, one that he had discussed during the campaign and had experimented with as governor of New York. Legislation creating the Civilian Conservation Corps was introduced immediately and passed both houses by the end of the month; the president signed it into law on the last day of March, less than a month after taking office. Roosevelt was uncertain about the other aspects of the program, which conflicted with his economy drive, but he was convinced by Frances Perkins, his secretary of labor, Harry L. Hopkins, his New York State Temporary Emergency Relief Administration (TERA) chief, and relief advocates in the Senate.[52]

The broader public works program was embodied in the National Industrial Recovery Act, which also created the National Recovery Administration (NRA); it was passed in June, establishing the Public Works Administration (PWA) with an appropriation of $3.3 billion for labor-creating public works to be allocated so as to drain the major reservoirs of unemployment. At first, the PWA was conceived as an integral part of the NRA, but Roosevelt, wary of giving too much control to NRA administrator Hugh Johnson, placed the PWA under cautious spender Harold Ickes and separated it from the industrial reorganization features of the NRA. Eventually, the PWA created many valuable and enduring public works, but in the short run, it did little to pump money into the economy or create jobs.[53]

Roosevelt invited Senators Costigan, La Follette, and Wagner to prepare a bill for direct relief. They responded with a measure calling for $500 million, half of which was to be distributed on the basis of local matching funds in a ratio of one federal dollar for every three state dollars spent in the preceding three months, and half of which was to be distributed on the basis of urgent need. Although the bill evoked the familiar protests of socialism and destruction of the federal system from conservatives, it passed the Senate at the end of March and the House three weeks later, winning large majorities in both houses. The president signed the bill on May 12, the same day that he signed the Agricultural Adjustment Act, and a week later announced the appointment of Harry Hopkins to head the Federal Emergency Relief Administration. Although he was basically unknown outside New York at the time of his appointment, Hopkins soon became almost a symbol of the New Deal. Tall, thin, brusque, a chain-smoker, poker player, and racetrack enthusiast, this Iowan turned big-city social worker had acquired sympathy and respect for poor people in settlement house work on New York's Lower East Side and administrative experience as assistant director of the Association for Improving the Condition of the Poor and director of the New York Tuberculosis and Health Association.[54]

Hopkins's major qualifications for the job, however, were as much matters of personality as of experience. He was intuitive, practical, and willing to spend money. He ignored obstacles and took risks in a job where caution could only have meant failure. Recalling Hopkins's performance in the early days of the FERA, Jerome Frank commented: "I think he did an unbeatable job. . . . Any man who had been trained in government administration wouldn't have dared do it. No man who didn't have courage would have done it. For he knew he was taking . . . very personal chances."[55] At first, Hopkins refused to appoint a lawyer for the FERA because he did not want to be hampered by technicalities, though he consulted informally with Frank. Eventually Hopkins did invite one of Frank's AAA lawyers, Lee Pressman, to serve as his counsel. Pressman's recollection of their conversation reveals much of Hopkins's style. After Pressman had agreed to join the FERA staff, Hopkins said, "I have only one instruction for you. You won't get instructions from me often. The first time you tell me that I can't do what I want to, you're fired. I'm going to decide what I think has to be done and it's up to you to see to it that it's legal."[56]

Legend has it that Hopkins, working from a desk placed in the hallway of the RFC building, spent $5 million in his first two hours in office. In any case, the FERA got under way with dispatch. Funds were disbursed to local public relief agencies through state Emergency Relief Administrations that were generally established by the governors at Hopkins's request. In a few instances, the FERA found it necessary to set up its own administration within a state, but in general, decentralization was the rule. The Washington staff remained small, and substantial authority was vested in the state administrators.[57]

The FERA placed great emphasis on preserving the dignity of relief recipients. Hopkins wrote of the effort to do so in a 1936 account of the development of federal relief:

> From the beginning, we strove to make methods of emergency relief differ from practices of local poor relief, which still held a heavy hand over many local agencies. . . . We asked for the establishment of respectable light quarters conveniently placed in the neighborhoods of those who had to use them. We tried to have the applicant received by an intelligent and sympathetic human being who did not . . . put a stigma upon the unfortunate person before him. We tried to see that

relief officials were people who understood that the predicament of the worker without a job is an economic predicament not of his own making; that his religion, race, or party is irrelevant. His need was the only thing that had to be established.[58]

In order to make sure that limited funds reached those most in need, "we had continuously to investigate families to see that no one obtained relief who could get along without it," Hopkins reported with some chagrin. While accepting the necessity for such investigations, he expressed dismay at the indignities involved in the process: "Hence we have to admit that relief investigators have entered the front door of millions of private homes hitherto holding themselves sacred against intrusion, and have pried into painful matters. . . . If we had not become so accustomed and, in a sense, so hardened to the fact of poverty, we should even now be astounded at our effrontery."[59]

Hopkins's concern for protecting the dignity of relief clients also guided his preferences regarding the form in which assistance was given. He preferred work relief, whenever possible. When work could not be provided, he urged the provision of relief grants in cash. Commissaries were in widespread use when federal emergency relief got underway, but Hopkins discouraged them on the grounds that they humiliated recipients and took business away from small retail grocers, many of whom had extended tremendous amounts of credit to the unemployed. "Of all forms of relief we have seen undertaken since the advent of our administration, I believe the commissary to be the most degrading."[60] Grocery orders were an improvement, but they still limited the recipient's freedom of choice in an effort to ensure that relief dollars were spent to satisfy basic needs. Hopkins preferred cash relief because "it is a man's own business how he spends it."[61] Gradually, under the leadership of the FERA, cash relief replaced commissaries and grocery orders in most communities. The basic FERA relief grant covered food, fuel, utilities, and minimal household supplies. Rent was paid only on an occasional basis. Neither hospital care nor other forms of institutionalization were included, although medications could be purchased. Theoretically, basic clothing was to be provided, but little was made available until the FERA established sewing rooms where unemployed women made garments from surplus cotton.

The complexities faced by the AAA and FERA staffs in launching their new agencies were not unique. Dozens of new agencies, bureaus, and programs were competing for office space, equipment, personnel, and the attention of the public and president. The result was an invigorating blend of confusion and excitement, which pervaded Washington in the spring of 1933. "The very air of Washington crackled," wrote Frederick Allen. "Suddenly this city had become unquestionably the economic as well as the political capital of the country, the focus of public attention." [62] The wife of a young Alabama lawyer who had come to Washington to join the Reconstruction Finance Corporation later recalled her husband's first few months with the new administration: "It was a time of tremendous activity and strain," remembered Virginia Durr. "But it was a terribly exciting time because Cliff and all the people he was working with felt like they were putting the world back together again, and all over Washington there was this feeling of putting the world back together again." [63] "The place hums and buzzes and quivers with talk," observed Anne O'Hare McCormick in early May. "You feel the stir of movement, of adventure, even of elation. You never saw before in Washington so much government, or so much animation in government." [64]

That much government required lots of people to administer it. After nearly four years of disappearing opportunity and dwindling hopes, no wonder the New Deal became a mecca for young professionals and job seekers of all descriptions. Some were simply unemployed and looking for work, but many were thoroughly idealistic, enlisting in what they considered an army fighting depression. George Peek described them as "young lawyers, college professors and social workers to whom the word had somehow gone out that a new dispensation had been given and for the first time the nation was looking to its great, serious, but hitherto unknown army of real thinkers. They came in," he stated, "prepared to brush aside the musty old dodos who had ruined the nation." [65] Newspaperman Tom Stokes recalled the younger members of the Washington press corps in the spring of 1933 who were intent on building the country over again and were "so confident and cocksure."

> So, too, were the young men who descended upon Washington from college cloisters and lawyers' offices and quickly found themselves places behind hundreds of desks and began to explore every cranny of the national economy, to probe its faults and to draw diagrams and blueprints of a new world. They were going to make the world over. [66]

Making the world over required enormous effort; Arthur Krock dubbed the New Dealers "colossal workers." [67] In a city full of hard-working rebuilders, none worked harder than the staff of the new General Counsel of the AAA. "Anything that has been written about the dizzying, frantic pace, the completely dedicated drive of the group with which Jerome was associated," Frank's widow recalled years later, "falls short of the reality."[68]

In this atmosphere of "tremendous activity and strain," personal bonds among participants develop and are endowed with special meaning. "We got to know quite a number of the young New Dealers and became very fond of them," Virginia Durr recalled, describing how such informal contacts led to ideas, plans, programs, and policies.[69] Informal social ties were to prove very significant in the creation of food assistance. Some networks that predated the advent of the New Deal were transferred to Washington. In agriculture, the long McNary-Haugen fight had produced a legacy of contacts among a whole generation of agricultural economists, farm state politicians, farm organization leaders, and Department of Agriculture staff. Similarly, the New Deal relief establishment was dominated by a group of New York City–based social workers, rooted in the settlement house tradition, who had worked together for many years for reform and social betterment. Through Rex Tugwell, who had come to know relief administrator Hopkins, Secretary of Labor Perkins, and other members of the social work group while working with the brain trust on Roosevelt's campaign, strong ties were forged between the new relief officials and the Ivy League liberals of the AAA.[70] Amid all this energy and effort, with the ties between the FERA and AAA staffs burgeoning in an atmosphere of innovation and almost palpable idealism, surely some response to the much-discussed paradox of want amid plenty was imminent.

CHAPTER SEVEN

The Little Pigs:
The Genesis of Relief
Distribution

The contrast between burdensome supplies of agricultural products and widespread deprivation did not immediately provoke
the new administration into arranging for distribution of surplus food to the hungry. The idea was certainly familiar from
the Farm Board wheat donations, and a specific proposal for a federal
agency to coordinate efforts to procure farm surpluses for the urban unemployed had been made to Roosevelt by an old friend in May and forwarded to Harry Hopkins at the time of his appointment.[1] Yet more than
six months of the new regime elapsed before an effort was made to apply
farm surpluses to relief. Not until implementation of the Agricultural Adjustment Act had horrified the public and bruised the consciences of segments of the AAA staff did the New Deal enter the surplus distribution
business.

The primary impetus for the initiation of food assistance was an emergency pig slaughter campaign undertaken by the AAA late in the summer
of 1933; the story begins, however, not in the pig pens but in the cotton
fields. By the time the Agricultural Adjustment Act passed in May, the
1933 crops of most staple commodities were well on their way to maturity. A drought in the West was curtailing the expected wheat yield, but
cotton, corn, and hogs were all promising bumper crops. Cotton seemed
the most immediate problem. An enormous surplus was already in storage, and the price had dropped to five cents a pound. While farmers
could be paid not to plant a portion of their acreage in the coming years, it
was too late to apply such preventive measures to the current crop. The

administration, unwilling to wait a year and a half for a rise in cotton prices, devised a drastic remedy. In June 1933, the AAA announced a campaign to plow under a quarter of the standing cotton crop. County extension agents supervised by the AAA undertook a whirlwind drive to sign up cotton planters. Participating growers agreed to plow up between 25 and 50 percent of their acreage prior to harvest in return for rental payments in cash or cotton options. That the campaign was successful enough to reach its goal is a testimony to the extremity of the situation and the pent-up desire for action released by the New Deal; 10 million acres—25 percent of the acreage planted in cotton—were plowed under in the summer of 1933.[2]

The plow-up created some vivid images. Farmers found it difficult to induce their mules—trained for years to walk between the rows—to trample on the growing plants.[3] For farmers who had cleared, plowed, and fertilized the land, and had planted and cultivated the crop, the plow-up was painful. Years later, the unpleasant memories lingered. "What bothered me about the Roosevelt time," recalled a sharecropper interviewed by Studs Terkel, "was when they come out with this business that you had to plow up a certain amount of your crop, especially cotton. I didn't understand, 'cause it was good cotton."[4] For observers aware of the clothing needs of the unemployed, the destruction of growing fiber seemed brutal. The newspapers circulated a story about an elderly black farmer who, after completing his plow-up, found a substantial number of bolls remaining above ground. He asked his neighbor of many years, a planter and a member of Congress, if it would be all right for him to gather the salvageable cotton to make himself a mattress. Advised by the congressman that it would be against the law, the older man queried, "Aint you white folks a little crazieh 'n usual jus now?"[5] Fact or fiction, the story captured the feeling of many that the plow-up was insane. "To have to destroy a growing crop," said Henry Wallace, "is a shocking commentary on our civilization."[6]

To the corn and hog raisers of the Midwest, however, the cotton plow-up suggested a possible solution to their own economic dilemma. Corn and hogs are linked in an intricate cycle. Much of the corn produced in the U.S. is marketed in the form of hogs; that is, it is fed to hogs on the same farm where it is grown. In the winter before Roosevelt's inauguration, hog prices had declined to their lowest level since the 1890s. As agricultural adjustment got under way, they were lower, relative to parity, than the prices of any other major agricultural commodity. Moreover, the number of farmers affected by these low prices was huge; more than 60 percent of U.S. farmers raised some corn or hogs.[7] In Iowa, approximately half of the gross income to agriculture came from corn and hogs. The new administration acknowledged that something had to be done to raise corn-hog prices, but this goal was not easily accomplished. Corn and hogs grow in cycles of different lengths; a corn crop requires six months to mature while hogs take twelve to sixteen months. If corn acreage were cut back before reductions in hog breeding could take effect, hog farmers would be faced with a feed shortage or forced to turn to other feeds. Furthermore, since not all feed corn is fed to hogs, any change in corn prices would affect other livestock as well; and not all hogs eat corn, so prices of other feeds had to be taken into account.[8]

Wallace decided against a plow-up campaign for corn and adopted a longer-range acreage adjustment policy instead. By July, forecasts suggested a small corn crop along with the curtailment of other feed grains caused by drought in the wheat country, providing a hiatus in which a long-term control plan could be developed. The hog forecasts, however, predicted a plentiful issue. Since pork products are perishable, huge surpluses of the sort that had occurred in cotton and wheat had never accumulated. Instead, prices had been reduced to move existing supplies into consumption. The forecasts suggested that more hogs would be ready for slaughter in 1933–1934 than in the two previous seasons, thus forcing prices even lower than the levels that had produced such unrest in the Cornbelt the previous year. Some means had to be found to reduce the supply of pork reaching the market.

The adjustment of pork supplies, however, was a difficult task. Farmers could not be encouraged to withhold live hogs from slaughter because they would have to be fed, and feed prices were rising. If current supplies were reduced by the removal of pork products from the market, price increases would be temporary because of the unreduced supply at the farms. If supplies were reduced at their source, the number of hogs bred to farrow, prices would not be affected before twelve to sixteen months. Longer-range plans were formulated to curtail the normal annual production and to seek outlets for existing supplies, and Wallace and his corn-hog section lieutenants began casting about for some means to forestall the impending market glut. The AAA turned to the producers themselves for suggestions.[9]

Wallace's general commitment to the involvement of farm leaders in the development of AAA programs was especially strong with regard to corn and hogs because no plan had been previously agreed upon. A series of meetings sponsored by the AAA and the farm organizations throughout the Cornbelt in June and July resulted in the creation of an ongoing organization, called the National Corn-Hog Committee of Twenty-Five, to represent corn and hog producers. At the end of July, the committee convened in Chicago to work out a plan. Its members suggested a number of methods of reducing pork supplies, the most startling of which was the "plowing under" of young and unborn pigs to prevent their reaching maturity. Along with several less-dramatic means, including the donation of pork products to the Red Cross, the committee suggested that the AAA offer benefit payments to induce farmers to market light pigs and piggy (pregnant) sows.

The administration reacted favorably to the National Corn-Hog Committee's recommendations for an emergency slaughter of young pigs and sows soon to farrow. Tentative plans were developed in late July and early August for the government purchase of 4 million pigs at weights between twenty-five and one hundred pounds and a million piggy sows at prices that would constitute a substantial incentive to market. The government hoped to reduce the pork tonnage for the 1933–1934 season by 16 percent through the removal of approximately one billion pounds of hogs. The campaign was officially announced by Secretary Wallace during a visit to the Chicago World's Fair on August 18, 1933, and the purchase of pigs and sows began a week later.[10]

The pig campaign was a remarkable venture from the outset, and one fraught with difficulties of both logistics and public relations. The smaller pigs slipped between the slats of stockyard pens creating what one reporter called a "nightmare" for stockyard workers: "all over the runways, sleek, fast, greasy pigs were running," pursued by "puffing humans," reported the *Milwaukee Journal*.[11] In some locations, the piglets escaped the stockyards and ran squealing down the streets of adjoining neighborhoods, arousing public sympathy for the "poor little pigs."[12] In Chicago, a huge piggy sow, nicknamed "Big Bertha," escaped and had to be shot as she charged a group of stenographers.[13] As word got around the hinterland that the government was paying premium prices for unfinished pigs, the designated terminal markets were flooded with piglets, "a new 'bonus army,' of porkers," one newspaper called them, that overcrowded stockyard holding pens and overtaxed the processing crews.[14] While teams of slaughterers and butchers worked all night to reduce the squealing backlog, and packers experimented with mass electrocution in lieu of the traditional method of sticking, or stabbing, the pigs, the AAA established a quota system, declaring that no more pigs would be bought for the account of the secretary of agriculture unless accompanied by a marketing permit.[15]

The permit system, hastily established without an opportunity for extensive public education, brought a new round of problems. Some farmers were unable to obtain permits to ship their pigs, and in some areas, commission dealers and speculators obtained large numbers of permits and then bought pigs from farmers on disadvantageous terms. Writing to Secretary Wallace about one such complaint from a constituent, Oklahoma Senator T. P. Gore expressed the strong feelings engendered in the Cornbelt by such profiteering and the permit system that fostered it. "There may be room to debate this whole policy of murdering pigs," he wrote, "but certainly if the Government is going to buy up these hogs and the taxpayers are going to pay twice what they are worth, the farmer who owns the pigs ought to get the benefits of the bounty or subsidy and not the speculators."[16]

Despite the permit problems, piglets kept pouring into the terminal markets, but only a trickle of sows accompanied them. Amid much speculation that farmers were holding back their piggy sows to have more piglets to sell at government supported prices the next year, the AAA reluctantly increased the quota of pigs in order to obtain the planned reduction in pork supplies. In the end, 6,188,722 pigs and 222,144 sows were slaughtered, 2 million more pigs than originally planned.[17] Meanwhile, farmers complained that the inspectors who determined whether sows were sufficiently pregnant to qualify for the bonus were rejecting obviously pregnant ones. Farmer after farmer wrote in to complain that his sows first had been judged ineligible for the bonus by the inspector and then docked by the packers for being pregnant. "The inspectors at the Cincinnati market could not tell a piggy sow," wrote one angry breeder. "I feel that the Government beat me out of $4.00 and that is the way the farmers feel about it. . . . You must not blame the farmers for not sending in their sows with the bonus inspectors you have hired."[18] Many wrote appealing to the Department of Agriculture to send them the bonus they had been unjustly denied. "Now if there is any way we could get this $12.00 it would just mean that much too us as we are under a big expense and do not have our 1932 taxes paid yet on account of sickness and poor prices," wrote one woman, explaining that her husband was hospitalized with throat cancer. "We live out in south central Nebrasky where there was no oats very little wheat and a poor corn crop this year," she added. "The western farmer has sure been hard hit."[19]

Not all letters were complaints; many farmers, especially those in the feed-short drought areas, were helped by the program. "If you could have been in my office the last few days and have heard the stories of farms where there is absolutely not one particle of feed for pigs, where they were just able to keep their pigs going long enough to get in on this bonus," wrote a South Dakota editor to the chief of the Corn-Hog Section of the AAA, "I know that you would be gratified that you are able to help out all of these farmers as much as you did." [20] The *Sioux City Journal* sponsored a "Golden Pig Jubilee" to celebrate "the return of prosperity to the middle west." Urging local businesses to conduct special golden pig sales, the paper declared that "already the federal plan to boost hog prices by curtailing the available supply of live pork has had a most beneficial effect on Sioux City businesses." The *Journal* estimated that a half million dollars in cash had been paid to farmers in the Sioux City area in the first few days of the emergency slaughter campaign and that another 10 million or more would follow. "Farmers are happy because for the first time in many months . . . they are in a position to buy hundreds of necessities that they have deprived themselves of during the sorely trying times of the last few years," and "businessmen are happy because this great outpouring of cash means increased sales and at least a partial return to normal business activity." [21]

Back at the stockyards, however, jubilation was tempered by a new set of problems arising from the glut of piglets. The AAA's plans had called for processing the sows and heavier pigs, those weighing eighty-one to one hundred pounds, into salt pork. Since the lighter pigs were too small to be dehaired with the mechanical equipment available at most packing plants, they were to be rendered into grease and tankage, a sort of liquified pig normally dried and used for fertilizer. To distinguish the pigs destined for butchering from those to be tanked, the packers were instructed to paint a stripe on the back of each pig after it was weighed— green for those large enough for normal processing and red for those headed for tankage. "In two days," quipped the Chicago *Tribune*, "Uncle Sam has become the world's largest buyer and painter of hogs." [22] But as the slaughter progressed and the anticipated numbers of sows and heavier pigs did not materialize, the humor occasioned by the pig painting requirement gave way to concern over disposal of the huge volume of tankage resulting from the red-striped pigs. The facilities for drying and storing tankage rapidly became clogged, and the market value of the fertilizer produced by the tanking process was too low to justify the construction of additional facilities. [23] By the first week in September, the Chicago papers

reported that "mountains of fertilizer—composed of ground up slaughtered pigs"—were piling up in dump yards and outside the packing
houses causing "something of a sanitary problem." [24]

Some of the undried tankage was carted away and used as landfill by
the Illinois Central Railroad in yards near Chicago's southern suburbs.
The results were vividly described by the *Chicago Tribune*, which made
no secret of its hostility to the program or the administration: "the re-
dolent ghosts of 200,000 little pigs, which were martyred by the government so that the rest of the swine in the United States might become more
valuable are haunting the residents of Hazel Crest," and other suburban
areas. "The warm sun has shown and the rains have fallen on this mass of
flesh, hastening the natural progress of decay and throwing to the breezes
a stench which the people of Hazel Crest declare is 'indescribably revolt-
ing,'" and engendering "vast swarms of big blue flies." [25] Chicago was
not the only city in which disposal of the tankage invited unfavorable
publicity. Throughout the Midwest, newspapers carried stories of pig carcasses burned, buried, and dumped in rivers and streams.

The AAA had anticipated a negative public reaction to the pig campaign, but the complications created by disposal of the tankage aggravated an already difficult public relations problem. "During the last few
days our newspapers in St. Louis and at St. Joseph Missouri have carried
stories about thousands of pigs that have been dumped into the River, and
it seems to me that this is mighty bad psychology for our cities at this
time," wrote William Hirth, editor of the *Missouri Farmer* to his old colleague from the McNary-Haugen fight, Chester Davis, now director of the
AAA's Production Division. "Surely these pigs could have been handled
in some other manner that would have left a better taste not only in the
mouths of those who are hungry in the cities, but likewise with our farmers." [26] While many of the press accounts may have been inaccurate—
"fantastic and false stories," [27] the AAA later called them—the charge
that a large quantity of the product of the emergency slaughter was
thrown away was undeniable. Eventually, 79 percent of the pigs and sows
slaughtered by number, or 61 percent by weight, were made into inedible
products, and only about two-fifths of the total yield of tankage could be
dried and stored. [28]

In their defense of the pig slaughter, Wallace and other AAA officials
primarily addressed those criticisms based on humane considerations, as
in the public condemnation of the agency's cruelty in slaughtering "inno-
cent little piglets." "They contended that every little pig has the right to
attain before slaughter the full pigginess of his pigness," grumbled the

secretary. "To hear them talk, you would have thought that pigs are raised for pets." [29] The AAA was surprised by this aspect of public sentiment; certainly neither the corn-hog section of the AAA nor the National Corn-Hog Committee of Twenty-Five had foreseen public sympathy for the pigs. As one participant recalled the committee's deliberations: "That was the start of the 'little pigs' episode: the murder of the little pigs. . . . Of course they were all used to killing pigs. That's part of our business and no one thought anything about it. . . . Pigs were all killed after all." [30] Other members of the committee, Historian Dean Albertson has reported, expressed similar feelings. [31] "I suppose it is a marvelous tribute to the humanitarian instincts of the American people that they sympathize more with little pigs which are killed than with full-grown hogs," commented Secretary Wallace. [32]

While the public's valiant defense of the rights of piglets caused some mirth and some pique within the administration, it could not obscure the more fundamental criticism of government-sponsored destruction of food in the face of desperate want. Among the hundreds of letters and telegrams received by the Corn-Hog Section of the AAA, the secretary, and the president during and after the emergency campaign, only a tiny fraction mentioned humane considerations, and several of these were serious letters from humane societies questioning the new methods of slaughter with which the packers were experimenting. Most of the communications were from farmers or packing houses asking how to get in on the program or complaining about inequities in its implementation. Among the many letters from those outside the hog industry, however, the overwhelming theme was the immorality of wasting food while people went hungry.

A substantial number of such letters came from the unemployed themselves, individually or through organizations. "Since there are millions of us still unemployed, and the winter which we are now facing has nothing but horror to offer, we are begging of you as a humanitarian of the highest degree, to stop this willful waste and allow the unemployed to have this meat," wrote the Canteen Township Improvement Association of East St. Louis, Illinois to Roosevelt. "We will take these pigs and use them to feed our families which very seldom see fresh pork, thereby saving the Government the huge expense of destroying this meat." Local relief had been suspended, noted the association's secretary, for lack of funds. [33] "Regarding this matter of killing hogs weighing less than 81 lbs and using them for fertilizer, I wish to say that I believe this is wrong, as the meat from these hogs could be used to feed the poor, and heaven above knows that they would be only too glad to have it to help them keep body and soul together," wrote an unemployed woman from Ohio who, along with her unemployed husband, received $2.20 a week from the county. "And as prices of food stuffs are rising every day, you can imagine how well we are fed on this amount," she added and enclosed a relief grocery order to underscore her point.[34] "I am writing to you to inquire if it is possible to get any of this pork, as I have been unemployed for many years and a lift along this line would be mighty welcome. I'll take a whole pig, dead or alive or made up into pork," wrote a man in Chicago.[35] An Ohio couple wrote to complain that their family had "not had a pork chop or any part of a hog in 2½ years. . . . We can't afford pork at the low price now, what would you expect us to eat at higher prices? . . . Why, oh why destroy what is so good to eat?" Nevertheless, they sent the president "blessings and fervent support."[36]

Especially poignant were the letters from supporters expressing incredulity and begging the president or the secretary of agriculture to put a stop to the malicious rumors that the little pigs were to be made into fertilizer. "There seems to be quite a bit of propaganda around here . . . in regards to the Emergency Hog Marketing Program. Such remarks as the hogs are purchased, slaughtered and sent to the soap factory or fertilizer plants, and other unwarranted waste of food products," wrote an American Legionnaire from Cincinnati. Suggesting that such rumors had been started by "some die hard Republican Politician," he asked for "all the information possible . . . so I can do my part in explaining the full details."[37] The manager of the Kansas Retail Grocers Association also wrote for information so that he could explain the new policy to members. "There are rumors in this city, . . . from the workers in the packing houses that these hogs are merely being thrown into the tank house for fertilizer. . . . Public opinion does not seem to be in favor of such activities. If they are the facts, in as much as there are some six thousand families in this city out of work, they cannot conceive the idea of destroying food."[38] A county Democratic committee chairman in Wisconsin wrote to the governor of his state reporting a story circulating "about the government buying hogs and burying or destroying them. . . . The story goes that they buried so many out back of the stock yards, and the stench was so great that the citizens objected. Of course the climax to the story is that the administration is spending millions of dollars for under-sized pigs and not even giving the poor an opportunity to eat them." Noting that "this story seems to grow as time passes," he asked "where I can get the information to stop this propaganda."[39]

Numerous letters quoted the prophesy "willful waste brings woeful want" and predicted dire consequences, natural, supernatural, or political, if the wasteful project continued. "We are on the eve of seven lean years," predicted a Kansas City prophet; "The lord never intended to have acres of valuable crops plowed under, when there were starving people all over the world, . . . it was not his intention a man should for the sake of money destroy crops by hand when we have failures of every sort staring in our face, pests have taken away plenty, floods have done likewise, storms, killing frosts." [40] "I fear the policy to reduce food supply's by killing 5,000,000 hogs is dangerous. . . . Hunger and revolution are neighbors," wrote a pastor in Iowa. [41] The Depression is not over, warned an Ohio man; "If this mad rush to curtail production should happen to be accompanied by a severe drought, an epidemic of hog cholera, or some other general misfortune, the country might find itself with a most distressing problem. As long as an adequate supply of materials is available, we can find some way to distribute it, but what could we do in case of an actual shortage, and what right have we to imagine that such a shortage can not occur?" [42] One especially restrained writer cautiously suggested that "if it is a fact that most of the pigs are going into tankage and grease, . . . then it occurs to me that some criticism of the administration might arise if it became generally known that perfectly good pork is being practically destroyed, while a lot of people are still in destitute circumstances and are having to be fed out of the public treasury." He became more passionate as he considered the possible consequences. "It seems to me that a lot of our God-fearing people might believe that the Almighty would not look with favor upon any government or any people sanctioning such destruction of food under such circumstances, and that the All Ruling Power might strike pestilence or some other calamity as Divine punishment." [43] Those predicting political repercussions were more blunt: "The people of Indiana were with you but such stunts as this . . . [are] turning them and not only against the plan you are working on but against the Party all the way through," wrote a distressed supporter in Indiana to the president. [44] "The hungry and needy have no representatives but Mr. President they helped to elect you and unless they receive consideration, . . . will demand a change very soon," wrote another political forecaster. [45]

That so many people wrote to suggest an alternative fate for the pigs destined for fertilizer tankage is a tribute to the resurgent activism of the American people and to the hope engendered by the early New Deal. The common suggestion, of course, was distribution to the unemployed. "We urge you to set up the proper machinery for immediate distribution of

every pig fit for human consumpation [*sic*] into the hands of the hungry
. . . this will . . . raise the physical and mental condition of the unemployed and rally the country as a whole," telegraphed an Indiana man to
the president.[46] People offered to help in various ways. One woman in
Illinois, writing to suggest that surplus grain be fed to the little pigs and
the pigs to the poor, volunteered to supply the president with a list of
families "who needs from one to three, if you decide to feed the hungry
instead of killing to keep up prices when there are so many who can not
buy meat as it is now priced."[47] The Allen County Unemployed Association, declaring it "a disgrace for the hungry people to witness the slaughter of pigs and have them turned into fertilizer," offered the labor of "experienced men who will be glad to give their time in the dehairing of
lighter weight pigs in order to give the suffering people in Allen county
something to eat."[48] A physician in Cleveland, describing a patient whose
family had been subsisting on vegetables from her brother's garden, proposed a "pig to a poor family" club to "put the meat where it will do
some good."[49]

While the implementation of such a plan would have been difficult in
Cleveland, it appeared feasible in some rural areas. "How the pigs would
help us if we could only get them to feed and kill," wrote a New Albany,
Indiana farmer; "It is surprising to know how many small farmers, in the
small farm sections of the state have not a single pig to be fed for [meat]
this year and no funds to buy with."[50] The director of extension service
for the state of Oklahoma wrote in to explain that the 1933 animal census
had shown that more than half the farms in the state had had no hogs at
all, and he suggested that the AAA work out a plan to "purchase pigs,
gilts and brood sows from those farms where surpluses exist and distribute these stock hogs to those farms which are without hogs to promote
the production of adequate and suitable home supplies of meat." The situation in Oklahoma, especially in the cotton-producing areas, he pointed
out, was completely different from the situation in the Cornbelt. "For
many years agricultural leaders in this state have been energetically and
systematically attempting to promote what has been commonly termed
the 'Cow, sow and hen' program or the production of the living on the
farm. Considerable progress has been made . . . and we are somewhat
concerned that this emergency program may entirely offset the progress
which has been secured. . . . Fundamentally," he concluded, "there is
not a surplus of hogs on the farms of Oklahoma as long as the children in
50,000 or 60,000 farm homes of the state are hungry for meat most of the
year."[51] The secretary of a Farmers' Union local in Cornville, Arizona

wrote in with a similar plan. Explaining that many of the farmers in his vicinity had lacked feed and funds to raise the normal number of sows, he reported: "They now have the feed, but no pigs; and feel that if in Arizona you contemplate the destruction of any of the pig family, that they would be extremely happy to provide food and lodging for such of the hog family as might about fill one car (hog car)." They would not offer the pork for sale, he assured the secretary, but "simply a supply for home use." [52]

Other writers had other propositions. The mayor of Cleveland wired for permission to carry out a plan he had developed with the packers to refrigerate the meat from the small pigs for distribution to the city's unemployed. [53] The chamber of commerce in Ponca City, Oklahoma suggested giving the slaughtered pigs weighing under eighty pounds "to the Indian tribes of this locality not only for their immediate meat supply but for them to jerk and cure, as is their custom, for their next winter use." [54] The American Association for China Famine and Flood Relief wrote to urge the administrator to allow the meat to mature and ship it to China, presenting "the prospect of developing foreign trade with China, which is probably the largest underdeveloped market today in the world." He raised the moral issue of waste amid want on the global scale: "the destruction of food and cotton, and especially pork, is all wrong and will bring nothing but harm in the future, especially when there are millions of people in the world who will be suffering and dying for lack of food and clothing this coming winter." [55] "Cannot the Government take these millions of hogs that they intend to kill and slaughter, and put them aside under contract to be fed to the poor after they are entirely fattened on Iowa corn?" inquired an Iowa lawyer. "The government will have to take care of the unemployed this winter anyway." [56]

"In any event," declared former Senator Atlee Pomerene after a brief discourse to a reporter on the joys of roast suckling pig, "when men, women and children are hungry, I say that no defense can be made either in law, morals or religion for throwing wholesome meat into a fertilizer vat. I tell you there are some things that are just too much." [57] Substantial segments of the press agreed; the wait-and-see attitude with which most papers had greeted Secretary Wallace's announcement of the Emergency Hog Marketing Campaign gradually grew into puzzlement, mirth, irony, and outrage. Shortly after the campaign began, a feature article in the *New York Times* reported the Cornbelt puzzled by agricultural adjustment. "What makes it all so puzzling is that it goes against the tradition that past generations of agriculture have handed down to the present as to

what constitutes a good husbandry. . . . What, one asks, is the value of
the 4-H pig clubs and the big litter contests, if it only results in the production of pigs which are to be wasted? . . . how can a country waste its
way back to prosperity." [58] Some papers worried that the plan would be
self-defeating because the higher prices would further reduce consumption. Others feared an actual food shortage; Secretary Wallace "is playing
with fire when he undertakes to curtail the nation's meat supply. . . . he is
setting about to create a food shortage in this country," warned the *Indianapolis Star*. The *Sioux City Journal* ran an ironic article entitled
"Nature Aids Farm Belt in Crop Destruction Plan," describing the "great
good luck" of states afflicted by drought and grasshoppers, since farmers
in these areas would have reduced output without toil. [59]

The strongest attack was launched by the *Chicago Daily Tribune*, which
grew increasingly hostile as the stench from the tankage disposal fiasco
mounted. The *Tribune*, initially skeptical of the plan but appreciative
of Secretary Wallace's open-minded attitude, adopted a critical stance
as the plan went into operation. "The city people must pay not only
higher prices because of an artificially created shortage but must pay
taxes to reward farmers generously for creating the shortage." Later, another editorial headline labeled restricted production "Another Farm Plan
on the Rocks," and the paper predicted that bounties for reduced output
would meet the same fate as futile efforts to peg prices under the Hoover
Farm Board. Farmers would subvert the plan and increase production
anyway, or higher prices would reduce demand: "The real hope of agriculture, today as always, is not in reducing output but in increasing the
demand . . . by restoring to our farmers their lost markets abroad." The
Tribune reprinted an editorial from the Marion, Indiana *Chronicle* responding to the pig slaughter and its accompanying tankage disposal
methods with outrage at "the enormity of the latest offense against every
law of God and man." Another editorial pointed out that the pig program
gave farmers an incentive to hold back their pregnant sows to have more
pigs for the next year and dubbed the whole campaign an "effort to make
a lean year out of a fat one." The paper ran a story on the tankage problems on page one, and later, an editorial on the "Economy of Costly
Waste" implied that the pig campaign was largely for show, "a huge
drama of administration purpose" and condemned the Roosevelt administration for the wasteful destruction of food. The editorial pointed out
the irony of concentrating the destruction "in Chicago, a city in which
the per capita cost of relief, supported by public revenues, is increasing
because the cost of foodstuffs is increasing. The sufficiency of the public

revenue to continue the feeding of the destitute becomes more questionable month by month," the paper continued, "and yet the festering carcasses of food animals drive inhabitants of this region to justified protests."[60] Although the Roosevelt administration had never considered the *Tribune* an ally, the paper's attack did not go unnoticed within the AAA. "The Chicago *Tribune* gave a great deal of publicity to our operations and embarrassed us considerably," wrote the chief of the meat processing section in an internal memorandum.[61]

On September 21, 1933, just a day after the *Tribune*'s scathing editorial, the White House announced a plan to use $75 million to procure surplus agricultural products to feed and clothe the unemployed over the coming winter. The press release that made the plan public linked it squarely to the pigs, indicating that the AAA would make "further" purchases of pork for distribution to the unemployed. "The announcement," read the official release, "followed the recent allocation by Mr. Hopkins of 100,000,000 pounds of cured pork which had been processed recently from millions of hogs purchased from surpluses by the Agricultural Adjustment Administration." The press release was short on details, but long on purposes. "By using funds of the Agricultural Adjustment Administration, supplemented by those of the Federal Emergency Relief Administration, and the nation-wide network of State and local relief administrations for distribution, a real effort to bridge the gap between supplies and consumption will be made." The president, according to the published statement, "considered such action as one of the most direct blows at the economic paradox which has choked farms with an abundance or farm products while many of the unemployed have grown hungry."[62]

Nine days later, after meeting with Hopkins at Hyde Park, Roosevelt announced a much broader version of the same program. "A Federal relief program shorn of red tape, in the interests of feeding, clothing, and providing coal for the needy during the coming winter, will be started within a week under plans approved today by President Roosevelt in a three hour conference with Harry L. Hopkins," reported the *New York Times*. "Mr. Hopkins declined to go into statistical discussions, but in talking with newspaper men emphasized rather the determination of the administration to protect the unemployed against hardship."[63] The next day, from his train en route to Chicago where he would address a convention of the American Legion, Roosevelt released a statement directing Harry Hopkins to establish immediately a nonprofit corporation to buy supplies for relief, emphasizing both the benefits to be delivered to the needy and the advantages of the plan to farmers. "The President has determined upon an Emergency Relief Corporation as the most effective instrument for accomplishment, promptly and on a big scale, of this service to the unemployed and to farmers. . . . The President believes the corporation can be organized quickly and in such a manner as to become the best agent for decisive action in the emergency." [64] The corporation was organized quickly, indeed. On October 4, the formation of the Federal Surplus Relief Corporation (FSRC) was announced to the public. A nonprofit, nonstock corporation had been chartered in Delaware by the Federal Emergency Relief administrator, the secretary of agriculture, and the administrator of public works to remove agricultural surpluses and distribute them for the relief of hardship caused by unemployment. [65]

The internal memoranda of the AAA indicate that plans for the FSRC were not yet fully formulated when the president first announced the program on September 21. In fact, only the day before the announcement, Wallace had requested of the department's solicitor an opinion as to the legality of a plan by which the FERA would use RFC funds to purchase surpluses removed from normal markets by the secretary of agriculture. The solicitor's opinion on the legality of a corporation to carry out the program was sent to the secretary on September 25, and even at this point, plans for the FSRC were not complete, since the proposed corporation was to be organized under the laws of the District of Columbia rather than the state of Delaware. [66] In fact, the White House announcement of September 21 apparently caught the AAA by surprise. An AAA press release issued the next day stated that: "The Agricultural Adjustment Administration will put into operation, as fast as they are developed, plans for supplying surplus farm products to needy and destitute people through the Emergency Relief Administration, Secretary Wallace said today. This action will be taken in order to carry out the program announced by President Roosevelt Thursday, for the twofold purpose of stabilizing farm markets and feeding the unemployed." [67]

While the president's premature announcement of the program may have been intended to test public reaction before a larger program was unveiled, his haste was certainly occasioned by the need to defuse mounting criticism as well. The outcry over the piglets was at its height, and the little pigs were not the only source of discontent in the fall of 1933; the postinauguration honeymoon was decidedly over. The weeks prior to the announcement had been marked by an increase in discontent with the progress of the recovery program, particularly among farmers who were affected by the NRA's influence on prices of items they purchased without being comparably affected by the AAA's influence on the prices of items they sold. The Farmers' Holiday Association revived talk of a farm strike, and delegations of southern cotton planters descended on Washington to protest the price of cotton and demand inflation. Furthermore, the processing tax on hogs was scheduled to go into effect on October 1, and an escalation of protest over the destruction of pork could be anticipated as consumers in the cities felt the pinch. In the same week in which he announced the purchase of agricultural surpluses for relief, the president stalled inflationists by announcing a scheme to lend farmers ten cents a pound on their cotton, in effect, a means of supporting the price of that commodity. Thus, the preliminary relief distribution announcement may have been intended to forestall charges of favoritism toward the producers of cotton as well as to emphasize the good that had come through the pork reduction campaign.

In any case, the move was beautifully timed. "Swift Roosevelt Blows Deal with Discontent" headlined a feature story in the Sunday *New York Times* a few days after the announcement. "Grumbling Silenced by Order Applying Food and Clothing Surplus to Relief and Pledge of Loan on Cotton," "Inflationists Headed Off," continued the subheads, "President's Practical Measures Advance Recovery Program, Strengthen Hold on Public and Check Nostrum Army." [68] Some editors warned that federal provision on so large a scale might lead states and cities to slacken their efforts to provide, but most were laudatory. "In this plan," reported the *Literary Digest* "is seen a means to end the most tragic and ironic phase of the depression— 'breadlines knee deep in wheat.' " [69] The Rochester *Democrat and Chronicle* declared that "no single feature of the Administration's recovery program will appeal more to the common sense and understanding of the country." [70] The *New York Times*, in response to the first announcement, pointed out that the new plan would not only help to relieve the unemployed and the farmer but would also "relieve our minds of the distressing 'economic paradox' of unprofitable surpluses existing side by side with extreme want." Noting that precedents for the action had been established by the distribution of Farm Board wheat and cotton, the *Times* went on to assert, "but even if there were not such precedents, the pressing paradox would suggest, if not compel, some such provision." [71]

Some commentators have made the assumption that the distribution of surplus agricultural products was undertaken by an astute administration eager to pacify an aroused public. Broadus Mitchell, for example, in his study of the Depression decade, summarized the episode thus: "The angry protests taught the AAA that the complacency of the people had its limits, and after this episode increasing care was taken to distribute 'surpluses' to the destitute."[72] In fact, the matter was not so simple. In the first place, the plans for relief distribution of the pork were made before the pig slaughter, with its attendant miseries, provoked widespread public disaffection. And in the second place, the criticism that provoked the development of broader surplus procurement and distribution plans and the establishment of an ongoing agency to administer them was nearly as vociferous within the administration as outside it.

The original proposals of the Corn-Hog Committee had included donation to the Red Cross of some of the stocks of pork products then in the hands of packers, and some members of the committee have contended that distribution for relief was always the intended destination of the little pigs from the emergency campaign as well. "They were going to save all the meat that could be saved and give it to the people on relief. That had been figured out in this original meeting. . . . and so it should be known."[73] Recollections, however, vary; AAA General Counsel Jerome Frank insisted that the original proposal would have turned the entire kill into grease and tankage, and both Frank and USDA economist Mordecai Ezekial remembered contacting Harry Hopkins to determine whether he could use the meat for distribution if it could be salvaged.[74] In any case, distribution of pork through the FERA was a firm part of the plan by mid August, a week before the actual slaughter began, and was included in press reports of Secretary Wallace's announcement of the program at the World's Fair.[75] But public indignation was not without impact. As the slaughter progressed and the outcry grew louder, the AAA placed increasing emphasis on plans for relief distribution in its press releases and replies to letters of inquiry and protest, and in the last week of the campaign, the weight limit for pigs to be processed for meat was reduced from eighty to seventy-one pounds to fill the quota of 100 million pounds of meat for which the FERA had contracted.[76]

Public outrage over the pigs was a major factor in the decision to extend surplus purchase and distribution to other commodities, but such external criticism also found fertile soil in the already bruised consciences of AAA officials and others within the Roosevelt administration who were profoundly ill at ease with the whole production control endeavor. One close friend described Eleanor Roosevelt as having "raised unshirted hell" within the administration about the destruction of food and fiber.[77] "Almost everyone I knew in the AAA felt strongly about the 'wrongness' of destroying surplus food at a time when many people were hungry and

unable to obtain anywhere near adequate subsistence," Alger Hiss recalled.[78] Jerome Frank described both Wallace and Tugwell as unhappy
with crop reduction, viewing it as a necessary evil until industrial production could increase.[79] "The feeling that man should live by providing
goods for his neighbors, not by withholding goods, goes very deep,"
wrote Wallace.[80] The pig slaughter, Frank remembered, "kind of hurt
Wallace as it was a pretty disgusting sort of thing to do that when people
were starving."[81] "The paradox of want in the midst of plenty was constantly in our minds as we proceeded with schemes like the emergency
hog slaughter," declared Wallace.[82]

"In examining the sources of new ideas in government," Adam Yarmolinsky has written in *The Presidential Advisory System*, "one observes
that the theory of simultaneous—and seemingly spontaneous—invention
applies here as elsewhere. The successful new ideas crop up all at once
from a number of sources."[83] The process by which the little pigs led to
the establishment of an ongoing program of surplus procurement and distribution with an independent operating base is a case in point; numerous
people have remembered the idea as their own or have attributed it to their
particular friends, protégés, heroes, or heroines. Jerome Frank, Lee
Pressman, and Alger Hiss in the AAA Legal Division have all been nomi-
nated by themselves or others.[84] Economic Advisor Mordecai Ezekial remembers the idea as his own;[85] Rex Tugwell, when interviewed, had "forgotten whether the idea first came from Jerome Frank or me."[86] Eleanor
Roosevelt is reported by many people, especially the female members of
the Washington press corps with whom she met regularly, to have initiated
the plan. "Of course all the male officials are convinced they would have
thought of it themselves" reporter Ruth Finney later wrote, "but they had
not done so up to the time she insisted it was the thing to do."[87] As
Eleanor Roosevelt replied when asked by a reporter for the *Christian Science Monitor* "whether it was her idea to buy up and distribute to the
unemployed the general farm surpluses, 'Nothing is ever one person's idea
entirely.'"[88] When the preliminary announcement of the surplus purchase
plan was made, AAA Administrator George Peek told the press that credit
for "enlarging the scope of this work beyond the plan already undertaken
for pork distribution" should go to Production Director Chester Davis,
Marketing Director William Westervelt, and Economic Advisor Louis H.
Bean.[89] The surplus commodity plan went through several stages—distribution of the pig meat, procurement of other surpluses for relief, and formation of a corporation to handle the transactions—and thus invited
original contributions from a number of people who might later remem-

ber the project as their own. In any case, official sanction for the project came from Roosevelt himself. On September 11, he wrote to Secretary Wallace, asking him to meet with Peek and Harry Hopkins and "possibly prepare a plan for purchase of surplus commodities such as butter, cheese, condensed milk, hog products and flour, to meet relief needs during the course of the winter." [90]

Even the idea of forming a corporation as the vehicle for surplus purchase and donation cropped up in several places. While Jerome Frank and the Legal Division were conceiving a corporation that would use funds from the general treasury and processing tax revenues and would handle distribution to the states as well as procurement and processing, staff members in the Production and Marketing Division of the AAA were developing plans for a corporation to use processing tax funds for the purchase of basic commodities to be donated to the FERA. The two plans differed in emphasis as well as financing with the Frank plan placing greater weight on the relief aspects of the project. Frank's corporation was the one actually formed, but confusion over the competing plans caused some hard feelings within the AAA. [91]

The ubiquitous claim to authorship of the plan suggests the popularity of the idea, the positive regard in which it was held and remembered by those involved. And this regard, in turn, suggests that the decision to purchase surpluses for distribution to the needy fulfilled some significant function in the lives of those involved. Adam Yarmolinsky's analysis is again appropriate; a new program may fulfill "the decision-maker's . . . desire to find a positive theme for the work of his agency." [92] "To many of us," Wallace wrote in 1934, "the only thing that made the hog slaughter acceptable was the realization that the meat and lard salvaged would go to the unemployed." [93]

As an effort to deflect public criticism of the pig slaughter in particular and the agricultural adjustment program in general, the establishment of surplus commodity distribution was only partially successful. The immediate flood of letters of protest did abate, and the press, as noted above, praised the new venture. But for many people the dramatic image of waste remained; "The cotton plowup and the slaughter of the little pigs," Leuchtenburg asserts, "fixed the image of the AAA in the minds of millions of Americans, who forever after believed that this was the agency's annual operation." [94] More than two years after the emergency hog marketing campaign, Wallace told a radio audience that "people are still interested in the six million pigs that were killed in September of 1933. In letters I have received following these radio talks, the pigs are mentioned more than any one thing except potatoes."[95] "I don't know," wrote Treasury Secretary Henry Morgenthau in his diary in 1938, "but I think from the day we started killing little pigs there has been a curse on this administration."[96]

The enduring stigma of the pig slaughter clung to Wallace especially. More than a decade later, when Wallace was a candidate for president, a campaign biographer felt constrained to defend his subject against charges stemming from the pig massacre. "Before we pass on to discuss his administration of the Department of Agriculture in more detail," wrote Frank Kingdon, "this is as good a time as any to take a look at the one recurring criticism of him that has been made, namely, that in his first year he inaugurated an economy of scarcity—usually summed up by reference to the six million little pigs that were killed in 1933."[97] Indeed, the pig slaughter did provide a continuing focus for a growing critique of the AAA's scarcity economics. As one member of the AAA press section recalled, "It typified the weakness of our entire structure, of the entire economic system; it was done in such a way that it stood out."[98] To many thoughtful people, the pig slaughter made clear the grim logic underlying domestic allotment: the balance between agricultural production and domestic consumption was to be restored by reducing production.

On the Left, dissenters from the scarcity approach to balance became increasingly articulate. In a world "still both hungry and cold," wrote Socialist Party standard bearer Norman Thomas early in 1934, "no Dean Swift ever wrote so complete a satire on civilization as the honest and troubled men who wrote in the pedestrian language of law the Agricultural Adjustment Act." Picturing human history as a long struggle against scarcity, Thomas characterized the New Deal agricultural program as a flight from abundance. "We do not know how to manage it, and therefore, by subsidized destruction, we return to familiar scarcity in order to give our farmers prosperity. We have 'breadlines knee deep in wheat,'" he lamented, "and our principal effort is to reduce the supply of wheat."[99]

For other critics on the Left, the AAA's production control features exposed the fundamental nature of capitalism. "Such attempts to cure economic ills by creating artificial scarcity through what is euphemistically called 'planned production' are not hard to explain," wrote *Nation* editor Mauritz Hallgren. "The productive forces of capitalism have reached the point where they seem to promise an era of abundance. But abundance, alas, has a depressing effect on prices," and thus on profits. "And a falling rate of profit threatens, not only individual industries, but the very foundation of capitalism." [100] In the same vein, Warren Vinton and Benjamin Stolberg in the *Economic Consequences of the New Deal*, argued that the abundant production in agriculture and the ensuing collapse of the farm price structure had become a "permanent threat to manufacturing prices," necessitating the reestablishment of scarcity. "And the organization of agricultural scarcity is exactly what the Agricultural Adjustment Administration is all about." [101]

For these critics, the distribution of farm surpluses to the poor was at best an afterthought to keep the blow from falling too heavily upon those least able to absorb it, at worst a sideshow to divert public attention from the real business of reestablishing scarcity. But for those within the administration, the FSRC resolved the painful paradox; "At last we had a mechanism through which the surplus could reach the hungry," rejoiced Wallace. "The new Corporation could not absorb all our farm surpluses, but it could give us new assurances that no one would go hungry or ragged because of any of our adjustment programs." [102] Rex Tugwell sounded the same theme when he told the 1934 meeting of the National Conference of Social Work that "the Surplus Relief Corporation helped us in the Department of Agriculture to solve the paradox of want in the midst of plenty. It made doubly certain that our program of crop reduction should not take place in a land where anyone went hungry." [103] In a sense, creation of the FSRC acted as a sort of moral safety valve that permitted the pig slaughter—and production control in general—to proceed. The fact remained that the government was engaged in the questionable process of reducing future meat supplies at a time when many families had been forced to do without meat altogether. Only about 100 million pounds of edible salt pork were salvaged for relief, as compared with an anticipated reduction of 16 percent, or more than a billion pounds, in pork supplies reaching the market during the 1933–1934 season, but somehow the symbolism caught hold, at least within the administration. "Not many people realized how radical it was—this idea of having the Government buy from those who had too much, in order to give to those who had too little, "wrote Wallace. "So direct a method of resolving the paradox of want in the midst of plenty could never have got beyond the discussion stage before 1933." [104]

CHAPTER EIGHT

The Federal Surplus Relief Corporation

Pragmatic, appealing, improvised, and flexible, the Federal Surplus Relief Corporation (FSRC) was in many ways an incarnation of the experimental spirit of the New Deal. Conceived in an informal conversation among friends and hastily established in an atmosphere of urgency, the new corporation was not the product of a careful policy-making process. It was seen by its creators as a temporary emergency measure to transfer agricultural surpluses to the unemployed until such time as the New Deal could bring about recovery, put the unemployed back to work, and restore balance to agriculture. In fact, the policies and constituencies established by the FSRC endured for decades and continue even now to influence domestic food assistance policy and politics. But at the time, both the problem and the solution appeared to be temporary, and speed was of the essence if the new agency were to do anything, as one reporter put it, referring to the little pigs, "to take the curse off a measure which was widely unpopular." [1]

The process by which the corporation was formed was described by Jerome Frank years later: "Tugwell and Harry Hopkins came over to my house on a Sunday. They were going to see the President the next day at Hyde Park. We talked out ways to accomplish this thing. . . . The idea was to have some joint operation between Hopkins and the AAA by which the AAA would buy the products and Hopkins would pay for processing them because AAA had no money for that purpose." Frank suggested forming a corporation. Hopkins obtained the president's blessing the next day, and "I was told to go full steam ahead and it would be done promptly," Frank remembers.[2] While Frank's recollections may have been simplified by time, the process he described is certainly a far cry from the laborious exchange of memoranda that would have been necessary among strangers or the rational progression of steps prescribed by program-planning texts. Haste and informality were to be the hallmarks of the incorporation process as well.

In an effort to avoid delay, the legal division staff omitted several steps in the incorporation process, omissions that were to cast a permanent shadow of doubt over the legality of the corporation. For example, the USDA solicitor's opinion as to the appropriateness of organizing under the laws of Delaware was not sought. Secretary Wallace had obtained an opinion affirming the legality of organizing such a corporation under the laws of the District of Columbia, but the process of obtaining a revised opinion regarding Delaware was not initiated until the new corporation was several months old. By that time, a precedent had been established by the formation of the Commodity Credit Corporation under Delaware law, but that corporation, the solicitor noted, had been formed pursuant to an executive order. He suggested that any doubt about the FSRC's legal status could be allayed by the issuance of an executive order ratifying it specifically.[3]

Obtaining an executive order or other written direction from the president to form the FSRC, however, was another step omitted by the legal staff. "Legend has it that authorization for the creation of the corporation was a note by the President on the back of a used envelope,"[4] a USDA official later commented, but when the corporation needed an executive order several years after its inception in order to continue to receive commodities from the secretary of agriculture, it was unable to produce one. In fact, an executive order was drafted early in November 1933 and, a later report concluded, "indubitably would have been signed by the President but for the fact that it was never presented to him, having been lost in the transmission of the papers to the member Cabinet officers and the Relief Administrator for their several approvals."[5] This disorder would be almost comic, were it not for the fact that the absence of a signed order later resulted in a virtual halt in the corporation's activities and a near cessation of the flow of commodities to needy people. In any case, three or four months elapsed before the loss of the executive order was discovered, and at that time, a new one was not requested on the assumption that the oral direction of the president had been sufficient. Another irregularity in the incorporation process occurred when Frank, rather than incur delay by applying to the comptroller general for the funds to pay the incorporation fee, supplied it himself. "I was bothered that if we organized this corporation, the Comptroller General would . . . raise hell and cause all kinds of difficulties. So I did something that maybe was politically immoral. I organized the corporation. It cost about thirty-five dollars to organize it and I paid it out of my own pocket. I never got the money back."[6]

The FSRC was chartered in the state of Delaware on October 4, 1933, as a nonprofit, nonstock corporation. Delaware was selected because, in Frank's words, "in Delaware you can get all the powers in the world in your corporate charter."[7] The state's corporation laws were, and are, among the most permissive; it was used as the legal home for a number of other federal corporations chartered early in the New Deal. The corporate form was selected, according to a speech prepared a decade later in the Department of Agriculture, "as a means of avoiding the red tape surrounding governmental activity" and to "facilitate prompt action."[8] The membership of the corporation was limited to "those persons who from time to time shall occupy the offices of Secretary of Agriculture, Federal Emergency Relief Administrator, and Federal Emergency Administrator of Public Works."[9] The Public Works administrator, Harold Ickes, was suggested by Hopkins and Tugwell, according to Frank, "because they knew he was friendly."[10]

The powers of the new corporation were derived from the Agricultural Adjustment Act, the Federal Emergency Relief Act, and Title II of the National Industrial Recovery Act. Its purposes, as stated in the Certificates of Incorporation were:

(1) To relieve the existing national economic emergency by expansion of markets for, removal of, and increasing and improving the distribution of, agricultural and other commodities and products thereof;
(2) To purchase, store, handle, and process surplus agricultural and other commodities and products thereof, and to dispose of the same so as to relieve the hardship and suffering caused by unemployment and/or to adjust the severe disparity between the prices of agricultural commodities and other commodities and products thereof.

An additional purpose was "to perform any and all functions, and exercise any and all powers, that may be duly delegated to it under the Acts of Congress specified above or any amendments to such acts."[11] In other words, as Jerome Frank later asserted, "The charter of the Federal Surplus Relief Corporation was big enough to do anything."[12]

Among the various things that the FSRC might do, however, no priorities were established, nor was any particular balance specified between the agricultural and unemployment relief aspects of the plan. Hopkins viewed the project primarily as a means of procurement for relief, a method of upgrading relief standards and improving the diets of the unemployed. "We will give them balanced diets. I can't give you a list of the types of food we plan to issue for the food will include everything necessary for healthful living," he told newspaper reporters in a press conference after his Hyde Park meeting with Roosevelt.[13] Wallace, on the other hand, had referred to the plan in internal memoranda as "the President's direction to me to cooperate with the Federal Emergency Relief Administration in removal of surplus commodities."[14] The fact that the secretary of agriculture and the Federal Emergency Relief administrator would emphasize different aspects of the program is not surprising, but it is nevertheless indicative of the pattern that developed, that reconciliation of their divergent points of view was not specified but was left to the hazards of interorganizational politics. Perhaps such specifications were not considered necessary among friends, but their absence eventually made surplus commodity distribution an open field upon which competing interest groups played for the benefits of public expenditure with spoils predictably going to the stronger, better-organized constituencies.

Nor were any standards of performance established for either the surplus removal or the food distribution aspects of the program. As a response to the paradox of want amid plenty, the corporation was doing its job if a portion of the surplus went to improve the diets of some of the unemployed. But the lack of performance standards reflects other aspects of the program's genesis besides its ambiguous goals. The FSRC was created by administrative action rather than through legislation, and the administrators who created it were legally limited to the powers conferred upon their agencies by existing laws. They could not have created a right to an adequate diet, or even a last defense against starvation, even if they had wanted to, because neither the Federal Emergency Relief Act, nor the Agricultural Adjustment Act, nor any other act of Congress had created such a right. Furthermore, Congress was not in session, and no evidence exists to suggest that those involved considered the possibility of seeking additional legislation. In the heady emergency atmosphere of the New Deal, few people were thinking in terms of creating new rights or establishing minimum standards. The Federal Emergency Relief Act, for example, not only lacked standards of adequacy and coverage, but did not even give the Emergency Relief administrator the power to set such standards. The new corporation's lack of performance specifications was consistent with the New Dealers' expectation that relief would be a temporary necessity, and with their general legal and administrative preference for flexibility and the avoidance of restrictions. In the long run, however, the standards and protections that the creators of the FSRC failed to provide were sorely missed.

The three corporate members met promptly after the FSRC was organized and elected themselves to the board of directors, with Harry Hopkins serving as president of the corporation, Henry Wallace as vice-president, and Harold Ickes as treasurer. The certificates of incorporation were amended almost immediately to increase the number of persons who might serve on the board from three to five, and William L. Myers, governor of the Farm Credit Administration, was elected to the directorate. Harry Hopkins's designation as president of the corporation was more than titular; he took an active role in both policy-making and management of the organization. Wallace was considerably less involved, though he remained enthusiastic about the venture. Ickes and Myers played relatively minor roles in establishing policy, although Ickes, as treasurer, oversaw the corporation's accounts.

In addition to the board of directors, the management personnel of the corporation included the assistant to the president and the executive officer. The former post involved implementing administrative and policy-making functions delegated by Hopkins. Jacob Baker, who occupied this position, was simultaneously head of the work relief operations of the FERA, and his role involved coordinating the activities and policies of the corporation with those of the relief administration. The executive officer of the corporation, Keith Southard, came to the FSRC from private industry; he was responsible for managing the daily operations of the corporation. Jerome Frank served as general counsel to the corporation, providing legal advice at the policy level, while William E. Linden as counsel handled routine legal matters. A procurement division, directed by Lieutenant Commander A. B. Clark, on loan to the corporation from the Naval Supply Corps, obtained bids and awarded contracts for purchase and processing of commodities in accordance with the supply procedures of the U.S. Navy. The distribution division, headed first by William A. Nielander and subsequently by William Nunn, arranged for the distribution of the commodities through state and local relief organizations.[15]

"We . . . had in front of us the question of getting underway quickly . . . there was no time to be lost," Keith Southard later reported to a conference of state and local commodity distribution directors.[16] The FSRC did get underway with remarkable speed; as early as October 16, the board of directors met to discuss possible purchases and by mid November, in Southard's estimate, the whole machinery was in place. In actuality, the FSRC functioned largely as a subsidiary of the FERA and was, for a while, housed at the same address. This arrangement was complicated, however, because the FERA lacked funds that could be used for the overhead and operating expenses of the corporation, and the FSRC lacked funds of its own. An initial plan for FSRC employees to be paid by the AAA as employees of its special commodities section while the secretary of agriculture covered offices expenses did not work out, and by early December, a new arrangement by which the FERA paid all the corporation's expenses and then billed the Department of Agriculture was in effect. This arrangement further cemented the close ties between the FSRC and the Emergency Relief Administration.[17]

The corporation's financial picture was complex, to say the least. As noted above, the FSRC initially lacked funds of its own, even the thirty-five dollars required to file its certificates of incorporation with the secretary of state of Delaware. With regard to the seven basic commodities designated by the Agricultural Adjustment Act, the secretary of agriculture could use processing tax funds to remove surpluses of these commodities but not to have them processed. Therefore, processing tax revenues, and advances from the U.S. treasury made in anticipation of processing taxes to be collected later, were used to purchase raw surpluses that the secretary donated to the FSRC, while FERA funds were used for processing and transportation to the states. Fundamentally, this arrangement was a continuation of the one that had been developed by the AAA and the FERA for the products of the emergency pig slaughter, and salt pork from the pig campaign was the first item handled by the FSRC. "Obviously pork was its first commodity, since pork was in a way the corporation's reason for being," wrote Hopkins.[18] During its first few months of operation, the corporation received from the secretary of agriculture 131 million pounds of cured pork, 45 million pounds of butter, and 3.5 million pounds of cheese at a total cost to the AAA of $20,481,000. Commodities designated as basic continued to comprise the bulk of FSRC operations, both by weight and by value, until additional funds were made available to the secretary of agriculture for surplus removal in 1935.

In order to provide greater variety for relief recipients, however, and to relieve markets of price-depressing surpluses of nonbasic agricultural products, the FSRC began to distribute substantial quantities of vegetables, fruits, dried beans, and poultry products. The cost of procuring as well as processing these commodities was borne by relief funds. The FERA made grants to the states for the specific purpose of commodity purchases. The FSRC then was designated to act as an agent for the states in purchasing and processing these commodities. In actuality, the states never saw the funds involved; the corporation advised them of the available commodities, and each state governor, as head of the State Emergency Relief Administration (SERA), executed an "Application of Governor for Supplemental Grants in Commodities and For Other Purposes" furnished by the corporation. Funds were transferred from the FERA to the FSRC where they appeared on the books as credits to the accounts of the states. By February 1, 1934, the FERA had spent a total of $23 million for the purchase and processing of nonbasic commodities and the processing of basic items donated by the secretary of agriculture. In addition, the SERAs, with the guidance of the FSRC, purchased some local surpluses with funds granted by the FERA; some of these products were then distributed to other states by the FSRC.[19]

These complicated financial arrangements with the SERAs appear to have been devised because the FERA was empowered to make grants to the states, not to a Delaware corporation. In addition, these arrangements served to protect the FSRC's operations from inspection by the U.S. comptroller general. Appointed by President Harding for a fifteen-year term in 1921, the comptroller general was answerable only to Congress. Since he could not succeed himself, Comptroller John McCarl, a Republican, felt no political loyalty to the Roosevelt administration, and he took a dim view of any New Deal expenditures not clearly and explicitly authorized by Congress.[20] As with Jerome Frank's original effort to sidestep possible objections from the comptroller by paying the FSRC incorporation fee from his own pocket, FSRC and USDA staff expended considerable effort and ingenuity to avoid precipitating an adverse ruling from Comptroller McCarl.

If the FSRC was an accountant's nightmare, it was a politician's dream; it promised something for everyone. The diets of the unemployed would be improved; "It was emphasized that the commodities given the unemployed will be in addition to amounts they are now receiving," declared the White House statement announcing the program. "They will add to and not replace items of relief already provided."[21] Farmers would benefit, both by direct government purchase of their unsaleable crops and by improved prices for the remaining portions. Processors could expect contracts to convert raw commodities into forms suitable for relief use, and "carefuly applied safeguards [would] forestall any disturbance of the regular channels of production, processing, and distribution." [22] Budget balancers, presumably, could anticipate reduced overall relief costs due to bargain prices and economies of scale, and both the public and the New Dealers would be relieved of the discomfort caused by contemplating waste amid want. Like the Economic Conservation Committee's peach butter project of several years earlier, surplus commodity distribution seemed to promise loss nowhere and gain everywhere.

But "this idea of having the Government buy from those who had too much, in order to give to those who had too little," [23] so appealingly simple in concept, proved remarkably complex in implementation. In all its operations, procurement, processing, transportation, storage, and distribution, the FSRC continually had to balance the needs and preferences of its various constituencies. And these, it turned out, included not only the producers of surpluses and the hungry unemployed, but also the producers of competing products, the processors, the wholesale and retail grocers, the purveyors of transportation, relief administrators at all levels, and of course, the taxpaying electorate.

The corporation's determination that its activities should benefit both producers and consumers was embodied in two fundamental policies. The first was the restriction of corporate purchases to items in surplus supply. The second was the distribution of FSRC goods over and above existing relief grants. "We shall not ordinarily buy any commodity unless you have given us a formal statement that a surplus of a given approximate quantity exists," Hopkins wrote Wallace in late October, "and shall buy or receive only such quantities as can be used by relief families over and above prior consumption." [24]

The determination of which commodities were in surplus supply was the responsibility of the Department of Agriculture while the FERA supplied information as to the additional amounts that could be distributed to relief clients without disturbing previous consumption. But what constituted a surplus? Apparently, the Department of Agriculture was not hampered in its calculations by what modern policymakers would call an operational definition; nowhere in the corporation's annual reports nor in the AAA's reports on surplus relief operations is a definition offered. A footnote to a FERA report on the FSRC attempted to clarify the matter as follows: "A surplus may be defined as that part of a supply which, at a given price, cannot be sold." [25] But this definition raises as many questions as it answers. Who was to set the "given price" at which any amount remaining unsold would be considered a surplus? If parity were used as the standard, virtually all major crops would have been considered available in surplus quantities. And what marketing area should be used? Could a given crop be in surplus supply in one area of the country and not in another? "Surplus foods are what the lawyers say they are," USDA food program administrator Rodney Leonard is reported to have said of the surplus purchase programs of the 1960s;[26] the FSRC seems to have established the same criterion at the outset of its operations. "In practice," the FERA report continued, "the surpluses purchased under the surplus commodity program originated in part under the marketing control agreements of the Agricultural Adjustment Administration. In other instances the presence of surpluses was determined by reference to the usual carry-over or the usual crop outturn and the price of the commodity."[27] The AAA had wide latitude in determining which crops were eligible for purchase. "We can have the purchase justified if we ask the Department of Agriculture to justify it or we can have it refused if we take that position," Jacob Baker wrote to Harry Hopkins about a purchase of Mississippi cane syrup urged by Mississippi's Senator Stephens. Baker recommended against the purchase: "My own inclination is against these local surpluses except as the Agriculture Department, on its own motion, brings them to our attention, or our own people tell us about them."[28]

The Department of Agriculture did indeed bring surpluses to the attention of the corporation on its own motion, recognizing in the FSRC a flexible tool for use in protecting the interests of farmers. For example, late in October, Secretary Wallace wrote to Harry Hopkins describing "a serious condition" among producers of such dried beans as great northerns, pintos, and pea beans: "The prices are such, that the producer who is compelled to sell immediately, must accept a price which in many cases will not pay his loans, with the consequent result that in many cases the bean farmer will become a client of your institutions." Wallace went on to report that the Department of Agriculture was in the process of arranging loans on a "fair market value" basis for bean producers, but these loans would take some time. He asked Hopkins to purchase $200,000 worth of dry beans to support the market until the USDA could complete its bean loan arrangements.[29] In effect then, the department was defining a surplus as a crop that could be marketed only at prices insufficient to cover the farmer's normal indebtedness. The corporation did purchase beans—8.5 million pounds of them by December 31, 1935.[30]

Despite the apparent flexibility of the Agriculture Department's definition of surplus, the limitation of FSRC purchases to officially declared surpluses was taken seriously. The corporation purchased eggs late in the fall of 1933, for example, but it declined to do so in 1935 when egg prices had reached 95 percent of parity and the number of cases in storage was well below the average number for the previous five years. Similarly, in the fall of 1934, in response to appeals from the prune industry, the corporation made an investigation of the marketing conditions for dried prunes and determined that the "commercial movement of this commodity was proceeding normally," and that no national purchase by the corporation was justified. On the other hand, the corporation did notify the states that prunes could be purchased at advantageous prices, and a year later, when a surplus did develop, the corporation purchased more than 23 million pounds of prunes.[31]

The designation of a commodity as a surplus did not guarantee its selection as a relief commodity, however; several other factors influenced the corporation's choices. The needs and preferences of relief clients were taken into account. After anemia was found to be widespread, for example, the corporation made special effort to obtain iron-rich liver for use in nursery schools serving the children of unemployed workers. Similarly, it undertook a major project of distributing dry skim milk in the Southeast where pellagra and other nutritional deficiency diseases were rampant, and it accompanied the distribution with an educational campaign involving relief, public health, and agricultural agencies.[32] Conversely, sensitivity to the needs and tastes of recipients sometimes dictated not purchasing a product. In a radio broadcast at the outset of the FSRC, Hopkins promised, "we will buy only the kinds of food products and other staples that the needy unemployed can use."[33] Despite significant pressure, the FSRC appears to have remained true to this principle; it refused to purchase surplus limburger cheese, despite the urging of the governor of Wisconsin, on the grounds that "limburger cheese is not universally used and we prefer, so far as possible, to distribute commodities which are natural foods for all, or very large sections of the population."[34]

The feasibility of distribution was another factor that had to be considered. Purchase of the large surplus of fluid milk was highly desirable from the relief recipient's point of view, and after the passage of the Jones-Connally Act in the spring of 1934, special funds were available to the corporation for the purchase of dairy and beef products for distribution. But the FSRC was never able to overcome the problem of distribution logistics that prevented it from handling fresh milk. Since fluid milk is a highly perishable commodity, distribution in fluid form would have required many local purchases and a system for prompt delivery; the FSRC would not have been able to make purchases at a few national markets as it did for butter and cheese. The possibility of using relief labor for delivery was discarded because opposition from unionized milk deliverymen was anticipated. Furthermore, many dairy farmers were already supplying some milk to local relief organizations, often under an arrangement by which the agency purchased some milk at full price and received additional amounts as outright donations. Any arrangement for FSRC purchases would need to respect the interests of the farmers who had thus cooperated with local relief organizations. Finally, precisely because milk is so perishable, the removal of surplus quantities has little long-term effect on prices. The corporation did purchase dry skim milk, as noted above, and both evaporated and condensed milk in cans.[35]

Not all the surpluses that might have proven desirable and feasible for relief distribution were purchased. The possible impact upon consumption of competing products also had to be considered. A plan to distribute peanut butter was shelved, for example, because "investigation showed that the surplus of peanuts was not as serious as the surplus of butter," and the FERA felt that supplying peanut butter for relief purposes would reduce butter consumption.[36] The corporation tried to select products for purchase that would benefit the grower rather than the middleman or the processor. Jacob Baker opposed the purchase of canned tomatoes, for example, on the grounds that "to have any effect on the market, we would have to buy $6 million worth, of which the growers would get $1.2 million, the packers, brokers and can manufacturers, getting the balance."[37]

The calculations that determined FSRC purchases, however, were by no means purely technical. Public opinion was a factor, as was the pressure exerted by growers and their allies. Concern about adverse public opinion discouraged the corporation from distributing poultry products, for example, although a surplus clearly existed. "Inasmuch as the Federal Emergency Relief Administration felt that it would be subjected to severe criticism for the purchase of poultry when other suitable foods were available at lower prices," read an AAA memorandum, "it was decided to abandon the purchase of poultry for relief purposes."[38] The same policy was applied to other foods classified as luxuries; plans for distribution of shrimp and oysters were abandoned. Similarly, a plan to purchase surplus tobacco for distribution to the unemployed, developed because of widespread reports that clients were trading relief supplies for tobacco, was discarded in anticipation of public condemnation, despite the fact that the tobacco would have been a donation, and, as Jacob Baker noted, "it would have cost practically nothing to distribute it."[39] Sensitivity to public opinion did not always prevail, however, and the distribution of such

luxury items as butter and fresh citrus occasioned much complaint about
the coddling of relief recipients.

Public reaction was less significant in shaping the FSRC's purchasing
agenda than the very concrete pressure exerted by the producers of agricultural surpluses. Almost as soon as the formation of the corporation
was announced, producers and handlers of all sorts deluged the corporation with letters and telegrams recommending the purchase of their particular products for relief. The FSRC files contain literally thousands of
these communications, and their sources reflect the whole infrastructure
of production, distribution, and political power in American agriculture.
Individual farmers, farmers' cooperatives and producers' associations,
agricultural extension agents, state agriculture department officials, distributors, processors, chambers of commerce, members of Congress,
state governors, and even cabinet members contacted the FSRC directly
or through Secretary Wallace, Harry Hopkins, friends in the government,
or even Roosevelt.

Some communications emphasized the farmers' deepening distress.
This letter from a New York State cabbage and potato farmer is typical of
many:

> Will you please use all the influence you have toward the Gov't buy-
> ing sauer kraut as a relief measure for the poor. We all know it is a very
> valuable food. In this county (Ontario) potatoes and cabbages are our
> main crop and today our Kraut factories are packed full of this valuable
> food (sauer kraut).
>
> Our potatoes didn't bring us half the cost of production last year and
> cabbages likewise and without the Gov't moves a lot of this large sur-
> plus kraut left over from last year, a lot of cabbage will undoubtedly
> remain in the fields this year because it will not be sold and many farm-
> ers will lose their farms.
>
> It seems to me it is high time (as long as the Gov't is spending so
> freely and taxing the people according) that something should be done
> for New York State also. Please investigate this sauer kraut situation
> and try to help us according.[40]

Many writers urged haste to avert some impending local disaster:

> This writer saw thousands of acres of potatoes freeze in this locality
> in 1932 because they were too cheap to make harvesting possible, yet
> thousands of people in the nearby city of Omaha were not able to buy
> them and went without. A parallel condition seems to me imminent at
> this time.[41]

Some stressed the nutritional value of their product for relief clients. "A pound of prunes," wrote a California grower to President Roosevelt, "has more food value than a pound of beef." He recommended that the government distribute ten pounds of prunes to each of 8 million relief cases.[42] Others stressed the low prices at which their product could be purchased: "May we respectfully invite your attention to the purchase of Reindeer Meat, in the interest of economy, since it is priced much lower than Beef and could be used to very good advantage."[43] Some stressed the importance of their product for growing children. The following telegram from Representative Clarence Cannon of Missouri, parliamentarian of the House of Representatives and a powerful member of the House Appropriations Committee, is typical.

> Earnestly urge allocation of $100,000 for purchase of apples in Missouri. Crop dropping off trees and price of number one fruit below cost of picking and packing. Will be needed by nation next year but a total waste without federal assistance. Most wholesome food available and greatly needed by relief agencies to balance rations. Especially imperative that children have fresh fruit and apples most economical available.[44]

The producers of Mississippi Ribbon Cane Syrup succeeded in enlisting the expert testimony of the state's director of public welfare who wrote to an acquaintance in the FERA:

> I wish you would go to Mr. Hopkins, Mr. Baker and Mr. Williams and tell them for me that a twenty-four pound sack of flour made up into real fluffy southern biscuits with about four pounds of surplus butter to the sack and spread with Mississippi Ribbon Cane Syrup is about all the relief that anybody needs in the way of real good eating.
> You might tell them to have somebody make them some real good biscuit about two inches thick, then punch a hole in one side of the biscuit and pur [sic] in some of this Mississippi Ribbon Cane Syrup and let it thoroughly soak into the biscuit and if they ever tasted any better eating than that I would like to know it.

He recommended the purchase of five hundred thousand gallons of Mississippi cane syrup and noted that "it would be a splendid thing if these purchases could be made between now and February 1st and thus enable some of these Mississippi syrup growers who have these surpluses on hand to get some money with which to pay taxes."[45]

Other writers tried to appeal to the FSRC's sense of fair play. "We understand that the Federal Surplus Relief Corporation has purchased or is considering the purchase of a large quantity of California dried prunes of the 1934 crop, and we are writing to bring to your attention a surplus of slightly over one million pounds 1934 crop Oregon dried prunes which our organization is carrying."[46] Some even appealed to the government's self-interest: "Erie County, Pennsylvania, again has a surplus of potatoes and would like very much to have an opportunity to market them not only through the regular channels, but to those persons being fed by the tax-payers money. The growers feel that they would be much more able to pay their taxes if they received a reasonably good market for thier [sic] potato crop."[47] The ingenuity expressed in the letters is impressive, the variation of the pleas was nearly endless, and the message was uniform—buy mine. One writer, apparently hoping to make government purchase an annual affair, summed up the situation cogently: "Last year and the year before, the Government purchased apples in this state and in the state of Oregon loose in cars. From the standpoint of the growers, this was a mighty fine thing."[48] Although the image of a relief diet composed of sauerkraut, prunes, and reindeer meat is amusing, the general picture painted by these letters is heartbreaking; crops were rotting in the fields because farmers couldn't afford to have them picked, farmers were losing their farms for lack of income that these crops could produce, and urban families were denied the potatoes, cabbages, and fruit needed to give their diets variety and nutritional balance. The pleas of the growers, no less than the desperation of the unemployed, reveal the full meaning of the paradox of want amid plenty.

Determining the general success of these pleas is difficult. Many of the corporation's purchase plans were initiated in response to appeals from producers, and many such appeals failed to lead to purchases. The corporation and the AAA took them seriously as a source of information, investigating many of them to assess crop conditions and desirability of distribution. During the drought of 1934, a Food Survey Committee was established in the Department of Agriculture under the chairmanship of Mordecai Ezekial to make an ongoing assessment of food supplies in order to identify both surpluses and shortages. Representatives of the FERA and FSRC, as well as staff members from the AAA, the Bureau of Home Economics, and the Bureau of Agricultural Economics, served on this committee. Once the committee was in operation, requests for purchases were routinely referred to it for consideration.[49]

Many producers, especially those organized into cooperatives or other associations, mobilized members of Congress to support their requests for purchase, and this strategy was effective in dealing with the politically astute New Dealers. Early in its existence, for example, the FSRC formulated plans to purchase potatoes in various potato-producing states, omitting Maine because no surplus of premium grade potatoes existed in that state. The Maine congressional delegation brought intense pressure to bear upon the administration. The result was a revised plan by which the corporation purchased second grade potatoes in Maine, although it purchased only premium potatoes in other areas, prompting the *New York Times* to comment that "among all the tubers of the world, the potatoes of Aroostook County are the most persistently cultivated, watched, defended, and represented at Washington." [50] Generally, pressure from producers did not result in such an obvious change in a previously recorded decision, and the extent to which FSRC purchases were influenced by such pressure is difficult to assess. But the lively correspondence that the corporation maintained with members of Congress indicates that the legislators believed such pressure was worthwhile.

For the most part, the corporation's files are remarkably free from allusions to politics, but one exceptionally candid memorandum, sent to Harry Hopkins over Jacob Baker's signature, suggests the nature of the interest with which members of Congress regarded the corporation's purchasing programs: "Senator Stephens writes . . . that Mississippi has this year one million gallons of surplus syrup instead of the 335,000 we bought last year and asks us to buy this million gallons of syrup and a million bushels of sweet potatoes. He asks a personal decision. . . . I take it that the Senator wants a decision before the run-off primary." [51] Baker recommended against the purchase, but the FERA later reported that Mississippi cane syrup had been bought from 4,807 farmers, enough to make a considerable difference in the outcome of an election; thus, the senator's desire for a quick decision from the FSRC can be appreciated. State relief administrators, under the corporation's supervision, normally purchased from a large number of small producers when buying local surpluses. Noting that "the buying of these local surpluses has had as its primary purpose the removal of these surpluses from commercial channels," the FERA reported that "the purchases were so handled, however, as to accomplish a secondary relief purpose. The commodities were purchased from small farmers who either had been forced to accept relief because of distress prices caused by glutted markets or were slowly approaching the necessity of applying for relief." [52] The logic seems undeniable, and so does the political payoff for a member of Congress who could claim partial credit for a decision to purchase.

Some of the FSRC's purchasing programs were initiated not by the Department of Agriculture nor by distressed growers but by the corporation itself. An exchange of correspondence between FSRC Executive Officer Keith Southard and Secretary of Agriculture Wallace suggests that the corporation actively sought surplus farm products on behalf of the needy and played a watchdog role to see that food was not destroyed. In August 1934, Southard wrote to Wallace concerning surpluses of products covered by marketing agreements or licenses, noting that some of the agreements permitted the surplus quantities to remain on the farms where they were "in effect, destroyed," while others collected them in the hands of control committees that were permitted to sell them after a specified time period had elapsed. Southard suggested that future marketing agreements or licenses direct that the surpluses in control of individual farmers be donated to the FSRC, and those in the hands of the control committees should, if commercial sale proved impossible, be offered to the corporation at a price that the FSRC would determine. While he did not affirm all of the details of Southard's proposal, Wallace agreed to the general idea that the corporation should serve as an outlet for control committee products and agreed to notify the FSRC of negotiations between the Department of Agriculture and producers and processors so that the corporation could send a representative.[53]

The corporation's largest procurement and processing operation, and one that put the organization on the map for many farm groups, was not prompted by relief needs nor by localized political pressure, but by the worst drought in American history. When the Agricultural Adjustment Act was drafted in 1933, the producers of beef had not wanted cattle included as a basic commodity, fearing federal interference in their industry. But as the great drought of 1933–1934 dried up not only feed grain crops but pastures and forage as well, the stock on the western ranges began to die of thirst and starvation. The cattle ranchers turned to Washington, and in April 1934, Congress passed the Jones-Connally Act that designated cattle as a basic commodity and authorized $50 million to permit the secretary of agriculture to make advances to the Federal Surplus Relief Corporation for the purchase of dairy and beef products for relief purposes and for the elimination of diseased beef and dairy cattle.[54] The Jones-Connally Act was the first official congressional recognition of the corporation. In Jerome Frank's words, the appropriation "legitimized" the FSRC: "it stopped being a bastard,"[55] a point that subsequently proved important in efforts to prove the legality of the FSRC's successor.

In the meantime, the Jones-Connally Act launched the corporation on the largest and most spectacular of its operations—the processing and distribution of livestock endangered by drought. The corporation had purchased some canned beef and live cattle before the Jones-Connally Act passed, but once cattle were designated basic, the secretary of agriculture purchased approximately 8.3 million head of cattle at a cost of $111,546,104. Approximately 1.5 million of these animals were found to be unfit for human consumption and were condemned and buried on the range, raising the specter of the little pigs and renewing charges of AAA-managed waste. The remaining 6,788,444 were turned over to the FSRC at the railroad shipping point nearest the range.[56]

Harry Hopkins recalled the speed and urgency with which the drought cattle operations were implemented:

> Western farmers, no longer able to stand back and watch their cattle suffer as the watering places and pastures failed them, were in a mood to make this federally managed retreat into a stampede. The cattle march took on the character of wartime speed. Appraisers worked desperately, while farmers pleaded with them to hurry. Men unrolled their beds in the offices to spend what was left of the night. At times, 3,000 cars of cattle a day moved out of St. Paul, in sixty trains of fifty cars apiece.[57]

Approximately 3.6 million head of cattle were processed directly by the corporation through contracts let to commercial packing houses. The remaining 3.2 million were allocated to SERAs for processing in work relief projects, for temporary pasturage until the processing facilities became available, or for use as milk or breeder cows in transient centers, self-help cooperatives, or rural rehabilitation programs. In the end, the FSRC acquired 657,396,312 pounds of fresh and canned beef with an estimated market value of $126,500,233. The hides from the drought cattle were originally retained by the processors as partial payment, but when they began to depress the market, the corporation decided to store them in refrigerated warehouses; the corporation acquired somewhat over 2 million cow and calf skins in this manner. In addition, purchases of sheep and goats yielded 20 million pounds of mutton and nearly 200,000 pounds of goat meat as well as a substantial quantity of sheep skins.[58]

Despite the large volume of beef and related products handled because of the drought, the corporation's purchases were small in comparison with overall national consumption. The AAA estimated in March 1935 that FSRC distributions up to that date had represented "roughly 3.5% of the normal annual consumption of pork and beef, 3% of butter, 2½% of cot-

ton, 1% of lard," and smaller percentages of such crops as apples, cabbages, potatoes, sorghum syrups, beans, cheese, and rice.[59] Although the
corporation did not keep records of the amounts reaching individual clients and families, rough estimates are calculable simply by dividing the
total amount distributed by the number of persons thought to be receiving
surplus commodities. In general, the corporation estimated that surplus
commodities reached between 50 and 90 percent of those on the relief
rolls, depending on the nature of the commodity and the adequacy of local distribution systems; and the relief rolls averaged nearly 18 million
persons during the months in which the FSRC procured and distributed
surpluses.[60] Using figures for the twenty-seven–month period between
October 4, 1933 and December 31, 1935, the average estimates are revealing. Since nearly all localities could handle canned goods, a reasonable assumption is that canned beef, the largest single item, reached most
of those on the rolls; if it reached 90 percent, they received about 23
pounds each, or less than a pound a month, on average. For fresh beef,
the average was lower: 6 pounds per capita for the entire period if only
half the relief caseload was reached, a likely situation since fresh beef
required refrigeration unavailable in many relief agencies. If 8.5 million
pounds of dried beans reached half of those on relief, then they received
slightly less than a pound each for the entire period. If the 9 million
pounds of apples had reached the entire relief caseload of 18 million persons, they would have received half a pound each or two small apples.
The corporation distributed enough flour to provide a little over 12 pounds
per capita to 90 percent of those on relief, or less than half a pound per
month. Butter was distributed for a period of about fifteen months at a
rate of about half a pound a month to half the people on relief. The pigs
that started the whole venture and their successors in subsequent purchases yielded a total of 297,579,000 pounds of pork—somewhere between a half a pound and a pound of meat per person each month, depending on how much of the relief caseload was reached. Since the flow
of most commodities was seasonal and irregular, monthly averages undoubtedly mask sizeable differences from month to month, but the figures
tell us something of the scale of the endeavor. In all, the corporation distributed approximately thirty-eight edible commodities for human consumption, in addition to livestock feed and inedible products, during the
twenty-seven months represented in these figures.[61]

In August 1935, Hopkins reported to Roosevelt that the commodities
distributed by the FSRC had cost the government $255,682,241.[62] This
figure represented an expenditure of approximately $.65 per month per

recipient, or a supplement of roughly $7.80 per person per year. As a point of comparison, the Department of Agriculture estimated that in 1934 the average low wage worker spent about $100 per family member per year on food and that the average relief case probably spent or received grocery orders worth about $60.00 per person annually.[63] Thus, the FSRC's activities represented a small but significant increment; "The volume of business done by this Corporation was never large," wrote Hopkins in 1936. "In addition to drought livestock we distributed something like $100,000,000 worth of foodstuffs in two years. . . . The magnitude of the corporation's business would never claim the attention of the success-story reader. . . . What gives the story its significance is that redivision and subdivision of these comparatively small amounts of food should be of such prime importance to any American family."[64]

The "redivision and subdivision" functions of the corporation— allocation, transportation, and distribution—were governed by a policy that came to be known simply as "over and above." Surplus commodities donated by the corporation were to be given to relief recipients "over and above" other forms of relief; they were to upgrade, not undermine, relief standards. And they were to be distributed only in such amounts as relief households could normally be expected to consume over and above their prior or normal consumption. Thus, they would represent an expansion of the total amount consumed.[65] In practice, of course, the "over and above" policy did not work out so neatly. "As a matter of fact the commodities were used in place of part of the usual relief in numerous localities in spite of the Federal orders to the contrary," reported Josephine Brown in her survey of Depression-era public relief. Her explanation for this widespread violation of federal rules is telling: "The relief funds were never sufficient for adequate benefits and surplus commodities merely meant that the available money could be eked out in order to give a little less inadequate aid to the same 'caseload' or to supply the same degree of inadequacy to a greater number of families."[66]

The other side of the "over and above" coin proved equally difficult to implement. How much cheese could be given to the families on relief without reducing their purchases of this product or those purchases made for them by relief agencies? Obviously, the actual amount would vary from family to family and agency to agency and would depend on such incalculable factors as the taste and nutritional wisdom of the social workers who had been writing the family food orders, the individual homemaker's adaptability and culinary skills, the family's ethnic heritage and food preferences, and the cost and availability of cheese in comparison to other protein sources. Despite public opposition to the provision of luxuries to families on relief, adding such relatively expensive items as meat to the diets of the poor without reducing previous consumption was easier than adding large quantities of such cheap, filling foods as cereals or beans. Ultimately, the FSRC faced the same question with which the congressional agricultural committees had struggled in the long slow process that led to the donation of the Farm Board wheat: how hungry are the poor?

In formulating its working decisions, the corporation necessarily relied heavily upon averages. A letter to Secretary Wallace prepared for Harry Hopkins's signature by the corporation's executive officer, for example, reveals the reasoning and the quantitative basis for a request for ten thousand tons of sugar per month for distribution. He reported that "approximately twenty-five pounds of sugar per average family is normal in the country at large," and figured that dividing the requested ten thousand tons of sugar monthly among a minimum of 4 million relief families would give each family approximately five pounds per month or no more than a fifth of their normal requirements. "It is the opinion of our Nutrition and Social Service Directors that the present relief budgets do not permit these relief families to obtain anything like the average sugar requirements, hence the distribution over and above other forms of relief to the extent of five pounds per family per month cannot affect commercial sales in any appreciable degree." In fact, Southard hoped that an even larger distribution might prove feasible.[67]

Not everyone affiliated with the FSRC was as enthusiastic about the sugar proposition as Southard. In fact, shortly after Southard prepared the letter requesting ten thousand tons per month, Philip Murphy, the chief of the AAA's Commodities Purchase Section, wrote to him stating that "attention should be called to the fact that, since sugar is a cheap source of energy, families on relief are already consuming more of it than is good for health and less of other important foods."[68] Murphy was writing in regard to a proposed purchase of cane syrup, suggesting that syrup should be distributed instead of, rather than in addition to, sugar, and thus he did not address the sugar venture itself. But he probably would not have supported the proposal that another five pounds a month be added to relief diets. Some people within the corporation felt that any distribution of sugar would violate the organization's mission. Writing to Southard early in 1934, William Nielander argued that "practically every experience in distributing sugar has shown that to do so would be direct substitution—which is the thing that the Corporation is endeavoring not to do." [69] Clearly, the determination of the amount that could have been—or ought to have been—distributed over and above prior consumption was not a matter of simple arithmetic. The corporation had to act upon incomplete and sometimes conflicting information about the needs and practices of relief recipients and bridge the gap between average figures derived from nutritional science on the one hand, and the daily coping behaviors of families trying to subsist on relief budgets on the other. As with the identification of crops as surplus, the corporation staff took the issue seriously but had considerable latitude within which to operate.

The task of identifying the people to whom surplus commodities could be distributed was shared by the federal government and the local relief agencies, with the FERA designating broad categories of eligibility and the local agencies determining which individuals and families fell within those categories. Originally, only individuals and families directly under the care of local Emergency Relief Administrations were eligible to receive the surplus foods. About a month after the corporation was organized, Hopkins sent a memo to governors and State Emergency Relief administrators extending commodity distribution to persons in need but not on public relief, selected by local ERAs and "agencies of proper standards designated by the local relief administration and approved by the State Relief Administrator." [70] In effect, this ruling made surplus commodities available to the clients of those private agencies selected by local emergency relief administrators, thus giving the local ERAs a measure of power over the family service agencies that constituted the social work establishment in many, if not most, localities. The ruling also created situations in which families in need, but not so desperate as to qualify for public emergency relief, might receive a category of assistance labeled "surplus commodities only."

Over the next few months, eligibility was extended to work relief clients on Civil Works Administration (CWA) projects, needy members of self-help cooperatives of the unemployed, and inmates of public charitable and health institutions. The extension of surplus commodities to CWA workers was subsequently limited to those whose needs had been individually investigated. The distribution of commodities to charitable institutions was broadened to include all institutions participating in or organized by the public relief program—the transient camps and emergency nursery schools, for example. Commodities were also made available to college students participating in college student relief employment projects, providing they were living alone, in cooperative arrangements with other students engaged in work relief, or were heads of households. [71]

Most of these extensions of eligibility were made fairly early in the corporation's existence when large quantities of pork and butter were awaiting distribution. The amount of a given commodity that could be given to a FERA client without disrupting normal purchases or inviting waste was limited, but outlets for the corporation's supplies could easily be expanded by extending the distribution to some of the millions of families not poor enough for relief but too poor to purchase an adequate diet.

Three major methods of distribution were available to local relief administrations to bring surplus commodities to their clients: commissaries, home deliveries, or distribution arrangements with local grocery stores. The choice of outlet was the prerogative of the state and local relief administrations, but the FSRC had a strong preference for the normal channels of trade—commercial wholesale and retail outlets—whenever possible. The corporation tried to avoid antagonizing food distributors, emphasizing that commodity distribution, because it was over and above normal purchases, would in no way diminish or compete with retail trade. Early in its existence, the FSRC invited national retail and wholesale food associations to send representatives to a conference where the operations of the corporation were explained and pledges of cooperation were exchanged. The wholesale grocers associations agreed to recommend to their affiliates that they handle—store and distribute—surplus commodities at a flat rate of ten cents per hundred pounds, and the retail associations agreed to urge members to handle surplus commodities without compensation. Although the ten-cent rate was clearly below cost, the corporation believed that both the wholesale and retail sectors of the industry would benefit by keeping commodity distribution within commercial channels. If the states were forced by cost factors to set up such independent distribution systems as commissaries for surplus commodities, it might prove cheaper for them to use these systems instead of cash or grocery orders for the remainder of the relief food budget as well, thus depriving grocers of the entire amount of custom represented by relief recipients.[72]

In a memorandum to relief administrators sent out about a month after incorporation, Jacob Baker stated the perceived advantages of distribution through normal channels. Expense was the first consideration discussed; "The flat rate of ten cents per hundred pounds for the wholesaling function and no compensation to the retailer can be secured almost everywhere," he reported. "Even with work relief labor and donated space and equipment, an independent method will frequently cost more than ten cents a hundred pounds in miscellaneous expenses alone." The convenience to relief families was also an important factor. "Relief clients can secure commodities without having to walk very far for them, and *when* they need them," he asserted, while a commissary would have difficulty issuing commodities even once a week, and "some of the food stuffs will be perishable." Finally, he predicted that less waste would be incurred in distribution because "the use of the regular channels puts the distribution in the hands of men who have years of experience in dealing with these products." He went on to request that states that anticipated using any other plan should advise him and submit an estimate of the costs involved. "We must be prepared to prove beyond question that the plan followed in each State is the most economical and practical one for the distribution of these surplus commodities."[73]

Despite the FSRC's preference for the normal channels, conditions around the nation varied widely, and commissaries were used fairly extensively for distribution of the corporation's wares. Furthermore, as experience with the various distribution systems accumulated, the corporation staff increasingly came to favor door-to-door delivery through work projects because this method protected the privacy and convenience of recipients. The door-to-door delivery method, developed first for sparsely settled rural areas, eventually was recommended for urban areas as well. The final choice, however, rested with the states, and throughout the existence of the FSRC and its successor, the dignity and convenience of relief clients competed with the claims of the wholesale and retail grocery industry, the omnipresent watchful eye of the taxpayer, and the preferences and sensibilities of relief administrators to shape a wide variety of delivery systems.[74]

Given the complexity of the corporation's activities and the number and variety of the interest groups affected by its work, it did a remarkable job. The tone, as well as the content of its surviving correspondence, suggests that the interests of all the major groups affected were regarded as legitimate and that great care was taken to balance and protect them. Nevertheless, no organization, no matter how skilled and tactful its staff, could serve so many masters to their complete satisfaction, and as the FSRC matured, it acquired an impressive and growing list of enemies.

CHAPTER NINE

The Corporation in Conflict: Competition with Private Enterprise

The corporation's troubles began even before the incorporation papers were filed. On October 3, the evening newspapers reported that the administration was considering extending the processing tax to pay for the expanded surplus distribution program, and the morning papers of the fourth repeated the story: "Additional processing taxes on food and farm products probably will be levied to finance the Government in relief work, Administrator Harry L. Hopkins announced yesterday. . . . Hopkins proposes to extend both processing and compensatory taxes over whatever commodities the relief corporation needs for distribution to the unemployed," reported the *Washington Post*. "There is no need for me to point out the wave of protest from the farm belt which such a statement of the policy will likely produce," wrote economic advisor Mordecai Ezekial in a memorandum to Secretary Wallace, recommending that "in the future all such announcements of relief policy which concern both organizations should be approved by our publicity director as well as by Mr. Hopkins before they are given to the press." Ezekial suggested a policy that might govern use of processing tax revenues for the purchase of products for relief: "We are justified in using processing taxes and compensatory taxes to divert supplies to the use of the unemployed in those particular cases when the farmers' net return is increased as a result. . . . We should," he continued, "make it perfectly clear in all our publicity that we can impose such taxes only in those cases where there is a definite gain to farmers in doing so." Since the processing tax was a volatile issue among farmers, Ezekial suggested that "all our publicity . . . should be so correlated as to develop and maintain the support of the farmers as well as of the city people behind our program." [1]

Ezekial's clarity, however, did not immediately pervade the administration. Ten days later, a reporter asked President Roosevelt if it were proposed "that a part of the new processing taxes should be shifted from the Agriculture Department to Harry Hopkins for Emergency Relief?" "Well," replied the president, "that's that old corn-hog thing." "That they divert part of the processing tax to Emergency Relief?" persisted the reporter. "I don't know," Roosevelt replied. "It is a terribly complicated problem. You had better check with them about it because it is possible, in the case of a tax on hogs, for example, to use a portion of that tax for Harry Hopkins' work, and the rest of it would come out of relief funds. It is so complicated that I do not dare talk about it." [2]

For some in the Farmbelt, the processing tax did not appear complicated at all. They viewed the proceeds of the processing tax as "farmers' money," a recompense owed them by consumers to redress the disparity between industrial and agricultural prices that had ruined so many farmers in the previous decade. For those who had labored in the McNary-Haugen vineyard, the processing tax was the fruit of the struggle for the "equalization fee" that had preoccupied agriculture's advocates for so many years. They were not about to see it used for general relief, especially since all the processing tax revenues that were not used for surplus removal activities went directly to participating farmers as benefit payments.

Even *Wallace's Farmer*, certainly as friendly toward the administration as any farm newspaper, paused amid its general rejoicing over the creation of the Federal Surplus Relief Corporation to note that: "From the farm standpoint, it is important that provision be made to use federal relief funds rather than processing taxes as the main source of revenue for this program. The feeding of the unemployed," the editor continued, "is the responsibility of the whole nation, and neither the consumer of farm products nor the producer should be forced to pay the whole bill." [3] The argument that use of the processing taxes for relief commodities would be unemployment relief at the expense of the farmer struck a familiar chord in Washington agricultural circles where only a few years earlier Gilbert Haugen had delayed the distribution of the Farm Board's wheat with a similar assertion that donation of the wheat would be "relief at the expense of the wheat growers." The argument was to become even more familiar as food programs evolved.

After the processing tax went into effect, it was found to be so burdensome to such state institutions as prisons and orphanages, which bought food in bulk, that an amendment exempting public charitable institutions from the tax was passed, and this exemption raised the issue once again. At a National Emergency Council meeting early in 1934, AAA Administrator Chester Davis told the president, the cabinet, and other heads of agencies that "I find quite a militant spirit among some of the farmers in a way opposing the idea that it is up to the farmer to finance the federal relief work." Describing a delegation of wheat growers from the Pacific Northwest in Washington to demand that the AAA support an amendment to end the processing tax exemption for relief commodities, he continued: "They claim what you were doing is taking away from the farmer the income and turning it over to relief." Davis assured Hopkins and other members of the council that the delegation's claim was "an extreme view with which we are not in sympathy," but he emphasized that the farmers' support for efforts to accomplish both farm and unemployment relief with a single program was limited.[4]

Farmers were not the only interest group worrying about the corporation's financing. The announcement of the creation of the FSRC generated sufficient apprehension among social work leaders that the American Association of Social Workers' Committee on the Current Federal Program sent a delegation for an emergency meeting with Hopkins. The relief administrator allayed their fears by explaining that, although a portion of the expenditure might come from his discretionary fund, the greater part would be derived from processing taxes. He reassured them that the proposed surplus commodity distribution program did not represent a wholesale diversion of cash relief monies to relief in kind.[5]

Not only the financing, but also the corporate powers and the fundamental legality of the FSRC provoked criticism during the corporation's early months. The original certificates of incorporation granted the FSRC broad powers under the Agricultural Adjustment Act, the National Industrial Recovery Act, and the Federal Emergency Relief Act of 1933. When the certificates were amended shortly after the corporation was established, both the list of empowering acts of Congress and the enumerated powers of the corporation were greatly expanded. The Reconstruction Finance Corporation Act of 1932, the Federal Farm Loan Act of 1916, the Farm Credit Act of 1933, the Emergency Relief and Construction Act of 1932, and Title I of the National Industrial Recovery Act were added to the legislation from which the corporation might derive power, and specific powers to deal in real property and commodities were added. Jerome Frank's comment, noted above, was not far from reality: "the charter of the Federal Surplus Relief Corporation was big enough to do anything." [6]

The press reacted to the expansive powers of the FSRC when the certificates of incorporation were finally made public on December 20, 1933. "It has a wider sweep than any other New Deal legislation," noted the *Boston Herald*. The *Baltimore Sun* described its powers as "almost limitless." The New York *Herald Tribune* called it a "new monster" that "opens up limitless possibilities for Federal interference and regulation." From Washington, the *New York Times* political correspondent reported that some "government legal experts" were speculating that the AAA, the Public Works Administration, and the FERA might be "made permanent through their absorption by the Surplus Relief Corporation . . . since it is to have 'perpetual existence.'" Others, according to the correspondent, "see in the Surplus Relief Corporation a plan to coordinate all farm recovery efforts by placing them within its jurisdiction." In addition to speculation on how the FSRC's broad powers might be used, some officials, the correspondent noted, "questioned . . . whether there is any authority in law for the delegation of AAA powers to the Surplus Corporation," since "corporations are not mentioned specifically among the agencies authorized by the Agricultural Adjustment Act." [7]

Although immediate anxiety over what the *Literary Digest* called the "vast powers of the FSRC" died down, the issue resurfaced in 1935 in an attack on government corporations launched by the Philadelphia Board of Trade and introduced to the Senate by Senators Hiram Johnson, Couzens, and Schall. Years later, Jerome Frank explained to an interviewer that "when a government department appoints an agent that agent has only the powers that the department has and only that part of the powers that are delegated. So it doesn't really make any difference what the charter of that company is. The power can't spread out to all the potentialities of the charter." Recalling attacks on the Commodity Credit Corporation similar to those endured by the FSRC, he concluded that it "was really alot of hooey. That was newspaper talk. The opposition used the argument against it that it had such wide powers, but that whole argument was really factitious . . . based on nothing." [8] Nevertheless, fear of the organization's vast and varied powers added one more to the number of anxieties and criticisms with which the FSRC had to contend.

While conservatives in general and the business community in particular may have objected to the entire idea of government corporations, the major trouble between the FSRC and the business world was not over philosophy or organizational form but over contested turf. The issue of competition with private enterprise was both a general criticism of the New Deal and a specific issue with regard to the activities of the FSRC. It was raised almost as soon as the corporation began its operations because some forms of distribution at the local level were far more congenial to retail and wholesale grocers than were others. The FSRC tried to protect itself, both by involving representatives of the grocery industry in its planning from the outset and by insisting that the final choice of method must rest with state and local relief authorities. It actively discouraged the use of commissaries and initially recommended that the commodities be distributed through local groceries. After experiments with home delivery, originally undertaken only in sparsely settled rural areas, proved popular with both relief clients and relief administrators, the corporation recommended use of this system wherever local conditions permitted. The FSRC never urged the creation of commissaries for distribution of its products. Local relief administrators, however, had to balance the possible inconvenience or embarrassment inflicted upon clients by commissaries with the demand for economy in relief. For some, the commissary, staffed largely with work relief clients, represented irresistible savings when compared with other methods, and the corporation was associated in many minds with the hated welfare stores.

The FERA received so many complaints about the commissaries that a separate file labeled "Commissary Complaints" was maintained. In the fall of 1934, a national retail grocers organization received the impression that the federal government was considering the adoption of commissaries throughout the nation, possibly because their use on a statewide basis was under consideration in Tennessee. The organization accordingly advised its state and local affiliates who promptly deluged Roosevelt, the FERA, and members of Congress with letters and telegrams of protest about the FSRC's alleged unfair competition with the private retail sector. Although the episode was based on misinformation, it revealed a great deal about the atmosphere in which the FSRC attempted to transfer surpluses to the needy. Many writers stressed the economy of distribution through local merchants: "Grocers can do job cheaper than any government agency" telegraphed a citizen in Santa Clara, California.[9] Other telegrams emphasized the jobs provided by grocers: "If government opens food commissaries will destroy food industry and put millions now self supporting in bread lines."[10] Echoing the growers who solicited FSRC purchases, other grocers reminded the government that their ability to pay taxes was dependent upon adequate business: "We certainly are entitled to this business if the government expects us to pay our taxes." [11] Some writers noted the potential inconvenience to relief clients if the relief administration switched to commissaries: "Distribution through stores gives larger selection saves time and individual self respect." [12] Basically, however, most writers argued that the commissaries were unfair to business in that they constituted government competition with private industry. They believed that merchants had a right to any business that relief clients might provide because, as the president of the Independent Grocers' and Merchants' Association wrote to Harry Hopkins,

> all during the depression the independent food dealers have been rendering a most excellent public service by the extension of credit to families whose earnings have either been greatly reduced [or] are entirely wiped out. In this way, they have kept out of the bread lines and off the relief rolls thousands of persons who, otherwise, would be on the rolls at an added expense to the Government. For this fine service, we feel that these merchants are entitled to whatever benefits it should be possible for them to derive from the handling of relief orders. [13]

Hopkins agreed with many of these ideas; he opposed the use of commissaries and urged the states to use other methods where possible. In responding to complaints he emphasized that the federal administration did not create commissaries: "The Federal Emergency Relief Administration is not establishing any commissaries in Tennessee, Georgia, nor any other State of the Union, and I am very glad to tell you that as a matter of fact I do not believe in commissaries. Our experience with them has in the main been unsatisfactory." [14]

Despite Hopkins's opposition to the use of commissaries, the choice of method in distributing relief in general and FSRC commodities in particular remained a state and local prerogative. Where commissaries were already in operation, the FERA directed those who wrote letters of complaint to take the matter up with the State Emergency Relief Administration. The federal agency replied to the many letters and telegrams protesting the alleged plan for nationwide conversion to commissaries with a form letter disavowing any knowledge of such a plan and explaining that the Tennessee Relief Administration had studied the possibility of converting to commissaries but had abandoned the plan.

The Tennessee episode is illustrative of the complexities faced by state relief administrations in their attempts to establish workable relief systems with as little cost as possible to the taxpayers. It also reveals the importance of state autonomy in selection of relief methods. When protest over the potential conversion to commissaries reached a peak, the press reported that Hopkins had vetoed the idea. The State Emergency Relief Administrator, Colonel Simpson, promptly denied that he had received any instructions from Hopkins to abandon the plan. In response to an inquiring telegram from Tennessee Senator McKellar, Hopkins's assistant Aubrey Williams contacted Simpson and then wrote to Hopkins: "I called Col. Simpson and he stated that he was working out a price arrangement with grocers in the state and that if he were forced at this point to say that they were not going to have commissaries, it would impair his bargaining power." [15] The threat of commissaries thus served to keep down the cost of using the normal channels of trade, and when a cost agreement was reached, the abandonment of the commissary scheme was announced.

Although the FSRC emerged from the commissary controversy relatively unscathed, in another major aspect of its work, the result was different. The corporation's involvement with "production-for-use" work relief projects, in which unemployed workers fabricated articles for distribution to those on relief, elicited both a general hostility and a series of specific attacks from the business community. Work relief in general troubled conservatives, especially business conservatives, throughout the New Deal period. Work relief was more expensive than direct cash payments or grocery orders because it involved an investment in materials, equipment, planning, and supervision. Furthermore, work relief was widely perceived by critics to be inherently in competition with private enterprise. The work supplied by relief labor, it was argued, ought to be purchased from private firms. In addition, work relief competed for the labor supply. While this last criticism was more a philosophical than a practical problem for business, since plenty of unemployed labor was available, the occasional instance in which an employer had difficulty in obtaining labor was often attributed to the presence of a local work project.

On the other hand, work relief was more consonant with widely held values than was the dole. It implemented the belief that able-bodied persons in need ought to make a contribution to society in return for relief, and it was thought to protect the skills and morale of the unemployed. Since the work ethic and the conservation of productive skills were among the primary tenets of the business ethic, many conservatives, as Arthur Schlesinger suggests, found themselves "in the unsatisfying position of deploring the moral consequences of relief while advocating the form of relief which by their own theory was morally most deleterious—

the cash handout, the detested dole." [16] On the subject of production-for-use schemes, however, business people were neither confused nor inarticulate. They were virtually unanimous in their opposition.

The production-for-use projects to which the business community so vociferously objected had their roots in self-help activities that originated spontaneously without government intervention. Early in the Depression, groups of unemployed workers had formed self-help cooperatives through which they produced goods and services for personal consumption and for barter. A typical activity was the exchange of the group's labor in harvesting a crop for a portion of the crop itself. Some of the groups established community gardens—often on donated land—in which they attempted to grow their own food. The garden and harvest projects led naturally to canning, and the preserved foods were sometimes traded with other co-ops for their products. The cooperatives used a variety of systems of organization, some issuing scrip, some relying on record-keeping or good will. Some of them became quite large; the Unemployed Citizens League based in Seattle, for example, had eighty thousand members in affiliates throughout the state of Washington. [17]

The movement drew considerable attention, not only because of its size, but also because of its commonsense appeal. As Jacob Baker has written, "There is a simple logic in an unemployed man's attempting to produce and distribute things for his family's needs." [18] Schlesinger notes that, "in time, it began to seem similarly logical for state governments to provide facilities to enable the unemployed to manufacture things necessary for their own existence." [19] When the Federal Emergency Relief Act was passed in 1933, it specifically authorized the administrator to make grants to aid "cooperative self-help associations for the barter of goods and services." [20]

Federal assistance to such cooperatives during the FERA period included aid to existing cooperatives and assistance to the states in organizing new ones. "Through this 'self-help' device," FERA official Edward A. Williams wrote later, "it was hoped that persons in the cooperatives might achieve better living standards than could be furnished through the granting of corresponding sums for direct relief." Limited assistance was also extended to cooperatives in the form of surplus commodities. Williams attributes the sparseness of the assistance to difficulties in management and organization of the cooperatives themselves and to "the general fear and hostility with which business groups viewed the production activities of the self-help co-operatives." He indicates that such hostility was "overcome to some extent by the ruling that co-operatives receiving

federal funds could not sell their goods in the open market," but that purchases made from cooperatives by state and local relief agencies for distribution to relief clients drew "great protest from dealers who asserted
that but for the co-operatives they might have sold the required goods to
the relief agencies." [21]

Despite such protests, use of the labor of unemployed people to produce
the items they needed spread beyond the cooperatives to the FERA Emergency Work Relief Program. Work relief activities had been in progress in
some states and localities even before the FERA was created; in fact,
more than a million relief recipients were engaged in some form of work
project when the federal relief program began its operation in May 1933.
Many of these, however, were forms of "make work" and were little different from the work tests used by relief agencies since the 1500s to determine the worthiness and motivation of an applicant. Pre-FERA work relief activities were nearly all projects aimed at unskilled or semiskilled
males, unsuited to the capacities of many of those in need.[22] The FERA
established regulations intended to upgrade work relief subsidized with
federal funds. Some success was achieved in raising wages and limiting
hours, but little progress was made in diversifying the projects until the
advent of the Civil Works Administration in November 1933.

By all accounts, the CWA was a remarkable episode in the history of
publicly sponsored work. It was conceived in November 1933 shortly
after the FSRC was incorporated, and by Christmas, more than 2 million
people were at work under its auspices. The number employed by the
CWA rose to a peak of 4 million in the first month of the new year. The
rapid mobilization of the CWA was accomplished in part by the wholesale
deputizing of state and local emergency relief personnel. Thus, the CWA
created a vehicle for major diversification and upgrading of work relief
methods, and it helped to overcome local resistance to projects for women,
professionals, artists, and others whose skills and capabilities did not fit
the mold of unskilled laborers. Since federal funds were being spent, adequate materials were supplied, and technical expertise was provided as
needed. Throughout the nation, the make-work activities were replaced
with projects that used available skills to make contributions of lasting
value. In its few months of operation, the CWA constructed or improved
five hundred thousand miles of secondary roads, forty thousand schools,
and one thousand airports; it created parks and playgrounds, dug swimming pools and ditches, cleaned out waterways, fought malaria-bearing
mosquitoes and other pests, installed sewers, conducted research, painted
murals, and taught people how to read and write.[23] The CWA also left a
legacy of pride among the federal relief officials who, within the span of a

few months, found or created useful work, in the words of an Army engineer who studied the program, for "nearly as many persons as were enlisted and called to the colors during our year and a half of World War mobilization." [24] As Hopkins later recalled, "a fraternity grew up among those who had worked in it." Corrington Gill expressed a similar notion: "I know that the CWA will always have a special place in the hearts of all of us who helped to bring it into being and fought to make its short life an example of what could be done for the unemployed." [25]

At the end of the winter of 1933–1934, the president, under mounting pressure from opponents of work relief and concerned about the budget, ordered the termination of the agency. "Nobody," he cheerfully told his National Emergency Council, "is going to starve in warm weather." [26] When the CWA was curtailed, some of its projects were salvaged by transfer to a newly created Emergency Work Relief (EWR) program within the FERA. Somewhat over a million people were employed on EWR projects in April 1934, and the number grew steadily to a peak of 2.4 million in January 1935. In that month, work relief provided 46 percent of all relief. Under FERA jurisdiction, the projects were converted to relief status; budgetary deficiencies, not wages, were paid, and only those determined through investigation to be eligible for relief could be employed. Efforts were made to preserve some of the gains made under CWA, however. The old pattern of federal-state relations through grants-in-aid was necessarily revived, but the federal administration played a larger role in planning and review of the projects than it had prior to CWA. Federal funds were made available to state and local projects for materials and skilled supervision. The FERA continued to urge the states and localities to implement projects for white-collar workers and women as well as construction workers and other laborers. Some of those involved hoped that a major expansion of productive projects could be achieved. As one man wrote after observing a CWA sewing room located in a wing of the Chicago Home for the Friendless,

> if only some way can be found to get goods into the empty hands of the millions who need so much. With an abundance of machinery, an abundance of power, an abundance of raw materials and an abundance of labor, there still are people by the millions without adequate food, clothing and shelter, to say nothing of things they want above the bare necessity class. [27]

The effort to provide work relief opportunities for women proved to be a major impetus for the development of production-for-use projects under the Emergency Work Relief Program. Women were generally considered ineligible for outdoor projects such as construction and road repair, and not all of those women in need had the skills for clerical assignments. Sewing, canning, and the fabrication of light household articles, however, were consistent with the perceived capabilities of women. By 1935, more than 60 percent of all of the women receiving work relief were engaged in production projects of various sorts; the percentage of male work relief recipients involved in such projects never reached 10 percent. Overall, production projects accounted for about 10 percent of expenditure under the Emergency Work Relief program.[28]

The production of clothing was the leading production-for-use activity. Sewing skills were fairly widespread, were easily taught, and could be implemented without elaborate equipment. Furthermore, after four years of depression, the clothing produced by sewing projects was urgently needed by unemployed workers and their families; most relief budgets provided only very scanty allowances for clothing, if any. "I wish I could find words adequately to express to you the immediate need for clothing in this area," field investigator Lorena Hickok wrote to Harry Hopkins from snowbound North Dakota in the fall of 1934. She described a middle-aged farmer who came to the relief office in clothes that obviously belonged to his son. "They're all we've got now," he told her. "We take turns wearing 'em." He had seven children. A few days later, she wrote from another North Dakota community where the temperature had already dropped to five degrees: "No bed linen. And quilts and blankets all gone. A year ago their clothing was in rags. This year they hardly have rags." [29] Understandably then, sewing rooms were among the first production projects established under the Emergency Work Relief program, and they expanded rapidly, continuing to provide between 30 and 40 percent of all production-for-use employment until the emergency work program was replaced by the WPA in 1935.

Hopkins described the sewing rooms as if they were only large-scale sewing circles. "They are not factories," he told reporters. "They are working rooms where a woman can go in and make a dress for her youngster and it would cost us about one fifth or one tenth of what it would if we purchased it." [30] The sewing rooms produced more than an occasional garment for home use, however. Between April 1, 1934 and July 1, 1935, they are estimated to have manufactured 14 million garments and reconditioned another 126,000.[31] When asked how much business private enterprise was losing through such projects, Hopkins answered, "None. We could not buy that dress anyway. We do not have the money." Nevertheless the program drew criticism from both retailers and apparel manufacturers. Hopkins pointed out that virtually all of the money paid as work relief wages immediately went to the private sector anyway, but he defended the sewing rooms and other production projects primarily on the basis of thrift: "I have no quarrel with anyone if they . . . give me all the money that we need. But without this work by the unemployed we would have to have far more money than we have now." [32] Although the sewing rooms were run by state and local relief administrations and supervised by the FERA, the corporation was implicated in these offenses against private enterprise in two ways. It procured and supplied most of the raw materials, and at the local level, the products were distributed as surplus commodities. Thus, the local retailer who felt deprived of relief clothing trade frequently faulted the corporation, as did state and national associations of retailers. [33]

Canning food from relief gardens and from locally procured or donated surpluses was another form of production-for-use that provided work relief for women. In these instances, the FSRC was even more implicated, for it not only assisted such projects by permitting them to use its facilities to trade canned goods with other work relief canning projects, but it actually sought, through discreet inquiries, to foster such projects. In the spring of 1934, the corporation's leadership anticipated that several states might undertake canning on a commercial scale. [34] Even when large quantities were involved, however, canning of fruits and vegetables never provoked the same opposition that met the other production-for-use projects, perhaps because canning garden produce was a time-honored American tradition associated with thrift and domestic virtue. "We have not yet found it necessary to ask the people to destroy some of their gardens so that we can buy for them," commented a relief administration official. [35] Nevertheless, the transfer of products canned by work relief projects among the states was conducted quietly in hopes of forestalling such criticism.

If FSRC and FERA officials hoped for an expansion of such productive projects, however, they were to be disappointed. Two projects undertaken in the summer and fall of 1934 elicited so much opposition that they nearly spelled the end of federal support for production-for-use altogether. Both were projects in which the FSRC was deeply involved, because both were undertaken to dispose of agricultural surpluses. At first, the mattress project, initiated in the summer of 1934, appeared to offer something for everyone. The cotton growers and the Department of Agriculture were anxious to find an outlet for surplus cotton. Ticking manu-

facturers were more than happy to sell large quantities of ticking to the
FSRC and agreed to purchase raw cotton equivalent to the amounts included in the ticking sold. A great deal of the work could be done by
hand, thus providing work relief employment to many people, especially
women, while avoiding the purchase or lease of expensive machinery.
The skills required were rudimentary, and a number of women in the
southern states had already been trained in mattress-making under an agricultural extension program conducted in 1933. Therefore, skilled su-
pervisors for mattress projects were already available in many localities.
Finally, families on relief were desperately in need of bedding; many had
not been able to replace household goods since before 1929 or had lost
them altogether in moving around the country searching for work.[36] As
Hopkins reported, "Relief workers have seen them sleeping on coffinlike
enclosures of sawdust, on springs covered with carpet, on the bare floor,
on chairs put together."[37] At the end of June, therefore, the FERA authorized the FSRC to use relief funds to purchase 250,000 bales of cotton.
The production of about 2 million mattresses and sheets, pillow cases,
towels, and comforters for a million families was anticipated.[38]

The FERA and the corporation were deluged with letters and telegrams
of protest from bedding firms, chambers of commerce, retailers, and
politicians. Although the letters varied in style, their themes were similar
and, by this time, familiar: relief mattresses would bankrupt the bedding
industry by destroying the market for mattresses, thus penalizing firms
that had remained in business through the depression years and throwing
their employees out of work. "For the sake of firms which have continued
in business in spite of reverses and unfavorable conditions, and employees who are engaged in the mattress industry," wrote the Alexandria
Bedding Company, "we urge you in the strongest manner possible to res-
cind your order and plans contemplated. If you do not do so you will rob
thousands of mattress factory employees all over the country of what
little work there is now available, merely adding thousands of additional
people to the relief rolls.[39] Furthermore, the manufacturers argued, FSRC
purchases of ticking and cotton would inflate the prices of these raw materials to the disadvantage of the mattress industry.

The FERA responses were reminiscent of the debates over the Farm
Board wheat and cotton two years earlier. The agency emphasized that
the relief clients to whom the mattresses would be distributed were in no
position to purchase them commercially: "this program to provide mattresses for people who are now in absolute want will have no material
effect upon the mattress market," wrote an FERA staff member to a com-

plaining congressman. "These relief clients are not now in the mattress market and have no immediate outlook for such purchases. Our investigations have shown that many of these people are now sleeping on straw or on the bare floor."[40] When the industry countered that the recipients might sell the mattresses to people who were in the mattress market, the relief administration replied that a "not for resale" label and severe penalties would prevent such illegal transfers.[41] In response to the industry's contention that due to the durable nature of mattresses, the FERA was depriving it of future business when the recipients should once again be employed, the FERA pointed out that many were so poor that they had never owned mattresses: "When normal industry does return this program may have served as an opportunity to acquaint these people with decent bedding."[42] Finally, the FSRC assured critics that it would make purchases in such a way as to avoid serious disturbance to the raw materials market. While the initial purchases were made through open bidding, a great deal of the cotton came from the cotton producers pool operated by the Department of Agriculture.

Although the reaction of mattress makers and their supporters in chambers of commerce and the National Association of Manufacturers did not persuade the FERA to cancel the program, it induced substantial caution. In September 1934, Jacob Baker wrote to the SERAs urging special care to prevent the mattresses from entering commercial channels and forbidding the relief organizations to distribute any of the mattresses to such institutions as hospitals serving needy persons. "Generally speaking," he wrote, "there is a local mattress concern that typically has supplied such institutions with mattresses. If our mattresses go into these channels it will mean that commercial mattress making concerns will lose business which they formerly enjoyed."[43] A few days later, Hopkins announced that the program would be terminated after approximately a million mattresses had been made, half the original estimate. The official explanation for the cutback was that an increase in the price of cotton had alleviated the need for surplus removal operations.[44]

Meanwhile, the drought that had dominated the corporation's procurement activities during the summer and fall of 1934 had also brought a new set of conflicts with business over production-for-use. The beef from the drought cattle liquidation program was canned in both commercial canneries and Emergency Work Relief Administration workrooms, the latter handling about one third of the total processing. These canning projects were on a larger scale than the produce canning operations, and they involved the purchase or lease of commercial capacity canning equipment. By August 31, 1935, the work projects had processed more than 195 million pounds of meat and meat products out of a total of 700 million pounds resulting from the cattle program. Once these canning facilities were established, state relief administrators understandably wanted to utilize them, and they protested when the FSRC transferred some cattle to commercial plants in order to speed up the processing. Commercial canners and the Department of Agriculture, on the other hand, protested because the cattle awaiting slaughter in the work relief projects were consuming feed grains made scarce by the drought, and commercial canning capacity was idle while many of the work projects were still bottlenecked.[45]

The beef canning projects were viewed with much greater alarm by the food processing industry than were the garden projects, though they generated far less controversy than the mattress program. Commercial canneries received a great deal of business from the FSRC and the SERAs and probably could not afford to alienate the relief agencies. In the case of the drought livestock, federally inspected commercial cannery capacity was fully booked before work relief projects were pressed into service. Private packing houses and canneries were awarded contracts for 3.6 million head of drought cattle, clearly a bonanza for the meat processing industry.[46] When asked whether the canning industry had suffered because of the work relief canning projects, Hopkins replied, "I doubt that it has. We are about the biggest customer of the canning industry in this country. We had about one billion cans of meat canned by commercial plants."[47]

The drought livestock operations left the FSRC with approximately 2 million cow and calf skins. The states also retained some cowhides as well as sheep and goat skins. Originally, corporation officials thought disposal of the hides would be an easy matter. Plans were developed for the hides to be commercially tanned and then manufactured into shoes for relief clients in idle shoe factories using relief labor. Despite Hopkins's indication that manufacturers would derive a profit from government use of their plants, both the shoe industry and the shoe retailers loudly protested, voicing familiar complaints. Work relief fabrication of shoes would reduce the sales of local shoe retailers and throw employees of shoe manufacturing concerns out of work and onto the relief rolls. Industry leaders charged the FSRC with competing with private enterprise and, in Arthur Schlesinger's words, "virtuously refused to rent the government the necessary machinery."[48] Although some leather goods were manufactured from the hides held by the states—shoes in Seattle and harnesses in Arkansas, for example—the plans for shoe manufacture on a national scale were eventually abandoned.[49]

The opposition of the shoe industry not only deprived unemployed workers and their families of needed footwear; it left the FSRC with hides for which it had no outlet. Shoe manufacturers and other industrialists who used leather as a raw material wanted the hides sold on the open market and claimed that a shortage would be created if they were withheld. Cattle ranchers, on the other hand, were worried that the release of the government hides would flood the market and depress the prices they received for cow and calf skins. There was some question as to whether the corporation could legally sell the hides, given the terms of the original USDA donation of the drought cattle to the FSRC. Secretary Wallace suggested processing the hides for relief on commercial contracts, a plan that shoe manufacturers might have supported but one to which retailers would certainly have objected.[50]

Meanwhile, the concentration of so many hides in government hands had an unsettling effect on the hide market. The sensitivity of the issue is revealed in a memo that Jacob Baker sent to Hopkins. He suggested that since the hide market was relatively strong, liquidation might begin soon to avoid further storage costs. He wrote,

> It seems to me that it is essential the matter be done without publicity and with no discussions leading to commitments with tanners or shoe-people. The sole public statement which could be used as a text by everybody is that we are liquidating our hides in an orderly manner so as not to disturb the market.
>
> Until we begin on a program of disposal the market will continue to suffer from little flurries due to rumors put out as to what we intend to do with our hides, resulting in quite a little speculation on its drops and rises. We are not responsible for that, but everybody that loses any money because of it takes a crack at us.[51]

The cracks that business and industry took at the FSRC and at the production-for-use projects escalated with the midterm election campaigns in the fall of 1934. "He tells me that the fears on the part of retailers, mattress manufacturers, furniture manufacturers, etc are being fanned at high pressure in the present political campaign," reported FSRC Distribution Director William Nunn of a conversation with the Washington representative of the National Retail Drygoods Association.[52] The fact that Upton Sinclair, running for governor of California on an essentially socialist platform, identified production-for-use projects as a necessary component of a socialist reconstruction of the American economy probably did little to ease the fears of business and industry. Early in October, under the auspices of the Illinois Manufacturers Association, sixty industrialists from across the nation gathered to launch an attack on the production projects. Their resolution urged the government to "abandon participation in business which competes with private enterprise." [53] A few days later, the National Association of Manufacturers (NAM) reported that a survey of its members found them "strongly disapproving" of such projects, and NAM joined the campaign begun by its Illinois affiliate. "Entrance of the government into manufacturing business in competition with its own citizens, even to supply relief for the unemployed, constitutes an extravagant use of the taxpayers money in further experimentations," declared the industrialists. They were certain that purchases from private firms would be cheaper. Relief, they asserted, was legitimate, "but to furnish the necessities required through government operated factories is the wrong way to do the right thing. Hundreds of firms have at great cost kept men on the payrolls when there has been no work for them," claimed NAM. "Now it is proposed to penalize these firms and their employees by not giving them work which must be done." [54] "[I]f it is desired to create special things to give away to the needy," editorialized the *New York Times* in reaction to the NAM statement, "it might still be more profitable for the relief agencies to turn such business over to going manufacturers who would also be obliged to hire more workers but who could do the business with far less waste." [55]

The FSRC usually was not singled out for criticism, since most critics referred either very generally to "the government" or very specifically to Harry Hopkins. Business opposition was an important influence on the FSRC, however, not only because it forced the curtailment of the mattress and shoe projects discussed above, but also because it created a chilling effect that inhibited the development of other projects uniting surplus commodities and surplus workers to produce the items needed by people on relief. Supplying raw material and containers for work relief projects never became a primary activity of the FSRC; approximately 13 percent of the corporation's total expenditure for commodities in the period ending July 31, 1935 was for work relief supplies exclusive of the drought cattle. [56] The corporation's experiences with production-for-use are of interest here because they clearly reveal the context of competing interests within which the corporation tried to "buy from those who had too much to give to those who had too little." In a sense, the FSRC operated in a gap in the normal American economy. In the face of the paradox of hunger and waste, direct transfers of food to people in need drew very little criticism. The production-for-use projects revealed the limits of this tolerance. Food might be thus transferred, but efforts to transfer nonfood surpluses without permitting industry to enjoy its customary profits met with powerful opposition.

Perhaps the difference between food and nonfood surplus transfers reflects the moral urgency of feeding hungry people. "Hunger is not debatable," Hopkins is reported to have said. Perhaps it reflects the distinction between consumable and durable goods, current and future markets. Food stuffs are rapidly consumed, but mattresses or shoes might last long enough to reduce future sales. As it turned out, unemployment remained high for much of the next decade, and many of the relief clients never found jobs again. When one considers the needs that remained unmet because of the opposition to production-for-use activities, it is not difficult to understand Hopkins's anger, expressed in a letter to a friend just after the mattress program was curtailed:

> I think most of these telegrams and others which I have received entirely miss the point; because if we were not making these mattresses in our work rooms, none of them would be manufactured in the mattress factories, so that by no stretch of the imagination can they be said to be losing any business. The plain fact of the matter is that many of these people would prefer that the unemployed have no mattresses. . . . The longer I stay here the more I am amazed at the complete lack of interest which a small minority of people have toward the urgent needs of the unemployed.[57]

Ironically, the midterm congressional elections showed that the Roosevelt administration had little to fear from business conservatives in 1934. The election was a major victory for the New Deal and for the Democratic party. A vast majority of the contested congressional seats and statehouses were won by Democrats. By the time the limited public support for the business critique of the New Deal was evident, however, the damage to the production-for-use approach had already been done.

Industrialists and retailers worried about government competition were not the only critics of the relief system of which the corporation was a part, however. Indeed, as Piven and Cloward have written: "No one liked direct relief—not the President who called for it, the Congress that legislated it, the administrators who operated it, the people who received it."[58] Farmers, especially large farmers who farmed their holdings with sharecroppers and day labor, were particularly vociferous in their criticism. Writing to Harry Hopkins of the opinions she encountered among planters in the Southeast while the CWA was still in operation, Lorena Hickok summarized the situation this way:

During the depression, the paternalistic landlord was hard put to it to "furnish" his tenants. He was darned glad to have us take over the job. But now, finding that CWA has taken up some of this labor surplus— both day labor and those tenants without farms, of whom there was always just a convenient number enough to aid the landlord in imposing his own terms on the tenants on his property—he is panicky, realizes that he may have to make better terms with his tenants and pay his day labor more, and is raising a terrific howl against CWA.[59]

What did the farmers want? Hickok tried to answer this question in another report:

The farmers, as nearly as I can figure them out, want everything pulled out except during their slack season, and each year they want it pulled out far enough ahead of the beginning of their work "so these Niggers will be good and hungry." In effect, they want us to take over the load they say they used to carry—that of keeping their peons alive during the slack seasons on pork and meal—and have everything nice and lovely so they can go on getting all the cheap labor they want when they want it without any responsibility toward that labor.[60]

Hickok reported exceptions, but such sentiments were prevalent among the large planters and truck farmers she had met.

Late in 1934, the delegates to an annual convention of the American Farm Bureau Federation joined the rising chorus of complaint about relief with a resolution that seemed to confirm some of Hickok's observations. They didn't like direct relief because it encouraged indolence; they accused it of having "promoted a desire on the part of some of our citizens to be unemployed." But they didn't like work relief either, because it exerted upward pressure on wages. The work relief wage scale, the resolution asserted, "must be kept in line with current practices in different localities" in order to avoid "the unfortunate experiences of the last two years in granting relief wages far above what agriculture or industry locally could pay."[61]

The unemployed did not like relief either, although obviously not because they thought the work relief wage scales were too high. Under the CWA, workers had averaged $15.04 a week; under the FERA, they received only $6.50. "We, the unemployed are fed up with relief," the head of the Unemployed Citizens Council in Fresno, California told Lorena Hickok late in the summer of 1934.[62] What they really wanted, for the most part, was a decent job at a decent wage. Short of that, they wanted work relief rather than direct relief, or at least both Hopkins and the president were convinced that they did. "In addition to want, the unemployed were confronting a still further destructive force, that of worklessness," wrote Hopkins of the pressures that had brought the CWA into being. This feeling was expressed by many, he explained, "but most particularly among the unemployed themselves. Letters came, delegations arrived, protesting against the indignity of public charity. . . . They were accustomed to making a return for their livelihood. It was a habit they liked and from which they chiefly drew their self-respect." [63]

At the other end of the system, the president and the budget office did not like paying for relief. Both Roosevelt and his relief administrator believed that the lower levels of government should play a larger role in financing public assistance. The states had participated to varying degrees in the financing of emergency relief, but on the whole, their participation accounted for only 13 percent of the total public relief expenditure in 1933 and slightly less the next year. Local governments had provided almost a quarter of the total in 1933 but less than one sixth in 1934. The coercive power of federal matching grants-in-aid had not proven successful in inducing the desired level of state participation; both the states and the federal government knew that the people who would suffer most if federal aid were withheld were the unemployed. [64] "One of the reasons why the Government got out of the direct-relief business," Hopkins told a Senate committee in 1936, "was because we believed in some cases the States were not bearing their fair share of this burden, and this was a method to assure that in certain sections, so far as this whole relief field was concerned, that the States particularly and the local communities, would provide their fair share of this burden." [65] The Roosevelt administration was increasingly uncomfortable with federally financed and administered direct relief. It was too costly, both in political and in financial terms, and yet it seemed to provide only inadequate aid at best.

While the corporation was usually not singled out in critiques of relief, one set of critics did select the corporation, or rather its wares, for special condemnation; with few exceptions, the leading social workers and relief administrators were adamantly opposed to relief in kind and blamed the corporation for continuing and spreading what they perceived as an archaic and regressive form of assistance. Much of the leadership of the social work profession in the decade before the Great Depression had been centered in the private family service agencies, and in these organizations, a great deal had been made of cash assistance as an essential tool for "conserving family independence and self respect." [66] Cash protected the clients' privacy and helped to make their lives as much like those of their nonrelief neighbors as possible. The articulate leadership of the profession had hoped, as the twenties drew to a close, to spread the practice of providing relief in cash from the voluntary to the public agencies. Instead, in the face of the overwhelming need unleashed by the Depression, they had seen their hard-won gains slip away as even the private agencies went back to distributing provisions. As the number of clients increased and funds became harder to secure, social workers found that they could not possibly become well enough acquainted with the majority of their clients "to determine with any degree of accuracy the client's capacity and willingness to spend money judiciously," observed Margaret Wead in a survey of changing relief practice under the impact of rising unemployment. "This made it seem necessary to insure that money actually went for basic necessities. Relief in kind became an indirect substitute for education in home economics and knowledge of clients." [67]

Despite such backsliding, much of the leadership of the profession held out staunchly for the dignity and capacity of clients. Dorothy Kahn, then the director of the Philadelphia County Relief Board, voiced the beliefs of many of her listeners when she spoke to the 1933 session of the National Conference of Social Work about the importance of cash:

> The great majority of persons now receiving public relief were, until recently, wage-earners. Even those who may have been dependent earlier upon relatives or upon social agencies for support were accustomed to the use of money. Money for them means the exercise of intelligence and discretion in providing for the fundamentals of existence for their families. It connotes household economy in the broadest sense. Around the family purse centers the education of children in wise and individual ways of spending, thrift, relative values, and the ethics of possession and sharing.

She went on to characterize the feelings of recipients of relief in kind:

> But if you are a vast relief organization, impersonal, designed for relieving the distress of hundreds or thousands like myself, these things you give me are leaden with the weight of your power, your choice, your restrictions, your arrogance—in fact, in assuming that you can meet my individual needs more wisely, merely because you have the purchasing power and I, for the time being, have not. [68]

When the FERA was established, and when Harry Hopkins, considered to be a progressive leader of the social work profession, was appointed administrator, many in the social work field hoped that the new relief administration would promote a restoration of professional standards in relief-giving in areas where relief had been debased by the Depression. They hoped to convert public agencies to a cash basis, and they were disappointed when the FERA became involved in disbursing relief in kind on a massive scale. They saw surplus commodity distribution as contradicting, and thus undermining, the FERA's effort to convince agencies on the lower levels of government to provide assistance in cash, and they resented the difficulties that surplus commodity distribution imposed upon already beleaguered relief administrators. Josephine Brown, in her history of public relief in the Depression decade, described the surplus commodity program in terms that convey the indignation felt by social workers within as well as outside the FERA:

> The Federal Administration, which was encouraging localities to give direct relief in cash and insisting, in the spring of 1934, that all work relief wages be paid by cash or check, continued to give relief in kind through a program which was financed almost entirely by Federal Funds and which was entirely under Federal control. This distribution of surplus commodities not only constituted relief in kind, but "package" or "basket" relief handed out through commissaries or at the corner grocery store where the recipients were bound to be publicly marked as "reliefers" to all their neighborhood. In order to regulate prices and take surplus goods off the market, the Federal Administration has been willing for six years to give direct Federal relief of the most demoralizing and stigmatizing type.[69]

The social work leaders who took this stand were not unaware of the pressing paradox of want amid plenty. In fact, a committee of the American Association of Social Workers charged with preparing a working document for an impending conference on "Governmental Objectives for Social work," explicitly considered the proposition that "surplus relief distribution should be continued," on the grounds that "it is the only answer to the paradox of people starving amidst warehouses crammed with food." With one wavering exception, the committee members dissented, choosing instead an alternative proposition: "Surplus relief distribution is illogical if adequate relief is being furnished." Arguing that adequate relief would itself reduce the surplus, the committee asserted that the commodity distribution project had been "loaded on the relief administrations rather to meet the needs of agricultural producers than the needs of the industrially unemployed," and recommended that an alternative method of eliminating surpluses be developed.[70] The delegate conference for which the committee was preparing subsequently affirmed the committee's recommendation, registering its opinion that the distribution of surplus commodities had "manifested serious social and administrative disadvantages and is an anomaly in an adequate cash relief program." [71]

The commissaries were considered the chief villains, and observers of the public relief scene noted that the availability of federal commodities not only permitted the continuation of the commissary approach but also occasioned its growth. "Undoubtedly the governmental policy adopted during the current depression of buying up surplus agricultural products and disposing of them through relief channels has served to extend commissary distribution," wrote Joanna Colcord, the director of the Charity Organization Department of the Russell Sage Foundation, after an extensive study of public assistance in cash and in kind in major cities across the nation. "Many communities, which might otherwise never have embarked on a commissary system, decided that they might as well take care of all relief in this fashion, since they already had a central depot issuing surplus goods." [72]

Hopkins, who shared the preference for cash relief, defended surplus commodity distribution with two arguments. First, the commodities were to be supplemental to other relief in whatever form and "because it was supplementary, it seemed never to have the stigma of charity which most people who receive relief feel so strongly." [73] Hopkins did not elaborate on the connection between the supplemental nature of the commodities and the lack of stigma, and many of his colleagues would have disagreed with him. But was probably correct; the FSRC files contain many letters from existing and potential relief clients, and while some are complaints about specific commodities or about ill-treatment by relief personnel, most are inquiries about how to obtain the surplus foods. A letter sent to Hopkins by a Michigan woman in February 1934 asked why the CWA workers with families of one to four people "are not allowed any of the butter and meats etc. which are sent into our county. . . . I know every one would sure be glad to get any am't of such things as it sure means a lot. I have 2 children one 3 and the other 8 months," she explained, "and you know with milk and such other things that infants must have $6.00 a week doesn't go very far." Her neighbors wanted the commodities, too, she reported: "Everyone seems to be complaining but no one would write to find out what is what." Like the letters sent to Henry Wallace offering to help dispose of the pig surplus, these letters reflect a sense that indeed little stigma existed in using what would otherwise go to waste. [74] Hopkins second line of defense was more convincing to his social work colleagues: "Millions of people were on a restricted diet, or in other words a diet capable of supporting life without any margin of safety. Meat prices rose, as they were bound to rise. Purchasing power lagged. Whatever food was to be had was that much food to the good." [75]

At its first birthday, then, the FSRC was under attack from industrialists and retailers, barely tolerated by social workers and relief administrators, and tainted by the general annoyance with which taxpayers and budget balancers viewed relief. Cattle ranchers tolerated it, at least for the time being, and hog farmers, potato planters, and citrus growers offered few complaints. Relief clients, despite the protective attitude of their social workers, were willing to help dispose of the surplus. The general picture that emerges, however, is one of an operation constrained on all sides by the necessity to avoid stepping on the toes of private enterprise. Even grateful growers were quick to complain if a competing product was purchased.

Predictably, this atmosphere engendered conflicts between the parents of the FSRC. "Tension existed in the relations between the Department of Agriculture and the Relief Administration," Richard Kirkendall has written of the two organizations at this period. "Officials in the department feared that the resettlement program under Hopkins' control might add to the farm surpluses and tried hard to prevent resettled farmers from engaging in commercial agriculture." On the other side of the fence, he notes, "members of the FERA . . . criticized Triple A on the grounds that it was promoting a displacement of tenant farmers, forcing them to turn to the relief agency for help." [76] In November 1934, economic advisor Mordecai Ezekial prepared a memorandum for Secretary Wallace discussing relations between the Department of Agriculture and the relief administration. "It has been found in practice that where we have tried to work to carry out operations with Agriculture laying down the policies and Emergency Relief putting them into effect, very great loss of time has resulted," he asserted. He specified conflicts arising from the drought cattle operations, citing a long delay on the part of the relief administration in setting up the program and noting the FERA's practice of holding back animals for slaughter in work relief projects even though commercial capacity was again available. Ezekial charged that delay by the relief organization had resulted in waste in food purchase operations: "Recommendations made months ago have not yet been acted upon. As a consequence much skim milk has gone down the sewer and apples have been boxed which should have been packed in bulk, and cabbages which

should have been distributed are still depressing prices." He hastened to
add that the delay in the FERA was not willful:

> It is recognized that the slowness in the Emergency Relief Administra-
> tion is not due to any lack of willingness on the part of the admin-
> istrators, but to the tremendous volume of administrative detail which
> falls upon their shoulders and the necessity of giving first attention to
> human relief.[77]

Nevertheless, the delays were sufficiently aggravating to the USDA that
Ezekial recommended against permitting a drought area feed distribution
program to be located in the relief administration or the FSRC. The inter-
agency alliance that had nurtured the corporation was beginning to erode.

The tensions within and around the FSRC were not disabling. The organization was continuing to procure surpluses and send them to the
states for distribution, continuing to strike "one of the most direct blows
at the economic paradox which has choked farms with an abundance of
farm products while many of the unemployed have grown hungry."[78] But
the strains, internal and external, were beginning to erode the cooperative
optimism of the early period and raise questions about the organization's
ability effectively to serve its several masters. The corporation was not
the only agency to experience these conflicts; indeed, they characterized
many of the instrumentalities created in the early New Deal. "The promises which heralded the 'new deal' are hard to fulfill," observed sociologist Robert MacIver in a thoughtful essay written in 1934. "The new
economic organizations will probably endure, but the vital question concerns the spirit that will animate them. . . . The new institutions are here,
but the essential point is—Who shall control them?"[79]

CHAPTER TEN

Transfer to the Department of Agriculture

On November 18, 1935, the Federal Surplus Relief Corporation was transferred to the direction of the secretary of agriculture. The corporation's offices were moved to USDA, and its name was changed to the Federal Surplus Commodities Corporation (FSCC). Transfer to the Department of Agriculture was more than a simple change in the locus of administration; it marked the beginning of a process by which food assistance was increasingly divorced from federal relief and integrated with the Agriculture Department's price support programs for commercial agriculture.

The 1936 *Annual Report* of the FSCC explained the move this way: "In 1935 it became apparent that the Corporation's greatest value was not as a relief organization, but rather as an agency to assist the Department of Agriculture in the execution of surplus removal programs conducted by the Agricultural Adjustment Administration." [1] Like many official explanations, this one raises as many questions as it answers: the corporations's greatest value to whom? And to whom did it become apparent? In order to answer these questions, we must examine in some detail the process that led to the decision to transfer the corporation.

The first discussions of the possibility of major changes occur in the FSRC's records in the latter part of 1934, and they indicate a shift of the corporation's priorities in an entirely different direction. In August, the corporation's executive officer, Keith Southard, submitted to Hopkins a "Forward Plan for Commodity Distribution" in which he noted the likelihood that commodities donated by the AAA would continue to be available in sufficient quantities to warrant a continuation of the distribution machinery established by the state relief administrations. Southard recommended that these surplus donations be supplemented by the regular distribution of "a minimum diet of staple foodstuffs," suggesting that relief funds, "perhaps to the extent of ten percent of the total Federal relief expenditure," be allocated to purchase and distribute a "minimum of balanced foodstuffs." He stressed the economies of the commodity distribution approach and its proven capacity to reach needy persons not on the regular relief rolls.[2]

In September, the Food Survey Committee, which had been established by the Department of Agriculture to assess food supplies as a part of the drought relief program, began discussing impending food scarcities and rising food prices anticipated in the wake of the drought. The committee expressed concern that the unemployed would find their already meager food budgets rendered even more inadequate by price increases and recommended an expanded role for the FSRC, envisioning a plan in which the corporation would supplement its commodity donations with large-scale purchases to be resold to the unemployed at cost in order to increase the purchasing power of their relief dollars. The committee was unsuccessful in an attempt to get Hopkins to endorse the plan and present it to the president, but the committee's minutes indicate that, as of the fall of 1934, the Food Survey Committee, which included representatives of the FSRC and the FERA as well as the Department of Agriculture, viewed the corporation primarily as a means of getting food to those in need.[3]

A shift in the direction of relief procurement was clearly the intent of the corporation's executive officer as late as December 1934. At a December 6 meeting of the FSRC board of directors, Hopkins asked what new programs were under consideration for the corporation once the drought livestock operations were completed. According to the minutes:

Mr. Southard stated that consideration had been given to the indicated shift from agricultural surpluses to purchases made specifically in relation to relief needs. In addition to such foodstuffs as may become available from expenditure of processing taxes or other moneys available to Agricultural Adjustment Administration, it is suggested that commodities be purchased specifically for purposes of continuing a regular supply of staples required by the needy and destitute on relief rolls as a reasonably balanced diet, and for such other fundamental needs such as cod liver oil for young school children, school lunch programs, etc., and to bring about full and economical use of the distribution organization and personnel, both Federal and State, which is already in existence and which is being continuously improved.

The minutes contain no record of a reaction, positive or negative, to this proposal. Hopkins concluded the meeting by asking the members of the board to "consider whether they have any suggestions to make . . . as to the further use of the Corporation for any . . . other purposes." In December 1934 then, the FSRC's future was far from settled. Seemingly, it was not yet "apparent that the Corporation's greatest value" was as a surplus disposal outlet.[4]

Several factors were probably important in provoking discussion of the corporation's future in the fall of 1934. The drought relief operations that were nearing completion had not only demonstrated the adaptability and usefulness of the corporation, they had also entailed a sizeable expansion of the FSRC staff that would now have to be reduced if new functions were not identified. At the other end of the system, the volume and value of the resulting meat had induced many state and local relief agencies to extend and improve their distribution operations. These distribution systems were now ready to handle a fairly large quantity of foodstuffs. At the same time, the harsh combination of drought and crop control had reduced or eliminated the huge surpluses of basic commodities that had prompted the FSRC's formation and constituted the focus of its early activities. The impetus of procurement operations was shifting to localized surpluses of fruit and vegetables purchased by state and local agencies under corporation supervision. Some adjustment would be needed to accommodate these changed conditions. Finally, the tensions between the Agriculture Department and the relief agency that had arisen over the processing of the drought cattle suggested a need to adjust relations between the FSRC's parents.[5]

Even if these tensions and changes had not raised questions about the corporation's future, however, plans for an overhaul of federal relief raised an element of uncertainty, both about the future of the FSRC as an organization and about surplus commodity distribution as an activity. During the fall of 1934, while the Committee on Economic Security was debating the form of the administration's social insurance plan, Roosevelt was meeting informally with Harry Hopkins, Harold Ickes, and Treasury Secretary Henry Morgenthau to plan a new federal relief program that would emphasize work for the unemployed. Probably the most crucial decision made, both for the long-term welfare of poor people and for the future of federal food assistance, was the decision to draw a distinction between "unemployable" and "employable" poor people. The former, under the new plan, would be turned over to the care of state and local agencies assisted by categorical federal grants-in-aid; the latter would be aided through a federally sponsored and administered work program. Theoretically, relief administered by the FERA had been intended for victims of depression-induced unemployment; in practice, FERA aid in most states had been extended to destitute families and persons, regardless of their employability or the cause of their misery. In practice then, this decision constituted a federal withdrawal from direct relief; the FERA estimated that about 1.5 million of the 5 million cases on the relief rolls at the end of 1934 contained no employable adult.

Roosevelt announced the fundamentals of the new plan in a message to the newly-reconvened Congress on January 4, 1935. Direct relief, he told the legislature, was "a narcotic, a subtle destroyer of the human spirit." Instead of continuing to sponsor "a spiritual and moral disintegration fundamentally destructive to the national fibre," the government must find work for those in need and able to work. "We must preserve not only the bodies of the unemployed from destruction but also their self-respect, their self reliance and courage and determination." Therefore, "the Federal Government must and shall quit this business of relief."[6]

In its place, Roosevelt proposed a massive works program that would provide jobs at a "security wage," higher than relief payments but lower than prevailing wages, for the 3.5 million "employable" unemployed on the relief rolls. Unlike traditional work-for-relief schemes in which payments were calculated on a budgetary deficiency basis, the compensation would be a wage in return for labor, not administered by a social worker and not adjusted to family size. In order to make sure that these jobs went to those most in need, however, potential employees would have to be certified as eligible for relief: the program would retain the means test to verify eligibility based on financial need. The work projects to be undertaken would be of permanent value to the broader community, but the president promised they would not compete with private enterprise. The works program would be financed by a federal appropriation of $4 billion, which he had requested in the budget submitted the previous day and $880 million remaining from previous appropriations.

Concerning the unemployables, Roosevelt told Congress that "most of them are unable for one reason or another to maintain themselves independently—for the most part, through no fault of their own. Such people, in the days before the great depression, were cared for by local efforts—by States, by counties, by towns by cities, by churches, and by private welfare agencies. It is my thought that in the future they must be cared for as they were before." The president promised that the security legislation that he would soon propose "will . . . be of assistance to local effort in the care of this type of cases." [7]

The Committee on Economic Security, which officially reported to the president on January 15, recommended federal grants-in-aid to the states to subsidize assistance to dependent children and impoverished aged persons not receiving benefits from the insurance provisions, which would not begin paying in any case until 1942. Such provisions would be discretionary at the state level; in effect, the federal government was offering to assist states if they chose to create old age assistance and mother's aid programs or to fund those already on their books. As far as other categories of "unemployables" were concerned, they were not to be the responsibility of the federal government. "With the Federal Government carrying so much of the burden of pure unemployment," the committee reasoned, "the State and local governments, we believe, should resume responsibility for relief." The Committee on Economic Security urged the states to substitute "modernized public assistance laws" for "their ancient, out-moded poor laws," and to "replace their traditional poor-law administrations by unified and efficient State and local public welfare departments." Finally, the committee suggested that the FERA was the most appropriate existing agency to administer grants-in-aid to the states. The Social Security Bill embodying the committee's recommendations was introduced into Congress on January 17. [8]

The uncertainty about the future of various aspects of the emergency relief program in general and the FSRC in particular, which had commenced when the president began talking about overhauling the relief program the previous summer, was, if anything, heightened by the introduction of the legislation. In the first place, the Emergency Relief Appropriation Bill, which was introduced in Congress a week after the Social Security Bill, was remarkably vague concerning both the activities that would be financed from the giant appropriation and the structure through which it would be administered. Indeed, the bill specified that the funds could be used for "relief" as well as "work relief" and said almost nothing at all about an administering agency. [9] Nor did Roosevelt have a clear plan waiting in the wings. He not only refused to describe the administrative setup but also to specify who would head the new works program. Most observers felt that the choice would be either Ickes or

Hopkins, but the president's failure to specify was very unsettling to both men.[10]

Congress added to the uncertainty when, early in its consideration of the work relief and social security bills, it decided that the FERA should not be designated to administer the grant-in-aid titles of the Social Security program, leaving that organization without a function or a future. Eventually, Congress assigned administration of the categorical assistance grants to the newly created Social Security Board, leaving the administration little choice but to liquidate the Emergency Relief Administration.[11] For the FSRC, this decision had major implications. On a daily basis, the FSRC had been operating largely as a subsidiary of the FERA. If the latter organization were liquidated, some change in the operating pattern would be necessary. The corporation's charter specified that its members "shall be the persons who from time to time may occupy the offices of Secretary of Agriculture of the United States, Federal Emergency Administrator of Public Works and Federal Emergency Relief Administrator, respectively." If the office of Federal Emergency Relief Administrator were eliminated by the new relief structure, a change in the corporate membership would be required. Finally, the corporation's finances had been derived from FERA grants to the states; when these were terminated, the corporation would have no money to pay for processing and shipping commodities, even if the AAA continued to donate items for distribution.

At a more fundamental level, the division of responsibility for those in need between the federal and state-local governments on the basis of employability and the choice of work projects as the most appropriate means of aiding the employable victims of depression called into question federally sponsored and subsidized distribution of groceries. The federal relief agency had strongly encouraged localities to switch from grocery orders and commissaries to cash relief and had insisted that work relief payments be made in cash. Part of the theory of the preferability of such work projects as those anticipated under the new relief setup over direct relief or traditional work relief was that the worker received an hourly wage that restored him or her to the roles of wage earner in the family and customer in the community. Hopkins later gave the following account of the importance of this difference:

> I should like to clarify the difference between work relief and a job on a work program such as CWA and WPA. To the man on relief the difference is very real. On work relief, although he gets the disciplinary re-

wards of keeping fit, and of making a return for what he gets, his need is still determined by a social worker, and he feels himself to be something of a public ward, with small freedom of choice. When he gets a job on a work program, it is very different. He is paid wages and the social worker drops out of the picture. His wages may not cover much more ground than his former relief budget but they are his to spend as he likes. I am told that all over the country the response was the same when people went off work relief (and we had over 2,000,000 on work relief) and on to Works Progress. The wife of the WPA worker tossed her head and said, "We aren't on relief any more, my husband is working for the Government." [12]

In this context, two questions of principle arise in regard to commodity distribution. Would the continued distribution of foodstuffs to workers on the new work projects compromise the attempt to restore to them the dignity of wage earning consumers? And if food assistance were deemed inappropriate for the employable unemployed under the new plan, would its continued provision to the unemployables be feasible or consistent with policy? That is, would unemployables be concentrated in sufficient numbers to permit distribution at any acceptable level of efficiency and would the continuation of federally sponsored commodity distribution contradict the policy of returning responsibility for unemployable persons in need to the state and local levels?

There is remarkably little evidence of discussion of these issues among the FSRC or FERA leadership during the first half of 1935. The idea of handling a regular flow of staple commodities, supplemented by such surpluses as might arise, as proposed by the Food Survey Committee the previous autumn, continued to attract attention, and in fact, both Baker and Southard wrote to Hopkins about it early in the year. "The Agricultural Department and the A.A.A. are, I think, still pretty firmly of the understanding and opinion that we shall continue taking commodities indefinitely," wrote Baker at the end of January, explaining that in response to that assumption the Commodity Distribution staff had worked up a plan for distribution that would "place the emphasis on the kind of commodities meeting relief requirements rather than those meeting agricultural production control requirements." Baker suggested that Hopkins might want to discuss the matter with Wallace, but his tone was diffident and indicated no particular support for the idea. [13] Southard's memo a few days later was more enthusiastic but still very tentative: "I think we might now re-define 'surplus' as 'depression excess,'" he suggested. "In other words take a realistic view of the cause of 'Surpluses,' not only Agricultural crops but also unused industrial productive capacity," and develop a "concentrated staple commodity distribution operation, to employables as low cost purchases and unemployables as gifts, utilizing both AAA 'Surpluses' and contract purchases from producers." [14]

Hopkins, however, must have responded somewhat coldly to the idea. He did not rule it out, evidently, since he asked Distribution Division Director William Nunn to prepare a detiled plan for including commodities in the budgets of relief clients. But apparently he gave his staff very little information about his expectations with regard to commodity distribution. From the middle of February through the early summer, virtually all communications with him bearing on the future of the corporation from FSRC staff contained specific references to the lack of certainty, as if staff members were trying to avoid seeming presumptuous. The corporation might publish a report on commodities distributed every six months as Ickes had suggested, wrote Southard, "provided we stay in business that long." [15] The corporate charter should be amended to permit the organization to function under the 1935 relief appropriation, Baker suggested, despite the fact that "the degree in which the Federal Surplus Relief Corporation will be utilized in the future is wholly uncertain." [16] A purchase of rice proposed by the Department of Agriculture was "a good proposition," wrote Baker in May, "if you have agreed to continuing any direct distribution of commodities." [17] Internally as well, the uncertainty was pervasive, with many decisions postponed until the size and shape of the new program and the role of commodity distribution within it should be specified.

The reasons why Hopkins left his staff in the dark about the future of surplus commodity distribution are not clear. In the early weeks of congressional consideration of the new legislation, during which time he was uncertain about his own future in the Roosevelt administration, he may well have wanted to hang onto the FSRC in case the works job went to Ickes. But when he realized, toward the end of March, that he would have a major role in the new system, that reason for holding onto the corporation was obviated. By that time, however, he was very busy and preoccupied with working out the details of the new program. On April 5, the day before the $4 billion relief appropriation cleared Congress, FSRC Executive Officer Keith Southard wrote Undersecretary of Agriculture Rex Tugwell a brief letter that suggests Hopkins was relatively uninterested in the direction of the corporation: "In talking about the future of FSRC with Harry, he suggested that whoever might be able to make use of it should be in control of it and run it. Up to this moment the old purpose seems to be pretty well running out." Southard suggested that a change in the charter permitting the president to name the three corporate members might transform the corporation into "a device ready-to-hand with all powers necessary to carry out the purposes of the Bankhead Tenant Farm bill, provided only that it is implemented with funds." Southard concluded with a comment implying a rather casual character to his idea: "I am sending you this suggestion for what it may be worth as a means to some of the ends which you have in mind." [18] At this point, the FSRC's future was up for grabs; its president was willing to give it to whoever could use it, and its chief operating officer was willing to see it removed from the commodity distribution business altogether.

In late April, Roosevelt announced his complex scheme for administering the new work relief program. In May, the executive order establishing Hopkins's Works Progress Division as an operating agency, the Works Progress Administration (WPA), gave the new unit the authority to initiate limited budget projects without going through the elaborate procedures of the allotments division headed by Ickes. Hopkins acted quickly to convert the WPA to the central thrust of the work relief effort. Explaining to a friend why Hopkins would not be considering new applications for aid from California's self-help cooperatives in the interim, Jacob Baker wrote in May, "his whole interest is in the new work program at the present time and he does not quite see how the cooperatives fit in with it." [19] The same comment might have been made about commodity distribution. Certainly, setting up the works program was an enormous undertaking and one that, unlike surplus commodity distribution, embodied both the principles and the hopes articulated by Hopkins and other leaders of the relief and social welfare community. [20] The resignation of Keith Southard, who left to take a job as executive officer of the Resettlement Administration also occurred in May, and no one was appointed to replace him.

Within the agricultural branch of the FSRC family, however, the shifting relief picture and uncertainty about the future of the FSRC provoked widespread discussion. "Some apprehension is felt by the Food Survey Committee lest the present program for purchase and distribution of food surpluses may be discontinued under the proposed work-relief plan, or so reduced in scope as to be ineffective in dealing with the surpluses," wrote Food Survey Committee Chairman Mordecai Ezekial to the members of the AAA Operating Council early in March. [21] In a series of letters, memoranda, and committee meetings, USDA and AAA staff discussed the importance of keeping the "relief outlet" available to agriculture. In the first place, they argued, government purchases had proven their capacity to support prices, but purchases required an outlet, which the FSRC had been providing. "In the year and a quarter that the Corporation has been operating it has handled such obviously necessary distribution as the pork from the pig program and the beef and mutton from the drought program," wrote AAA staff member Jonathan Garst to Secretary Wallace in a well-reasoned appeal for maintenance of the commodity relief program. "The Corporation has become an accepted outlet for the unmarketable portions of agricultural crops." [22]

Surpluses held on the farms or by control committees under marketing agreements that restricted shipments presented an even more pressing problem. "The only alternative outlets for the supplies to which such restrictions give rise are outright destruction, dumping abroad, manufacturing into by-products, or distribution for relief or charitable purposes," Garst noted. "Destruction may be as defensible as factory shut-downs," he continued, "but it is more offensive to the general public." Dumping would incur opposition, and conversion to by-products was often wasteful, he argued. And of the two modes of transfer to the poor, "the organized system of the Federal Surplus Relief Corporation with its past experience would appear preferable to haphazard charitable distribution agencies." [23] The Food Survey Committee was also concerned about the surpluses to be held by control committees, positing "physical destruction or rotting" and "diversion to low-value by-products" as the only feasible alternatives to relief. "It would seem highly undesirable that the AAA program involve the physical destruction of any surplus next year, even if these surpluses should be due to favorable weather," wrote the committee. "Food costs will probably be high through much of the year and it would be politically as well as humanistically undesirable to destroy food supplies at the same time many millions of persons were on low relief or work-relief incomes." Pointing to the problems engendered by sporadic supplies, "with dribbles at some times and gluts at other times," the Food Survey Committee recommended a larger and more regular commodity distribution program that would "provide a sufficient flow of commodities to justify setting up and keeping in continuous operation local machinery for its distribution to those on relief." [24] The committee suggested that $100 million to $150 million of the proposed appropriation of $4 billion be allocated to commodity purchase and distribution, of which about $50 million would go for actual surpluses, while the remainder would be used to maintain a continuous supply of staples. [25]

As of the early spring of 1935 then, USDA was contemplating a food assistance program funded from the relief appropriation and designed to distribute both needed staples and expected surpluses. Furthermore, the continuous flow of staple commodities was anticipated to require funds at least equal to and possibly as great as double those necessary for the purchase and distribution of surplus commodities. Even in the depths of USDA, it was not yet "apparent that the corporation's greatest value was not as a relief organization, but rather as an agency to assist the Department of Agriculture in the execution of surplus removal programs." What was apparent was the public relations value of commodity distribution, its role in the maintenance of a favorable climate of public opinion toward agricultural adjustment. Equally apparent was the Food Survey Committee's concern with the nutritional situation of relief clients. Throughout these discussions, the needs of the poor were consistently addressed. The Department of Agriculture's Bureau of Home Economics supplied figures that permitted the Food Survey Committee to calculate the sorts of diets that families of various sizes might be expected to purchase if work relief wages averaged $50 per month as suggested in the Senate hearings. It concluded that many families would need a supplement to bring their food consumption up to even minimal standards of adequacy, and the nutritional needs of relief families formed an essential part of its argument for continuing distribution.[26]

Even while the Food Survey Committee and the AAA Operating Council considered the need for a continuing program of food distribution, the internal politics of the Department of Agriculture deprived relief recipients of some of their staunchest supporters within the agricultural camp. The pervasive differences of perspective between the liberal reformers centered in the offices of the General Counsel and the Consumers' Counsel and the more conservative staff members, especially those in the commodity sections, came to a head early in 1935 over the protection of sharecroppers and tenant farmers under AAA production adjustment programs.[27] Throughout 1934, reports from the field and in the press indicated that farm tenants and sharecroppers in the Cotton Belt were being victimized under the acreage reduction contracts. In the first place, many of them were not receiving the meager share of rental and benefit payments to which they were legally entitled; in the second place, they were being forced off the land. AAA regulations to the contrary, as farmers reduced the number of acres under cultivation they often reduced the number of tenants as well, a move that was illegal under the contracts but apparently widely practiced. The extent of AAA-related displacement is difficult to measure, because it accelerated a trend, already under way, of conversion from a year-round tenant system to the use of migrant and day labor, but almost all serious studies found the rate of displacement to be substantial.[28] Nor should it have come as a surprise. As two observers noted in the first volume of *Rural Sociology*, "There are few people gullible enough to believe that the acreage devoted to cotton can be reduced by one-third without an accompanying decrease in the laborers engaged in its production."[29]

The displacement had a multiplier effect because many of the displaced sharecroppers remained nearby, enlarging the pool of available agricultural day labor and thus making conversion to such casual labor increasingly feasible. By raising cotton prices the AAA provided landlords with another incentive for such conversion because paying low wages in cash became cheaper than paying in shares of an increasingly valuable crop. And day labor had no rights to a share of benefit or parity payments under the AAA contracts, so landlords had yet another incentive to make the transition.[30] Within the AAA, reports that activities under the acreage reduction program were seriously penalizing tenants and further enhancing the power of their landlords aggravated the tensions between the reformers and the more traditional agrarians. The Legal Division under Frank's leadership had been arguing for some time for a stronger interpretation of a vaguely worded protective clause in the cotton contracts; interpretation would have required landlords to show cause for any evictions, in effect to retain the same tenants unless they could prove that a dismissed tenant was a "nuisance or a menace."[31] The Cotton Section and other conservative elements resisted the idea, fearing that this interpretation would deter cotton planters from participating in the program.[32]

In January, the Southern Tenant Farmers Union that had formed largely in response to landlord abuses under the AAA and that had done much to publicize the plight of the sharecroppers sent a delegation to Washington to plead for help. When efforts to persuade AAA Administrator Chester Davis and Secretary Wallace to take action to protect the tenants failed, the Legal Division asserted its prerogative of final say in matters of contract interpretation. Early in February, while Davis was out of town, a formal legal opinion on the meaning of the protective clause was issued, and Frank wired state AAA offices that landlords were to be required to retain their tenants. "The explosion in the South was immediate," Sidney Baldwin reports in his study of the Farm Security Administration, "and from the Middle West Davis hurried back to Washington with an ultimatum for Wallace—the liberals had been conspiring against him and would have to go." [33] Wallace reluctantly acquiesced, and Frank, Pressman, Shea, Howe, and Jackson were fired. Hiss, who had authored most of the controversial opinion, was inexplicably omitted from Davis's hit list but resigned in protest. The fact that the firings extended beyond the Legal Division to include the Office of the Consumers' Counsel lends credence to the argument that Davis's action was not so much a response to the offending interpretation as to the entire social reform perspective. "Liberals," according to Leuchtenburg, "viewed the 'purge' of the Frank faction as the end of an era, the triumph of the planters and processors over the advocates of a 'social outlook on agricultural policy.' " [34]

Frank continued as counsel for the FSRC, and Pressman joined Hopkins's staff, continuing to handle matters relating to the corporation, but relief-minded urban liberals no longer had a stronghold within the AAA. Tensions between the parents of the FSRC continued. The relief agency had long been critical of the impact of AAA programs on impoverished croppers and tenants, many of whom turned to relief for survival after being displaced, but the purge escalated this tension to a more personal level. Hopkins's invitation to Pressman was interpreted, by Pressman at least, as a slap in the face to Wallace: "the entire New Deal was extremely angry at Wallace's action," he wrote to Frank's widow years later. "This is proven in that it was Harry Hopkins who, up until that point, had operated without an attorney, but when the issue arose he brought me in as General Counsel of the F.E.R.A." [35] Other accounts also recall that the incident engendered acrimony among the New Dealers.

The tensions among the members of its board of directors may explain the absence of any discussions of the FSRC's future in the minutes of the spring meetings of the board. Hopkins and Ickes were in conflict over the form—and the control—of the new federal relief program. Wallace and Ickes were fighting over a proposal by Ickes to move the Forestry Service from the Agriculture Department to the Department of the Interior and rename the latter the Department of Conservation. And both Hopkins and Ickes were furious at Wallace over the AAA purge. For whatever reason, no record of such discussion exists either in the FSRC minutes or in the meeting of the National Emergency Council in which all three participated. [36]

Meanwhile, the drought-induced curtailment of the huge nationwide surpluses that engendered the FSRC had resulted in a shift in emphasis to purchases of local and regional market gluts by state and local relief agencies using FSRC purchase authorities. In July, the FERA Monthly Report noted that "the procurement division of the Federal Surplus Relief

Corporation has done no purchasing whatsoever for several months." [37] During the spring months, differences also erupted between the FSRC Director of Procurement, on loan to the corporation from the Navy, who was required to use Navy supply procedures, and the USDA technicians designated by the secretary to advise the procurement officer with regard to specific commodities. As a result of these differences, the Department of Agriculture established its own Procurement Division, which operated independently of the FSRC. According to USDA policy formulated late in the spring, the Procurement Division would purchase all surplus commodities to be paid for by USDA funds and then donate them to the FSRC for distribution.

The failure to specify plans for the corporation's future, especially in the context of such internal and external changes, began to evoke questions from state and local personnel; letters inquiring what to expect began to arrive, but little information was available. "I don't know that there is any information I can give you," Baker wrote the administrator of the Michigan Emergency Welfare Relief Commission at the beginning of June. "The Agriculture Department wants to have us distribute a lot of commodities—but they may not want us to very badly. I don't think Mr. Hopkins will want to use much Relief money for the purpose," he continued, "and I don't know whether Agriculture will be willing to furnish money for it." He concluded with a vague prediction, hedging his bets: "I should say that the chances are not great that Commodity Distribution will be as important as it has been. At the same time, I would be very hesitant to say that we won't distribute any. I'm sure this helps you a lot." [38]

As the uncertainty persisted, it began to disable the corporation. Early in July, the corporation's distribution chief, William Nunn, wrote to Jacob Baker:

The creation of the Works Progress Administration and announcements of the forthcoming liquidation of the relief administration without any reference to the purchase and distribution of surplus commodities has (a) not been consistent with plans being carried out by the Department of Agriculture, and (b) has tended to break the morale of state commodity distribution divisions as indicated by conflicting plans, including a premature attempt to eliminate work projects for conservation of local food surpluses, a frantic searching for jobs by state directors of commodity distribution and their staffs in Work Progress Administrations and other Government agencies, and a noticeable reluctance on the part of relief administrations to accept further allocations as made by the Distribution Division of the Federal Surplus Relief Corporation, of surplus commodities now being purchased by the Department of Agriculture.[39]

Nunn included a proposed reorganization plan that specified that the secretary of agriculture should become president of the corporation and the executive officer should be someone from the Emergency Relief Administration. He suggested that the state directors of Commodity Distribution and their staffs be attached to the Washington office of the Distribution Division and operate state systems of distribution on the basis of WPA projects. The memorandum was not entirely clear about financing but implied that the costs of distribution would be largely born by WPA funds while both agricultural and relief funds would be used to purchase surplus commodities. In addition, Nunn anticipated that amendments then under consideration in Congress would enable the corporation to engage in buying and selling in the open market in order to stabilize market conditions and that these latter functions would "place the Corporation much more closely with the Department of Agriculture than with the Relief Administration." Nunn urged that the plan be regarded as "a basis for some real thinking as to the future of this Corporation."[40]

A week after Nunn circulated his memo, Jacob Baker in his role as assistant to the president of the FSRC finally called a conference of major FSRC operating staff "for the purpose of transmitting to these men the information he had as to the future of the Federal Surplus Relief Corporation and to find out from them the present status of work in each of their departments." The digest of this conference notes that Baker "stressed the following points:

1. Distribution to be arranged by October 15, 1935 so we'll give no more after direct relief is cut off
2. The necessity of finding a method of distribution after that time so that it does not appear as Federal Relief
3. The necessity of arranging at once for a statistical differentiation between those getting commodities only and direct relief cases.[41]

Baker urged the transfer of distribution operations to state programs as soon as possible and indicated that transportation would be funded by grants to the states for that purpose. He indicated that the two Navy officers in charge of Procurement and Disbursements were to continue until written orders to the contrary. Finally, Baker asked the staff to inform him if they had any ideas "about maximum distribution and effective distribution with a minimum of responsibility to the Federal Government." [42] As late as mid July then, no clear plan for continuing commodity distribution beyond the final FERA grants to the states existed, although the desirability of doing so was affirmed. The major concern of the relief establishment seems to have been avoiding the appearance of ongoing direct federal relief. The Department of Agriculture still wanted to keep the "relief outlet" open and wanted to accomplish its own procurement if farm funds were used, but the department made no offer to provide funds for the procurement of crops other than the basic items.

Up on Capitol Hill however, events were transpiring that would resolve the issue of financing a continuation of surplus commodity distribution and would shape domestic food assistance for decades. House Agriculture Committee Chairman Marvin Jones introduced an amendment to the Agricultural Adjustment Act that embodied a novel approach to the farm surplus. The surplus, Jones believed, was "the heart of the farm price problem." [43] And the problems of the producers of surpluses were aggravated because they received no benefit from the tariff but had to pay for it on the items they bought. He proposed, therefore, that a certain proportion of tariff receipts be reserved to finance surplus disposal. He suggested a figure of 30 percent because, he later explained, "there were about 30 per cent of the American people who at that time lived on farms or were primarily interested in farming." [44]

The House Agriculture Committee had spent much of the spring working on a bill containing a wide range of amendments to the Agricultural Adjustment Act, most of which had to do with the secretary's powers to issue licenses and to enter marketing agreements with groups of producers. The most controversial feature of the bill concerned the right of persons and firms to sue the government for the return of illegally collected processing taxes. Consideration of the bill had been stormy, with farm organizations demanding measures to strengthen the original act and processors attacking it, especially the processing tax. Deep divisions within the committee had surfaced over the licensing provisions, and the Supreme Court decision in May that had invalidated the National Industrial Recovery Act raised further questions about the validity of the processing tax. [45] Jones proposed the novel approach to the surplus problem to his tired committee, which voted unanimously to report the amendment out as part of the larger package. [46]

Jones's later recollections may have simplified events, but one can imagine that the plan had immediate appeal to the House Agriculture Committee, many of whose members, like Jones, had served in Congress through the McNary-Haugen years. The FSRC operations had demonstrated that surplus purchases could indeed support prices and that distribution of such purchases could be readily accomplished. The special genius of the idea, however, was in obtaining the money to finance such purchase and distribution from the tariff collections. The National Agricultural Conference and a number of farm leaders in their individual testimony before the committee had advocated raising funds for such surplus diversion operations by authorizing the levying of processing taxes without rental or benefit payments.[47] The customs receipts idea, however, would achieve the same end without the complexities or political liabilities of the processing tax. More important, perhaps, farm representatives perceived it as much-delayed justice, a long overdue compensation for years of hardship imposed by the tariff protecting industrial goods. The idea must have been doubly appealing to those who had first defended the McNary-Haugen equalization fee and then the processing tax by comparing them to the tariff, only to be told that the same arguments did not apply. Although Jones explained his idea to the committee in full, he did not notify the Department of Agriculture nor anyone else in the administration. When Secretary Wallace testified before the House Rules Committee in late May in support of the package of Triple A amendments, he appeared surprised by the proviso. "He struck oil and didn't know it," Jones commented.[48] Jones recalled that he encountered no opposition to the measure on the House floor, and the House passed the bill containing what would become Section 32 of Public Law 320 in July. The Senate, however, rejected the proviso; "I think largely because no one explained it," Jones wrote in his memoirs.[49] This rejection left the fate of Section 32 to be resolved by a conference committee.

Meanwhile, with the possibility of additional funding for surplus disposal in the offing and the approach of the date for the final grants to the states growing near, the relief and agricultural agencies finally began to make definite plans for the surplus relief corporation. Unfortunately, the FSRC's records for this period are incomplete. A letter in the USDA solicitor's file reveals that late in July, before the House and Senate conferees met to consider their disagreements, the AAA had inquired as to the legality of a name change. "It now appears that it will be necessary for the Agricultural Adjustment Administration to take a more prominent part in the affairs of the Federal Surplus Relief Corporation," wrote Jesse Tapp, director of the AAA Division of Licenses and Marketing Agreements, to Solicitor Thomas. "In this connection, it would be desirable in many respects to have the name of the corporation changed to the Federal

Surplus Commodity Corporation or the Federal Surplus Farm Products Corporation, or some similar name in order to minimize the relief aspect of the Corporation's activities." Tapp asked Thomas to advise him as to whether such a name change would be legal and how it might be effected.[50]

Henry Wallace's papers contain a handwritten, undated note from Harry Hopkins that probably embodies the final decision to transfer the corporation to agricultural control. While the absence of a date precludes precisely fixing the decision in relationship to the Section 32 legislation and other events, the note does suggest something of the informality with which the choice was made:

> Henry:—
> I feel like the devil & want to go home after this conference.
> We believe Surplus Relief Corp should be managed & operated by your department & change name to Surplus Commodity Corp. Can we have meeting as Wednesday.
> Harry[51]

Henry Wallace's recollections of the change confirm that the decision was Hopkins's and suggest a similar informality. Asked about the corporation, Wallace replied: "That was really under Harry Hopkins in the first instance. For a while he ran it, and eventually he kicked it over to us—but for quite a while it was more his baby than it was ours."[52]

On August 6, a few days after the Senate and House conferees had restored Jones's customs receipts provision to the AAA amendments, Triple A Administrator Chester Davis sent Federal Emergency Relief Administrator Harry Hopkins a letter and a "Memorandum of Understanding Regarding the Purchase and Distribution of Surplus Agricultural Commodities." The letter noted the approval of Section 32 by the House and Senate conferees and emphasized the "increasingly apparent" desirability of maintaining outlets for surplus commodities. Davis indicated his belief that "the problem can be handled in such a way as to avoid any conflict between your program for eliminating Federal direct relief and the necessity which we face of finding proper domestic or foreign outlets for surplus farm commodities."[53] The accompanying memorandum proposed changes in the name of the corporation, its operating divisions, its officers and in the composition of its membership and its board of directors, which would bring the agency under USDA control. It also specified the continuation of the over and above policy and the restriction of recipients to those in the care of relief agencies. It stated that "the Works Progress

Administration agrees to cooperate as far as practical by approving properly prepared work projects for the orderly liquidation of existing inventories, and for the distribution of such additional purchases as are made." [54] The letter and memorandum were transmitted by Undersecretary Rex Tugwell who indicated that the Resettlement Administration was "vitally interested" in distribution of surplus commodities to the farm families under its care and that as administrator he would like his name added to the revised board of the corporation. Both Davis and Tugwell's letters mention Hopkins's discussions of the future of the corporation with President Roosevelt, and Tugwell suggested that Hopkins should review the attached plan and "determine whether or not this meets with the President's wishes." [55] Apparently it did because the plan outlined by Davis was basically the one adopted.

In one of those quirks of fate that have characterized the history of food assistance, Marvin Jones settled any remaining doubt about the financing of commodity distribution. A last minute trade between Jones and Alabama Senator John Bankhead converted the Section 32 authorization into a highly unusual permanent appropriation, the first in American history. The process by which the provision was transformed into a permanent fund of "farmers' money" was recalled in 1968 by Jones in a speech commemorating the thirty-fifth anniversary of the signing of the original Agricultural Adjustment Act. Because Section 32 has had such far-reaching implications for food assistance, and because Jones's recollections provide such a fascinating example of the American policy-making process, the relevant section of his address is presented here at some length:

> I pencilled out Section 32 at my desk and included it in a legislative bill with many other provisions. Then we had to go to conference with the Senate, where Senator John Bankhead headed up the Senate conferees. He was primarily interested in extending a bill that I didn't like much anyway.
>
> Well, we came to my Section 32 provision, and John said to let it go over—it was a controversial thing—and for us to take up his act. I said I didn't think I wanted to do that. I wasn't too sure I was for an extension of his act. I said let's take up Section 32 first.
>
> John looked at me and said "you don't have any compromise in your make-up—you want everything just like you want it!"
>
> So I said, "I will make you a proposition. If you let me write Section 32 like I want it, and agree to that, then I'll agree to extend your Bankhead provision when we get to it."
>
> And he got up and walked back and forth by the table and pulled his

hair. I said "What is the matter, John? Don't you have any compromise in your makeup?"

And he wheeled around and said, "All right, I'll agree to that."

So I sat down there and I struck out "there shall be authorized to be appropriated" and wrote "there is hereby appropriated," and I made it a permanent piece of law.[56]

Jones explained that he returned to the House with the conference report and was granted the waiver of all points of order. After the bill was passed, Treasury Secretary Henry Morgenthau "discovered it, and he hit the ceiling." Morgenthau threatened to ask the president to veto the bill, but Jones pointed out that "he couldn't veto Section 32 without vetoing the whole bill—and we had more things in there that the President wanted than anybody would dream about."[57]

Subsequently, the president recommended its repeal in a budget message, and Jones went to see him. His explanation of the reasoning behind the provision reflects the ideology that would govern the expenditure of Section 32 funds.

> I told the President that Hamilton said the tariff would not benefit the farmer and there should be a bonus, either paid on the exportation or on his production at home, to bring things into balance.
>
> I said, "Mr. President, now I don't believe in the philosophy of Alexander Hamilton, but he was intellectually honest. And it was his report that gave me this idea."
>
> President Roosevelt said, "That is not a bad idea, is it?" I said "No, it is a good idea."
>
> And he became as enthusiastic as anybody else—and then the critics didn't have a chance. They were never able to touch it.
>
> Anyway, I'm a little proud of getting the Section 32 provision for agriculture. And from all reports, it has served its purpose wonderfully.[58]

With Section 32 on the books, the AAA was given both a new incentive and a means to keep the "relief outlet" open. The provision authorized the secretary of agriculture to use the special fund to "(1) encourage the exportation of agricultural commodities . . . (2) encourage the domestic consumption of such commodities or products by diverting them . . . from the normal channels of trade and commerce; and (3) finance adjustments in the quantity planted or produced for market of agricultural commodities."[59] One means by which the secretary could implement clause two of this legislation was by purchasing agricultural commodities and distributing them to people who would not otherwise be able to purchase and consume them. Thus, Section 32 both guaranteed that substantial funding would be available for commodity distribution programs in the Department of Agriculture and ensured that any such programs funded from Section 32 revenues would have to be justified in terms of their benefits to producers. The provision linked commodity distribution historically to McNary-Haugenism and the fight for equality for agriculture, and it reinforced the pre-eminence of producers in the department to which the FSRC was being transferred.

No evidence exists of any dissent to the decision to transfer direction of the corporation to USDA. The press, without much comment, reported the change when it occurred, and the FSRC files contain no letters or memoranda suggesting changes in the plan. Once again, the needs of agency decision makers meshed conveniently to produce a solution that appeared inevitable. The FERA needed to rid itself of commodity distribution so as to terminate all federal direct relief with the final emergency relief grants to the states. The AAA needed to maintain the outlet for agricultural surpluses that the corporation had provided in order to continue price supporting purchases and avoid the embarrassment of rotting crops or physical destruction of surpluses. The Department of Agriculture, not the works program, would be criticized if such waste occurred. Transfer to the Department of Agriculture provided Secretary Wallace with a means to implement the new Section 32 legislation and to counter criticism of crop reduction, and it provided Harry Hopkins and his associates with an escape from the direct relief business without depriving hungry people access to the nation's farm surpluses.

Once the decision was made, the process of transfer was accomplished through changes in the composition of the corporation's membership and its board of directors and through relatively minor amendments to its charter. In a series of meetings between mid September and late November, the corporation was reorganized "to adapt it more closely to the President's announced plan to replace direct Federal relief with work relief." [60] Agriculture officials replaced relief officials in the membership of the corporation, and the board of directors was expanded to seven persons, five of whom were USDA officials with Hopkins and Baker remaining on the board to represent the relief perspective. The new board accepted the resignations of all the corporation's officers and, amending the by-laws to create new offices, filled all but one with Department of Agriculture staff members. AAA Administrator Chester Davis was elected president of the corporation and Jesse Tapp, director of the AAA's Division of Licenses and Marketing Agreements, was selected to fill the newly created office of executive vice-president.[61] In accordance with Hopkins's request that the name of the organization be changed "to something which includes the word 'commodities' so that it is identified in the public mind with our farm program rather than with our relief program, although the commodities themselves . . . will be distributed through local and state relief agencies," the name was changed to the Federal Surplus Commodities Corporation.[62]

Although Hopkins and Baker remained on the board of the FSCC, nominally at least, the general attitude of the relief establishment toward the transfer appears to have been governed by a desire to comply with the president's decision to "quit this business of relief." In September, Wallace wrote to Hopkins raising the issue of the potential distribution of surplus commodities to WPA workers and their families. This issue was important for the future of commodity distribution, not only because the unemployed workers eligible for WPA jobs were much more numerous than the unemployables, but also because the Department of Agriculture believed that unemployables were not concentrated in sufficient numbers to make the maintenance of relief outlets feasible in any but a few large cities. Aubrey Williams answered the letter in Hopkins's absence, indicating that the FERA would neither direct that the WPA workers be made eligible for surplus commodities nor "place any barrier at all" in the way of public and private local and state relief agencies that "may decide to give surplus commodities they may have available to the members of large families, some of whom may be working on Works Progress Administration jobs, or members of large families, some of whom may be working in private industry." Williams's concluding statement is revealing: "Since the President has directed us to get out of relief we wish to withdraw from situations that require statements on policy matters of this sort."[63]

In reality, the WPA eventually made substantial contributions to the maintenance of surplus commodity distribution by operating numerous state and local work projects which handled the actual distribution of the food. By mid 1936, less than a year after the transition, more than two thousand local, district, and state work projects for the distribution of surplus commodities were in operation or had been approved. The total cost to the federal government of these projects was estimated at $19,800,000 for the year, while state and local sponsors had pledged $2,855,000. Because federal commodity purchases during 1936 were severely restricted by drought and other factors, the WPA funds committed actually exceeded the Section 32 funds that were spent.[64]

Nevertheless, the WPA maintained a low profile in regard to surplus commodities. Nowhere in the corporation's annual reports for calendar year 1936 or fiscal year 1937 is the WPA involvement mentioned. The provision of jobs for the able-bodied unemployed did not violate the new relief policy in any way. In some aspects, commodity distribution ideally suited the conditions of the WPA; it was labor intensive, required only limited skills, was appropriately sponsored by local governments, and made a contribution to the health and welfare of the nation. But the fact that the WPA's important participation in the program received no mention in the corporation's public reports suggests a cosmetic element in the hasty departure of relief officials from the FSCC; the break between federal relief and surplus disposal appeared cleaner than it was.

The desire to make a clean break was also apparent in Hopkins's role in an effort to obtain an executive order ratifying the transfer of the corporation. The corporate members thought that such an order might be helpful in averting any difficulties with the comptroller general that might arise when federal funds under Section 32, rather than state funds derived from FERA grants, were used to purchase and process commodities.[65] An order, which Hopkins found satisfactory, was drafted, but he declined to present it to the president because "it is primarily related to the future, rather than the past, of the Corporation."[66] A week later, the corporation's members wrote to the president requesting a formal executive order, but the letter was misplaced. Consequently, the meeting at which the changes were formalized was held without the president's written approval because, as the USDA solicitor later explained in his attempt to obtain a retroactive order, Ickes and Hopkins were "anxious to be relieved of their duties."[67] Hopkins in fact, attended none of the November meetings of the corporate members or of the board of directors at which the amendments to the certificates of incorporation were ratified and the personnel changes were completed.

Sociologist Robert McIver's question, cited at the close of Chapter 9, concerning control of the new institutions seems to have been answered without a contest in the case of the Federal Surplus Commodities Corporation. The organization would be controlled by the Agriculture Department and adapted to its purposes. The relief establishment had realized that continuing a visible role in the surplus commodity program would undermine its effort to shift responsibility for relief to the states and localities. And the AAA had realized that it must have some outlet for the visible surpluses to which its marketing agreement programs gave rise in order to avoid public criticism of wanton waste.

The Agriculture Department's interest in maintaining the relief outlet is clear enough, but the relief administration's determination to shed the program is more problematic. Clearly, the decision involved more than a mere cosmetic change. As the 1935 *Annual Report* of the corporation stated, "the controlling factor in the determination of policies became the removal of agricultural surpluses and the encouragement of domestic consumption rather than providing for the needs of the unemployed."[68] This emphasis proved to have far-reaching consequences. In both the short and the long run, as we shall see in the remaining chapters, agricultural hegemony meant a severe limitation of the program's ability to meet the needs of poor people. The relief administration's decision to turn the corporation over to the sole custody of its agricultural parent appears to have been a significant disservice to the poor; it requires some explanation.

Was the demotion of food assistance from an end to a means an unavoidable byproduct of the congressionally mandated termination of the FERA? The history detailed above suggests that the assumptions underlying the new relief policy rather than the termination of the FERA administrative structure determined the fate of the FSRC. The FERA, in fact, remained extant as a legal entity until 1938 in order to fulfill commitments and discharge obligations made during its active period; it could probably have continued to participate in food assistance on the same basis had such participation not contradicted the administration's position on relief. Furthermore, it was the public rationale supporting the new policy of work for the able bodied and state and local responsibility for the unemployables, rather than the policy itself, that would have been eroded by continued federal food assistance.

The notion of ideology is useful in explaining the connection between the new relief arrangements and the transfer of surplus commodity distribution to USDA. An ideology may be defined as a set of beliefs that explains or justifies an institution or policy; it contains beliefs that cannot be demonstrated to be true. The federal withdrawal from direct relief drew upon an ideology for support; Hopkins's assertion that needs arising from causes other than unemployment had an "obvious local character" exemplifies this ideology.

Visible continued federal participation in food assistance as a relief measure would have violated two tenets of the relief ideology that gained ascendancy in 1935. First, if federal food relief were given to unemployables, the administration's contention that these people were solely a state and local responsibility would be vitiated. This element of the ideology was, of course, not new in 1935. It was at least as old as the Elizabethan poor law and had prevailed in the U.S. until municipal bankruptcy, widespread suffering, and growing disorder had prompted federal provision for relief in 1933. The effort to reestablish the traditional pattern after two and a half years of federal general relief, however, required an extensive re-articulation of the ideology. "Local responsibility can and will be resumed, for after all, common sense tells us that the wealth necessary for this task existed and still exists in the local community and the dictates of sound administration require that this responsibility be in the first instance a local one," Roosevelt told Congress when he announced the new relief scheme.[69] For the federal government to continue to distribute groceries as a relief activity appeared inconsistent both with the contention that the localities had the resources to do the job and with the assertion that it was their responsibility to do so. Their distribution as a by-product of agricultural surplus removal, however, was simple American thrift: waste not, want not.

At the practical level, the Roosevelt administration anticipated significant resistance by state and local governments to assuming the care of the unemployables, and it wished to avoid doing anything that would suggest to them that the federal government would continue to relieve them of what it perceived to be their responsibility. Roosevelt felt strongly about this issue, as Treasury Secretary Morgenthau discovered in the summer of 1935 when he reported to the president that Georgia was the only state to have returned its unemployables to local care. Morgenthau recorded in his diary that Roosevelt went "into a long harangue . . . how for years there had been ten families in Hyde Park, that the town had always taken care of them but now the federal government is taking care of them and that there is no reason why these ten families should not be thrown back on the town and that there must be thousands of communities who have similar situations and who could take care of their chronic unemployables."[70]

Would a continuation of federal surplus commodity relief have undermined the effort to turn the responsibility and the cost of relief for unemployables over to the lower levels of government? After all, social security grants were perceived as aiding, not hindering, this change. Almost no record of discussion of this matter exists in the FERA or FSRC files, other than Baker's brief comment to his staff about the necessity of finding a means to continue distribution after the cessation of grants to the states "so that it does not appear as Federal Relief." However, an account from several years later suggests that relief officials felt strongly that commodity distribution under relief auspices would deter state provision. In 1938, during a relief emergency in which local funds were exhausted in several midwestern cities, Secretary Morgenthau proposed transferring some WPA funds to direct relief and expanding the distribution of surplus commodities. Hopkins opposed the transfer of WPA funds on the grounds that the federal government should do nothing that might keep the states involved from appropriating their own funds to meet the crisis. Two weeks later at a meeting with the president, Hopkins's deputy Aubrey Williams opposed expanded surplus commodity distribution, according to the minutes recorded in Morgenthau's diary, on the grounds that "the State and local governments would throw the whole problem of relief of unemployables back into the lap of the federal government." Morgenthau recorded that Williams felt strongly that any such move "would bring about very undesirable repercussions similar to those which he said occurred a few years back before the works program was initiated." [71] If relief officials in 1938 were concerned that surplus commodity distribution might be interpreted as federal resumption of direct relief sufficient to deter states from appropriating money, presumably they would have taken a similar view in 1935.

Under closer scrutiny, however, the practical arguments do not hold up. After all, the federal government did continue shipping surplus foods to state and local relief agencies. If the availability of this food were going to deter local provision, it would probably do so regardless of the name of the shipping agency. The focus on changing the agency's name and on the public perception of commodity distribution—"so that it does not appear as federal relief," "so that it is identified in the public mind with our farm program rather than our relief program," and "in order to minimize the relief aspect of the Corporation's activities" suggest that ideological rather than practical considerations were paramount in the relief agency's desire to rid itself of the corporation. Relief officials were anxious to appear consistent with the rationale justifying federal withdrawal from direct relief.

In regard to food assistance for employables, the various AAA memos quoted above indicate that the Roosevelt administration was aware that the proposed WPA security wage rates would not be sufficient to permit larger families dependent upon a single WPA worker to obtain an adequate diet. Federal food assistance to WPA employees would not have violated the administration's efforts to return responsibility for unemployables to the lower levels of government. It would, however, have contradicted the effort to make WPA jobs as much like private employment as possible and undermined the myth that the federal government was providing work, not relief, for the unemployed. As Aubrey Williams wrote to Henry Wallace:

we do not feel we are justified in directing that Works Progress Administration workers as such shall receive any relief benefits. It is intended that they shall be in the situation of workers on jobs and that the Government's responsibility to them shall be discharged in its payment to them of security wages.[72]

Again the emphasis was on the appearance of consistency. In reality, Williams left the way clear for, and in fact gave subtle support to, the distribution of surplus commodities to large families dependent upon WPA by comparing it to the distribution of commodities to large families dependent upon private employment. Again the agricultural aspect provided a convenient resolution. Williams suggested that the FSCC work with local agencies to develop arrangements "to meet the requirements of the Agricultural Adjustment Administration."[73] Who could object if local agencies decided to permit WPA families to supplement their hard-earned diets with commodities removed from the market to assist troubled farmers?

A third element of relief ideology that was probably important in the transfer was by no means new in 1935. It was the perception, widely shared by professional social workers, that relief in kind constituted the most degrading, least desirable form of relief. Surplus commodity distribution had been subjected to especially harsh criticism, as we have seen, because it occasioned the extension of commissaries in some localities, and because, even where local retailers handled the goods, the privacy of clients was violated. Josephine Brown, for example, characterized surplus commodities as not only "relief in kind, but 'package' or 'basket' relief . . . of the most demoralizing and stigmatizing type."[74] For the most part, social workers did not actively resist the surplus commodities, but neither did they treat federal food assistance as an opportunity to expand public provision for those in need by capitalizing on widely held values surrounding food and waste, as poor people and their advocates have done with great success in recent decades. C. M. Bookman, addressing the National Conference of Social Work in 1934, expressed an ambivalence that was probably characteristic of concerned relief professionals:

> At the very time the FERA was recommending cash relief instead of relief in kind, it found itself sponsoring the largest program of relief in kind ever undertaken in this nation. This program was contrary to approved practices, but under conditions then existing it appeared to be a wise procedure. However, the more or less indiscriminate distribution of surplus products undoubtedly had a demoralizing influence upon many of those receiving them, and should cause us to take careful

thought before again making any wholesale distribution of surplus products as a relief measure.[75]

It is not surprising that social workers within the FERA or through their professional organizations did not object to the transfer of commodity distribution to USDA.

The suggestion that the social workers' dislike for relief in kind was part of an ideology is not intended to disparage the concern for the freedom and dignity of clients that accompanied this point of view. The problem was not the concern for clients but rather the way in which this concern was mystified by the prestige of cash. Receipt of benefits in kind is stigmatizing and demoralizing only if it is socially defined that way; no evidence exists that the members of cooperative associations of the unemployed who received their returns in kind experienced them as degrading. Furthermore, the relief grants made available to families on relief were so low that they permitted the exercise of very little real choice. The addition of surplus commodities served to increase the recipient's choices by supplying a portion of the required nourishment. The development of home delivery systems protected both the convenience and privacy of clients. And what little record exists of clients' reactions to the surplus commodities suggests that they welcomed the commodities in much the spirit in which they were offered. Clients undoubtedly preferred relief in cash, but they do not seem to have regarded the surplus foods as incompatible with that preference.[76] So long as the narrow view of food assistance was a professional convention, it was relatively harmless. If, however, it contributed to the failure of social workers and relief advocates to take an interest in the fate of the FSRC or to the hasty departure of relief officials form the corporation and their hands-off attitude after its transfer, then the cash ideology may be seen as an element in the process that freed the corporation for a complete takeover by agricultural interests.

CHAPTER ELEVEN

Accommodation to Agricultural Priorities

The immediate impact of the shift to Section 32 funding and USDA direction was an almost complete cessation of the flow of commodities. According to the "Memorandum of Understanding" worked out between Davis and Hopkins, the Commodities Purchase Section of the AAA was to absorb the Procurement Division of the corporation once the transfer was complete. In any case, the Commodities Purchase Section had been making all purchases involving USDA funds for several months because of differences over procedure between the AAA staff and the Naval supply officer who headed the Procurement Division. Accordingly, early in October, the chief of the Commodities Purchase Section requested an opinion from the Department of Agriculture's solicitor as to the authority of the secretary under Section 32 to purchase such agricultural commodities as cabbages and potatoes and donate them for relief. The solicitor ruled that "there can be no question that the purchase of agricultural commodities and their donation for relief purposes constitutes a diversion of such commodities from the normal channels of trade and commerce within the meaning of Section 32." He approved the proposed means of purchase and indicated that he had no legal objection to the plan as submitted by the section chief. He concluded, however, with a recommendation that proved fateful for commodity distribution: "since the question is one which involves the expenditure of public moneys, I believe it would be advisable to submit the proposal to the Comptroller General for his decision upon the availability of funds under Section 32 for the purposes specified." [1] In due course, the secretary of agriculture submitted the proposed plan to the comptroller general, and the comptroller general promptly rejected the proposal on the grounds that even though growers might benefit from such activities, they were primarily relief activities for which funds were available under the Emergency Relief Appropriation Act of 1935. Furthermore, he ruled, the purchase and donation of fruits and vegetables would constitute not a diversion from the normal channels but an increase in the flow through the normal channels.[2]

The Department of Agriculture pointed out that distribution for relief was specifically mentioned in the committee report accompanying the bill,[3] but the comptroller held firm, temporarily halting plans to finance commodity distribution with Section 32 monies. The Department of Agriculture requested and obtained supplemental legislation specifying that in implementing Clause 2 of Section 32, the secretary of agriculture might make purchases of agricultural commodities without regard to Section 3709, a law specifying low bid procedures to be used for government purchases. The legislation also stated clearly that Section 32 funds might be used for purchases for donation to the FSCC.[4] This clarifying legislation was not obtained until mid February 1936, however, delaying the availability of Section 32 funds for nearly four months.[5]

Fortunately, the FSCC was not wholly dependent upon Section 32 funding to carry on its activities. It had inherited an inventory of canned beef and cowhides, and supplies of several basic commodities purchased with processing tax revenues. In addition, responding to a request from distribution director William Nunn, the AAA donated to the corporation stocks of grain that had accumulated from a seed conservation program during the drought of 1934. Some commodities continued to reach needy families during the conflict with the comptroller general, but as the corporation's acting director of procurement wrote to an inquiring senator in January 1936, since "funds under Section 32 are not now available, our program of necessity has been considerably restricted and the purchases accordingly limited."[6]

Conflict between the comptroller general and the FSCC was not limited to the use of Section 32 funds. The comptroller required evidence of the president's formal authorization of the corporation's name change. Pending an executive order or other formal authorization, he refused to audit the accounts of the FSRC, establish an accounting system for the new corporation, designate a symbol under which the FSCC might make contracts (thus depriving the agency of the possibility of auditing through the General Accounting Office), or provide the corporation's procurement officer with information about freight rates, which was essential if the FSCC was to comply with General Accounting Office procedures governing shipping.[7] The comptroller's unwillingness to recognize the FSCC greatly hampered its activities in its early months.

The executive order that the comptroller general required had been drafted, as noted above, to prevent just such objections. After Hopkins declined to present it to Roosevelt and the letter from the three corporate members was misplaced, the order was apparently submitted through AAA channels as Hopkins had suggested. As with all executive orders, it was submitted to the attorney general who reviewed it and in turn submitted it to the budget director for approval. The budget director objected to language stating that the FSRC had been organized originally "under direction of the President." He noted that no executive order directed the organization of the corporation. The budget director conceded that the FSRC had been mentioned in another executive order and that Congress had authorized the secretary of agriculture to make advances to the FSRC, so he indicated that the lack of an original executive order was not crucial. He further objected to basing the proposed new executive order upon the Emergency Relief Appropriation Act of 1935 since Congress, in considering the act, had removed language authorizing the president to create corporate entities to implement it and had stated instead, that the chief executive must use agencies "within the government." The budget director doubted whether the FSRC was an agency within the government as defined by the act and therefore had reservations as to the authority of the president to authorize a change in name or other changes in the corporation.[8]

The attorney general in turn returned the executive order to the Department of Agriculture, which drafted a memo arguing that the president did indeed have the authority to direct changes in the charter of the corporation. According to USDA, the president had orally directed the original incorporation, and the corporation was an agency within the government because it had been set up pursuant to acts of Congress.[9] The Justice Department continued to object to the executive order so long as references to the Emergency Relief Appropriation Act of 1935 were included in the corporation's charter. Therefore, in January and February 1936, the FSCC board of directors met to amend the certificates of incorporation to remove the objectionable references. Before the amendments were filed, Congress recognized the FSCC by name, thus rendering the executive order unnecessary.

Unfortunately for people in need, this conclusion to the saga of the executive order did not occur until an entire winter of depression had passed—the winter of transition from direct federal relief to the new system of federally sponsored public works, social security, and state and local care of unemployables. "The period of transition, after the liquidation of the FERA at the end of 1935," Josephine Brown has written,

> stands out as a time of confusion and near chaos in the history of public relief. It was a time of uncertainty, insecurity and even terror for the relief client who could not get a work relief job and who had no sure niche in the developing categorical programs. Suffering was acute in too many sections of the country. Funds for general relief were inadequate or entirely lacking in state after state.[10]

Although the FERA collected information and made plans to make final grants to the states large enough to tide them over the winter months, a substantial grant to the Resettlement Administration for the care of needy farm families and the greater-than-expected costs associated with the works program sharply reduced the funds available for the final grants. They were considerably smaller than had been anticipated, and many states were unprepared to take up the slack. A filibuster by Louisiana Senator Huey Long prevented Congress from appropriating money for the promised federal matching funds under the categorical assistance programs of the Social Security Act before the adjournment of Congress, so these funds did not become available until February 1936. Relief agencies dealt with the shortage of funds in the only ways they knew. "The average benefits per family showed a marked decrease," Brown reports, "and hundreds of thousands of applications for relief were refused because of lack of funds to provide even minimum food allowances."[11] In this context, a steady flow of commodities might have made a crucial difference to many poor families, had the intransigence of the comptroller general and the niceties of the law not tied the corporation's hands.

The hardships created by lack of funds were compounded by legislative and administrative confusion. In most states, participation in the new relief scheme required new legislation. All the states except Virginia convened their legislatures in 1935, and most passed some form of welfare legislation in hopes of taking advantage of the social security legislation. Much of the legislation was hastily drafted, and some of it was unworkable. In seventeen states and the District of Columbia, the termination of FERA found a Department of Public Welfare ready to assume at least part of the responsibility of the State Emergency Relief Administration. In another fourteen, the SERA continued for a time using state funds, and in some, the agency was later dissolved and responsibility for general relief was left entirely to the local units. In others, the SERA continued until it was integrated with a newly created state social security agency or an existing public welfare department. In the remaining seventeen states, the SERA was promptly liquidated, and no state agency was established with responsibility for general relief.[12]

In many states, these arrangements left the FSCC without state-level outlets for commodities. Even where state departments of public welfare existed or were created, they often lacked the authority to receive and distribute surplus foods. The FSCC found it necessary to make arrangements with a large number and variety of state and local, public and private relief agencies in order to establish adequate outlets for its commodities. Many of these local agencies developed WPA projects for the actual distribution of the surplus foods; some 2,095 individual WPA food distribution projects were in operation in 1936.[13] Two years passed before the corporation could report that state relief agencies in all states had "secured sufficient authority to carry on commodity distribution as an integral part of their relief activities."[14]

Although some of the hardship that characterized the winter of 1935–1936 originated from problems of state adjustment to federal withdrawal from direct relief, much of it was integral to the new relief structure and was not as easily remedied as a state's failure to provide authority for its welfare department to distribute surplus food. The new relief structure assumed that states would establish general relief programs to provide for persons in need who were not eligible for such categorical programs as Aid to Dependent Children (ADC), but it did not require them to do so or establish any standards governing such programs. State coverage of general relief needs was haphazard and inadequate throughout the Depression and subsequent decades. A statement by social worker C. M. Bookman to the 1940 session of the National Conference of Social Work summarized the shortcomings of general relief five years after the termination of federal direct relief:

> General relief . . . has been so inadequate that there is today a widespread condition that has been aptly described as "slow starvation." It has weakened the resistance of thousands of men, women, and children; has contributed to the development of physical deficiencies, illness, and defects; has broken human morale and, to a very serious extent, destroyed employability. . . . The present reliance on the state

and local community to finance general relief is unsound, inhuman, and disastrous.[15]

Numerous studies of relief conditions conducted by the American Association of Social Workers and its state and local affiliates, by the WPA, and by various magazines and civic and charitable groups in the years after the liquidation of the FERA found that even those families who received general relief were frequently in dire need. In many states, actual relief grants represented only a portion, often half or less, of the amounts that had been budgeted as necessary for minimum basic needs. In Denver, where most relief grants fell to 40 percent of the prescribed standards in June 1937 and remained at that low level through 1940, a study by the Dietetics Department of the School of Medicine at the University of Colorado revealed that the diets of relief families were severely deficient in most of the ingredients essential to health. The diets studied provided 51 percent of the needed calories, 30 to 40 percent of the necessary protein and iron, 20 to 30 percent of the calcium and vitamin A requirements, 10 to 20 percent of the standard for vitamins B and G, and only 5 and 6 percent, respectively, of vitamins C and D.[16] The situation in Denver may have been extreme, but reports from many sections of the country compiled by Donald Howard in the early 1940s suggested that the diets of families dependent upon general relief were insufficient to preserve health and were in dire need of supplementation. Even where relief grants budgeted amounts sufficient to purchase a minimally adequate diet, studies revealed that provisions for other needs such as fuel, clothing, and shelter were so inadequate that the family's food budget often provided these essentials, with consequent damage to nutrition.[17]

Explanations for the inadequacies of general relief are as varied as the political and intellectual perspectives brought to bear on the question. Hoover would probably have said that the moral infrastructure of neighborly assistance and local self reliance had been destroyed by two years of the federal dole. Franklin Roosevelt, sounding much like his predecessor, felt that small communities like his hometown of Hyde Park, New York were shirking their responsibilities in hopes of a free ride from the federal government.[18] Piven and Cloward contend that the parsimony and irregularity of general relief functioned to make low wage work attractive by comparison.[19] One could point to the actual poverty of some localities in which poor people were being taxed to support very poor people or to the inequities of the tax structure itself or to the taxpayers' weariness induced by years of hard times. One could fault the ideology that regarded the poor as thriftless and morally responsible for their destitution. The powerlessness of poor people, the indifference of the comfortable, the inability or unwillingness of social workers and other advocates to articulate forcefully the appalling conditions, and the unresponsiveness of elites calloused by the normalization of suffering were probably all factors. In essence, the entire system of ideology and perceived interests that supports inequality in prosperous times tolerates its extremes during periods of economic dislocation.

Aubrey Williams, the FERA administrator, captured this complexity of factors when he spoke to the National Conference of Social Work in 1934 about public attitudes toward relief:

> As to the attitude of the public toward the poor and toward our programs, I may say quite frankly that one of the most subtle and difficult problems with which the administration has had to deal has been the attitude of the public toward what constitutes adequate relief. This should surprise no one since it is a fact of long standing that the well-to-do and those who have their share and more of the necessities of life are notoriously incurious concerning the conditions of those in need. We cannot escape the painful fact that there is in America today an attitude of mind which is attempting the stratification of standards of living—the erection of one level for workers, another for professional workers, another for executives, and still another for owners and purveyors of capital. And when anyone finds himself without income, he is put outside these classifications and is no longer expected to have normal wants.
>
> The historical attitude toward poverty is still more widely prevalent than is easy to believe. In the last several years the worldly demotion of previously comfortable people has opened the eyes of themselves and their intimates to the fact that poverty is contagious. But there are still responsible public officials and still sizeable portions of the public who hold the opinion that the poor man is individually and morally at fault, and that in the mass poverty is as unpleasant and irremediable as bad weather.[20]

In addition to these attitudinal factors, the matching grant provisions of the Social Security Act probably worked against the provision of adequate general relief by encouraging state legislatures to draw federal funds to the state by allocating available relief funds to the categories designated to receive social security assistance. Similarly, the WPA program gave local governments an inducement to allocate local relief monies for the sponsor's share of WPA projects rather than for general assistance.

Even inadequate general relief, however, was preferable to no relief at all, and no relief, or virtually no relief, was the fate of uncounted but apparently large numbers of employable persons for whom no WPA jobs were created. The federal government's insistence that unemployables were a state and local responsibility led naturally enough to resistance at the lower levels of government to providing any relief at all for employables. Among the employable unemployed unable to obtain WPA assistance were workers whose skills were inappropriate for available WPA slots, workers who were aliens, workers who lost their WPA jobs when WPA appropriations were cut back, and workers who were discharged at the end of eighteen months after Congress imposed an eighteen-month limit on WPA benefits in 1939. They included workers who lived in towns where WPA projects were scarce or not sponsored at all. Some states and localities did provide assistance to such unfortunate people under general relief programs, but many did not.

Since surplus commodities could be provided to families eligible for relief and to those near the relief line as well as those actually receiving assistance, many destitute families whose needs were unmet by the major relief programs came to depend on the federal surplus foods for basic survival. Families with an employable member certified as eligible for WPA for whom no job was available, for example, could be given surplus commodities. Although some statistics on cases receiving "surplus commodities only" were kept, the numbers and conditions of persons in this relief category are hazy and incomplete. In some cases families were assigned to this category because they were perceived by relief officials to require no further assistance, but in many, probably most, cases, families receiving surplus commodities only qualified for additional relief that was simply not available. In a 1940 study in Florida, more than half of the families granted surplus commodities during a two-week period had no income at all, and an additional third had incomes between a dollar and five dollars per week. One careful observer of relief conditions after 1935 described the meaning of the "surplus commodities only" category:

> To many the term "surplus commodities only" frequently encountered in descriptions of social programs in many sections of the United States, is only a three-word phrase tacked on to round out the story of what happens to an unknown number of needy families which for some reason or other are not given relief. To observers having first-hand knowledge of relief conditions, the phrase is a hollow-sounding expression which usually means that a community is failing to meet its responsibilities toward needy, hungry, poorly clad, and miserably

housed men, women, and children. To those who know most intimately the significance of "surplus commodities only," it means slow starvation, cold, and demoralizing destitution.[21]

If the number of people struggling to subsist on surplus commodities only was comparatively small, the number whose diets might well have benefited from the FSCC's commodities was large. The 1935–1936 Survey of Consumer Expenditures revealed that 14 percent of the nation's families—4 million families composed of 14 million persons—had incomes of less than $500 per year and an average yearly income of $312. These families spent, on the average, about five cents a meal per person or about half of what a "reasonably adequate diet" was estimated to cost. Later in the 1930s, the Surplus Marketing Administration studied families receiving relief and families with a WPA worker and found food expenditures in both groups well below the levels considered necessary to obtain nutritional adequacy.[22] On the basis of fairly extensive analyses, the Department of Agriculture's Bureau of Home Economics estimated, at the turn of the decade, that about a third of all families in the United States had diets that failed to meet minimum nutritional standards for one or more nutrients. Most of the dietary inadequacy was due to lack of purchasing power.[23] In this context then, of widespread dietary insufficiency and a disturbing amount of severe deprivation, the FSCC undertook the task of shifting the emphasis of commodity distribution from relief to agricultural surplus disposal.

USDA's assumption of control of the corporation involved a change in the focus of the corporation's activities as well as a change in the locus of administration. The 1935 annual report of the corporation describes the change as follows:

The transfer of the direction of the Corporation from the Federal Emergency Relief Administration to the Department of Agriculture involved a shift of emphasis from the relief to the agricultural aspects of the functions of the Corporation, although it did not affect the continuity of its operations. The controlling factor in the determination of policies became the removal of agricultural surpluses and the encouragement of domestic consumption rather than providing for the needs of the unemployed.[24]

The shift in policy priorities became more definite as time passed. Early in 1937, an article prepared for newspaper publication by a corporation staff member noted that "although feeding of the hungry is important in

these projects, it should be emphasized here that in the 3¼ years of practice the removal of surpluses in the hands of growers and distributors, and
the stabilization of markets has gradually become the paramount objective." [25] In January 1937, Congress recognized the corporation's growing
integration with USDA by designating it "an agency of the United States
under the direction of the Secretary of Agriculture." [26]

Under some circumstances, the FSCC found it useful to suggest that
surplus removal was virtually its only objective. Notes on a meeting with
a group seeking FSCC's influence in favor of the establishment of a WPA
project for commodity distribution are revealing. Distribution Division
Director James Brickett told the group that "we are engaged in a surplus
removal program and the distribution of commodities is incidental."
When the group pressed further, asking if FSCC approval of such a
project would carry any weight, Brickett replied that it would not since
"the Corporation was divorced from the Relief end of the Administration," and noted that since November 1935 "the psychology has changed
altogether." Brickett then added, "What I am thinking is that I would like
to indicate in some way or other that the Department of Agriculture is not
interested in the distribution of commodities as much as they are interested in the economic value that surplus removal programs are a benefit to
agriculture. The objectives of the Department is [sic] to divert surpluses
where they are affecting market conditions and prices. They naturally are
interested in seeing that commodities are distributed to those who need
them in order to accomplish the objective of the diversion program." [27]

While all of these statements were designed for public consumption
and must be understood as such, a later internal departmental memorandum reviewing the history of the distribution programs came to a similar
conclusion. It characterized the programs' operating assumptions during
the 1936–1938 period as follows:

> distribution to needy people was simply a convenient outlet for com-
> modities purchased because of a surplus situation. . . . In this period
> monetary aid to growers was probably the primary aim in practice.
> Grower distress or threat of distress was the principal spur to action.
> The removal of a part of the supplies depressing prices was the basic
> means of aiding growers. [28]

The integration of commodity distribution with basic USDA policy
was reflected in the organizational structure that emerged from the transition as well. The Distribution Division of the corporation remained intact, but the Procurement Division was basically absorbed by the AAA.

Just as the FSRC had operated at the same location and with many of the same staff members as the FERA, the 1935 annual report of the FSCC noted that "following the change in the management of the Corporation, the Commodities Purchase Section of the Agricultural Adjustment Administration, which handled the procurement of all commodities donated for distribution, was coordinated with the Procurement division of the Corporation so that both are now in the same location and under the supervision of the same personnel." [29]

Changes in the corporation's personnel were another means by which the FSCC was integrated more fully with the Department of Agriculture. Although AAA Administrator Chester Davis was elected president of the FSCC, his day-to-day involvement was quite limited. [30] The actual management of the operation was turned over to Jesse W. Tapp, the head of the Division of Marketing and Marketing Agreements and later head of the Surplus Marketing Administration. Davis later characterized Tapp as "a top-flight executive" who he defined as "somebody who will take an assignment and see that it's neatly buttoned up and completed and will follow through getting things done that need to be done and do it effectively." [31] Tapp succeeded Davis as the president of the corporation in 1936. Just as the corporation during the FERA period was influenced by Hopkins's social work background and Jacob Baker's interest in work relief and cooperative enterprise, so Tapp's agricultural background and business experience were probably influential after the transfer.

Tapp was born and raised on a large Kentucky tobacco farm and majored in farm management and agricultural economics in college; he worked in finance for the National Investors' Corporation before joining the AAA in 1933. His memoir in the Columbia Oral History Collection contains few references to the FSCC, which he apparently perceived as a convenient means of implementing Section 32. His recollections of the Department of Agriculture in the 1930s indicate his commitment to agriculture and his focus on the operational rather than the policy aspects of programs and controversies. In discussing the purge that ousted the liberal reformers from the offices of the Consumers' Counsel and the General Counsel, Tapp's comments repeatedly stressed his sense that the reformers were interfering with a job that needed the full attention of "the group that was trying to make the programs work." He identified this group as the "agricultural economists and agriculturally trained people who were staffing those organizations, who knew agriculture and who were primarily interested in developing an agricultural program," apparently in contrast to the legal staff who "had no farm background . . .

knew very little about agriculture . . . were not much interested in agriculture." He indicated that some of the objectives of the social reformers may have been worthwhile, but that the agricultural group "didn't want the agricultural program to carry such a heavy load it would bog down." Even if the AAA programs had "rather limited objectives, nevertheless they were the kind of objectives in agricultural adjustment and marketing adjustment which were very important to farmers, where timeliness of action was important, where the income of segments of agriculture was heavily dependent not only on prompt action but action that necessarily was confined to the specific agricultural objectives." [32] With his management background, his focus on agriculture, and his emphasis on one objective at a time, Tapp's leadership of the FSCC was directed wholeheartedly and systematically toward assisting farmers. "As time passed, and these programs lost some of their purely relief aspects and gained more emphasis on the surplus removal side," notes an FSCC newspaper release, "there has been more and more of a systematizing of the whole business, from the removal of the surpluses to their consumption by relief clients."

On the procurement side of the ledger, the FSCC developed an elaborate rationale governing the amounts, locations, and prices of its purchases. At the same time, it moved to involve farmers and farm organizations as advisors to the purchase process. "Purchasing representatives of the Commodities Purchase Section," notes the news story mentioned above, "assist in the formation of advisory committees, usually composed of prominent producers and producer representatives and state and federal government agents in the area involved." [33] In 1938, the corporation issued an annual report considerably more extensive than any previous yearly accounting, and attempted to explain its operations, emphasizing the fact that FSCC purchases were made to stabilize the entire market for a given commodity rather than to aid individual growers:

> The surplus-removal programs can promote orderly marketing and increase grower returns by purchasing sufficient quantities at the principal producing points in the area that determines the price. The purchase is the equivalent of either a corresponding reduction in supply or increase in demand and the beneficial effects are usually felt by all producers whether inside or outside the principal commercial areas. The fact that the effects of purchases are distributed throughout the industry, even though the purchases themselves may not be, is not always understood. It is sometimes hard to convince an individual with a small quantity to sell that the corporation must concentrate its buying in

areas where it can obtain large supplies in short periods of time if it is successfully to improve the return that he and other growers are receiving for their crop.[34]

In addition, the corporation worked with growers to assist them in the development of cooperative marketing arrangements and the use of grading, packaging, and inspection to bring order to the marketing of their products.

Similarly, the FSCC invested considerable effort in attempts to increase the efficiency and decrease the costs of its own operations. The 1935 annual report indicated that a decrease in administrative expenses of approximately 30 percent had been achieved by closing several midwestern offices at the end of the drought-cattle program and the coordination of the Procurement Division with the Commodities Purchase Section. A year later the FSCC was able to report further improvements:

> Experience in handling special problems of rapid procurement and distribution has enabled the Corporation to deal effectively with perishable commodities and suddenly developed emergency conditions. Careful planning of operations and constant simplification of procedures and organization have overcome hampering technicalities and difficulties. The Corporation has functioned as a complete operation and administrative unit in procuring surplus commodities, arranging for their immediate transportation and distribution to the States on a carlot basis or for their processing when necessary, and in providing for auditing, accounting, and paying expenses.[35]

Apparently the FSCC's ability to move quickly in emergency situations was much appreciated by distressed farmers. One group of Massachusetts apple growers wrote to thank Secretary Wallace for the FSCC's prompt action in relieving them of apples blown from their trees during a hurricane:

> With the gravest crisis ever faced by us through the destruction of our crop plus the damage to orchards and buildings, we were in a state of bewilderment as to how to dispose of the tremendous quantity of apples that had to be salvaged quickly to prevent the entire loss of this crop.
> The Surplus Commodity Corporation was the only organization that could handle the problem, and the quick and efficient manner in which the work was done was gratifying to us all.
> It was a great job well done.[36]

One of the growers involved sent a copy along to President Roosevelt with a cover letter that made his appreciation quite vivid: "I have had the privilege of handling about sixty carloads of apples shipped by the small growers in this vicinity. I wish you might have accompanied me on my personal visit to the homes of these men, and have seen their expressions of gratitude. You would have felt highly repaid for this great service rendered in a time of such great distress." [37]

The FSCC also worked to convince the states to centralize responsibility for intrastate distribution in a single agency. States were encouraged to develop and exchange commodity distribution newsletters (Nebraska published one called "Comma Ditty"), and efforts were made to shift distribution operations from the emergency style that had characterized the FSRC to a more businesslike basis. The 1936 annual report summarized these efforts:

> Information concerning inventories, methods, procedures, forms, costs, and facilities has been carefully assembled and analyzed, in order to assist the States in developing the most efficient, adaptable and economical means of distributing the commodities donated. Through the dissemination and interchange of this information, the Corporation and the States cooperating closely together have been able to cut down distribution costs, increase the speed of distribution, and provide for more equitable disposal of the commodities. [38]

The same combination of focus on agricultural problems and businesslike procedure that enabled the corporation to respond so effectively to the distress of growers beset by hurricanes probably contributed to its extreme caution in drawing upon Section 32 funds. Although the legislation itself does not use the term "surplus" and in no way restricted the corporation's purchases to surpluses, it was apparently interpreted so by FSCC officials. "Of course, we do not buy agricultural commodities," Tapp told a congressional committee, "unless there is a surplus and prices are relatively low." [39] According to a later study of commodity distribution conducted by a departmental committee, "objectives of activities have been guided by administrative policy for carrying out agricultural legislation. So long as agricultural policy was itself concerned with surpluses of individual commodities, administration of domestic food and cotton disposal activities was predominantly influenced by these problems." [40]

Tapp apparently continued to take a strict view of the purposes to which Section 32 funds might be used even after other USDA officials began to explore a broader interpretation of the law. In late 1938, a departmental committee was convened to consider methods of promoting increased consumption of agricultural products by low income families. Eventually, the committee got around to discussions of subsidizing such consumption through a "two price" system—discussions that eventually led to the creation of the Blue and Gold food stamp plan. O. C. Stine, one of Tapp's colleagues, recalls that Tapp "posed the idea that it was a misuse of Three A funds. The funds that would be available for use were the Section 32 funds which were intended to be used for disposal of surpluses by exportation or diversion in the United States. He said farmers look on these funds as belonging to them. He said that it was not an agricultural relief program but that it was a consumer relief program." [41]

Because the transition to USDA control occurred during a period when drought and other weather conditions prevented the accumulation of many of the surpluses that had occurred earlier, the narrow construction of Section 32 meant, in practice, that comparatively little money was spent. Testifying before the House Committee on Agriculture in 1937, Jesse Tapp reported that in the previous fiscal year only $11 million of the available $109 million had been spent. When asked for further information to explain "why the Secretary of Agriculture and your corporation did not use that money for the purpose for which Congress said it should be used," Tapp replied: "I would say the principal reason for that has been the droughts of 1934 and 1936. Surpluses were reduced by these natural conditions so that it was not necessary to use large amounts of the fund to maintain price levels." At another point in his testimony, Tapp revealed at least part of the reason for the corporation's temperance: "We have the feeling that if we were to spend all of Section 32 funds regardless of crop conditions and supply conditions that we could very well be criticized for such action." [42] Tapp's recollection of the incident suggests that he perceived the limited spending as thrift.

> I remember making a report to the appropriations committee on the use of the funds. One or two of the members of the committee were inclined to be very critical because I hadn't spent all this money that they had made available. But some Congressman from the South with a sense of economy came to my rescue and complimented us on not spending the money if we didn't find the appropriate uses which would warrant its use. [43]

The impact of such caution on the availability of commodities for distribution to the states was definitive. In the 19½ months following the corporation's transfer to USDA, only $22 million of the available Section 32 funds were spent.[44] During this period, the number of families certified as eligible to receive surplus commodities fluctuated at 2 million. Using this figure as a rough average, $22 million over 19½ months divided among 2 million cases yields a monthly expenditure of about $.56 per case or about $.16 for each of the 3½ "statistical persons" in each case. These expenditures were for purchase, processing, and transportation; the retail value of the commodities would have been higher, though not much. Fortunately, not all of the commodities distributed by the FSCC during this period were derived from these limited Section 32 funds; substantial inventories of canned meat and more limited quantities of other non-perishables had been inherited from the FSRC, but the total quantities were not large. In 1936 for example, distribution totaled approximately 400 million pounds of food. Again using a rough average of 2 million families, the FSCC sent out approximately 16⅔ pounds per month per case or a little less than 5 pounds for each person. Comparable figures are not available for 1937, but a report submitted by the president of the FSCC to its board of directors covering the last six months of 1937 suggests that commodities were again in short supply.

> During the purchasing period, the relief load has been such that commodities have moved immediately into distribution. The inventories as of Dec. 3, 1937, were very small and consisted only of purchases made during the latter part of the month of December. As a matter of fact, there has been much urging on the part of state relief agencies to increase the volume of merchandise going through their hands. In some instances, certain states have been completely out of commodities for a period of several weeks. Under such conditions it is rather difficult to maintain proper distribution machinery which is essential to the type of program conducted by this Corporation.[45]

In 1938, both surpluses and distribution rates rose sharply. The average distribution a month per family for the fiscal year ending June 30, 1938 was 45 pounds and for the last six months of the fiscal year—52 pounds. The corporation hastened to assure that these commodities would not interfere with the normal market: "If this aid is considered strictly on a poundage basis and with no references to the varieties of foodstuffs required, even this higher rate represents only approximately one eighth the total number of pounds a family needs to maintain a minimum adequate diet."[46]

Agricultural priorities also led to an adjustment of the basis upon which commodities were allocated to the various state and local relief organizations. The 1936 annual report summarized the change:

> Allocation of surplus commodities by the Corporation has been based not only upon the relative number of certified eligible relief cases in the States, but . . . upon several other factors as well. . . . Because of the agricultural problems involved, commodities procured in a surplus area have not been distributed in another geographical area in which the same commodities are grown. Since a primary purpose of distribution is to increase domestic consumption, whenever possible commodities have been allocated to areas in which they are not ordinarily used to a great extent, thus they have reached individuals comparatively unfamiliar with their use.[47]

Thus people in a given area of the country were denied an available commodity from another region simply because it was also grown locally, regardless of whether prices for the local variety were within their reach. When the corporation neglected this deference to local growers, reaction could be quite sharp. A telegram received by Roosevelt from an irate Georgia congressman illustrates the point.

> Carload apples purchased in Massachusetts by Federal Surplus Commodities Corporation at Clarkesville Georgia now for distribution. Local people not given opportunity to sell apples for same purpose. I am protesting this strongly. People do not understand it and I am being swamped with telegrams and letters of protest from best citizens. Same thing occurred recently in my home city Gainesville Ga., when carloads of Irish potatoes and cabbages were sent here. Please have this investigated and stopped causing confusion and dissatisfaction. These products all produced here in quantities.[48]

The FSRC may well have been under similar pressure, but once the corporation was transferred to USDA, its decision makers were more vulnerable to criticism from farmers and farm representatives than they had been under the former arrangement.

The practice of shipping commodities to areas where they were relatively unfamiliar was a matter of considerable pride for the corporation. As the FSCC's distribution officer, James Brickett, commented in a letter to the head of Montana's Public Welfare Department, "commodity distribution is creating new consumers who, upon leaving the relief rolls become purchasers of those commodities through their retail grocers." Brickett recommended that this aspect of the FSCC's work be emphasized in a press release that the Montana official was preparing on the subject of commodity distribution.[49] Relief homemakers, however, may have been less enthusiastic about receiving unfamiliar foods. A story prepared for newspaper release notes cheerfully that "grapefruit from Florida and Texas were Sanskrit to relief clients in Oklahoma, Nebraska, . . . and other states."[50] While most of these strange foods were nutritious, the combination of introducing unfamiliar foods and avoiding items that competed with those produced locally must have brought extensive change of diet to families who had to rely upon government surplus foods. Disregard for the habits and preferences of recipients continued to hamper the effectiveness of food assistance in combating malnutrition throughout the existence of the commodity distribution program.

The corporation's allocative policies had the effect of further limiting the variety of diets already restricted by the range of a given season's surpluses and the FSCC's narrow interpretation of Section 32. The effect was intensified by the fact that state and local agencies were instructed to refuse any commodities for which they did not have the proper storage facilities, or any that they chose, for any reason, not to handle. Sharp imbalances resulted in some sections of the country. In 1937 for example, Assistant Secretary of Agriculture Paul Appleby reported that a WPA administrator in the Midwest had complained that "children in relief families have been getting so much grapefruit juice that it runs out their ears. . . . The WPA feels the need for many commodities that they are not getting, and seems to be rather swimming around in a sea of citrus juice." He suggested that perhaps the secretary's office should call for periodic reports from the FSCC.[51] Information from the Southwest also showed a severe lack of variety. In April 1939, for example, recipients in San Antonio were getting only wheat and graham flour, and in September 1938, they received only grapefruit juice.[52]

The over-and-above policy drew more careful attention from the FSCC than from its predecessor. The 1938 annual report describes the addition of a complex series of regulations specifying the maximum amount of each commodity that could be distributed to a given family:

> To assure that surplus commodities will not re-enter commercial channels and that distribution will not interfere or compete with commercial commodities, the rates at which they may be distributed are rigidly prescribed. These rates are graduated according to size of family and also include provisions for those instances when similar commodities are being distributed simultaneously. . . . Each commodity is studied and a rate determined that will prevent the donated commodi-

ties from cutting into the normal purchases of the families. . . . Any competition with commercial sales is strictly guarded against not only through such precautions as labels and limited rates of distribution, but through investigation of all instances of reported competition.[53]

Because these rates governed each commodity individually rather than the total commodity bundle, families living in areas where only a few commodities were distributed suffered a double restriction: both the total amount of food they received and its variety were limited. Taken together, the various regulations governing allocation and distribution combined to restrict the quantity and variety of commodities available to families in need and to create large fluctuations in the amounts and kinds available from month to month.

One other aspect of the corporation's transfer to USDA deeply affected the program's benefits to needy people. The USDA, regarding relief distribution as an outlet for agricultural surpluses, took no part in the determination of eligibility for the foods. The determination was left entirely to the local agencies and the states where they chose to establish statewide standards:

> The Corporation has issued instructions that it will recognize the certification, by accredited State social service agencies or similar local bodies, of people in need who may be described as coming under the heading of recipients of direct relief, of old age assistance, of aid to dependent children, of aid to blind, and of Farm Security Administration aid, Works Progress Administration security wage workers, and those families not on relief but whose income level places them on the relief border line. The determination of which of these groups are to receive surplus commodities is the responsibility of the local certifying agencies. It is also their determination which decides which families qualify for consideration as members of these groups and which are thereby certified as being eligible to receive surplus commodities.[54]

This permissive approach resulted in disparities from region to region, state to state, and county to county. Because the FSCC did not claim any role in such determinations, it did not keep systematic information as to the nature or classification of its recipients. After surveying reports from various states and localities concerning the inclusion of WPA workers among those eligible, policy analyst Donald Howard noted, in his major study of the WPA and federal relief, that policies ranged from automatic inclusion to automatic exclusion. In between were numerous localities that offered the surplus foods to WPA workers only if they had large families. Howard noted that the policy of denying surplus commodities to all WPA employees, even those with numerous dependents, most often occurred in the South, precisely where they were most needed because WPA wages, scaled to local prevailing wages, were lowest.

What is perhaps most striking about the use of commodities to supplement WPA earnings is that policies regarding their distribution are likely to be most stringent in the very areas where wages are lowest and where other relief provisions are least nearly adequate. These restrictive policies are frequently justified on the ground that WPA workers already enjoy so much more liberal benefits than other classes of relief recipients particularly those receiving general relief that further additions to their wages are indefensible. Thus, the very breakdown of general relief programs which the federal government had done nothing to prevent, has mitigated against the use of commodities which have been purchased and made available by the federal government for the purpose of providing WPA workers (among others) additional food which is necessary to piece out their admittedly inadequate resources.[55]

In light of these findings, the haste of the FERA officials in withdrawing from the corporation and their unwillingness to participate in policy decisions concerning eligibility resulted in a missed opportunity to safeguard the welfare of WPA workers, although such safeguards would have been largely theoretical in the absence of larger purchases.

The inequities and potential abuses involved in local determination of eligibility were reinforced by the shortage of commodities during periods in which few surpluses were purchased. The 1938 annual report notes that:

The relief caseload trend as reported to the Corporation cannot be considered alone as an indication of relief conditions in the States. These figures are materially influenced by the quantity of commodities available. During periods when the supply of commodities was inadequate for the needs of the States there was little incentive for them to certify all families whose economic condition would qualify them as being eligible. When supplies became larger, the States expanded their activities to assist a larger part of the people in need.[56]

In the short run then, the transfer of food assistance to USDA was a setback for poor people. In the simplest terms, after the transfer, fewer people received food, and they received less of it. The Department of Agriculture did not share the emergency orientation of the FERA; its faithfulness to the bureaucratic procedures and legal niceties that Hopkins and Frank had adroitly sidestepped subjected surplus commodity distribution to what appears to have been a predictable adverse ruling by the comptroller general.[57] Commodities were reduced to a trickle just at the time when the difficult transition to state and local care of the unemployables was creating severe hardships among the poor. Even when Section 32 funds were cleared for use in commodity distribution, their disbursement was subjected to an extremely narrow interpretation that meant that they were used only to relieve major surpluses. Crop reduction measures of various sorts and bad weather combined to limit the production of surpluses, so that overall distribution was cut by at least half in terms of weight and by an even greater figure in terms of value.[58] Furthermore, the variety of foods distributed was decreased, commodity by commodity maximum distribution rates were imposed, and foods were allocated in the hopes of creating new markets and avoiding competition with local growers rather than on the basis of the needs of relief recipients. Clearly, the transfer of control of surplus commodity distribution to the Department of Agriculture signified a reduction in the program's responsiveness to poor people.

Nevertheless, subsequent developments would illustrate that the problem for relief clients was not so much the corporation's transfer to the Department of Agriculture as the Department of Agriculture to which the corporation was transferred. The Department of Agriculture that was put in charge of transferring crop surpluses to needy consumers was the same department that was working overtime to implement a policy of restricting agricultural output to raise the prices paid by all consumers. In one sense, USDA was trying to create the very problem that commodity distribution was originally supposed to ease—consumers' inability to afford a nutritionally adequate diet. The agricultural sector revealed, perhaps more vividly than any other, the conflict between the interests of consumers and those of producers that is inherent in a capitalist economy. "It became obvious," Jerome Frank later recalled, "that so far as the farmers usually were concerned, if they could get an increase in price for the farmer they didn't care whether the consumer got squeezed."[59] Henry Wallace alluded to the fundamental nature of this conflict when he defended crop restriction with the comment that "agriculture cannot survive in a capitalistic society as a philanthropic enterprise."[60]

Interviewed some years later about the various groups in the Department of Agriculture, Wallace's Special Assistant Paul Appleby summarized a prevailing sentiment within the department: "Perhaps we ought to pay more attention to the non-farmer interests here, but I don't seen how.

After all, this is the Department of Agriculture. We do have to prosecute the farm interest and uphold it quite a bit." [61] Jerome Frank reported American Farm Bureau Federation President Ed O'Neal to have stated it quite simply: "What in the hell have we got to do with the consumer. This is the Department of Agriculture!" [62] Up until the purge of the liberals in the spring of 1935, of course, a significant minority consistently raised issues of consumer protection and the broader public interest, but in the aftermath of the fight over tenant farmers, the office of the Consumers' Counsel fell into more conservative hands and the narrower interpretation of the Agriculture Department's responsibilities gained ascendancy. Mordecai Ezekial and some of the other members of the Food Survey Committee continued to articulate the need for expanded consumption among the nation's lower income consumers, but they did not occupy such a crucial position as the one held by the General Counsel's office, which had, of necessity, passed upon all contracts and legal matters. And once the Food Survey Committee was disbanded at Tapp's suggestion, its members appear to have had relatively little impact upon the commodity distribution operations.

If USDA was free, for a time at least, to concentrate wholeheartedly upon raising farm prices, it was not free from internal competition for the benefits of agricultural adjustment. The effort to achieve higher prices had been undertaken on a commodity by commodity basis, which entailed an effort to protect the market for each individual commodity and made the department resistant to solutions to farm income problems that would have involved shifting consumption from lower to higher value products. It played into and reinforced a politics of agriculture that pitted commodity against commodity and region against region. Asked by Treasury Secretary Morgenthau to declare wheat a surplus so that the FSCC could supply bread to families left destitute by the bankruptcy of the relief system in several midwestern cities, Wallace replied that he could not do it because it would be "bad politics," it would "run into a jam with the Corn Belt." [63] The commodity by commodity approach constrained the department's efforts on behalf of poor people in a number of ways and was certainly a factor in the FSCC's decision to impose maximum distribution rates for individual commodities, a decision that had the effect of keeping total food assistance far below the levels that poor people needed and could have consumed without reducing the normal purchases for which they had no money.

The Department of Agriculture's unfettered priority on obtaining higher prices for farm products meant that food assistance would be made available only to the extent that it could be demonstrated that it improved the returns received by farmers. In principle, food assistance had always been constrained by the necessity to avoid any reduction in returns to growers as reflected in the over-and-above policy. The change was a matter of degree, a matter of which risk would be taken in an inherently uncertain situation: the risk of providing clients with slightly too much food and thereby reducing other purchases, or the risk of providing them with less than they needed and could consume without materially reducing other food expenditures. An agricultural agency committed, and politically accountable, to farmers would prefer the latter risk while relief administrators might prefer the former.

Theoretically, even a thoroughly farmer-identified agricultural establishment might have promoted a vigorous surplus commodity distribution program, because a significant number of those who received surplus commodities were themselves farmers. Relief provisions in rural areas and in agricultural states tended to be even less adequate than those in urban and industrial sections, and displaced farm tenants and under-employed agricultural day laborers were among the "unknown number of needy families" subsisting with the aid of "surplus commodities only" or eking out a living from some combination of commodities, cash relief, and wages or cropping. Within the AAA, however, the large, commercial farmer was the client. "It was true, of course," Paul Appleby reflected years later, "that the Three-A as a working organization was militantly pro-agriculture and militantly for the larger farmers and was much less interested in the lower economic level farmers and very little interested in farm tenants and farm laborers and so on. It was an organization whose function had to do with the more successful farmers by and large," he explained. "Their orientation was that way and the pressures that were on them from the public scene were from that kind of people. A lot of those pressures on the Three-A were from within the Three-A itself and they existed throughout a very large part of the Three-A. That was essentially the fight which occasioned the purge of '35." [64]

Before the purge, Frank and his cohorts had, with some regularity, pointed out the extent to which the adjustment programs were aiding the big farmers rather than those most in need and questioned the acceptability of such policies. As Frank later recalled the issue, "it was the usual story that the big boys always played up the plight of the little farmer because giving the little man an inch meant giving the big boy a yard. It seemed to me that anything we did in the AAA of a stopgap character that would meet a farm revolution would be justified. But once you were by that it was time to readjust and straighten out the kinks and see that you really were accomplishing what the New Deal ought to be accomplishing." [65] The purge effectively ended such questioning from within the AAA, although the issue of the distribution of the benefits of agricultural adjustment continued to be a focus for critics outside the administration.

Shortly after the purge, the voice of social reform within USDA was further muted by the establishment of the Resettlement Administration as an independent agency. Created in April 1935, the Resettlement Administration was charged with the task of responding to rural poverty, particularly the needs of sharecroppers and tenant farmers displaced by the changes in agriculture. The basic idea, as implied in the agency's name, was to move impoverished farm families who had been farming on submarginal land to better acres and to provide them with help in becoming independent. It combined the subsistence homestead projects that had been developed in the Department of the Interior, the Land Policy Section of the AAA, and the FERA's rural rehabilitation work. Rex Tugwell, an outspoken proponent of the broader view of the legitimate aims of agricultural policy, was appointed head of the Resettlement Administration, and although he continued to occupy the position of undersecretary of agriculture, he devoted most of his time to the new organization. While the creation of a unified, independent agency may in fact have given those concerned with rural poverty and land tenure a greater visibility in the Roosevelt administration, it reduced their influence within the Agriculture Department where the FSCC was housed.

The combined effect of the purge, the creation of the Resettlement Administration, and the withdrawal of relief officials from involvement with the Federal Surplus Commodities Corporation resulted in allowing USDA a free hand in adjusting commodity distribution to its own priorities, which, as Appleby noted, were shaped by "the pressures that were on them" from the larger farmers. Increasingly, these pressures were not simply supportive of large-scale commercial farming; they were overtly anti-relief. In 1934, for example, the American Farm Bureau Federation's annual convention passed a long resolution on relief that read in part:

> The farmers of our nation may be willing to produce products which supply food and clothing and shelter, at no profit to themselves for our citizens who are incapable of working or who of necessity are unemployed. We cannot approve a continuation of plans and operations connected with federal relief projects during the last two years which have

in many instances promoted a desire on the part of some of our citizens to be unemployed, and have in other instances developed an alarming thought in the minds of many voters that the government owes them a living irrespective of whether or not they do anything to justify the governmental relief given them.

Not all the federation's criticism of relief was so philosophical in nature. The same resolution went on to assert that "the wage scale on all work relief projects must be kept in line with current practices in different localities so that the unfortunate experiences of the last two years in granting relief wages far above what agriculture or industry locally could pay shall not be continued." The resolution commended the organization's board of directors for its "courageous and patriotic statement on these troublesome questions," the substance of which was that: "they who work, eat; they who will not work on government or other projects at wages which our nation can afford to pay, shall not eat." [66] Three years later in 1937, the American Farm Bureau Federation (AFBF) was even more explicit, calling for an end to "gigantic federal relief rolls and expenditures." Relief, the farm organization argued, "should be turned back to the states and their respective sub-divisions at the earliest practicable date." And again, work relief wages were a sore point: "The wage scale for those on relief should not be such as to make relief work a career but rather to encourage a return to private employment, even though not of a specially remunerative or desirable character." As long as federal relief continued, the AFBF argued, WPA regulations "should provide for equalization of hours of labor and wages on relief projects to the custom of the community. Men enrolled on relief should not be penalized for accepting temporary employment by extreme difficulty in returning to the relief rolls." [67]

These statements and those of other farm organizations reflect a deep-seated conflict in the relationship between large farmers and relief. On the one hand, the farmers were ideologically conditioned to abhor the idea of promoting idleness, and they were adamantly opposed to any form of relief that exerted upward pressure on agricultural wages or threatened to disrupt old systems of landlord-tenant relations. On the other hand, as they converted from farming with tenants to day labor, they were increasingly dependent upon relief to sustain the agricultural labor pool in winter months and other slack times.

Relief quickly became an indispensable support to a collapsing plantation system in the South. As early as 1934, rural sociologist Rupert Vance

wrote to a colleague that "it may come to be that the greatest efficiency of
the Southern planters consists in securing government subsidy to uphold
a system that might otherwise break down of its own weakness. . . . With
the one hand the cotton landlord takes agricultural subsidies and rental
benefits from his government, with the other he pushes his tenants on relief." [68] And in the Far West, a similar dependence was developing in regard to migrant labor. Clarke Chambers has summarized the situation in
California that he studied in considerable detail:

> California agriculture depended upon a supply of migratory labor. If
> sufficient harvest hands were to be available at harvest time, a large
> mass of labor had somehow to be financed through seasons of low la-
> bor demand. Government relief payments to migratory labor, then,
> constituted an indirect subsidization for farm employers. [69]

Local control of relief, especially of eligibility and benefit levels,
would generally permit locally powerful, large farmers to insure a willing
labor supply by reducing or eliminating the flow of public assistance during planting, harvest, and other periods when labor was needed. Thus,
farm employers pressed for local control and for ease of reinstatement for
recipients who accepted temporary employment. Cotton and tobacco
planters in the South found it relatively easy to influence the local relief
machinery. In his study of the Southern Tenant Farmers Union, for example, Donald Grubbs reported that one of the experiences that radi-
calized the union's founders, H. L. Mitchell and Clay East, was observing
"how readily the local planters gained control of [the New Deal relief
programs] and used them solely for taking care of the planters' 'best' tenants and foremen during the off season." [70] In California, Chambers reported, large growers were able to secure the cooperation of the state
relief administrator (who later became executive secretary of the Associated Farmers, a militantly anti-labor organization of larger farm labor
employers) in a "prevailing wage" policy that met their conditions. When
a more liberal state administration came in under Governor Culbert
Olson, the State Farm Bureau Federation and the Associated Farmers
launched a concerted effort to secure county level administration of state
relief funds, an effort that was thwarted only by the governor's veto. [71]

Given this orientation among the farm organizations and their close
ties to the Department of Agriculture, it is not surprising that the department spent funds conservatively in the administration of food assistance,
nor that it left a great deal of discretion to state and local relief agencies in

implementing the program at the local level. Even when Secretary Wallace began to turn away from the Farm Bureau and toward the Farmers' Union, which was far more supportive of relief and much more concerned about the plight of smaller farmers than was the larger organization, many AAA staff members continued to maintain close ties to the Farm Bureau, because durable bonds had been formed in the long McNary-Haugen fight. Chester Davis was close to the Farm Bureau, as was Jesse Tapp. Tapp's commercial farming background, his conservative political orientation, and his academic training, may have made him particularly unlikely to emphasize the relief aspects of the corporation's work. But in general, farm-reared, farm-trained staff members were certainly more likely to be responsive to farm organizations than to the observations of social critics or the pleas of relief officials.

Even if Tapp's attitude represented an extreme case of the agricultural mindset, it is no surprise that highly placed staff members in the Department of Agriculture awarded a high priority to the achievement of what they regarded as agricultural goals. James Schlesinger has noted the difficulty that many government agencies experience in adopting a wider, less-traditional view of their function. His example, drawn from the history of the U.S. Forestry Service, provides an instructive comparison with the case under study:

> The Forestry Service is charged not only to manage the forests efficiently for production purposes, but to provide recreation for the public. However, the Forestry Service is dominated or strongly influenced by professional foresters, sometimes known as "timber beasts." Foresters certainly love trees and productive forests as such, and may view the town dwellers who invade their forests as a nuisance to be tolerated. Consequently, the suggestion is hardly surprising that the Forest Service has overinvested in timber production and underinvested in recreation.[72]

The point is that a program is influenced not only by the fundamental policies of the agency that administers it, but also by the training and background of its staff. The staff, in turn, is likely to have been selected on the basis of qualifications relevant to the agency's overall goals. But this situation is not immutable. Sufficient public or congressional pressure would probably induce the Forestry Service to hire fewer "timber beasts" and more woodland recreation specialists. In the 1970s, pressure from the "hunger lobby" secured the appointment of food assistance experts with a demonstrated concern about the nutrition of poor people to

administer the food assistance programs of the Department of Agriculture. In the aftermath of the transfer of the corporation in the mid 1930s,
however, no such pressure existed.[73]

The apparent lack of public or even congressional interest in the policies of the corporation probably resulted from a number of factors. In the
first place, the New Deal involved a great deal of activity, and the corporation was not the main concern for most constituencies. Those interested
in agriculture were absorbed in finding an alternative to the processing
tax after it was invalidated by the Supreme Court. Those concerned with
relief focused their attention on the works program and the Social Security Act that together represented the culmination of years of effort. On
the Left, where the plight of the sharecropper and the problem of farm
tenancy were of considerable interest, the focus was on enabling tenants
to become owners, not on the distribution of groceries. Among the general public, the basic idea of transferring surpluses to those in need had
much commonsense appeal, but the public was not inclined to scrutinize
the details of the corporation's performance. In a very real sense, the corporation did its public relations job simply by existing and provding a
visible symbol for the prevention of waste. It was something to which agricultural administrators could refer when questioned about crop restriction amid destitution; people paid very little attention to the size of its
efforts or the distribution of its benefits.

The corporate form and the unusual permanent appropriation embodied in Section 32 further protected the commodity distribution operations from scrutiny. The program did not go through the normal process
of seeking an annual appropriation. It issued an annual report, of course,
but since Congress had no specific decisions to make concerning it, the
reports were rarely studied by busy legislators. Indeed, when FSCC
President Tapp was called before the House Agriculture Committee because the corporation's mandate was about to expire, the representatives
on the committee seemed surprised to learn that the corporation had been
spending so little of the available Section 32 funds.[74] And without regular
congressional appropriation hearings or other congressional attention,
little opportunity existed for the public to be made aware of the details of
FSCC's activities.

Even if greater public awareness of the gradual adjustment of the corporation's priorities had prevailed, however, few objections would have
been raised. Organizations of the unemployed were already losing their
strength by 1935 as the social security legislation, tax reform bill, and the
WPA drained the support of liberals who had earlier supported the de-

mands of such militant organizations as the Workers' Alliance. The alliance itself seems to have paid little attention to the commodity distribution program except as a source of WPA jobs in distribution projects. And among the general public, as Aubrey Williams declared in the statement quoted above, the old victim-blaming attitudes toward poverty were resurgent as the economy improved. Farmers, however, continued to tap a reservoir of public concern and respect. Agricultural economist Varden Fuller, commenting on several decades of experience with farm income support measures, noted that "the political support essential to the actions taken has apparently depended heavily upon a pre-existing and long surviving endowment of sympathy for 'the farmer,' who according to prevailing ideology, was unfairly treated by the economic system and therefore entitled to protection and redress." Fuller points out the failure of the public to differentiate among farmers in its support of farm income measures. "What is remarkable is that so much political sympathy for the farmer as an undifferentiated eclectic abstraction has not been matched by an equal concern for the really poor as against the not-so-poor within agriculture." [75]

Given the priorities of the Department of Agriculture to which the surplus commodity distribution program was transferred, the lack of public scrutiny or effective pressure from organized relief recipients, and the very effective pressure from the farm organizations, the perspective that relief administrators had provided in the FSRC was sorely missed in its successor. Theoretically, even a program that placed a high priority on meeting the needs of producers might have continued to serve the poor as well. But in the absence of any standards protecting the relief aspects of the program or any voice advocating the interests of poor people, USDA was free to adjust the program to provide more benefits—or the appearance of more benefits—to farmers without any need to calculate the loss to relief clients. The imposition of rigid commodity by commodity ceilings on distribution that applied regardless of the total number of commodities being distributed was a case in point. The benefits to farmers of such a rule were largely theoretical, but to an impoverished family trying to get by on surplus commodities and inadequate relief payments, the loss of potential assistance was real and crucial. By 1938, the FSCC was so hemmed in by such regulations that it could not respond even to dire emergencies and reports of near starvation.

CHAPTER TWELVE

Food Assistance: The Legacy of New Deal Policy Choices

I n June 1937, the Roosevelt administration, once again flirting with the seductive notions of a balanced budget and a restoration of business confidence, dramatically cut spending and sharply reduced the WPA rolls. As summer gave way to autumn, the stock market fell off precipitously, and the layoffs began, initiating an economic nightmare variously called a recession or a depression, depending upon how closely one was associated with the administration. By March 1938, 4 million people had been thrown out of work.[1]

Predictably, the cities and states, which had only grudgingly shouldered responsibility for relief of the unemployables, were unprepared for the large number of families rendered destitute by each new round of layoffs, and the WPA had nowhere near enough slots to go around. In an accelerated version of the aftermath of 1929, local relief agencies exhausted their resources, and cities exhausted their statutory borrowing limits. In the Midwest, where the steel and auto industries were especially hard hit, stark destitution was obvious by Christmas. In Cleveland, relief stopped altogether for the first six days of the New Year, and the behavioral indices of hunger— scavenging and begging—were once again reported.[2]

In January, a special census of unemployment shocked the administration with the news that between 7.5 and 10 million people were out of work and the prediction that more people would soon be unemployed than had been when Roosevelt was elected in 1932. Comparisons with that dreadful year began to appear with great frequency, and nowhere were the similarities more marked than in relief activities. "Relief needs are approaching those of the darkest days of 1933, and in some areas such as Cleveland and Detroit, may actually be greater," reported *The Nation*.[3] "The fact is," declared the *New Republic*, "the present depression has thrown us into an emergency very nearly as serious as the breakdown of relief administration this country experienced in 1931 and 1932." The liberal periodical went on to paint a picture grimly familiar to those who had observed the crumbling of local relief at the beginning of the decade: relief agencies were inundated "with applications they have neither the funds nor the personnel to handle," more and more people were receiving less and less adequate relief, and "the appropriations for relief are everywhere being curtailed." However, the *New Republic* pointed out one new element in the situation: "Everybody is sick of the problem. The emergency of 1932 has not been passed, but the public enthusiasm over meeting the crisis has largely died down." State legislatures, the editor predicted, would be reluctant to increase appropriations for relief.[4]

In April, Roosevelt reversed his position on balancing the budget and asked Congress for $3.5 billion for public works and other pump-priming activities. But neither cities nor relief clients could live on expectations of federal aid, and by May, while Congress considered the president's request, a full scale relief crisis was in progress in the Midwest, and severe deprivation was reported in many of the southern states. Reporting on a tour of the Midwest in the summer of 1938, journalists Samuel Lubell and Walter Everett summarized the situation this way:

> Relief in a good part of the United States is crumbling under the impact of the recession like a town rocked by a series of earthquakes. In some cities relief agencies have already slammed their doors against thousands in dire need. Akron's reliefers must keep body and soul together on twelve cents a person for a day's food. Cleveland's poor are still begging from door to door and foraging in garbage cans. Detroit's jobless sick must trust to God or nature if their illnesses require any but the cheapest drugs. Evictions have become a daily routine in Chicago. Distress and suffering are spreading like the plague.

The hard-pressed communities responded as they had in the early years of the depression, Lubell and Everett reported, by cutting grants:

> Food, clothing, and shelter budgets for families receiving direct relief have been lopped so drastically and so generally that it is impossible to measure the results in human suffering. After the first few days

of traveling through "dole slums," we came to expect that children six, seven, and eight years old would have legs as spindly as the starving Armenians for whom we used to contribute our pennies. Regional WPA officials estimate that in Ohio, Indiana, Michigan, and Illinois budgets have been slashed on the average 20 to 50 per cent. And that cut has been made since the start of the recession, when "economy" had already lowered relief standards below the level of adequacy set by private charities.[5]

Nor was the suffering confined to the industrial centers of the Midwest. In most of the southern states, relief had been cut to levels below subsistence. The average monthly relief grant had dropped to eight dollars in Alabama, six dollars in Georgia and Arkansas. In Little Rock in February, social workers discovered that two thousand families with no income were not receiving aid and were on the verge of starvation.[6]

Meanwhile, echoes of 1932 were heard in another sphere. With the end of the drought, agricultural abundance was returning to haunt the Roosevelt administration. As with the Farm Board years, surpluses of wheat and cotton were especially troublesome. If the nation had another good crop year, Henry Wallace told the cabinet glumly in 1938, "we would be sunk."[7] Within the administration, the irony of mounting surpluses and lengthening breadlines was especially troubling to Treasury Secretary Henry Morgenthau. "There's something wrong," he told the president. "On one hand they're worrying about 750 million bushels, and, my God, what you do on the other hand—you've got 250,000 people starving in Cleveland and two weeks from now you're going to have the same thing in Chicago. Why can't we do things? Why can't we act the way we used to?"[8] "I don't know whether its too late to change the philosophy of this Administration around," he told the surgeon general, Thomas Parran, after discovering that Wallace was requesting one hundred thousand dollars to finance wheat reduction and export subsidy: "that instead of trying to cry . . . and bemoan the fact that we're going to have a wonderful wheat crop—instead of thanking the Lord for the blessing— that we go out and instead of paying the farmers to grow less that we . . . go out and buy and give it to the people who are undernourished."[9]

Morgenthau was worried not only about the needless suffering of the unemployed but also about potential damage to the president's image; "his people aren't on their toes, and this thing is just going to crack up in their face, and instead of being ahead of the game they wait until this thing blows up and somebody blows up the City Hall or murders the Mayor of Cleveland—something like that; then they get worried," he told his staff in exasperation. Convinced that no one else would act, Morgenthau embarked upon a campaign to secure money and commodities for the stricken areas. "I want to be able to call up the Mayor . . . in Cleveland, and say 'Mayor, I'm sending you a million dollars for food and so many bushels of wheat and so many quarts of milk, so much rice, so much food, so much this, so much beef'—whatever they want. 'That will take care of you from now until the legislature meets.' " [10]

Money, it soon became obvious, was out of the question. The only available money that could be used for relief purposes was a WPA reserve. Morgenthau had an informal chat with Harry Hopkins who said flatly that he would not carry out instructions to transfer WPA funds to cash relief. "We're not going back to direct relief" he declared, and Morgenthau told his staff the next morning, "I was simply amazed . . . how angry he got at the thought that somebody was trying to suggest direct relief." [11] The treasury secretary and his staff were indeed suggesting direct relief because, as they saw it, WPA was giving "twice the money to every other person." The relief was more adequate and the work beneficial, but the money could not be stretched to cover the rising tide of relief applications. "Food before work," as one of Morgenthau's lieutenants stated it. [12] By the early spring of 1938, substantial segments of the social work profession were voicing similar opinions. [13]

The WPA leadership, however, remained adamant. The day after Chicago closed its relief stations for lack of funds, Harry Hopkins issued a statement asserting that the federal government "had done more than its share to mitigate the relief crisis in Cleveland and Chicago." Hopkins laid the responsibility for the situation squarely at the doors of the state legislatures of Ohio and Illinois. The emergency would be met without further federal action, he said. "No one is going to starve; the legislatures will take care of that." [14] Any effort to help the situation, Aubrey Williams told the president a week later, "would simply mean that the State and local governments would throw the whole problem of relief of unemployables back into the lap of the Federal Government." [15]

When the president suggested surplus commodities as a means of helping both WPA workers and unemployables, and FSCC President Tapp indicated that both groups were currently receiving surplus foods, Williams somewhat reluctantly agreed not to obstruct expanded commodity distribution. According to Morgenthau's notes on the conference, Williams "said he thought it was very important that the explanation of this direct relief distribution of surplus commodities be made to the public in terms of relief to agriculture, and that it be made clear that it is a program for the disposition of agricultural surpluses." His primary concern, according to the minutes, "was that the public should not get the impression that a switch was being made from a works program to a direct relief program by the Federal Government." [16] Hopkins made a similar distinction in an informal conversation with Morgenthau in which he indicated his unwillingness to be a party to direct relief. Morgenthau asked him, "How would you feel if we bought the food and gave it to them in order to help Wallace use up some of this surplus wheat that he's so worried about?" As Morgenthau reported to his staff the next morning, " 'Oh,' he said, 'that's an entirely different matter, if we do it on that basis.' " [17]

Although Morgenthau continued to look for ways and means of freeing some cash to aid the distressed areas, he turned his attention primarily to surplus commodity distribution where he confronted a host of policies, priorities, rules, and regulations that limited the FSCC's ability to respond to the needs of hungry people. He had asked Wallace to buy fresh milk for families whose relief grants had been cut off, Morgenthau told Eleanor Roosevelt, but Wallace said that he could not rule that milk was a surplus. [18] "Section 32 is so technical," Morgenthau's assistant told him, "that I can't tell you its provisions, but there has to be a declared surplus on the market before Secretary Wallace can use Section 32 money." [19] In fact, Section 32 was not very technical, and Congress had limited its use only by providing that no more than a quarter of any year's funds could be used for a single commodity, but by 1938, a mystification had set in that was to obscure the flexibility of Section 32 for many years. [20]

Morgenthau knew that wheat was in surplus, however, since it was Wallace's request for money to finance crop reduction or export subsidy that had turned his attention to the paradox in the first place. But when he told Secretary Wallace that he was interested in finding ways to increase the domestic consumption of wheat, Wallace replied that it was "out of the question." In the first place, Wallace argued, it would not be good from a dietary standpoint, and "it's bad politics." "Get this," Morgenthau told his staff indignantly, quoting the secretary: "bad politics, because if you got people to eat more wheat, you immediately would run into a jam with the Corn Belt. All I could do was not to just curse in his face," concluded Morgenthau. "I felt like saying 'I'm talking about feeding human beings, and not hogs.' " [21]

Stymied on acquiring bread and fresh milk for the time being, the treasury secretary turned his attention to the products the FSCC was already shipping. On May 18, when Chicago closed its relief stations and terminated cash assistance, the papers announced that ninety-one thousand

Chicagoans would get only surplus commodities for the rest of the month. "Families of four will receive four pounds of prunes, two pounds of dried beans, four pounds of butter, twelve pounds of cabbage, eight stalks of celery, thirty pounds of oranges and two pounds of rice," reported the *New York Times*, noting that they would have received the same amounts even if cash assistance had been continued.[22]

Morgenthau sent an assistant to discuss with FSCC officials the possibility of increasing commodity distribution in the hard-hit areas. She reported that the corporation used a maximum distribution rate derived from the difference between the Department of Agriculture's emergency diet and the next higher standard, the adequate diet at minimum cost. "The FSCC standard," she reported, "assumes the issue of relief orders to supply basic needs, and gives only the additional food requirements for the next higher standard. If the relief orders are not issued, they are not issued." In reality, she found distribution had been generally below the FSCC rate and only apples, butter, oranges, potatoes, and rice were being distributed in the Cleveland area. "The Corporation has this justification for its refusal to give more commodities, that it has been struggling since 1935 to prevent relief authorities all over the United States from using surplus commodities in place of local relief funds."[23] When the secretary indicated displeasure that staples such as beans and flour were not on the list, she hastened to clarify: "it is not the fault of the Surplus Corporation. They're doing what they're told to do. . . . By the Secretary of Agriculture and the Relief Administration."[24]

Another logic to the ceilings on amounts distributed was revealed in an internal FSCC memorandum. Noting that the quantities released did not meet the requirements for an adequate diet, Distribution Director James Brickett pointed out: "The complete lack of other resources of many recipient families however indicates that any real increase in the present distribution rates of the food stuffs now available will greatly increase the likelihood that a portion of the commodities will be traded for other goods and services to provide in part other essential requirements of the families' budget, provision for which is now lacking." Brickett recommended increasing the variety of commodities distributed in preference to increasing the volume of the items already being shipped.[25]

Morgenthau's efforts were not entirely fruitless. The corporation did begin shipping flour and dried milk to the Midwest, and it stepped up its purchase and distribution operations significantly. In fact, distribution for the last six months of fiscal 1938 averaged about 50 percent higher than that in the first half of the year.[26] But a more elaborate plan for expanded distribution was quietly shelved, Morgenthau later told his staff, as soon as he stopped riding herd on it. "The minute I turned my back Harry went to Wallace and said they couldn't do it because that is admitting everything you have done is wrong. . . . If we feed the undernourished the surplus food stuffs, that was admitting the plan was a flop, and we'd better not do it." [27]

Essentially, what Morgenthau learned was that if people were hungry, the federal government would send a food item only if it had been officially declared a surplus, did not compete with another politically powerful commodity, and could be justified as a Section 32 purchase. Even then, the quantities shipped must not be large enough to provide an incentive for trading or bootlegging, to induce reduction of local relief effort, or to permit substitution by clients for normal purchases, whether or not the normal purchases were actually being made. And the overall program could not be large enough to be interpreted as a return to general federal relief or to undermine the basic overproduction logic of the farm program. "It just turns my stomach to hear Henry Wallace want a hundred million dollars to have the people grow less wheat . . . with people not getting enough to eat. Now, there's just something cock-eyed, crackpot, about this administration. I mean it just goes against all decency and human understanding that they should be trying to find ways and means to grow less," the treasury secretary summed up his frustrations. "And there's people going hungry in America, all over America. Now there's just something—the combination of Wallace and Hopkins refusing to do any direct relief—just something ungodly about it." [28] The FSCC's limited ability to respond to the relief crisis of 1938 proved to be a fairly accurate preview of the performance of federal food assistance, as far as poor people were concerned, for the next three decades. The factors that tied the corporation's hands in 1938 became enduring aspects of domestic food assistance policy and politics. The rules and regulations designed to protect the interests of farmers on the one hand, and those designed to enforce state and local responsibility for general relief on the other, continued to constrain food assistance for most of the next thirty years and still influence it today.

In order to appreciate the legacy of New Deal policy choices in food assistance, a brief review of subsequent developments is necessary. The mounting surpluses that upset Secretary Morgenthau evoked concern within the Department of Agriculture as well, and with the threat that mounting European hostilities might disrupt the export market, USDA began looking for means to expand domestic consumption, especially among lower income consumers. Early in 1939, Wallace appointed Milo Perkins as president of the FSCC and administrator of the Surplus Marketing Administration. Under Perkins's leadership, the corporation began to pursue vigorously the goal of better diets and expanded food consumption for the third of the nation that Roosevelt had described as "ill housed, ill clad, ill nourished."[29] Surplus purchase and distribution operations mounted so rapidly that expenditures in fiscal 1940 were almost ten times as great as they had been in fiscal 1937, and new outlets for surplus commodities were created through an aggressive USDA campaign to stimulate the establishment of school lunch programs.[30] Early in 1939, an innovative food stamp program was initiated by the department on a trial basis; the plan used stamps of two colors to channel subsidized consumption to items declared to be in surplus by the secretary of agriculture. Immediately popular with wholesale and retail grocers, relief administrators, and those clients who could afford to participate, the Blue and Gold Stamp Plan spread rapidly during the first two years of the new decade, reaching almost 4 million people by May 1941.[31]

The remarkable expansion of food assistance at the turn of the decade lends support to the point made in the previous chapter that the problem with the corporation's transfer to USDA control in 1935 was not so much transfer to the Department of Agriculture as the dominant interests of the Department of Agriculture to which food programs were transferred. No inherent reason prevents a department of agriculture from administering a program of food assistance responsive to the needs of the poor, and for a brief period in the late 1930s and early 1940s, the anticipated closing of foreign markets and a growing emphasis upon good nutrition as an aspect of national defense combined to provide the U.S. Department of Agriculture with a compelling rationale for such a program. War, however, soon revealed the fundamental vulnerability of food assistance programs tied to agricultural surpluses. As allied purchasing agents and the needs of the armed forces escalated demand, surpluses gave way to scarcities, and food programs suffered a predictable fate. Direct distribution dwindled to a trickle. The Food Stamp Program was terminated, and the School Lunch Program, more popular with Congress because it was linked to the defense nutrition idea, was converted to a cash indemnity basis. Unemployment decreased at the same time, of course, but the truly unemployable needed food assistance more than ever as food prices rose sharply under the pressure of wartime scarcities.[32]

War also brought the end of the WPA, which meant the end of the federal contribution to the cost of intrastate commodity distribution. The states, suddenly faced with the labor costs of distribution in an increasingly tight labor market, turned to the counties for a share of the funds needed to continue the service. USDA first ruled that the states might require participating counties to bear a share of the costs and then, that participation must be optional if participating localities were required to spend local tax revenues to secure benefits. As a result, many of the poorest counties where the need was greatest withdrew altogether from the direct distribution of surplus commodities to needy families. Despite the vigorous expansion in 1939 and 1940 then, food assistance emerged from World War II in much the same shape it had emerged from the transfer to USDA in 1935. The corporation itself was dissolved in 1942, its dwindling functions consolidated into the Agricultural Marketing Administration within USDA.[33]

Although the School Lunch Program was established on a separate, permanent legislative basis by the National School Lunch Act of 1946, the family food assistance programs did not really recover from wartime cutbacks until concern about poverty in America surfaced in the 1960s. Surpluses mounted again after the war, stimulated by high price supports and generous crop loan programs, but efforts to revive the Food Stamp Program failed repeatedly, and the commodity distribution program remained hampered by the reluctance of state and local units to bear the cost of distribution. In 1949, Congress authorized the donation of surpluses held by the Commodity Credit Corporation to state and local welfare agencies and school lunch programs. In 1954, Public Law 480 authorized the donation of American food surpluses to relief agencies serving developing nations and their sale to such nations in return for local currencies, thereby somewhat reducing the supply available for domestic distribution programs. Eisenhower's Secretary of Agriculture Ezra Taft Benson expanded direct distribution, agreeing in 1953 that USDA would pay the shipping costs to the states, but by 1960, the quantity distributed still stood at only about 654 million pounds, or about 20 million more than had been distributed in 1935. The commodity bundle in the late 1950s consisted almost entirely of staple grains and nonfat dried milk with an occasional ration of butter or cheese.[34]

Proponents of the Food Stamp Program were never quite reconciled to its demise. In 1944, Senators Aiken of Vermont and La Follette, Jr. of Wisconsin introduced legislation to reestablish the Food Stamp Program on a much broader basis, not restricted to persons receiving relief. Their National Food Allotment Plan would have permitted any household to exchange 40 percent of its income for stamps sufficient to provide it with a minimally adequate diet. The Senate Agriculture Committee appointed a subcommittee and held a hearing on the proposal, but the committee took no action, and the plan never reached the Senate floor.[35] Food stamp legislation was introduced into every subsequent Congress where, in the context of declining interest in poverty and the shifting priorities of postwar agricultural policy, it seldom got out of committee, until the Food Stamp Act of 1964 finally established the current program. During the Depression, the activities of the Farm Holiday Association and the AAA had placed agricultural policy on the public agenda, and during the war, the importance of American food supplies to the allies and the institution of civilian rationing had kept it there. But in the 1950s, agricultural policy was widely regarded as a complex, technical, and arcane field of little interest to urban voters. The House and Senate agriculture committees were composed almost entirely of members from farm states and rural districts, and they, along with USDA administrators and the powerful farm organizations, had nearly a free hand in determining farm policy.[36]

A few dissenting voices were heard. Throughout the 1950s, Congresswoman Leonor Sullivan repeatedly introduced bills calling for the establishment of a food stamp plan, and regularly reminded the secretary of agriculture that he had authority to start such a program under Section 32 without additional legislation. The department, however, adopted the position that direct distribution was more beneficial to farmers and less expensive than the food stamp approach and opposed re-creation of the program. Even when Representative Sullivan's persistence finally resulted in legislation specifically authorizing a new Food Stamp Program, the Department of Agriculture failed to implement it. The secretary continued to believe that direct distribution was the better tool for achieving the purposes of Section 32, and there was little public interest to push the department and Congress into revaluating this stand.[37] With no activist federal relief administration to speak for the poor and poor people themselves unorganized and politically unconscious, no pressure was exerted on the department to take their interests seriously, and as we have seen, no standards or guarantees were built into the food assistance program to protect them.

With a new decade came a new president and a new secretary of agriculture. John Kennedy had seen the inadequacies of the Commodity Distribution Program firsthand while campaigning in depressed areas of Appalachia, and his first executive order doubled the number of foods on the surplus commodity list. In his first month in office, Kennedy directed the Department of Agriculture to begin work on a pilot food stamp program in order to obtain information and experience for the formulation of a permanent program. The pilots departed from the Blue and Gold model of 1939–1943 in that the stamps were of only one color and could be used for any domestically produced food item. The program was designed to increase total food consumption rather than to direct consumption toward surpluses. The experimental programs were judged a success, and in 1963, Representative Sullivan introduced an administration-sponsored Food Stamp Bill seeking a separate legislative base and funding not derived from Section 32 for a Food Stamp Program on a national scale.[38]

The difficult progress of this measure through various congressional committees revealed the persistence of the political commitments and ideas that had hampered food assistance since the wartime cutbacks. The bill's opponents argued that it represented an incursion of the federal government into an area rightly controlled by the states, that the administration would use the discretion granted the secretary of agriculture to force desegregation of southern retail outlets, and that the plan would pamper the lazy. In echoes of earlier discussions, its opponents contended that it would not sufficiently benefit farmers to be considered an appropriate activity for the Department of Agriculture, that it would not significantly reduce the stocks of price-depressing surpluses, and that it would shift to the federal treasury those costs born by the states and localities under the commodity distribution program.[39] Even the escape from the confines of Section 32 funding did not immediately weaken the farmers' money concept. Appropriations administered by the Department of Agriculture, reasoned the members of the House Agriculture Committee, would be "charged against agriculture" in the public mind. Even members who supported the plan were concerned; Chairman Harold Cooley, for example, who had supported food stamp legislation since the mid 1950s, indicated a wish "that some way could be found to charge this up to welfare and not the farmer. With a $6 billion budget," he continued, "the city people criticize us and complain that the farmers are a bunch of parasites, bloodsuckers and many other unwarranted epithets. As a matter of fact, more of this goes to the cities than it does to the country people. The benefits are more for the city people."[40] The bill was finally passed in 1964, but only after a compromise was arranged between urban liberals and rural conservatives: the former would vote for wheat and cotton price supports, if the latter would permit the food stamp legislation to pass.[41]

Although the new legislation provided for funding from the general revenues and was intended to expand general consumption by the poor rather than to dispose of specific surpluses, the opposition of conservatives and the farm orientation of the agriculture committee were not without effect: the new program was designed to secure and expand the farmer's market among the poor; it did not provide a floor under consumption nor guarantee access to food. As in the commodity distribution program after its transfer to agricultural hegemony, any conflict between the needs of the poor and those of the producers had been resolved in favor of the latter. The purchase requirement was set so high that many of the poorest families were excluded, while the value of bonus stamps was restricted by the fear that they might be used to replace previous consumption—the old "over and above" principle in modern dress. As journalist Nick Kotz later summarized the early development of the Food Stamp Program under Secretary of Agriculture Orville Freeman, "At every turn, Freeman appeared to mold and defend the Department's food Programs in terms calculated to soothe his congressional overseers." [42]

The mid sixties also saw the beginning of an expanded child nutrition program. The new interest in poverty that had surfaced in the early sixties provoked a widespread investigation of the effects of inadequate income on many aspects of individual and social life, including the academic performance of poor children. Investigators searching for an explanation for the lower achievement of impoverished children found empty stomachs instead of low intelligence quotients. Arguing that the school lunch program came too late in the day to provide fuel for crucial morning learning hours, educators and poverty warriors asked for a school breakfast program. Congress responded in 1966 with a small pilot program, targeted at schools in very poor neighborhoods.

However, the notion that agricultural abundance meant adequate food for all was slow to recede. Even after the civil rights movement and Michael Harrington's *The Other America* opened the eyes of many to the existence of widespread poverty and deprivation in the U.S., even after Lyndon Johnson declared "unconditional war" on this poverty, the public still felt that the American poor, however "culturally deprived" and "underprivileged" they might be, were fortunate in comparison to their Third World counterparts because "at least they get plenty to eat." Most Americans, as George McGovern noted in 1969, "assumed that hunger and malnutrition are the afflictions of Asia and other faraway places." [43] Even people who recognized that abundant production did not mean adequate distribution frequently assumed that real hunger was prevented by a government program. Robert Kennedy summarized this sentiment in a 1968 speech: "but surely, it is said, surely the government which can send wheat to combat famine in India is feeding the hungry at home." [44] There-

fore, in the late 1960s, when hearings and field investigations conducted
by well-known senators reported hunger and malnutrition in America,
many people were shocked. A dramatic tour of destitute communities in
the Mississippi Delta by Robert Kennedy and Joseph Clark was followed
in quick succession by a CBS television documentary, *Hunger in America*, and by *Hunger USA*, a report by the Citizen's Board of Inquiry into
Hunger and Malnutrition in the United States. A Senate Select Committee on Nutrition and Human needs was established, and a National Nutrition Survey implemented by the Department of Health Education and
Welfare at the direction of Congress began an assessment of the nutritional status of low income populations in ten states. Hunger had become
a public issue.

The rediscovery of hunger was greeted with expressions of outrage that
must have sounded familiar to those who remembered the Depression, for
the fundamental contradiction was the same—want amid plenty, waste
amid want. "Starvation in this land of enormous wealth is nothing short
of indecent," Robert Kennedy told an audience of college students.[45] "I
think, today in an affluent society, it is an absolute disgrace that we have
over 10 million Americans living on a diet of less than two-thirds of the
minimum nutrients required for good health," declared Senator Charles
Goodell in a statement to the opening session of the Senate select committee.[46] "There is no shortage of food," Secretary of Agriculture Orville
Freeman told the Senate committee. "Quite the Contrary. Clearly we are
fighting now and will continue to fight the problem of overproduction—
and not of shortage—in agriculture. . . . The single question that remains is whether we have the skill, ingenuity, and determination to get
the food to where it is needed."[47] "Hunger . . . exerts a special claim on
the conscience of the American people," declared George McGovern, not
only because of the suffering involved, but also because "it outrages the
Puritan ethic to have billions spent to stop food from being grown and
finance surplus storage while other Americans languish under the blight
of malnutrition."[48]

Turning their attention to the federal food assistance programs that
people had assumed were preventing the predictable effects of poverty on
diet, critics found them providing too little food to too few people with
too little equity and sensitivity to the poor. In 1967, the surplus commodity distribution and food stamp programs combined were reaching
less than a fifth of those with incomes below the federal poverty line. Neither program provided enough assistance to secure an adequate diet. Eligibility and benefit levels varied not only from state to state, but from

county to county, among counties that chose to participate. Eligibility criteria were not limited to income or need. In one Indiana township, for example, any family with a dog was excluded from receiving surplus commodities. And from all across the country came reports of local administrative practices displaying a remarkable indifference to the needs, convenience, and dignity of actual and potential participants: long waiting lines, inaccessible distribution points, few protections for the rights of participants or applicants, and no recourse for those who believed themselves unfairly treated.[49]

When investigators began to probe for explanations behind the descriptions of program inadequacies, they found the legacy of New Deal policy choices. The underlying factors that rendered federal food assistance inadequate against hunger in the land of plenty were the same factors that had constrained the FSCC's response to the relief crisis of 1938. Food assistance programs were still linked to surplus disposal and farm income support, still administered by an agency in which expertise, orientation, and constituency all reinforced the priority placed on aid to commercial farmers, still devoid of standards to protect the relief aspects of the programs, still overseen by congressional committees hostile to welfare measures and jealous of the prerogatives of big agriculture, especially where agricultural appropriations were at stake, and still subject to an unusual degree of local control. In the commodity distribution program, the composition of the commodity bundle was still dependent upon the vagaries of weather and markets and the power of competing producer groups, not upon the nutritional needs of participants. The Section 32 mindset had been reified by the passage of time. The federal relief establishment was no longer expressing concern about food assistance being interpreted as a return to federal general relief, but in the Food Stamp Program, the cost to the federal treasury was a significant constraint upon program growth, and USDA officials expressed considerable concern that states would use the program to shift welfare costs to agriculture.[50]

Fortunately for poor people, this story does not end, as tales of the discovery of the misery of the poor so often do, with a committee and an investigation. In the aftermath of the rediscovery of hunger in America in the late sixties, a process of reform in food assistance began that continued for a decade and achieved a remarkable expansion in program benefits and in the responsiveness of food programs to the poor. By the early 1980s, the Food Stamp Program was serving one in ten Americans, and expenditures for family food assistance had grown forty-seven fold. Uniform national eligibility and benefit levels had been established, and the Food Stamp Program had been extended to every county in the nation. Benefits had been expanded to conform to the agriculture department's standard for a minimally adequate diet, and a whole series of legally enforceable rights and protections had been established for participants and applicants. Finally, after a decade of effort by food assistance reformers, the purchase requirement was eliminated; food stamps equal in value to approximately the difference between a third of a participant's income (the supposed average normal expenditure) and the cost of a minimally adequate diet were distributed with no charge to recipients.[51]

The tremendous expansion and reform that made food assistance a major form of income support for poor people was essentially a process of undoing the constraints inherited from the program's Depression origins. That is, first the iron link between food assistance and surplus disposal was weakened by the creation of the Food Stamp Program, and its funding from general revenues rather than Section 32 set the stage for a gradual relaxation of the farmers' money idea. The development of an extensive "hunger lobby," a network of individuals and organizations that monitors food program performance and works through litigation and legislation for expansion and extension of food assistance benefits, provided a countervailing force to the power of agribusiness lobbyists. The establishment of the Senate select committee provided a congressional forum outside the agriculture committees for oversight of the programs, and the membership of the agriculture committees themselves became more heterogeneous with more representation of urban and consumer viewpoints. Within USDA, the creation of the Food and Nutrition Service to administer food assistance programs and other consumer-oriented activities replaced the integration of food assistance with agricultural marketing activities. Local control was terminated by a series of congressional acts and administrative regulations that returned control of food programs to the federal level. Although critics still find many faults with federal food programs, in a sense they have become the federal general relief that Hopkins resisted. Food stamps are the only federal noncategorical assistance program in the U.S. that can readily be translated into income equivalents.[52] In the years since the rediscovery of hunger, food assistance has become the federal floor under consumption, however inadequate, that was so sorely missed after the federal withdrawal from direct relief in 1935. The fact that the recent cutbacks in food assistance initiated by the Reagan administration have resulted in a growing need for soup kitchens, food pantries, and other emergency provisions suggests the extent to which poor people have come to rely upon this form of subsistence.

The reform and expansion of food assistance, however, came too late for a whole generation of the American poor. Since so much of the inadequacy of domestic food assistance programs that shocked the nation in the late 1960s can be traced to policy decisions made in the Great Depression, some accounting is necessary. What became of the high hopes and good intentions with which the New Dealers faced the unparalleled opportunities of 1933? How did a program that was intended to "resolve the paradox of want amid plenty" become merely a means of disposal for unmarketable products?

First, there was the "paradox" definition itself and the specific historical circumstances that generated and dramatized it. In the long run, the link between food assistance and farm surpluses proved a severe limitation on the ability of the programs to meet the nutritional needs of the poor. Looking back, one can easily fault the link to agricultural surpluses for the nutritional inadequacies of the commodity bundle, the subordination of relief to agricultural goals, and the domination of the programs by producers. In the context of the Depression, however, these factors were not obvious. The contradiction of wasted food and widespread hunger was so intolerable that it was difficult to see beyond the enormity of the contradiction to its deeper causes. The destruction of foodstuffs, the milk poured into ditches by striking dairy farmers, the burning of kerosene-soaked oranges in California, the other scattered dramatic incidents of deliberate waste fueled a sense of outrage and frustration that made planning beyond the urgent task of distributing those surpluses to the hungry difficult.

The Farm Board's stabilization operations, by concentrating a huge supply of the primary ingredient of the "staff of life" in government hands at public expense, politicized the paradox, providing a visible focus for widespread anger. The inability of even the staunchest foes of federal relief to resist the appeal of the wheat, the long line of speeches in which the members of the House of Representatives explained that they would not normally approve such a measure but could not, under the circumstances, vote against it, and President Hoover's acquiescence and later attempts to claim credit for the donations suggest just how compelling the contrast of waste and want was. The wheat rotting at government expense became a symbol of irrationality. And if the wheat proved irresistible after a protracted process of debate, is it any wonder that the sudden, surprising martyrdom of the piglets, with their squeals and stinking tankage, reified the contrast between surplus and need? In the face of so striking a contrast, raising questions about the long-term effects of binding food assistance to farm surpluses would have been difficult. The

Roosevelt administration had to act quickly: the pigs had created a public relations debacle. A clear symbol was urgently needed if the administration was to distinguish itself from its tarnished predecessor and rehabilitate its own image. The obvious, humane act was to distribute the pork to the unemployed—"The pressing paradox," as the *Times* commented, "would suggest if not compel some such provision." If the distribution for relief was to accomplish its mediating function, however, it needed to be obvious and visible. A new agency, complete with fanfare and initials, was quickly created to do the job, thus institutionalizing the paradox concept in an organization. That the organization established to transfer the food to the needy was created with so few standards, so little specification of its goals and priorities, was also in part an outcome of the paradox notion. With the problem defined as the paradox of want amid plenty, the agency was doing its job if it used a portion of the available surplus to relieve some of the need. The lack of standards was also a reflection of the atmosphere of the early New Deal and the specific need for haste created by the piglets, in part a function of the relatively untried corporate form. The FSRC was in some ways an archetypical embodiment of the much discussed pragmatism of the New Deal. The new agency was created specifically for a new task and was appealing, comprehensible, and unhampered by unnecessary legal constraints. In the long run, however, the absence of standards, the failure to specify minimum rights or to protect the relief functions of the project left the corporation open to control by commercial agriculture. Nothing in its charter prevented Harry Hopkins from declaring that "whoever can use the corporation should take it and run it."

Once the corporation was established, however, a new historical situation was created. The pressure was relieved, both the political pressure generated by the public outrage over the pig slaughter and the individual psychological and moral pressure experienced by well-intentioned people implementing distasteful policies. The heavy reliance of the secretary of agriculture and the AAA staff on the relief distribution venture in replying to critics of production control suggests the extent to which the creation of the Federal Surplus Relief Corporation served this function. It served it by merely existing, without much regard to the actual size of the surplus donation project. With the federal government visibly engaged in a program to transfer the surpluses to the hungry, people whose sensibilities had been violated could breathe a sigh of relief and resume normal activities: "It will relieve our minds of the distressing paradox." Once the pressure was relieved, the likelihood of more fundamental action evaporated. The limited transfers of surplus foods to the needy accomplished by the Federal Surplus Relief Corporation and its successors did not resolve the paradox of want amid plenty nor remove the underlying contradictions, but the establishment of the program did go a long way toward solving a sensitive public relations problem and conferring legitimacy upon an otherwise profoundly questionable and widely questioned policy.

Once the pig crisis was past, a familiar and predictable pattern was set in motion. The new organization began to develop its own clientele, and this clientele, with its interest in continuing to receive the benefits of surplus purchase and distribution, further precluded, for a time at least, more fundamental approaches to the problem of poverty-related malnutrition. In fact, several groups of clients existed. Farmers, who became the program's priority beneficiaries, were initially skeptical about the FSRC and hostile to the use of the processing tax to finance it. But the distribution of tangible benefits is seldom lost on a highly organized, politicized interest group, and groups of producers, especially those organized into commodity marketing cooperatives, soon caught on to the substantial benefits to be derived from relief purchases. "Last year and the year before, the Government purchased apples in this state . . . loose in cars. From the standpoint of the growers, this was a mighty fine thing." It proved to be a fine thing as well for agricultural administrators who had to find some acceptable means of eliminating the unmarketable portions of crops covered by marketing agreements and other surpluses removed in price support operations. In the long run, as we have seen, the desire of farm organizations, USDA marketing administrators, and farm representatives in Congress to continue this mighty fine thing led them to oppose the recreation of food stamps in the postwar era and throughout the 1950s and led to many of the constraints that hampered the current food stamp program in its early years.

Relief recipients, presumably, were also a clientele for the surplus commodity corporation, and if they had been as powerful and well-organized as farmers, they might have retained some voice in the commodity distribution program and shaped it to meet their needs more fully. But power, organization, and legitimacy were precisely the commodities they lacked, and their fortunes in the competition for the benefits of collective action were thus heavily dependent upon their advocates in the halls of power—the relief administrators. These men and women, however well intentioned, were myopic about food assistance. Committed by professional training and years of effort to obtain cash relief for their charges, they regarded commodity distribution as little better than an evil necessitated by the peculiar circumstances of 1933, and they were happy to be rid of the responsibility for perpetuating this archaic form of aid. In their commitment to cash as the only modern, acceptable, dignity-preserving form of assistance, they missed an opportunity to protect a significant federal floor under the inadequate provisions made by the states and localities. Recent history has proven them wrong. Not only has the nation devised a whole series of relatively dignified provisions in kind—public housing, Medicaid, food stamps, school meals—but these programs account for the greater part of federal outlay for means-tested programs (programs directed specifically to the poor). Poor people now receive considerably more aid from the federal government in kind than in cash. And though cash of equal value might still be preferable, to recipients as well as to administrators, the welfare politics of the last two decades strongly suggest that in the context of our attitudes toward the poor and our interest group–dominated policy process, programs in kind will obtain more for the poor than cash strategies alone.

The superiority of cash, as we have seen, was not the only ideology fogging the vision of the relief establishment in 1935. Another was the distinction between unemployed and unemployable, which became a self-evident basis for abandoning the latter to the uncertain mercies of local communities due to the "obvious local character" of their needs. In order to shore up this shaky explanatory edifice and communicate to governors and state legislators the firmness of its intent, the Roosevelt relief administration declined any part in the management of surplus commodity distribution, turning over the corporation—lock, stock, and barrel—to the waiting arms of the Agriculture Department. Arguing conclusively about events that never occurred is difficult, of course, but the later history of food assistance suggests that continued active involvement of relief officials in surplus commodity distribution might have made a difference. Unfortunately for poor people, relief officials viewed such continuing involvement as inconsistent with the president's intention to get out of the relief business.

Section 32 further sealed the corporation's fate. Not only did it ensure that the program would be transferred to the Department of Agriculture, but it also ensured that there commodity distribution would be dedicated to the needs of producers, since Section 32 was farmers' money. The historic argument over the disadvantages accruing to farmers from the tariff, the long McNary-Haugen fight for equality for agriculture, the desperation of farmers dramatized by the Holiday Association, the endless discussion of parity, the articulate power of the farm organizations, and the legacy of the farm bloc combined to make this peculiar concept seem plausible and acceptable. With Section 32 funds regarded as farmers' money, any additional appropriations for Section 32 purposes, and eventually all appropriations administered by USDA, were reasonably regarded as farmers' money.

Once the transfer was accomplished, the conversion of the program to a convenient outlet for products acquired in surplus removal operations was predictable. In a system in which agencies compete for funds through congressional committees, administrators will try to please those committees, and the membership of the congressional agriculture committees became, over the postwar decades, increasingly conservative and anti-welfare, while remaining militantly pro-agriculture. The congressional committee assignment system reinforced that process: throughout the 1950s, the House Agriculture Committee had only one member from a nonfarm district. This pattern not only assured a relative uniformity of opinion within the committee, but it also tended to shield the committee's actions from public view. By the mid 1950s when Leonor Sullivan was pursuing reestablishment of the Food Stamp Plan, the widespread perception was that the farm problem was a technical matter concerning parity ratios, something that was neither comprehensible nor interesting to urban consumers. And as the public lost interest in agricultural policy, the relationships among the Agriculture Department, the congressional agriculture committees, and the farm organizations came to approximate a closed system. "When political scientists of the 1950's and the 1960's studied the U.S. Department of Agriculture . . . , they found that it epitomized an 'iron triangle' bureaucracy," political scientist Jeffrey Berry has noted. "It had close relationships with the agriculture committees in Congress and with the many interest groups representing farmers. The three sides of this triangle worked together in harmony behind the scenes to formulate national agricultural policy,"[53] and they had little incentive to concern themselves with the poor. Thus, with the remarkable exception of the Blue and Gold Food Stamp Plan, the die was cast with the transfer. The strictures of the iron triangle set in, and they continued to constrain the performance of food assistance until a countervailing triangle arose with the rediscovery of hunger in the late sixties. In between, an entire generation of poor people went hungry, hidden from view by enormous piles of grain, invisible to the public, and a convenient receptacle for the agricultural policy makers preoccupied with finding storage space for unmanageable surpluses.

Who were these poor people? In one sense, they too were a New Deal legacy. When poverty investigators took a closer look at the desperately poor people who had been subsisting on surplus commodities only, they discovered the Depression's displaced sharecroppers and tenant farmers and their children and grandchildren. They found them still on the margins of agriculture, providing a residual seasonal labor force, on hand for a few weeks' work at planting and harvest or traveling with the migrant labor caravans. They also found them unskilled and unemployed in the large cities. The long-term agricultural trend toward "get big or get out" had been accelerated by agricultural adjustment; not only had many farm tenants been displaced when landlords removed the acres they had been farming from production, but large farmers had used their government crop loans and price support payments to mechanize, further displacing agricultural labor. Agricultural subsidies had made farming increasingly attractive to huge agribusiness conglomerates that employed mechanization on an advanced scale. With the demise of the Farm Security Administration in 1943, a casualty of war and the hostility of the Farm Bureau Federation, had come the end of any serious effort by the federal government to assist poor farmers in retaining or regaining their independence. The armed services and jobs in war industries had provided income for a time for some of those displaced, but the adjustments of the postwar era proved them to be temporary havens for many, especially black and Hispanic workers. The nation's failure to plan for those released from agriculture, together with policies that accelerated the displacement of farm labor and the replacement of small farms by large, bred much of the poverty and hunger that exploded upon the nation's consciousness in the 1960s.

And so the paradox came full circle. The coexistence of hunger with huge surpluses elicited widespread anger and demands for action, which turned to outrage when the federal government undertook the pig slaughter to forestall a market glut and raise the price of pork. The government responded with a program to transfer a portion of the surplus to a portion of those in need, and with the pressure of conscience and public opinion eased, agricultural New Dealers resumed the distasteful business of reducing output and driving up prices. The measures they used to achieve this dubious aim accelerated the displacement of marginal farmers from their meager livelihoods, adding them to the ranks of the rural and urban poor who would become dependent upon federal food assistance after other federal relief was withdrawn. They would thus suffer most from the inadequacies of the food programs that emerged from the New Deal. Meanwhile, the mere existence of a federal surplus commodity distribution program continued to confer legitimacy upon the broader farm program and to relieve minds of the paradox. For the nation's poorest citizens, the legacy of New Deal food assistance was, once again, hunger in the midst of plenty.

SOURCES

The major sources of data for this study are the records of the Federal Surplus Relief Corporation and its successor, the Federal Surplus Commodities Corporation, which are part of Record Group 124, Records of the Surplus Marketing Administration, in the National Archives. They consist of correspondence, memoranda, draft reports, occasional pamphlets, and newspaper clippings—all the surviving paper records of the day-to-day activity of a busy agency. The most useful entries were the records of Jacob Baker, assistant to the president of the FSRC, those of Keith Southard, the corporation's executive officer until 1935, and the various correspondence files, especially those containing correspondence with members of Congress. They are designated FSRC Files and FSCC Files in the endnotes that follow.

The records of the secretary of agriculture in Record Group 16 were also essential; these are designated Secretary of Agriculture's Files. The records of the Legal Division of the AAA, which contain much useful material for this study, are also part of Record Group 16, as are the files of the Solicitor of the Department of Agriculture. These are designated AAA Legal Division Files and USDA Solicitor's Files, respectively.

The files of the Agricultural Adjustment Administration in Record Group 145, the records of the Agricultural Stabilization and Conservation Service, were very valuable; within this collection, extensive use was made of the records of the emergency hog marketing program, and these are designated Hog Emergency Files.

The records of the Federal Emergency Relief Administration in Record Group 69 provided useful information on the FSRC's involvement with production-for-use projects and helped to fill in the missing pieces of the process leading to the corporation's transfer to the Department of Agriculture. Jacob Baker's Chronological File proved to be an especially useful entry. Records from this group are designated FERA Files.

For the pre–New Deal period, the records of the President's Emergency Committee on Employment and the minutes of the Federal Farm Board were consulted, along with the Secretary of Agriculture's Correspondence File and the records of the Senate Committee on Agriculture and Forestry. The PECE Files in Record Group 73 are particularly fascinating.

Several other manuscript collections were consulted in addition to the records at the National Archives. The most important was the Franklin Delano Roosevelt Library, Hyde Park, New York. In addition to the president's own papers, those of Eleanor Roosevelt, Harry Hopkins, and Henry Morgenthau were useful. Material from the Herbert C. Hoover Presidential Library in West Branch, Iowa, was obtained in photocopy form through correspondence. The Social Welfare History Archive at the University of Minnesota provided much useful material on the attitudes of social welfare leaders; especially useful were the files of the Government and Social Work Division of the American Association of Social Workers in the National Association of Social Workers Collection. The Charles McNary papers at the Library of Congress were useful. The Jerome N. Frank papers at Yale University Library were fascinating although they touched only briefly on the creation of the FSRC. The files maintained by the Agricultural History Branch of the Economic Research Service of the United States Department of Agriculture, USDA, Washington, D.C., were very helpful; they included the minutes of the Food Survey Committee which provided useful insight into the policy debates that led to the transfer of the corporation to its new home in the Department of Agriculture.

Oral histories were also an important source for this study. The Columbia University Oral History Collection is particularly rich in memoirs of New Deal agricultural officials; those consulted included, Paul Appleby, Samuel Bledsoe, Virginia Durr, R. M. Evans, Mordecai Ezekial, Jerome Frank, Marvin Jones, Lee Pressman, O. C. Stine, Jesse Tapp, Rexford Tugwell, Henry Wallace, Claude Wickard, and Milburn L. Wilson. These are all designated COHC in the notes that follow. Several published collections of oral histories also proved useful. Studs Terkel's *Hard Times* was invaluable, as were two collections based on the work of the WPA writers project, *These Are Our Lives* and *Such as Us*. Margaret Jarman Hagood's fascinating study of the lives of tenant farm women, *Mothers of the South*, while not confined to the oral history genre, provided valuable insights.

Among published sources, those which were used most consistently as primary sources were the *Congressional Record*, House and Senate Committee Hearings, the *Annual Reports* of the FSRC and the FSCC, the published papers and addresses of Presidents Herbert Hoover and Franklin Roosevelt and a number of Department of Agriculture publications including *The Yearbook of Agriculture*, *Agricultural Statistics*, and various reports pertaining to the AAA. Two books by major participants in the events recorded here, Harry Hopkins's *Spending to Save: The Complete Story of Relief* and Henry Wallace's *New Frontiers* were especially helpful. A number of periodical series were used quite extensively, including the *New York Times*, the *Commercial and Financial Chronical*, *Wallace's Farmer*, *Better Times*, *The New Republic*, *The Nation*, *Today*, *Fortune*, *Current History*, the *Literary Digest*, *Proceedings* of the National Conference of Social Work, *The Bureau Farmer*, *The Nation's Agriculture*, and the *Annual Report*s of the American Farm Bureau Federation.

The brevity of these notes does not permit a listing of the secondary sources without which such a study is impossible. They include general works on the Depression and New Deal, more specialized studies of relief and agricultural policy and politics in this period, and for background, studies of farm organizations, of American agriculture, and of social welfare history and policy. Several specialized items, to which the reader may turn for other perspectives on the Federal Surplus Relief Corporation, however, should be noted here. One dissertation on the subject, Irvin M. May's study entitled "The Paradox of Agricultural Abundance and Poverty: The Federal Surplus Relief Corporation, 1933–1935," and two published articles: C. Roger Lambert, "Want and Plenty: The Federal Surplus Relief Corporation and the A.A.A.," *Agricultural History* 46 (1972) and Irvin M. May, "Cotton and Cattle: The FSRC and Emergency Work Relief," *Agricultural History* 46 (1972) were useful. Similarly, two published accounts of the emergency pig slaughter are available: George T. Blakey, "Ham That Never Was: The 1933 Emergency Hog Slaughter," *The Historian* 30 (1967–1968); and D. A. Fitzgerald, *Corn and Hogs Under the Agricultural Adjustment Act: Developments Up to March 1934* (Washington: Brookings Institute, 1934).

NOTES

INTRODUCTION

1. *New York Times*, January 1, 3, 4, 1933.
2. Corrington Gill, *Wasted Manpower* (New York: W. W. Norton, 1939), p. 138.
3. Oscar Ameringer, testimony in Congress, subcommittee of the House Committee on Labor, *Unemployment in the United States*, 72d Cong., 1st sess., 1932, pp. 98–99.
4. Walter Lippmann, "Poverty and Plenty," *Proceedings* of the National Conference of Social Work, 59th sess., 1932 (Chicago: University of Chicago Press, 1932), pp. 234–235.
5. Henry A. Wallace, *New Frontiers* (New York: Reynal and Hitchcock, 1934), p. 183.
6. Rexford Tugwell, "Relief and Reconstruction," *Proceedings* of the National Conference of Social Work, 61st sess., 1934 (Chicago: University of Chicago Press, 1934), pp. 40–41.
7. *Congressional Record*, 72d Cong., 1 sess., 1932, p. 5196.
8. Maurice Leven, et al., *America's Capacity to Consume* (Washington: Brookings Institution, 1934), pp. 121–124.
9. Wallace, *New Frontiers*, p. 184.
10. Howard Zinn, *New Deal Thought* (New York: Bobbs-Merrill, 1966), p. xvi.
11. Norman Thomas, *After the New Deal, What?* (New York: Macmillan, 1936), p. 33.
12. Barton J. Bernstein, "The New Deal: The Conservative Achievements of Liberal Reform" in B. J. Bernstein, ed., *Towards a New Past: Dissenting Essays in American History* (New York: Vintage Books, 1969), p. 264.

CHAPTER ONE

1. Ida Moore, "Old Man Dobbin and His Crowd" in *These Are Our Lives* (New York: W. W. Norton, 1975), p. 190.
2. Murray R. Benedict, *Farm Policies of the United States 1790–1950: A Study of Their Origins and Development* (New York: Octagon Books, 1966), pp. 116, 247, 356–357; see also Earl O. Heady, *A Primer on Food, Agriculture and Public Policy* (New York: Random House, 1967); Gilbert C. Fite, *George N. Peek and the Fight for Farm Parity* (Norman: University of Oklahoma Press, 1954).
3. Harry Braverman, *Labor and Monopoly Capital: The Degradation of Work in the Twentieth Century* (New York: Monthly Review Press, 1974), pp. 109, 433, 434.
4. Margaret Jarman Hagood, *Mothers of the South: Portraiture of the White Tenant Farm Woman* (New York: W. W. Norton, 1977), p. 10.

5. For a cogent discussion of farm tenancy in the United States, see David Eugene Conrad, *The Forgotten Farmers: The Story of Sharecroppers in the New Deal* (Urbana: University of Illinois Press, 1965), pp. 3–18, and Donald Grubbs, *Cry From the Cotton: The Southern Tenant Farmers Union and the New Deal* (Chapel Hill: University of North Carolina Press, 1971), pp. 3–16, 25.

6. Writing of the insecurity of tenure in the early years of the Great Depression, Norman Thomas commented: "If [the lease was] out of the family, it set up a system of what in Ireland was called rack-renting; that is, the tenant had no security of claim on improvements. It is only our own of civilized nations which still tolerates rack-renting." Norman Thomas, *America's Way Out: A Program for Democracy* (New York: Macmillan, 1931), p. 180.

7. Hagood, *Mothers of the South*, p. 22.

8. W. O. Foster, "Five Year Lease" in *These Are Our Lives*, p. 59.

9. Benedict, *Farm Policies*, pp. 114–116.

10. U.S. Department of Commerce, Bureau of the Census, *Historical Statistics*, series K361–375 (Washington, D.C.: U.S. Government Printing Office, 1975), p. 491.

11. Benedict, *Farm Policies*, pp. 167, 168.

12. Remley J. Glass, "Gentlemen, the Corn Belt!" *Harper's*, July 1933, p. 201.

13. Benedict, *Farm Policies*, p. 168.

14. Murray R. Benedict, *Can We Solve the Farm Problem?* (New York: Twentieth Century Fund, 1955), pp. 5–7; Benedict, *Farm Policies*, pp. 168–170.

15. Benedict, *Farm Problem*, pp. 6–7; Fite, *George N. Peek*, pp. 3–13.

16. William H. Lyon, testimony in Congress, reprinted in George McGovern, ed., *Agricultural Thought in the Twentieth Century* (Indianapolis: Bobbs-Merrill, 1967), p. 87.

17. Fite, *George N. Peek*, p. 4.

18. Benedict, *Farm Problem*, p. 7; Theodore Saloutos and John D. Hicks, *Twentieth Century Populism: Agricultural Discontent in the Middle West 1900–1939* (Lincoln: University of Nebraska Press, 1951), p. 100.

19. Lyon, in McGovern, *Agricultural Thought*, p. 87.

20. Marvin Jones Memoir, COHC, pp. 192–193.

21. Grant McConnell, *The Decline of Agrarian Democracy* (Berkeley: University of California Press, 1953), pp. 39–41; Wesley McCune, *The Farm Bloc* (New York: Greenwood Press, 1968), pp. 145–157.

22. John A. Crampton, *The National Farmers Union: Ideology of a Pressure Group* (Lincoln: University of Nebraska Press, 1956); McConnell, *The Decline of Agrarian Democracy*, pp. 37–39, 146; McCune, *The Farm Bloc*, pp. 193–221; Benedict, *Farm Policies*, p. 134.

23. McConnell, *The Decline of Agrarian Democracy*, pp. 44–65; Benedict, *Farm Policies*, pp. 176–180; McCune, *The Farm Bloc*, pp. 165–192.

24. Benedict, *Farm Policies*, pp. 181–186; McConnell, *The Decline of Agrarian Democracy*, pp. 57–59.

25. Benedict, *Farm Problem*, pp. 6, 7, 84, 85.

26. Lyon, in McGovern, *Agricultural Thought*, p. 91.

27. George N. Peek and Hugh S. Johnson, *Equality for Agriculture* (Moline, Illinois: H. W. Harrington, 1922).
28. The most extensive study of the McNary-Haugen campaign is in Fite, *George N. Peek*; see also Saloutos and Hicks, *Populism*, pp. 372–403; Arthur Schlesinger, Jr., *The Crisis of the Old Order, 1919–1933*, vol. 1 of *The Age of Roosevelt* (Boston: Houghton Mifflin, 1957), p. 100.
29. *Congressional Record*, 69th Cong., 2d sess., February 25, 1927, 68, p. 4771.
30. Fite, *George N. Peek*, pp. 193–202; Benedict, *Farm Policies*, pp. 235–238.
31. One such free trade voice was that of Norman Thomas who wrote in 1931,

> It cannot be said at present that the justifiable discontent of farmers has taught them any economic wisdom. They are awakening to the disastrous effect of a high tariff policy on them, not to ask a reduction of tariffs in the interest of cheaper goods that they must buy and better world trade, but to demand tariffs for themselves or indirect export subsidies through the debenture plan on those export crops like wheat and cotton which cannot be protected by an import tariff. [Thomas, *America's Way Out*, p. 183.]

32. Albert U. Romasco, *The Poverty of Abundance: Hoover, the Nation, the Depression* (New York: Oxford University Press, 1965), p. 101.
33. Benedict, *Farm Problem*, pp. 85–89; Romasco, *Poverty of Abundance*, pp. 108–114.
34. Carl Sandburg, *The People, Yes* (New York: Harcourt, Brace, 1936), p. 75.

CHAPTER TWO

1. *Prairie Farmer*, November 9, 1929, p. 21, quoted in James F. Evans, *Prairie Farmer and WLS* (Urbana: University of Illinois Press, 1964), p. 141.
2. Schlesinger, *Old Order*, pp. 174, 175; Benedict, *Farm Problem*, pp. 10, 11; Dean Albertson, *Roosevelt's Farmer: Claude R. Wickard and the New Deal* (New York: Columbia University Press, 1961), p. 65.
3. Benedict, *Farm Problem*, pp. 92, 101–132.
4. Schlesinger, *Old Order*, p. 185.
5. Benedict, *Farm Problem*, pp. 49, 138–139.
6. John Stokes to the Rockefeller Foundation, December 20, 1930, *Records of the President's Emergency Committee on Employment* (hereafter PECE), Record Group 73, National Archives.
7. Oscar Heline in Studs Terkel, *Hard Times: An Oral History of the Great Depression* (New York: Avon Books Discus, 1970), p. 252.
8. Ruth Loriks in *ibid.*, p. 266.
9. Harry Terrell in *ibid.*, p. 250.
10. Paul Webbink, "Unemployment in the United States, 1930–1940," *Papers and Proceedings* of the American Economic Association, vol. 30, 53rd annual meeting, 1940 (American Economic Review, 1941), pp. 250–251.

11. Irving Bernstein, *The Lean Years* (Boston: Houghton Mifflin, 1972), pp. 489–491.
12. Marion Elderton, ed., *Case Studies of Unemployment* (Philadelphia: University of Pennsylvania Press, 1931), pp. xxx–xxxi, xli–xlvii; Schlesinger, *Old Order*, pp. 167–168; see also Louis Adamic, *My America, 1928–1938* (New York: Harper, 1938), pp. 283–293.
13. Clarke A. Chambers, *Seedtime of Reform: American Social Services and Social Action 1918–1933* (Minneapolis: University of Minnesota Press), p. 146.
14. E. Wight Bakke, *The Unemployed Worker: A Study of the Task of Making a Living Without a Job* (New Haven: Yale University Press, 1940), pp. 266–268.
15. Josephine Brown, *Public Relief, 1929–1939* (New York: Holt, 1940); Blanche D. Coll, *Perspectives in Public Welfare: A History* (Washington: U.S. Government Printing Office, 1970); Walter Trattner, *From Poor Law to Welfare State* (New York: Free Press, 1979).
16. Brown, *Public Relief*, p. 10.
17. Herbert Hoover, "Address to the Welfare and Relief Mobilization Conference," *Public Papers of the Presidents, Herbert Hoover, 1932–1933* (Washington: U.S. Government Printing Office, 1976), p. 294.
18. Herbert Hoover, "Lincoln's Birthday Address," text of radio address as printed in the *New York Times*, February 13, 1931.
19. Herbert Hoover, "Address to the Welfare and Relief Mobilization Conference," *Public Papers*, p. 294.
20. Bernstein, *The Lean Years*, pp. 302–304; E. P. Hayes, *Activities of the President's Emergency Committee for Employment* (Concord, New Hampshire: Rumford, 1936).
21. Frances Piven and Richard Cloward, *Regulating the Poor: The Functions of Public Welfare* (New York: Pantheon, 1971), pp. 48–49; Schlesinger, *Old Order*, pp. 164–165; Gilbert Seldes, *The Years of the Locust: America, 1929–1932* (Boston: Little, Brown, 1933), pp. 9–11, 54–56, 161, 162; Harris G. Warren, *Herbert Hoover and the Great Depression* (New York: Oxford University Press, 1959).
22. Arthur Mann, *LaGuardia: A Fighter Against His Times, 1882–1933*, vol. 1 (Philadelphia: J. B. Lippencott, 1959), p. 290.
23. Brown, *Public Relief*, pp. 73–74; Margaret Wead, "Drifts in Unemployment Relief," *The Family*, November 1932, pp. 225–226.
24. Wead, "Drifts," p. 226.
25. Joanna C. Colcord, "The Commissary System," *The Family*, November 1932, pp. 235–240.
26. Helen Hall, *Unfinished Business* (New York: Macmillan, 1971), p. 51.
27. Dixon Wecter, *The Age of the Great Depression, 1929–1941* (New York: Macmillan, 1952), p. 16; Caroline Bird, *The Invisible Scar* (New York: David McKay, 1966), p. 26; H. L. Lurie, testimony in Congress, subcommittee of the Senate Committee on Manufactures, *Federal Aid for Unemploy-*

ment Relief, 72d Cong., 2d sess., 1933, pp. 64–67; Adamic, *My America*, pp. 296, 297.

28. These are but a few of the many examples of informal assistance measures undertaken by individuals and groups. Many anecdotal accounts of the Great Depression contain descriptions of such efforts. The samples cited here come from: Bird, *The Invisible Scar*, pp. 24–25; Robert Bendiner, *Just Around the Corner: A Highly Selective History of the Thirties* (New York: Harper & Row, 1967); Edward Robb Ellis, *A Nation in Torment: The Great American Depression, 1929–1939* (New York: Capricorn Books, 1971), pp. 125–131; *Amsterdam News*, September 14, 1932.

29. Bernstein, *The Lean Years*, pp. 292–302; "No One Has Starved," *Fortune*, September 1932, pp. 19–28.

30. Karl de Schweinitz, testimony in Congress, subcommittee of the Senate Committee on Manufactures, *Federal Cooperation in Unemployment Relief*, 72d Cong., 1st sess., 1932, pp. 20, 21.

31. "No One Has Starved," pp. 22, 23.

32. Frances Piven and Richard Cloward, *Poor People's Movements: Why They Succeed, How They Fail* (New York: Vintage Books, 1979), pp. 60, 61.

33. "No One Has Starved," pp. 27, 28.

34. "Notes and Comment," *The Social Service Review* 6 (December 1932), pp. 637–639.

35. Quoted in Mauritz Hallgren, *Seeds of Revolt: A Study of American Life and the Temper of the American People During the Depression* (New York: Knopf, 1933).

36. Dynamite Garland in Studs Terkel, *Hard Times*, p. 115.

37. Dorothe Bernstein in *ibid.*, p. 123.

38. Quoted in Hallgren, *Seeds of Revolt*.

39. Adamic, *My America*.

40. Bernstein, *The Lean Years*, pp. 416–420.

41. Piven and Cloward, *Poor People's Movements*, pp. 49–60.

42. Adamic, *My America*, p. 309.

43. Dixon Wecter, *The Age of the Great Depression*, p. 36.

44. Daniel Willard, "The Challenge to Capitalism," *Review of Reviews* 83 (May 1931), p. 61.

45. Bernstein, *The Lean Years*, pp. 362–363; James L. Fieser to Herbert Hoover, June 1, 1931, PECE; Edmund Wilson, "Red Cross and County Agent," in *The American Earthquake* (Garden City: Doubleday, 1958), pp. 249–266.

46. Charles Hurd, *The Compact History of the American Red Cross* (New York: Hawthorne Books, 1959), p. 209.

47. Wilson, "Red Cross and County Agent," p. 252.

48. David E. Hamilton, "Herbert Hoover and the Great Drought of 1930," *Journal of American History* 68 (March 1982), pp. 850–875; Robert Cowley, "The Drought and the Dole," *American Heritage* 23 (February 1972), pp. 16–19, 92–99.

49. Woods to Payne, February 14, 1931, PECE.

50. *Congressional Record*, 72d Cong., 1st sess., 1932, p. 1186.

51. Hamilton, *Hoover and the Drought*, pp. 852–853; "Arkansas's Fight for Life," *Literary Digest*, February 28, 1931; Charles Morrow Wilson, *The Fight Against Hunger* (New York: Funk and Wagnalls, 1969), pp. 92, 93.

52. See Braverman, *Labor and Monopoly Capital*, for a discussion of the destruction of self-provisioning skills and resources that accompanied the commodification of food.

53. Hall, *Unfinished Business*, p. 48.

54. Bernstein, *The Lean Years*, p. 363.

55. Quoted in Hallgren, *Seeds of Revolt*.

56. Cowley, "The Drought and the Dole"; Hamilton, "Hoover and the Drought," pp. 869–870.

57. Bernstein, *The Lean Years*, pp. 378, 422; Wilson, *The Fight Against Hunger*, pp. 100–105.

58. Eleanor Flexnor, "Yes, There Is Starvation in New York City," *Better Times*, April 11, 1932, p. 4; Bernstein, *The Lean Years*, pp. 329–332; Harry Hopkins, *Spending to Save: The Complete Story of Relief* (New York: W. W. Norton, 1936), pp. 79–82.

59. Judge Will Cummings, statement quoted in the Chattanooga, Tennessee *Times* and the *Congressional Record*, 72d Cong., 1 sess., 1932, p. 1406.

60. "Using Surplus Grains," editorial in the Mount Vernon, Ohio *Republican News* and reprinted in the *Congressional Record*, 72d Cong., 1st sess., 1932, p. 1407.

61. Herbert Hoover, "Statement on the Purposes and Methods of the Cabinet Committee on Unemployment," October 21, 1930, *Public Papers*, p. 438.

62. *Congressional Record*, 72d Cong., 1st sess., 1932, p. 5191.

63. J. R. McCleskey to William G. McAdoo, October 25, 1930, PECE.

64. Quoted in Schlesinger, *Old Order*, p. 225.

65. Samuel Bledsoe Memoir, COHC, p. 47.

66. "Less Work—More Pay," *The Nation*, October 15, 1930, p. 393.

67. Romasco, *Poverty of Abundance*, p. 3.

68. Oscar Ameringer, *If You Don't Weaken: The Autobiography of Oscar Ameringer* (New York: Henry Holt, 1940), p. 449.

69. James Truslow Adams, "America Faces 1933's Realities," *New York Times Sunday Magazine*, January 1, 1933.

70. Walter Lippmann, "Poverty and Plenty," pp. 234–235.

71. H. G. Wells, excerpted in the *New York Times*, November 9, 1930.

72. Adams, "American Faces 1933's Realities."

73. "To Bring Back Prosperity," *Wallace's Farmer and Iowa Homestead*, December 20, 1930, p. 1954.

74. *Congressional Record*, 71st Cong., 2d sess., 1930, quoted in Jordan A. Schwarz, *The Interregnum of Despair: Hoover, Congress and the Depression* (Urbana: University of Illinois Press, 1970), p. 30.

CHAPTER THREE

1. President's Emergency Committee for Employment, "Food Conservation for Relief of the Unemployed," no. 9 in the *Community Plans and Activities* series, issued in pamphlet form as occasional papers, n.d., p. 3.

2. *Kansas City Times*, July 19, 1933.

3. PECE, "Food Conservation," p. 5.

4. Virginia Durr Memoir, COHC, pp. 64–65.

5. *Chicago Daily Tribune*, September 11, 1933.

6. Hayes, *Activities of the President's Committee*, pp. 112–114.

7. Economic Conservation Committee of America, brochure, copy with McCleskey correspondence in PECE.

8. McCleskey to Woods, November 6, 1930, PECE.

9. *New York Times*, October 24, 1930; Clyde Warburton, Secretary National Drought Relief Committee, to Fred Croxton, November 25, 1930, PECE; Sam R. McKelvie, Federal Farm Board, to Col. Arthur Woods, October 23, 1930, "Summary of Suggestions—1930–31," typescript in PECE.

10. *San Francisco Chronicle*, October 21, 1930, clipping with McCleskey correspondence in PECE.

11. *New York Times*, October 24, 1930.

12. W. G. McAdoo to Charles L. McNary, November 12, 1930, telegram, McCleskey correspondence in PECE.

13. *New York Times*, December 2, 1930.

14. J. R. McCleskey to Col. Arthur Woods, November 24, 1930, PECE.

15. McCleskey to McAdoo, October 25, 1930, PECE; McCleskey to Herbert Hoover, October 20, 1930, PECE; McCleskey to Herbert Hoover, telegram, October 20, 1930, PECE; McCleskey to Herbert Hoover, telegram, December 5, 1930, PECE; McCleskey to Woods, December 6, 1930, PECE; McCleskey to Ray L. Wilbur, Secretary of the Interior, December 8, 1930, Grain File, Hoover Papers, Herbert Hoover Presidential Library (HHPL).

16. A. E. Taylor to R. L. Wilbur, December 18, 1930; R. L. Wilbur to Lawrence Richey, secretary to the President, December 22, 1930, Wheat File, Hoover Papers, HHPL.

17. Woods to McCleskey, telegram, December 10, 1930, PECE.

18. Joe T. Robinson, testimony in Senate Committee on Agriculture and Forestry, *Relief for Drought Stricken Areas*, 71st Cong., 3d sess., 1930, p. 9 (hereafter cited as Senate, *Relief for Drought Stricken Areas*).

19. McAdoo to McCleskey, December 8, 1930, PECE.

20. Hamilton, "Hoover and the Drought," pp. 864–865. Hamilton calls the President's reversal "one of the gravest blunders of his presidency," and attributes the decision to "the fear of a large budget deficit, of making unsound loans, and of establishing precedents for federal relief programs."

21. Herbert Hoover, *Public Papers of the Presidents, Herbert Hoover, January 1 to December 31, 1930* (Washington: U.S. Government Printing Office, 1976), pp. 556–557.

22. McCleskey to Woods, December 10, 1930, PECE.

23. Senate, *Relief for Drought Stricken Areas*, pp. 44–56; House Committee on Agriculture, *Drought and Storm Relief*, 71st Cong., 3d sess., December 5, 17, 1930, pp. 71–74 (hereafter cited as House, *Drought and Storm Relief*).

24. *Congressional Record*, 71st Cong., 3d sess., December 12, 1930, pp. 628–629.

25. Senate, *Relief for Drought Stricken Areas*, pp. 10, 12, 53; *Congressional Record*, 71st Cong., 3d sess., January 14, 1931, p. 2192; Hamilton, "Hoover and the Drought," p. 871.

26. Hamilton, "Hoover and the Drought," p. 866.

27. Senate, *Relief for Drought Stricken Areas*, pp. 46, 53.

28. Senate Committee on Agriculture and Forestry, *Distribution of Surplus Wheat for Relief Purposes* 71st Cong., 3d sess., December 11, 1930, pp. 1–13. Unless otherwise specified, all quotations in the discussion of this hearing come from this document.

29. Senator John B. Kendrick of Wyoming in Senate, *Relief for Drought Stricken Areas*, p. 16.

30. Senate Committee on Agriculture and Forestry, *Report to accompany S.J. Res. 210*, committee print no. 1341, January 21, 1931.

31. *Congressional Record*, 71st Cong., 3d sess., January 26, 1931, pp. 3196, 3197; *Commercial and Financial Chronicle*, January 31, 1931, p. 765.

32. Haugen to McCleskey, December 3, 1930, PECE.

33. *Congressional Record*, 71st Cong., 3d sess., January 8, 1931, pp. 1645–1647.

34. Hamilton, "Hoover and the Drought, pp. 869–871; "Country Crying for Relief from the Relief Fight," *Literary Digest*, February 14, 1931, p. 9; Cowley, "The Drought and the Dole," pp. 94–98; "The Trend of Events," *Outlook*, February 11, 1931, pp. 205–207; "Backstage in Washington," *Outlook*, February 18, 1931, p. 251.

35. House Committee on Agriculture, *Reforestation Act Amendment, Peanut Statistics, Farm and Unemployment Relief, Agricultural Credit Corporation, Experimental Farm in Mobile County, Ala., National Arboretum Appropriations*, 71st Cong., 3d sess., January 28, 1931, pp. 74–81 (hereafter cited as House, *Farm and Unemployment Relief*). Unless otherwise specified, all quotations in the discussion of this hearing come from this document.

36. Haugen to McCleskey, December 3, 1930, PECE.

37. Senate, *Distribution of Surplus Wheat for Relief Purposes*, p. 4.

38. William Gibbs McAdoo to Arthur Capper, December 8, 1930, reprinted in *Ibid.*, p. 9.

39. Marvin Jones Memoir, COHC, p. 206.

40. See the *Congressional Record*, 71st Cong., 3d sess., January 8, 1931, pp. 1646, 1647 for evidence of Fish's somewhat strained relations with his colleagues.

41. House Committee on Agriculture, *Wheat Distribution*, 73d Cong., 1st sess., January 4, 5, March 1, 1932, p. 12.

42. House, *Farm and Unemployment Relief*, p. 81.

43. Arthur Hyde to Senator Charles McNary, December 27, 1930, Senate Agriculture Committee Files, Legislative files, National Archive and Records Service (NARS).

44. Senate, *Distribution of Surplus Wheat for Relief Purposes*, p. 5.

45. Woods to McCleskey, December 10, 1930, PECE.

46. "Country Crying for Relief from the Relief Fight," *Literary Digest*, February 14, 1931; *Congressional Record*, 71st Cong., 3d sess., January 29, 1931, p. 3478; "The Trend of Events," pp. 205–207.

47. Hamilton, "Hoover and the Drought," p. 871.

48. Hoover, *Public Papers, 1931*, pp. 50–53.

49. *Commercial and Financial Chronicle*, February 21, 1931; Hamilton, "Hoover and the Drought," pp. 872–874.

50. W. G. McAdoo to Senator Arthur Capper, reprinted in Senate, *Distribution of Surplus Wheat for Relief Purposes*, p. 13.

51. J. R. McCleskey to Col. Arthur Woods, December 10, 1930, PECE.

CHAPTER FOUR

1. Charles Traux to James Stone, reported in the *New York Times*, March 27, 1931.

2. *New York Times*, July 29, 30, 31, 1931.

3. *New York Times*, July 22, 30, 1931.

4. Frances Piven and Richard Cloward, *The New Class War* (New York: Pantheon, 1982), p. 107.

5. *New York Times*, August 19, September 20, October 4, October 6, November 9, 1931.

6. *Commercial and Financial Chronicle*, January 2 and 9, 1932.

7. All citations in the discussion of this debate are to the *Congressional Record*, 72d Cong., 1st sess., January 4, 1932, pp. 1181–1194. Page numbers for individual quotations are as follows: Gore, p. 1187; King, p. 1188; Tydings, p. 1184; Norris, p. 1191; and Copeland, p. 1186.

8. Robert Smith to R. B. Howell, January 4, 1932, telegram reprinted in the *Congressional Record*, 72d Cong., 1st sess., January 4, 1932, pp. 1189–1190.

9. *Ibid.*, pp. 1192–1194.

10. *Ibid.*, January 7, 1932, pp. 1406, 1407.

11. *New York Times*, January 6, 1932.

12. House Committee on Agriculture, *Wheat Distribution*, 72 Cong., 1st sess., January 4, 5, March 1, 1932, p. 9.

13. *Ibid.*, pp. 22, 28.

14. *Ibid.*, pp. 37, 39, 40.

15. The records of the Social Work Conference on Federal Action on Unemployment, for example, show no discussion of the wheat measure before its passage except a brief discussion with Senator Costigan who had proposed dis-

tribution of 20 million bushels of the Farm Board wheat in an address to the National Consumers League. The social work leaders expressed concern about the difficulties involved in distributing relief in kind. (Files of the Government and Social Work Division, American Association of Social Workers, National Association of Social Workers Collection). Similarly, the records of the National Social Work Council contain no discussion of the wheat measure prior to its passage, and only casual reference to it once distribution was begun (National Social Work Council Records, National Social Welfare Assembly Files). Both these collections are located in the Social Welfare History Archive, University of Minnesota.

16. House, *Wheat Distribution*, p. 45.
17. *Commercial and Financial Chronicle*, February 13, 1932, p. 1135.
18. *Congressional Record*, 72d Cong., 1st sess., February 12, 1932, p. 3821.
19. American Farm Bureau Federation, Board of Directors, Minutes of the meeting of March 10–12, 1932," folio in National Agricultural Library, Beltsville, Maryland.
20. Herman Falker, Millers National Federation to Walter H. Newton, Secretary to the President, March 7, 1932, Grain File, Herbert Hoover Presidential Library.
21. *New York Times*, February 9, 1932.
22. *Congressional Record*, 72d Cong., 1st sess., February 12, 1932, p. 3821.
23. *New York Times*, February 24, 1932.
24. Editorial from the *Washington News* and the *Cleveland Plain Dealer* were inserted by Capper into *Congressional Record* 72d Cong., 1st sess., February 12, 1932, pp. 3807, 3808. See also the *New York Times*, March 1, 1932 and W. H. Bowker to Hamilton Fish, March 1, 1932, reproduced in the *Congressional Record*, 72d Cong., 1st sess., March 2, 1932, p. 5191.
25. House, *Wheat Distribution*, pp. 47–79.
26. "It is embarrassing," declared Mr. White of Ohio on the floor of the House two days later, "to ask for food for livestock when people are starving. . . . I am willing that some of this wheat go to the livestock, but let us have some of it for the destitute people in this country who are in desperate need." *Congressional Record*, 72d Cong., 1st sess., March 3, 1932, p. 5192.
27. *New York Times*, March 2, 1932; *Congressional Record*, 72d Cong., 1st sess., March 3, 1932, p. 5188. All the quotations in this section come from *Congressional Record*, March 3, 1932. Page numbers for specific quotations are as follows: Pou, p. 5188; Fish, p. 5191; Jones, p. 5194; Norton, p. 5210; Lonergan, p. 5211; Crowe, p. 5211; Jones, p. 5194; Reed, p. 5210; Glover, p. 5196; DePriest, p. 5213; Garber, p. 5209; Johnson, p. 5212; Flannagan, p. 5198; Adkins, pp. 5199, 5200; and Hope, p. 5198.
28. *New York Times*, March 4, 5, and 6, 8, 1932; "Is the Wheat Gift a Dole?" *Literary Digest*, March 19, 1932, p. 12.
29. *New York Times*, March 8 and 9, 1932.
30. For committee discussions pertinent to these subsequent donations see Senate Committee on Appropriations, *Distribution of Government-Owned*

Wheat and Cotton, 72d Cong., 1st sess., July 8, 1932 and House Committee on Agriculture, *Cotton Distribution*, 72d Cong., 2d sess., December 13, 1932. Discussion on the floor of Congress occurred repeatedly in both Houses in June and July. See *Congressional Record*, 72d Cong., 1st sess. In general, the debate over the second donation focused upon a demand by Representatives LaGuardia and Cellar of New York for a provision permitting the Red Cross to exchange some of the flour for finished products containing wheat. Since many urban families were without facilities to bake bread, the New York congressmen argued that such a provision was necessary to allow New York and other large cities to receive a fair share of the wheat. The bill was eventually passed with an exchange provision despite the vigorous opposition of a number of wheat district representatives.

31. See, for example, his "Address to the Welfare and Relief Mobilization Conference," September 15, 1932, in which he stated, "With the possibility of still larger tasks and lessened individual local resources for the next winter, before the close of the last Congress I secured to the Red Cross 85 million bushels of wheat, 500,000 bales of cotton and an authorization to the Reconstruction Finance Corporation to advance $300 million to such states as could not finance themselves to care for distress." Hoover, *Public Papers and Addresses*, p. 431. *See also* Herbert C. Hoover, *The Memoirs of Herbert Hoover, The Great Depression, 1929–1941* (New York: Macmillan, 1952) p. 152.

32. Piven and Cloward, *The New Class War*, chapter 4.

33. *Congressional Record*, 72d Cong., 1st sess., March 3, 1932, p. 5208.

34. Benedict, *Farm Problem*, pp. 111, 112; Brown, *Public Relief*, p. 126.

35. *New York Times*, May 27, 29, and November 13, 1932 and "Red Cross Flour," *New York Times*, May 30, 1932.

36. *Congressional Record*, 72d Cong., 1st sess., June 16, 1932, p. 13196.

37. Arthur Hyde to Charles McNary, June 10 and 11, 1932. Senate Agriculture Committee Files, Legislative files, NARS; James C. Stone to Charles McNary, June 9, 1932, reprinted in Senate Committee on Agriculture and Forestry, *Distribution of Government-Owned Wheat for Relief Purposes*; House, *Cotton Distribution*, pp. 7, 8.

38. *Congressional Record, 72d Cong., 1st sess., June 16, 1932, p. 13199.*

CHAPTER FIVE

1. Ellis, *A Nation in Torment*, p. 150; John Kazarian, "Starvation Army," *The Nation*, April 12, 1933, p. 396.

2. Bernstein, *The Lean Years*, pp. 454, 455; Schlesinger, *Old Order*, pp. 264, 265; William E. Leuchtenburg, *Franklin D. Roosevelt and the New Deal, 1932–1940* (New York: Harper & Row, 1963), pp. 13–16.

3. Harris Gaylord Warren, *Hoover and the Great Depression*, p. 208.

4. Leuchtenburg, *FDR and the New Deal*, pp. 10–14; Schlesinger, *Old Order*, pp. 413–437; Franklin D. Roosevelt, *Public Papers and Addresses of Frank-*

lin D. Roosevelt, vol. 1 (New York: Random House, 1938), pp. 654, 657, 663, 664. See especially, Roosevelt's Radio Address on Unemployment and Social Welfare, Albany, New York, October 13, 1932, *Public Papers and Addresses*, vol. 1, pp. 786–795 and Herbert Hoover, *Public Papers*, pp. 431, 528.

5. Roosevelt, *Public Papers and Addresses*, vol. 1, p. 810.
6. Hoover, *Public Papers*, p. 53.
7. See, for example, his September 1932, "Address to the Welfare and Relief Mobilization Conference," in Hoover, *Public Papers*, pp. 429–433, esp. 431; also, his campaign address in Cleveland, Ohio, October 15, 1932, *Public Papers*, pp. 519–543, esp. 528.
8. President's News Conference of November 6, 1932 in Hoover, *Public Papers*, pp. 771, 772.
9. Benedict, *Farm Policies*, pp. 269–272; Saloutos and Hicks, *Populism*, pp. 404–434.
10. Schlesinger, *Old Order*, p. 266.
11. *Iowa Union Farmer*, March 9, 1932, reprinted in Saloutos and Hicks, *Populism*, p. 443.
12. John L. Shover, *Cornbelt Rebellion* (Urbana: University of Illinois Press, 1965), pp. 1–57; Saloutos and Hicks, *Populism*, pp. 435–451.
13. Boland M. Jones, "Farmers' Holiday Doomed to Failure." *New York Times*, August 21, 1932. "If a group of hard-boiled dairymen in the neighborhood of Sioux City had not dumped several truckloads of milk all over the clean Iowa highway, the Corn Belt might never have realized that a great farm holiday was being carried on in its midst. It had been going along for a week without enough noticeable effect to make a headline. Then it came in contact with this local dairymen's strike, the milk was spilled and it splashed all over the front pages of Corn-Belt newspapers," wrote Mr. Jones from Omaha.
14. Shover, *Cornbelt Rebellion*, pp. 53–57.
15. Oscar Heline in Studs Terkel, *Hard Times*, p. 253.
16. Raymond Moley, *The First New Deal* (New York: Harcourt, Brace & World, 1966), p. 245.
17. Roosevelt, *Public Papers and Addresses*, vol. 1, p. 697.
18. *Ibid.*, p. 853.
19. *Ibid.*, pp. 699, 704.
20. *Ibid.*, pp. 655, 664.
21. *Ibid.*, p. 655.
22. *Ibid.*, p. 646.
23. *Ibid.*, p. 657.
24. *Ibid.*, p. 711.
25. Hoover, "Remarks to Newspaper Editors," October 4, 1932, *Public Papers, 1932–1933*, p. 489.
26. Bernstein, *The Lean Years*, pp. 508–511; Shover, *Cornbelt Rebellion*, p. 54; *New York Times*, November 12, 1932; *New York Amsterdam News*, Election Edition, November 9, 1932.

27. Louise V. Armstrong, *We, Too, Are the People* (Boston: Little, Brown, 1938), p. 41.

28. Farm Holiday Association Memoirs, COHC. Interviews conducted by Lowell K. Dyson with John Bosch, Richard Bosch, and Donald Murphy.

29. *The Nation*, February 15, 1933, p. 162.

30. *New York Times*, January 22, 1933.

31. Ed O'Neal, "Farm and Home Hour, " radio address, February 11, 1933 reprinted in the *New York Times*, February 12, 1933.

32. Russell Lord, *The Wallaces of Iowa* (Boston: Houghton Mifflin, 1947), p. 317; Bernstein, *The Lean Years*, pp. 416–425; Schlesinger, *Old Order*, pp. 448, 459; Leuchtenburg, *FDR and the New Deal*, p. 25; Piven and Cloward, *Regulating the Poor*, pp. 61–62.

33. Piven and Cloward, *Regulating the Poor*, p. 67; *New York Times*, January 4, 1933; Senate, subcommittee of the Committee on Manufactures, *Federal Aid for Unemployment Relief*, 72d Cong., 2d sess., January 1933, pp. 64–67.

34. Stuart Chase, *The Road We Are Traveling: Guidelines to America's Future as Reported to the Twentieth Century Fund* (New York: Twentieth Century Fund, 1942).

35. See, for example, Gerald W. Johnson, "The Average American and the Depression," *Current History* 35 (February 1932), pp. 671–675; George R. Clark. "Beckerstown: 1932. An American Town Faces the Depression," *Harpers*, October 1932; and Marquis Childs, "Main Street Ten Years After," *The New Republic* January 18, 1933, pp. 263–265.

36. *The Nation*, February 15, 1933.

37. Kazarian, "Starvation Army" p. 396.

38. George R. Leighton, "And If the Revolution Comes . . . ?" *Harpers*, March 1932, p. 466.

39. Cary McWilliams in Studs Terkel, *Hard Times*, pp. 278, 279.

40. Leuchtenburg, *FDR and the New Deal*, p. 22.

41. Piven and Cloward, *Poor People's Movements*, p. 12.

42. Leuchtenburg, *FDR and the New Deal*, pp. 30–38; Schlesinger, *Old Order*, pp. 464–485.

43. James MacGregor Burns, *Roosevelt: The Lion and the Fox* (New York: Harcourt, Brace, 1956), p. 147.

44. Frederick Lewis Allen, *Since Yesterday: The 1930's in America, September 31, 1929–September 3, 1939* (New York: Harper & Row, 1940), pp. 78–81. For other accounts of the banking collapse and the atmosphere of crisis it engendered, see Schlesinger, *Old Order*, pp. 474–479 and Warren, *Hoover and the Great Depression*.

CHAPTER SIX

1. Arthur Schlesinger, Jr., *The Coming of the New Deal*, vol. 2 of *The Age of Roosevelt* (Boston: Houghton Mifflin, 1958), p. 8.

2. For lively accounts, see Leuchtenburg, *FDR and the New Deal*, pp. 41–62 and Schlesinger, *New Deal*, pp. 1–23.

3. Richard S. Kirkendall, *Social Scientists and Farm Politics in the Age of Roosevelt* (Columbia: University of Missouri Press, 1966), p. 56.

4. Rexford Tugwell Memoir, COHC, p. 44; Clifford V. Gregory, "Birth of the AAA," *The Bureau Farmer*, August–September 1935, pp. 2–3, 11–12; Conrad, *The Forgotten Farmers*, pp. 2–22.

5. Tugwell Memoir, COHC, pp. 44, 45.

6. Marvin Jones Memoir, COHC, p. 559.

7. Oscar Heline in Studs Terkel, *Hard Times*, p. 254.

8. Theodore Lowi, *The End of Liberalism: Ideology, Policy, and the Crisis of Public Authority* (New York: W. W. Norton, 1969), p. 103.

9. Rexford G. Tugwell, *The Brains Trust* (New York: Viking Press, 1968), p. 450.

10. Christina McFayden Campbell, *The Farm Bureau and the New Deal* (Urbana: University of Illinois Press, 1962), pp. 50–58, 63–65; Conrad, *Forgotten Farmers*, pp. 27, 28, 35, 36. For an interesting discussion of the failure of the leaders of the large farm organizations to recognize the consumer interests of impoverished farmers, see the Jerome Frank Memoir, COHC, pp. 92–93.

11. Campbell, *Farm Bureau*, pp. 52, 53.

12. McConnell, *Decline of Agrarian Democracy*, pp. 10–35 passim; Lowi, *End of Liberalism*, pp. 104–107.

13. Jones Memoir, COHC, p. 580.

14. Benedict, *Farm Policies*, pp. 267–269, 283–284. For a detailed account of the evolution of the domestic allotment plan and its adoption by the incoming Roosevelt administration, see Kirkendall, *Social Scientists*, chapters 1–3.

15. Fite, *George N. Peek*, p. 287; Kirkendall, *Social Scientists*, pp. 27–28, 57–58.

16. Tugwell, *Brains Trust*, p. 209.

17. *Ibid.*, p. 453.

18. Benedict, *The Farm Problem*, p. 227.

19. *Ibid.*, p. 278.

20. Roosevelt, *Public Papers and Addresses*, vol. 2, p. 74.

21. Marvin Jones Memoir, COHC, p. 570.

22. *New York Times*, March 22, 1933.

23. Kirkendall, *Social Scientists*, p. 52; *New York Times*, February 7, 1933.

24. "Putting it to the Touch," *New York Times*, March 19, 1933.

25. Frank R. Prina to the *New York Times*, February 14, 1933; Forbes R. McCreery to the *New York Times*, March 22, 1933; Caroline Kent to the *New York Times*, January 16, 1933.

26. *New York Times*, March 20, 1933.

27. Ernest K. Lindley, *Half Way With Roosevelt* (New York: Viking Press, 1936), p. 116.

28. *New York Times*, March 17, 20, 1933; Conrad, *Forgotten Farmers*, pp. 29–36.

29. *New York Times*, March 22, 1933; Schlesinger, *New Deal*, pp. 40, 41.

30. *New York Times*, March 22, 1933.
31. Schlesinger, *New Deal*, pp. 41, 42; Leuchtenburg, *FDR and the New Deal*, p. 49, 50.
32. Oscar Heline in Studs Terkel, *Hard Times*, p. 255.
33. Schlesinger, *New Deal*, pp. 42–45.
34. For assessments of the impact of the Agricultural Adjustment Act, see: Benedict, *Farm Policies*, pp. 297–298, 310–315, 335–337, 514–520; Benedict, *Farm Problem*, esp. pp. 431–480; Theodore Saloutos, "New Deal Agricultural Policy: An Evaluation," *Journal of American History* 61 (September, 1974), pp. 345–355; Willard W. Cochrane and Mary E. Ryan, *American Farm Policy, 1948–1973* (Minneapolis: University of Minnesota Press, 1976), esp. pp. 363–371.
35. Varden Fuller, "Politics and Income Distribution in Agriculture," in Vernon Ruttan, Arley D. Waldo, and James P. Houck, eds., *Agricultural Policy in an Affluent Society* (New York: W. W. Norton, 1969), p. 256.
36. Lindley, *Half Way*, p. 134; Cochrane and Ryan, *American Farm Policy*, pp. 363–371.
37. Leuchtenburg, *FDR and the New Deal*, p. 51.
38. Lord, *The Wallaces of Iowa*, p. 343. For discussion of Peek's selection, see Kirkendall, *Social Scientists*, pp. 65, 66.
39. Schlesinger, *New Deal*, pp. 46–49; Kirkendall, *Social Scientists*, pp. 65–67.
40. Schlesinger, *New Deal*, pp. 49–51.
41. Peek's viewpoint on this controversy is recounted in George N. Peek and Samuel Crowther, *Why Quit Our Own?* (New York: Van Nostrand, 1936), pp. 20–23, 112–120, 140–156; Frank's recollections of the conflict with Peek are preserved in his memoir in the COHC, esp. pp. 92–120.
42. For two cogent summaries of the personalities and ideologies prominent in the New Deal Department of Agriculture, see Sidney Baldwin, *Poverty and Politics: The Rise and Decline of the Farm Security Administration* (Chapel Hill: University of North Carolina Press, 1968), pp. 54–58 and Dean Albertson, *Roosevelt's Farmer: Claude Wickard and the New Deal* (New York: Columbia University Press, 1961), pp. 74–77.
43. Milburn L. Wilson Memoir, COHC, p. 1108.
44. Marvin Jones Memoir, COHC, p. 590.
45. *Ibid.*
46. M. L. Wilson Memoir, COHC, pp. 1108, 1109.
47. Peek and Crowther, *Why Quit Our Own?*, pp. 20.
48. Benedict, *Farm Policies*, pp. 335, 336.
49. Albertson, *Roosevelt's Farmer*, p. 76.
50. Peek and Crowther, *Why Quit Our Own?*, p. 107.
51. Frank Memoir, COHC, pp. 111, 115.
52. Leuchtenburg, *FDR and the New Deal*, pp. 52, 53; William W. Bremer, *Depression Winters: New York Social Workers and the New Deal* (Philadelphia, Temple University Press, 1984), pp. 126–129.
53. Schlesinger, *New Deal*, pp. 99, 103–109.

54. Leuchtenburg, *FDR and the New Deal*, p. 120; Schlesinger, *New Deal*, pp. 265, 266.
55. Frank Memoir, COHC, p. 37.
56. Lee Pressman Memoir, COHC, p. 20.
57. Leuchtenburg, *FDR and the New Deal*, p. 121; Schlesinger, *New Deal*, p. 267.
58. Harry Hopkins, *Spending to Save: The Complete Story of Relief* (New York: W. W. Norton, 1930), pp. 100–101.
59. *Ibid.*, p. 117.
60. *Ibid.*, p. 104.
61. *Ibid.*, p. 105.
62. Frederick Allen, *Since Yesterday*, p. 89.
63. Virginia Durr Memoir, COHC, pp. 80, 82.
64. Anne O'Hare McCormick, "Vast Tides That Stir the Capital," reprinted in Marion Turner Sheehan, ed., *The World at Home: Selections From the Writings of Anne O'Hare McCormick* (New York: Knopf, 1956), p. 195.
65. Peek and Crowther, *Why Quit Our Own?*, p. 112.
66. Thomas L. Stokes, *Chip Off My Shoulder* (Princeton: Princeton University Press, 1940), p. 362.
67. Arthur Krock, "Washington," in Hanson Baldwin and Shepard Stone, eds., *We Saw It Happen* (New York: Simon and Schuster, 1938), p. 19.
68. Florence Kiper Frank, interview with author, July 2, 1973, New Haven, Connecticut.
69. Virginia Durr Memoir, COHC, p. 82.
70. Bremer, *Depression Winters*, pp. 3–14, 171–179; Gertrude Springer, "The New Deal and the Old Dole," *Survey Graphic* 22 (July 1933), pp. 347–352, 385, 388.; Lee Pressman Memoir, COHC, pp. 9–15; Frank Memoir, COHC, pp. 120–122.

CHAPTER SEVEN

1. Jim Kieran to F. D. Roosevelt, May, 1933, Hopkins Papers; F. D. R. to Kieran, May 8, 1933, Hopkins Papers; Roosevelt, "Memo for the Federal Emergency Relief Administrator," Hopkins Papers, Franklin Delano Roosevelt Library.
2. Gladys Baker, Wayne D. Rasmussen, Vivian Wiser, and Jane Porter, *Century of Service: The First 100 Years of the United States Department of Agriculture* (Washington: U.S. Government Printing Office, 1963), p. 143; Henry Wallace, *New Frontiers*, pp. 172–175.
3. Samuel Bledsoe Memoir, COHC, pp. 69, 70.
4. Emma Tiller in Studs Terkel, *Hard Times*, p. 270.
5. Charles P. Stewart, "Nature Aids Farm Belt in Crop Destruction Plan," *Sioux City Journal*, October 3, 1933.
6. Wallace, *New Frontiers*, pp. 174, 175.
7. D. A. Fitzgerald, *Corn and Hogs Under the Agricultural Adjustment Act:*

Developments up to March 1934, pamphlet (Washington: Brookings Institution, 1934), p. 2.

8. *Ibid.*, p. 3.
9. *Ibid.*, pp. 4–8; George T. Blakey, "Ham That Never Was: The 1933 Emergency Hog Slaughter," *The Historian* 30 (1967–1968), pp. 41–46.
10. Fitzgerald, *Corn and Hogs*, pp. 10–18; Saloutos and Hicks, *Populism*, p. 476; *Chicago Daily Tribune*, August 19, 1933.
11. *Milwaukee Journal*, August 27, 1933, p. 6.
12. Leuchtenburg, *FDR and the New Deal*, p. 73; *Chicago Daily Tribune*, August 25, 1933, p. 32; "Birth Control Causes Rush to Market," *Newsweek*, September 2, 1933, p. 22.
13. *Sioux City Journal*, September 14, 1933.
14. *Chicago Herald American*, August 26, 1933.
15. Saloutos and Hicks, *Populism* pp. 476, 477; *Chicago Daily Tribune*, August 26, 1933, p. 17.
16. T. P. Gore to Henry Wallace, September 14, 1933, Hog Emergency Program Folder in AAA Files, 1933–1935, Record Group 145, National Archives (hereafter cited as Hog Emergency Files).
17. Fitzgerald, *Corn and Hogs*, pp. 35, 38.
18. Thomas Hunter to Henry Wallace, September 25, 1933, Hog Emergency Files.
19. Mrs. Jacob Keller to A. G. Black, September 19, 1933, Hog Emergency Files.
20. W. R. Ronald to A. G. Black, August 30, 1933, Hog Emergency Files.
21. *Sioux City Journal*, August 31, September 2, 1933.
22. *Chicago Daily Tribune*, August 25, 1933.
23. Fitzgerald, *Corn and Hogs*, pp. 37–39; Claude R. Wickard, "Memorandum to Mr. D. P. Trent," April 20, 1934, Hog Emergency Files; Alfred Stedman to F. J. Reynolds, August 12. 1936, Hog Emergency Files.
24. *Chicago Daily Tribune*, August 31, September 8, 1933.
25. *Chicago Daily Tribune*, September 19, 1933.
26. William Hirth to Chester Davis, September 12, 1933, Hog Emergency Files.
27. A. D. Stedman to F. J. Reynolds, August 12, 1936, Hog Emergency Files.
28. Fitzgerald, *Corn and Hogs*, pp. 35–39.
29. Wallace, *New Frontiers*, p. 180.
30. R. M. Evans Memoir, COHC, p. 81.
31. Albertson, *Roosevelt's Farmer*, p. 68.
32. Henry Wallace, "Pigs and Pig Iron," radio address, November 1935, reprinted in Henry Wallace, *Democracy Reborn* (New York: Reynal and Hitchcock, 1944), p. 104.
33. Canteen Township Improvement Association, East St. Louis, St. Clair County, Illinois, to Franklin D. Roosevelt, September 12, 1933, Hog Emergency Files.
34. Mary C. Roberts, Dayton, Ohio, to Hugh S. Johnson, August 24, 1933, Hog Emergency Files.

35. C. W. Ermler to Secretary Wallace, December 15, 1933, Secretary of Agriculture's Correspondence, Record Group 16, National Archives.

36. Mr. and Mrs. George Biddle to Franklin D. Roosevelt, August 29, 1933, Hog Emergency Files.

37. Clyde C. Bedwell to the Secretary of Agriculture, September 14, 1933, Hog Emergency Files.

38. C. M. Sandstrom to Charles Brand, September 5, 1933, Hog Emergency Files.

39. John Garvin to Governor A. G. Schmederman, October 2, 1933, Hog Emergency Files.

40. Louie H. G. Dobler to Secretary Wallace, August 20, 1933, Hog Emergency Files.

41. J. W. Bulger to President Roosevelt, August 12, 1934, Hog Emergency Files.

42. Lawrence Stahl to Secretary Wallace, October 8, 1933, Hog Emergency Files.

43. G. A. Gurley to Henry Wallace, September 5, 1933, Hog Emergency Files.

44. Ray W. Hedges to President Roosevelt, September 4, 1933, Hog Emergency Files.

45. Chas. H. Newkirk to Franklin D. Roosevelt, September 29, 1933, Hog Emergency Files.

46. Claude E. Thompson to FDR, September 7, 1933, Hog Emergency Files.

47. Mrs. Belle Lutz to F.D.R., September 5, 1933, Hog Emergency Files.

48. H. Hilger, Allen County Unemployed Association to Hugh R. O'Donnell, Federal Emergency Relief Administration, September 16, 1933, Hog Emergency Files.

49. Chas. H. Hay, M.D. to Secretary Wallace, August 25, 1933, Hog Emergency Files.

50. G. George Ganatt to Franklin Roosevelt, August 26, 1933, Hog Emergency Files.

51. D. P. Trent, Director, Cooperative Extension Work, to Henry A. Wallace, August 25, 1933, Hog Emergency Files.

52. F. C. Jordan, Secretary, Farmers' Educational and Cooperative Union of America, Oak Creek Local Number 1, Cornville, Arizona, to Henry Wallace, September 6, 1933, Hog Emergency Files.

53. Ray T. Miller to Henry Wallace, telegram, September 2, 1933, Hog Emergency Files.

54. C. M. Sarchet, Secretary, Chamber of Commerce, Ponca City, Oklahoma, to the Department of Agriculture, August 29, 1933, Hog Emergency Files.

55. Wirt W. Hallam, President, American Association for China Famine and Flood Relief, to George N. Peek, September 12, 1933, Hog Emergency Files.

56. Frank Maher to Secretary Wallace, August 11, 1933, Secretary of Agriculture's Correspondence.

57. Charles W. Lawrence, "Slaughter of Sucklings Makes Pomerene Angry," newspaper clipping attached to letter from Chas. H. Newkirk to FDR, September 29, 1933, Hog Emergency Files.

58. Boland M. Jones, "Corn Belt Puzzled by Farm Policy, *New York Times*, August 27, 1933, sec. 4, p. 8.

59. A sample of editorial reaction is presented in "Killing the Hog and Saving the Farmer," *Literary Digest*, September 2, 1933, p. 6; Stewart, "Nature Aids Farm Belt.

60. *Chicago Daily Tribune*, August 21 and 28, September 9, 13, 14, 19, and 20.

61. Guy C. Shepard, Chief, Meat Processing Section, "Memorandum to Mr. James E. Jones," December 6, 1933, Hog Emergency Files.

62. *New York Times*, September 22, 1933; Franklin D. Roosevelt, *Complete Presidential Press Conferences of Franklin D. Roosevelt*, vol. 2 (New York: Da Capo Press, 1972), p. 280.

63. *New York Times*, October 1, 1933.

64. *New York Times*, October 2, 1933.

65. *New York Times*, October 5, 1933; Federal Surplus Relief Corporation (FSRC), "Certificates of Incorporation," AAA Legal Division Files, Record Group 16, National Archives.

66. Henry Wallace to Seth Thomas, September 20, 1933; Seth Thomas to Henry Wallace, September 23, 1933, AAA Legal Division Files.

67. AAA Press Release, September 22, 1933, copy in AAA Legal Division Files.

68. Turner Catledge, "Swift Roosevelt Blows Deal With Discontent," *New York Times*, September 24, 1933, sec. 4, p. 1.

69. "The Government Program for Direct Relief," *Literary Digest*, October 14, 1933, p. 8.

70. Quoted in *ibid*.

71. "Plenty and Want," *New York Times*, September 23, 1933.

72. Broadus Mitchell, *Depression Decade: From New ERA through New Deal, 1929–1941* (New York: Holt, Rinehart & Winston, 1962), p. 190.

73. R. M. Evans Memoir, p. COHC, 82; see also Claude Wickard Memoir, COHC, p. 607.

74. Frank Memoir, COHC, pp. 40, 117; Mordecai Ezekial Memoir, COHC, p. 71.

75. *Chicago Daily Tribune*, August 19, 1933.

76. Fitzgerald, *Corn and Hogs*, p. 20; Guy C. Shepard, "Memo for Mr. Davis," September 27, 1933, Hog Emergency Files.

77. Ruby Black, *Eleanor Roosevelt: A Biography* (New York: Duell, Sloan, and Pearce, 1940), p. 199.

78. Alger Hiss, personal communication, February 21, 1974.

79. Frank Memoir, COHC, p. 80.

80. Wallace, *New Frontiers*, p. 139.

81. Frank Memoir, COHC, p. 118.

82. Wallace, *New Frontiers*, p. 183.

83. Adam Yarmolinsky, "Ideas into Programs," in Thomas E. Cronin and Sanford Greenberg, eds., *The Presidential Advisory System* (New York: Harper and Row, 1969), p. 94.

84. Frank Memoir, COHC, pp. 117, 118; Lee Pressman to Florence K. Frank, March 9, 1959, copy supplied to author by Florence Frank.
85. Mordecai Ezekial Memoir, COHC, p. 71.
86. Tugwell Memoir, COHC, p. 51.
87. Ruth Finney quoted in Joseph P. Lash, *Eleanor and Franklin* (New York: W. W. Norton, 1971), p. 383. See also, Ruby Black, *Eleanor Roosevelt, A Biography* (New York: Duell, Sloan, and Pearce, 1940), p. 199; Tamara K. Hareven, *Eleanor Roosevelt: An American Conscience* (Chicago: Quadrangle Books, 1968), pp. 62, 257.
88. "Mrs Roosevelt Links President to Nation's Common People," *Christian Science Monitor*, October 6, 1933.
89. *New York Times*, September 23, 1933.
90. Memorandum from the President for the Secretary of Agriculture, September 11, 1933, Roosevelt Papers, Roosevelt Library.
91. Jerome Frank to W. I. Westervelt, October 24, 1933, draft of letter, Frank Papers, Yale University; Robert Littlejohn to Jacob Baker, October 4, 1933, FSRC Files.
92. Yarmolinsky, "Ideas into Programs," p. 95.
93. Wallace, *New Frontiers*, p. 183.
94. Leuchtenburg, *FDR and the New Deal*, p. 73.
95. Henry Wallace, "Pigs and Pig Iron," radio address reprinted in Wallace, *Democracy Reborn*, p. 103.
96. Henry Morgenthau, Jr., the Morgenthau Diaries, book 125, p. 34, Roosevelt Library.
97. Frank Kingdon, *An Uncommon Man: Henry Wallace and 60 Million Jobs* (New York: Readers Press, 1945), p. 60, 61.
98. Sam Bledsoe Memoir, COHC, p. 69.
99. Norman Thomas, "Starve or Prosper!" *Current History*, May 1934, p. 135.
100. Mauritz Hallgren, *The Gay Reformer: Profits Before Plenty under Franklin D. Roosevelt* (New York: Knopf, 1935), p. 147.
101. Warren Vinton and Benjamin Stolberg, *The Economic Consequences of the New Deal* (New York: Harcourt, Brace, and World, 1935).
102. Wallace, *New Frontiers*, p. 183.
103. Rexford Tugwell, "Relief and Reconstruction," *Proceedings* of the National Conference of Social Work, 61st sess., 1934 (Chicago: University of Chicago Press, 1934), pp. 40, 41.
104. Wallace, *New Frontiers*, pp. 183, 184.

CHAPTER EIGHT

1. Kathleen McLaughlin, "Mrs. Roosevelt Goes Her Way," *New York Times Magazine*, July 5, 1936.
2. Frank Memoir, COHC, pp. 117, 118.
3. Jerome Frank to Mr. Wenchel, January 5, 1934, AAA Legal Division Files; Seth Thomas, USDA Solicitor, "Memorandum for the Secretary,"Copy of Opinion 13523, January 12, 1934, AAA Legal Division Files.

4. "Food Procurement Programs of the Food Distribution Administration," Speech for Delivery February 22, 1943, copy in Files of the Agricultural History Branch, USDA, FSCC file, folder 9 B3b).

5. J. P Wenchel to Solicitor Mastin G. White, "Memorandum on question of authority of the President to authorize a change in the charger of the Federal Surplus Relief Corporation," December 5, 1935, AAA Legal Division Files.

6. Frank Memoir, COHC, pp. 117, 118.

7. *Ibid.*, p. 142.

8. "Food Procurement Programs of the Food Distribution Administration," p. 1.

9. FSRC, "Certificates of Incorporation" Hopkins Papers, Roosevelt Library.

10. Frank Memoir, COHC, p. 118.

11. FSRC, "Certificates of Incorporation."

12. Frank Memoir, COHC, p. 120.

13. *New York Times*, October 1, 1933.

14. Henry Wallace to the Attorney General, n.d., AAA Legal Division Files.

15. Irvin M. May, Jr., "The Paradox of Agricultural Abundance and Poverty: The Federal Surplus Relief Corporation, 1933–1935," (Ph.D. diss., University of Oklahoma, 1970) pp. 75–79.

16. "Report on Conference on Commodity Distribution, October 4 and 5, 1933," typescript in FSRC Files, Record Group 124, National Archives (hereafter cited as FSRC Files).

17. Harry Hopkins to Henry Wallace, November 13, 1933 and Hopkins to Wallace, December 4, 1933, FSRC Files.

18. Hopkins, *Spending to Save*, p. 156.

19. "Report of the Federal Surplus Relief Corporation, October 4–December 31, 1933," typescript, FSRC Files; U.S. Agricultural Adjustment Administration, *Agricultural Adjustment: A Report of Administration of the AAA, May 1933–February, 1944* (Washington: U.S. Government Printing Office, 1934).

20. "They Stand Out from the Crowd," *Literary Digest*, November 25, 1933, p. 9.

21. Text of White House statement as reprinted in the *New York Times*, September 22, 1933.

22. *Ibid.*

23. Henry Wallace, *New Frontiers*, p. 184.

24. Harry Hopkins to Henry Wallace, October 24, 1933, FSRC Files.

25. FERA, "The Federal Surplus Relief Corporation," *Monthly Report*, July 1935 (Washington, D.C.: Government Printing Office, 1935), p. 25.

26. Rodney Leonard, quoted in Nick Kotz, *Let Them Eat Promises: The Politics of Hunger in America* (Englewood Cliffs, New Jersey: Prentice Hall, 1969), p. 71.

27. FERA, "The Federal Surplus Relief Corporation", p. 25.

28. Jacob Baker to Harry Hopkins, September 1, 1934, FSRC Files.

29. Wallace to Hopkins, October 25, 1933, FSRC Files.

30. FSRC, *Report for the Calendar Year 1935* (Washington: U.S. Government Printing Office, 1936), pp. 10, 11.

31. FERA, "The Federal Surplus Relief Corporation," p. 25.
32. Southard to Nunn, October 31, 1934, FSRC Files; "Food and Nutrition Work of the FERA," press release, July 15, 1935, FERA Files, Record Group 69, National Archives (hereafter cited as FERA Files).
33. Harry Hopkins, "Emergency Relief in the U.S.," radio address delivered over NBC, October 11, 1933, FERA Files.
34. Southard to Murphy, August 13, 1934, FSRC Files.
35. May, "The Paradox," pp. 154, 155.
36. "Operations of the Special Commodities Section during period May 12 to Nov 30, 1933," narrative report, p. 11, files of the Commodities Purchase Section of the AAA, Record Group 145, National Archives.
37. Baker to Hopkins, August 20, 1935, FERA Files.
38. "Operations of the Special Commodities Section," p. 12.
39. *Ibid.*, p. 10; Jacob Baker to W. A. F. Stevenson, AAA, November 10, 1933, FSRC Files.
40. Charles D. Snyder to Secretary Wallace, August 10, 1935, FSRC Files.
41. J. M. O'Hara, Manager, Plains Producers Cooperative, Inc., Alliance, Nebraska, to William L. Nunn, September 20, 1935, FSRC Files.
42. F. A. Sherman, Santa Clara, California, to Franklin D. Roosevelt, September 8, 1935, FSRC Files.
43. Otto Schuler, Assistant Treasurer, Nathan Schweitzer Co., Inc., to Harry Hopkins, October 9, 1935, FSRC Files.
44. Clarence Cannon, Elsberry, Missouri, to William L. Nunn, Director Commodity Distribution, FSRC, September 20, 1935, FSRC Files.
45. George B. Power to Ellen S. Woodward, January 25, 1934, FSRC Files.
46. John F. White, Manager, North Pacific Cooperative Prune Exchange, to FSRC (n.d.), FSRC Files.
47. P. S. Crossman, County Agent, Erie County Extension Association, to W. L. Nunn, September 12, 1935, FSRC Files.
48. Roy Anthon, Underwood Fruit and Warehouse Company, to FSRC, October 8, 1935, FSRC Files.
49. See the Minutes of the Food Survey Committee, the Agricultural History Branch, Economic Research Service, USDA.
50. "The Glory of Aroostook," *New York Times*, October 15, 1933.
51. Jacob Baker to Harry Hopkins, September 1, 1934, FSRC Files.
52. FERA, "The Federal Surplus Relief Corporation," *Monthly Report*, July 1935, p. 24.
53. Wallace to Southard, October 1934, FSRC Files.
54. For an in-depth exploration of the issues raised by the drought cattle episode, see C. Roger Lambert, "The Drought Cattle Purchase, 1934– 1935: Problems and Complaints," *Agricultural History* 45 (1971), pp. 85–93; see also, D. A. Fitzgerald, *Livestock Under the AAA* (Washington: Brookings Institution, 1935), pp. 183–191.
55. Jerome Frank Memoir, COHC, p. 118.
56. AAA, *Agricultural Adjustment, 1933 to 1935* (Washington: U.S. Government Printing Office, 1936) pp. 66, 67; FSCC, *Report of the Federal Surplus*

Commodities Corporation for the Calendar Year 1935 (Washington: U.S. Government Printing Office, 1936), p. 4, 5.

57. Hopkins, *Spending to Save*, p. 158.
58. AAA, *Agricultural Adjustment*, p. 67; Hopkins, *Spending to Save*, pp. 157, 158; FSCC, *Report, Calendar 1935*, p. 4, 5; Edwin G. Nourse, Joseph S. Davis, and John D. Black, *Three Years of the Agricultural Adjustment Administration* (Washington, D.C.: Brookings Institution, 1935), p. 201.
59. Mordecai Ezekial to Members of the AAA Operating Council, "Memorandum from the Food Survey Committee," March 6, 1935, FSRC Files.
60. FSCC, *Report, Calendar Year 1935*, p. 4. The figure of 18 million persons on the relief rolls is my calculation based on monthly totals reported in Theodore Whiting, ed., *Final Statistical Report of the Federal Emergency Relief Administration* (New York: Da Capo Press, 1972), p. 78. I have omitted months in which the Civil Works Administration greatly reduced the rolls, because many CWA employees continued to receive commodities. The 18 million persons represented between 4 and 5 million families or cases.
61. FSCC, *Report, Calendar Year 1935*, pp. 10, 11.
62. Harry Hopkins to Franklin Roosevelt, "The Genesis, History and Results of the Federal Relief Program," memorandum, August 23, 1935, FERA Files.
63. "Under-Consumption of Food among Families on Relief," attachment to a memorandum from the Food Survey Committee to members of the AAA Operating Council, March 4, 1935, Food Survey Committee Minutes, Agricultural History Branch Files, USDA.
64. Harry Hopkins, *Spending to Save*, p. 155.
65. Harry Hopkins to Henry Wallace, October 24, 1933, FSRC Files.
66. Brown, *Public Relief*, p. 255.
67. Harry Hopkins to Henry Wallace, September 8, 1934, FSRC Files.
68. Philip G. Murphy to Keith Southard, September 18, 1934, FSRC Files.
69. Wm. A Nielander to Southard, February 5 1934, FSRC Files.
70. Harry Hopkins to All Governors and State Emergency Relief Administrators, November 6, 1933, FERA Files.
71. Joanna C. Colcord, "Report on Current Relief Program, *Proceedings* of the National Conference of Social Work, 61, 1934, p. 112; Keith Southard to Winifred Chappele, March 6, 1934, FSRC Files; Jacob Baker to All State Emergency Relief Administrators, September 14, 1934, FSRC Files.
72. FSRC, "Report of the Federal Surplus Relief Corporation, October 4 to December 31, 1933," FSRC Files.
73. Jacob Baker to All Governors and State Emergency Relief Administrators, November 6, 1933, FERA Administrative Memoranda Series, FERA Files.
74. William L. Nunn to Baker and Southard, "State Distribution Systems," December 7, 1934, FSRC Files.

CHAPTER NINE

1. Mordecai Ezekial to Henry Wallace, October 4, 1933, Secretary of Agriculture's Files.

2. Roosevelt, *Press Conferences*, vol. 2, pp. 341, 342.
3. *Wallace's Farmer and Iowa Homestead*, October 14, 1933.
4. Lester G. Seligman and Elmer E. Cornwell, Jr., eds., *New Deal Mosaic: Roosevelt Meets with His National Emergency Council, 1933–1936* (Eugene: University of Oregon Books, 1965), p. 122.
5. Linton B. Swift to the Members of the Committee on Federal Action on Unemployment, American Association of Social Workers, October 7, 1933, Files of the Division of Government and Social Work, National Association of Social Work Papers, Social Welfare History Archive, University of Minnesota.
6. Jerome Frank Memoir, COHC, p. 120.
7. "The Vast Powers of the FSRC," *Literary Digest*, January 6, 1934, p. 8; *New York Times*, December 21, 22, 1933.
8. Jerome Frank Memoir, COHC, p. 143.
9. Joseph F. George, Santa Clara, California, to President F. D. Roosevelt, FERA Files.
10. Baltimore Wholesale Grocery Company to F. D. R., FERA Files.
11. Oshkosh Retail Grocers Association to H. L. Hopkins, October 9, 1934, FERA Files.
12. Arizona Wholesale Grocers Association to FERA, n.d., FERA Files.
13. J. M. Hartan and D. A. Landress to Harry L. Hopkins, September 14, 1934, FERA Files.
14. Harry L. Hopkins to Senator Walter George, October 23, 1934, FERA Files.
15. Aubrey Williams to Harry Hopkins, memorandum, n.d., FERA Files.
16. Schlesinger, *New Deal*, p. 276.
17. Bernstein, *The Lean Years*, pp. 416–419.
18. Jacob Baker, "Work Relief: The Program Broadens," *New York Times Magazine*, November 11, 1934, reprinted in Carl N. Degler, ed., *The New Deal* (Chicago: Quadrangle Books, 1970), p. 160.
19. Schlesinger, *New Deal*, p. 179. But Bernstein concludes that such state aid to self-help cooperatives was a result of threatened bloc voting and/or disruptive tactics rather than logic; Bernstein, *The Lean Years*, pp. 416–419.
20. The Federal Emergency Relief Act of 1933, reprinted in Doris Carothers, *Chronology of the Federal Emergency Relief Administration, May 12, 1933 to December 31, 1935* (New York: Da Capo Press, 1971), p. 2.
21. Williams, *Federal Aid For Relief*, pp. 145, 146.
22. Gill, *Wasted Manpower*, pp. 159, 160.
23. Schlesinger, *New Deal*, pp. 268–270; Williams, *Federal Aid*, pp. 113–115; Arthur W. MacMahon, John D. Millett, and Gladys Ogden, *The Administration of Federal Work Relief* (Chicago: Public Administration Service, 1941), pp. 18–19.
24. Lt. Colonel John C. H. Lee, "The Federal Civil Works Administration: A Study Covering Its Organization in November 1933 and its Operation until 31 March, 1934," quoted in Schlesinger, *New Deal*, p. 271.
25. Hopkins, *Spending to Save*, p. 124; Gill, *Wasted Manpower*, p. 169.

26. Seligman and Cornwell, *New Deal Mosaic.*
27. John H. Millar, excerpt from unpublished article, February 1934, FERA Files.
28. P. A. Kerr, "Production-For-Use and Distribution in Work Relief Activities," FERA, *Monthly Report*, September 1935, pp. 1–11; Williams, *Federal Aid*, pp. 124, 125; Whiting, *Final Statistical Report*, pp. 44, 55.
29. Richard Lowitt and Maurine Beasley, eds., *One Third of a Nation: Lorena Hickok Reports on the Great Depression* (Urbana: University of Illinois Press, 1981), pp. 61–70.
30. "Relief Factories; An Issue," *U.S. News*, October 15, 1934, p. 5, clipping in FSRC Files.
31. Kerr, "Production-For-Use," pp. 3, 9, 10.
32. "Relief Factories; An Issue," *U.S. News*, p. 5.
33. Nunn to Baker, October 26, 1934, FSRC Files.
34. Jacob Baker, memorandum to Keith Southard and William Nielander, May 1, 1934, FSRC Files.
35. Digest of telephone conversation between Mr. Fellows and Mr. Myer, Bureau of Foreign and Domestic Commerce, June 21, 1934, FSRC Files.
36. Kerr, "Production-For-Use," pp. 10, 11; May, "The Paradox," pp. 206, 207; Searle F. Charles, *Minister of Relief: Harry Hopkins and the Depression* (Syracuse: Syracuse University Press, 1963), pp. 68–69. For graphic descriptions of the need for bedding among families who had gone years without replacing household goods, see Lorena Hickok's letters to Eleanor Roosevelt and Harry Hopkins from North Dakota in Lowitt and Beasley, *One Third*, pp. 55–70.
37. Hopkins, *Spending to Save*, p. 159.
38. Baker, "Work Relief: The Program Broadens," pp. 160–164; "Relief Factories; An Issue," *U.S. News*, p. 5.
39. Alexandria Bedding Company, Alexandria, Louisiana, to Harry L. Hopkins, n.d., FERA Files.
40. Perry A. Fellows to George W. Blanchard, July 24, 1934, FERA Files.
41. "Relief Factories; An Issue," *U.S. News*, p. 5.
42. Fellows to Blanchard, July 24, 1934, FERA Files.
43. Jacob Baker to SERAs and State Directors of Commodity Distribution, September 18, 1934, FERA Files.
44. FERA Press Release Number 922, reprinted in Carothers, *Chronology*, p. 66; "Relief Factories; An Issue," *U.S. News*, p. 5.
45. Southard to Hopkins, September 1, 1934, FSRC Files; Baker to Southard and Nunn, November 2, 1934, FERA Files; Kerr, "Production-For-Use," pp. 7, 8; FERA, "The Federal Surplus Relief Corporation," pp. 22, 23; Lambert, "The Drought Cattle Purchase," pp. 88, 89.
46. Westbrook to Hopkins, June 27, 1934, FSRC Files; FSCC, *Report, Calendar Year 1935*, p. 5; Nourse et al., *Three Years of the AAA*, p. 201.
47. "Relief Factories; An Issue," *U.S. News*, p. 5.
48. Schlesinger, *New Deal*, p. 278; Philip Murphy to Keith Southard, memoran-

dum, September 18, 1934, FSRC Files; "Shoes for Needy; Private Industry to Make Them Up," *U.S. News*, September 10, 1934, clipping in FSRC files.

49. Kerr, "Production-For-Use," pp. 8, 9.
50. Keith Southard to Harry Hopkins, April 15, 1935; Lee Pressman to Keith Southard, May 1, 1935; Jacob Baker to Chester Davis, July 30, 1935, FSRC Files.
51. Jacob Baker to Harry Hopkins, n.d., (spring 1935), FERA Files.
52. William L. Nunn to Jacob Baker, October 26, 1934, FSRC Files.
53. "Fight Gov't in Private Business," *New York Times*, October 4, 1934.
54. "Factories for Idle Fought as Unsound," *New York Times*, October 8, 1934.
55. "Making Jobs," *New York Times*, October 9, 1933.
56. FERA, "Federal Surplus Relief Corporation," pp. 19, 20, table B.
57. Harry L. Hopkins to Clark Howell, September 22, 1934, quoted in May, *The Paradox*, p. 224.
58. Piven and Cloward, *Regulating the Poor*, p. 80.
59. Lorena Hickok to Harry Hopkins, February 14, 1934 in Lowitt and Beasley, *One Third*, p. 187.
60. Lorena Hickok to Harry Hopkins, February 10, 1934, in *ibid.*, p. 185.
61. American Farm Bureau Federation, "Resolutions, 1919–1947" (mimeograph typescript, bound, n.d., in the pamphlet collection of the New York Public Library), p. 79.1.
62. Lorena Hickok to Aubrey Williams, August 17, 1934 in Lowitt and Beasley, *One Third*, p. 311.
63. Hopkins, *Spending to Save*, p. 109.
64. *Ibid.*, p. 98; E. A. Williams, *Federal Aid*, pp. 170, 229–239.
65. Senate Committee on Appropriations, *Hearings on H.R. 12624, First Deficiency Appropriation Bill for 1936*, 74th Cong., 2d sess., 1936, p. 3.
66. Joanna C. Colcord, *Cash Relief* (New York: Russell Sage Foundation, 1936), p. 10.
67. Wead, "Drifts," p. 225.
68. Dorothy Kahn, "The Use of Cash, Orders for Goods, or Relief in Kind in a Mass Program," *Proceedings* of the National Conference of Social Work (Chicago: University of Chicago Press, 1933), pp. 273, 274.
69. Brown, *Public Relief*, pp. 233, 234.
70. Minutes of the Subcommittee on Future Program of the Committee on Federal Action in Social Welfare of the American Association of Social Workers, January 17, 1934, National Association of Social Work papers, Social Welfare History Archives, University of Minnesota.
71. "Recommendations of the Conference on Governmental Objectives For Social Work, February 17, 1934, copy in the files of Subcommittee on Future Program of the Committee on Federal Action in Social Welfare of the AASW, NASW papers.
72. Colcord, *Cash Relief*, pp. 20, 22.
73. Hopkins, *Spending to Save*, p. 105.
74. Mrs. Mike Supanich, Mohawk, Michigan, to Honorable Harry L. Hopkins, February 28, 1934, FSRC Files.

75. Hopkins, *Spending to Save*, p. 158.
76. Kirkendall, *Social Scientists*, p. 85.
77. Mordecai Ezekial, Memorandum to Secretary Wallace, November 1, 1934, Secretary of Agriculture's Correspondence.
78. *New York Times*, September 22, 1933.
79. Robert M. MacIver, "Social Philosophy," in William F. Ogburn, ed., *Social Change and the New Deal* (Chicago: University of Chicago Press, 1934), p. 112.

CHAPTER TEN

1. FSCC, *Report of the Federal Surplus Commodities Corporation for the Calendar Year 1936* (Washington: U.S. Government Printing Office, 1937), p. 1.
2. Southard to Hopkins, August 4, 1934, FSRC Files.
3. Minutes of the Food Survey Committee, Meetings of August 29, August 31, September 7, September 18, and October 9, 1934; "Memorandum from the Department of Agriculture on Food Purchases," Agricultural History Branch Files, USDA.
4. Minutes of the Meeting of the Board of Directors of the Federal Surplus Relief Corporation, December 6, 1934, Hopkins Papers, Roosevelt Library.
5. Ezekial to Wallace, November 1, 1934, Secretary of Agriculture's Files.
6. Roosevelt, "Annual Message to Congress, January 4, 1935, *Public Papers and Addresses*, pp. 19–20.
7. *Ibid.*, p. 20.
8. Committee on Economic Security, *Report to the President*, June 15, 1935, reprinted in Brown, *Public Relief*, pp. 303–304.
9. Donald Howard, *The WPA and Federal Relief Policy* (New York: Russell Sage Foundation, 1943), p. 809.
10. Arthur Schlesinger, Jr., *The Politics of Upheaval*, vol. 3 of *The Age of Roosevelt*, pp. 343–347.
11. Brown, *Public Relief*, p. 312.
12. Hopkins, *Spending to Save*, p. 114.
13. Baker to Hopkins, January 31, 1935, FERA Files.
14. Southard to Hopkins, February 2, 1935, FSRC Files.
15. Southard to Hopkins, February 14, 1935, FSRC Files.
16. Baker to Hopkins, May 7, 1935, FERA Files.
17. Baker to Hopkins, May 9, 1935, FERA Files.
18. Southard to Tugwell, April 5, 1935, FSRC Files.
19. Baker to Winslow Carlton, May 10, 1935, FERA Files.
20. The emerging works program contained many flaws, not only in its implementation but also in its basic design. Many social work leaders who had consistently urged that work, not relief, was the appropriate response to unemployment were disappointed in the new program, and Hopkins, a master of the art of pragmatic compromise, was not able to realize his fondest hopes. Nevertheless, the works program was far more consonant with the leading thought among social workers and relief administrators than was sur-

plus commodity distribution. For a revealing discussion of social workers' criticisms of the work programs of the New Deal, see Bremer, *Depression Winters*, esp. ch. 11, pp. 126–141.

21. Mordecai Ezekial, "Memorandum From the Food Survey Committee," to members of the AAA Operating Council, March 4, 1935, AAA Legal Division Files.

22. Jonathan Garst to H. A. Wallace, January 29, 1935, Secretary of Agriculture's Files.

23. *Ibid.*

24. Food Survey Committee, "Preliminary draft of a report of Department of Agriculture to the National Emergency Council," March 1935, AAA Legal Division Files.

25. *Ibid.*; Ezekial, "Memorandum from the Food Survey Committee," March 4, 1935, AAA Legal Division Files.

26. Food Survey Committee, Preliminary draft of report to NEC, and minutes of winter 1935 meetings, Agricultural History Branch Files, USDA.

27. Baldwin, *Poverty and Politics*, pp. 76–81.

28. For a cogent summary of attempts to assess the displacement effect, see Grubbs, *Cry from the Cotton*, pp. 24–26. For a more extensive review, see Conrad, *Forgotten Farmers*, esp. pp. 50–82.

29. Fred Frey and T. Lynn Smith, "The Influence of the AAA Cotton Program upon the Tenant, Cropper and Laborer," *Rural Sociology* 1 (December 1936), p. 489, quoted in Grubbs, *Cry from the Cotton*, p. 25.

30. Grubbs, *Cry from the Cotton*, pp. 22–25; Conrad, *Forgotten Farmers*, pp. 78, 79.

31. Grubbs, *Cry from the Cotton*, pp. 45, 46.

32. Baldwin, *Poverty and Politics*, p. 81.

33. Baldwin, *Poverty and Politics*, p. 81.

34. Leuchtenburg, *FDR and the New Deal*, p. 139.

35. Lee Pressman to Florence K. Frank, March 9, 1959, letter in possession of the author.

36. Burns, *Roosevelt*, p. 372; Schlesinger, *New Deal*, pp. 79, 80, 346–349; Schlesinger, *Politics of Upheaval*, pp. 343–347.

37. FERA, "The Federal Surplus Relief Corporation," p. 23.

38. Jacob Baker to William Haber, June 1, 1935, FERA Files.

39. William Nunn, memorandum to Jacob Baker, July 5, 1935, FSRC Files.

40. *Ibid.*

41. "Digest of Conference in Mr. Baker's Office," July 11, 1935, FSRC Files.

42. *Ibid.*

43. Jones Memoir, COHC, p. 867.

44. *Ibid.*, p. 869.

45. For a discussion of the attack on the AAA from the viewpoint of the legislation's advocates in the American Farm Bureau Federation, see Edward A. O'Neal, "Major Issues Facing Agriculture," *The Bureau Farmer*, May 1935, pp. 4, 12.

46. Jones Memoir, COHC, pp. 870, 880.

47. House Committee on Agriculture, *Hearings on a bill to Amend the Agricultural Adjustment Act, H.R. 5585*, 74th Cong., 1st sess., February 26, 27, 28, March 1, 5, 6, 1935, pp. 132, 228–232, 336–338.

48. Jones Memoir, COHC, p. 880; House Committee on Rules, *Hearings on a bill to Amend the Agricultural Adjustment Act, H.R. 8052*, 74 Cong., 1st sess., May 23, 1935, pp. 19, 20.

49. Marvin Jones in Joseph M. Ray, ed., *Marvin Jones Memoirs, 1917–1973: Fifty-Six Years of Continuing Service in All Three Branches of the Federal Government* (El Paso: Texas Western Press, 1973), p. 112.

50. Jesse Tapp to Solicitor Seth Thomas, July 29, 1935, USDA Solicitor's Files.

51. A copy of this note was provided by Dr. Gladys Baker of the Agricultural History Branch of USDA who indicated that the original was in the papers of Henry Wallace in the possession of his family.

52. Henry Wallace Memoir, COHC, vol. 2, p. 262.

53. Chester Davis to Harry Hopkins, August 6, 1935, FSRC Files.

54. Chester Davis, "Memorandum of Understanding Regarding the Purchase and Distribution of Surplus Agricultural Commodities," August 6, 1935, FSRC Files.

55. R. G. Tugwell to Harry L. Hopkins, August 6, 1935, FSRC Files.

56. Marvin Jones, Speech Marking the 35th Anniversary of the Signing of the Agricultural Adjustment Act, May 15, 1968, Agricultural History Branch Records, USDA.

57. *Ibid.*

58. *Ibid.*

59. Public Law 320, 74th Cong., August 24, 1935. 49 Stat. 774.

60. FSRC, Minutes of Special Meeting of the Board of Directors, October 24, 1935, Harry Hopkins Papers, Roosevelt Library.

61. *Ibid.*; FSCC, Minutes of the Special Meeting of the Board of Directors, November 12, 1935, FSCC Files; Minutes of FSRC Board Meeting, September 16, 1935, Hopkins Papers, Roosevelt Library.

62. FSRC, Memorandum of a Meeting of the Board of Directors, September 16, 1935, Hopkins Papers, Roosevelt Library. A more detailed account of the transfer process is included in Janet E. Poppendieck, "Breadlines Knee Deep in Wheat: The Initiation of Federal Domestic Food Assistance" (Ph.D. diss., Brandeis University, 1978).

63. Aubrey Williams, Acting Administrator, FERA, to Henry Wallace, October 24, 1935, Secretary of Agriculture's Files.

64. James E. Brickett, "Memorandum to Mr. F. R. Wilcox, June 29, 1936, FSCC Files.

65. Chester Davis to Henry Wallace, November 7, 1935, AAA Legal Division Files.

66. Jacob Baker to Mr. Linden, October 28, 1935, AAA Legal Division Files.

67. Mastin G. White to Golden W. Bell, December 19, 1935, AAA Legal Division Files.

68. FSCC, *Annual Report, 1935*, p. 1.
69. Roosevelt, *Public Papers and Addresses*, p. 20.
70. John Morton Blum, *From the Morgenthau Diaries: Years of Crisis, 1928–1938* (Boston: Houghton Mifflin, 1959), pp. 243–244.
71. Transcript of a staff meeting, May 13, 1938, Morgenthau Diaries, book 124, pp. 401, 402; George Haas, Memorandum of meeting at the White House, May 31, 1938, Morgenthau Diaries, book 126, pp. 320–322, Roosevelt Library.
72. Aubrey Williams to Henry Wallace, October 24, 1935, Secretary of Agriculture's Files.
73. *Ibid.*
74. Brown, *Public Relief*, pp. 233, 234.
75. C. M. Bookman, "The Federal Emergency Relief Administration: Its Problems and Significance," *Proceedings* of the National Conference of Social Work, 1934, p. 20.
76. See, for example, the account of surplus commodity distribution in a community in northern Michigan in Louise V. Armstrong, *We Too Are The People* (Boston: Little, Brown: 1938).

CHAPTER ELEVEN

1. Mastin G. White, Memorandum to the Administrator, October 15, 1935, AAA Administrator's Files, Record Group 45, National Archives.
2. J. R. McCarl, Comptroller General of the United States, to Henry Wallace, undated fragment of letter, FSCC Files.
3. House of Representatives, *House Report*, 74th Cong., 1st sess., 1935, p. 1241.
4. Public Law 440, 74th Cong., February 11, 1936, 49 Stat 1118.
5. Even this legislation did not fully satisfy the comptroller, who still believed that donation for relief did not constitute diversion. Consequently, on February 29, 1936, the seventy-fourth Congress passed Public Law 462 (49 Stat 1151), which provided that the secretary of agriculture should have the final authority to determine what constituted "diversion," "normal production," and the "normal channels of trade and commerce."
6. H. C. Albin to the Honorable Burton K. Wheeler, January 31, 1936, FSCC Files.
7. Mastin G. White to Golden W. Bell, December 18, 1935, AAA Legal Division Files.
8. D. W. Bell, Acting Budget Director, to the Attorney General, n.d., AAA Legal Division Files.
9. J. P. Wenchel, "Memorandum on question of authority of the President to authorize a change in the Charter of the Federal Surplus Relief Corporation," December 17, 1935, AAA Legal Division Files.
10. Brown, *Public Relief*, p. 325.
11. *Ibid.*, p. 318.

12. *Ibid.*, pp. 318–322.
13. Jesse W. Tapp to Harry Hopkins, June 29, 1936, FSCC Files.
14. FSCC, *Annual Report of the Federal Surplus Commodities Corporation for the Fiscal Year 1937* (Washington: U.S. Government Printing Office, 1937).
15. C. M. Bookman, "The Essentials of an Adequate Relief Program, *Proceedings* of the National Conference of Social Work, 67th sess., 1940 (New York: Columbia University Press, 1940), pp. 161, 165.
16. Jean Sinnock and others, *The Denver Relief Study: A Study of 304 General Relief Cases Known to the Denver Bureau of Public Welfare on January 15, 1940*, reported in Howard, *WPA and Federal Relief*, p. 93.
17. Howard, *WPA and Federal Relief*, pp. 85–96.
18. Blum, *From the Morgenthau Diaries*, pp. 243, 244.
19. Piven and Cloward, *Regulating the Poor*, pp. 116–117, 123–145.
20. Aubrey Williams, "A Year of Relief," *Proceedings* of the National Conference of Social Work, 1934, pp. 159–160.
21. Howard, *WPA and Federal Relief*, p. 72.
22. Norman Leon Gold, "Food Needs and Economic Surpluses," speech to the Nutrition Forum, Chicago, February 10, 1941, typescript in FSCC Files.
23. Milo Perkins, "The Challenge of Underconsumption," pamphlet reprinting an address to the National Farm Institute (Washington: U.S. Government Printing Office, 1940), pp. 3–5.
24. FSCC, *Report, Calendar Year 1935*, p. 1.
25. Hugh S. Ahern, typescript of an article prepared for submission, February 20, 1937, p. 6, FSCC Files.
26. Public Law 165, 75th Cong., June 23, 1937, 50 Stat 323.
27. James Brickett, Notes on Conference with a group from the Commodities Local of the City Project Council, Mr. Green, Chairman, FSCC Files.
28. Department of Agriculture, "Report of the Interbureau Planning Committee on Distribution Programs," December 19, 1941, mimeographed copy, Agricultural History Branch Files, USDA.
29. FSCC, *Report, Calendar Year 1935*, p. 2.
30. Davis's recollections of the corporation make an interesting comparison with those of Frank, Pressman, or Tugwell. Davis notes only that: "I was elected president of the Federal Surplus Commodities Corporation. That was evidence of the trend away from RFC and toward the Department operations. It was one of the Branches of the Commodity Credit Corporation. It was just an operation." Chester Davis Memoir, COHC, p. 443.
31. Davis Memoir, COHC, p. 373. Not all of his associates recalled Tapp so fondly. The group centered in the general counsel's office perceived him as a representative—or at least a defender—of the interests of large agribusiness and canning corporations affiliated with the powerful California Gianinni family and the Bank of America (Pressman to Florence Frank, March 19, 1959, in possession of author). Jerome Frank's recollections are particularly colorful:

Even in this secret record I do not want to commit my views on Mr. Tapp. Let's just say that instead of a "city slicker," he was a country slicker . . . everywhere in his sweet and gentle manner, Jess was putting his coils around things so that you never knew just what was happening. You had to watch every minute because something would be brought to you in innocuous form that he knew to be exactly what he had been told you would never accept as legally valid. (Frank Memoir, COHC, pp. 151, 152).

32. Jesse W. Tapp Memoir, COHC, pp. 1–28, 83, 84, 89, 94–98, 103, 104, 112, 113, 122, 123, 136, 143.
33. Hugh S. Ahern, typescript of article, FSCC Files.
34. FSCC, *Report of the Federal Surplus Commodities Corporation for the Fiscal Year 1938* (Washington: U.S. Government Printing Office, 1938), pp. 5, 6.
35. FSCC, *Report, Calendar Year 1936*, p. 2.
36. Amos A. Merril, B. C. Shaw, and others, to Henry Wallace, November 4, 1938, Roosevelt Papers, Roosevelt Library.
37. Amos A. Merril to President Franklin D. Roosevelt, November 8, 1938, Roosevelt Papers, Roosevelt Library.
38. FSCC, *Report, Calendar Year 1936*, p. 3.
39. House Committee on Agriculture, *Hearings on S. 2439*, 75th Cong., 1st sess., June 11, 1937, p. 9.
40. USDA, "Report of the Interbureau Planning Committee on Food Distribution Programs," p. 26, Agricultural History Branch Files, USDA.
41. O. C. Stine Memoir, COHC, p. 381.
42. House Committee on Agriculture, *Hearings on S.2439*, 75th Cong., 1st sess., June 11, 1937, pp. 9, 13, 24, 25.
43. Tapp Memoir, COHC, p. 154.
44. USDA, "Report of the Interbureau Planning Committee on Food Distribution Programs," p. 25.
45. FSCC, "Report of the Federal Surplus Commodities Corporation, July 1, 1937 through December 31, 1937," p. 1, typescript in FSCC Files.
46. FSCC, *Report, Fiscal Year 1938*, p. 11.
47. FSCC, *Report, Calendar Year 1936*, p. 4.
48. B. Frank Whelchel, Gainseville, Georgia, to the President, October 24, 1938, telegram, FSCC Files.
49. James E. Brickett to I. M. Brandford, October 19, 1938, FSCC Files.
50. Ahern, typescript, p. 5.
51. Paul Appleby to R. M. Evans, April 29, 1937, Secretary of Agriculture's Files.
52. Howard, *WPA and Federal Relief*, p. 71.
53. FSCC, *Report, Fiscal 1938*, p. 13.
54. *Ibid.*, p. 10.
55. Howard, *WPA and Federal Relief*, pp. 211, 212.
56. FSCC, *Report, Fiscal 1938*, p. 10.
57. Mastin G. White to Golden W. Bell, December 19, 1935, AAA Legal Division Files.

58. Figures concerning the amounts of commodities shipped by the corporation are difficult to compare; some are by weight, some by bushels and other measures. Some annual reports provide figures on items purchased, others on items distributed. The comparative weight given here is derived from Ahern's manuscript that reports that the corporation shipped 2 billion pounds of foodstuffs in the period October 1933 to the beginning of 1937, of which four hundred thousand pounds were shipped in 1936.

59. Frank Memoir, COHC, p. 23.

60. Wallace, *New Frontiers*, p. 139.

61. Paul Appleby Memoir, COHC, p. 95.

62. Frank Memoir, COHC, pp. 22, 23.

63. Henry Morgenthau, Transcript of staff meeting, May 25, 1938, Morgenthau Diaries, book 126, pp. 172, 173, Roosevelt Library.

64. Appleby Memoir, COHC, pp. 97–98.

65. Frank Memoir, COHC, p. 158.

66. American Farm Bureau Federation, "Resolutions, 1919–1947," pp. 79.1, 79.2.

67. *Ibid.*

68. Rupert Vance to William Watts Ball, September 15, 1934 quoted in Grubbs, *Cry from the Cotton*, p. 26.

69. Clarke A. Chambers, *California Farm Organizations: A Historical Study of the Grange, the Farm Bureau and the Associated Farmers, 1929–1941* (Berkeley: University of California Press, 1952), p. 82.

70. Grubbs, *Cry From the Cotton*, p. 28.

71. Chambers, *California Farm Organizations*, pp. 82–97.

72. James Schlesinger, "Systems Analysis and the Political Process," *Journal of Law and Economics* 11 (October 1968), p. 195.

73. For a discussion of the activities and impact of the hunger lobby of the 1970s, see Jeffrey M. Berry, "Consumers and the Hunger Lobby," in Don F. Hadwiger and Ross B. Talbot, eds., *Food Policy and Farm Programs*, Proceedings of the Academy of Political Science, vol. 34 (New York: Academy of Political Science, 1982), pp. 68–78; Janet E. Poppendieck, "Policy, Advocacy and Justice: The Case of Food Assistance Reform," in David and Eva Gil, eds., *Toward Social and Economic Justice* (Cambridge, Mass.: Schenkman, 1985).

74. House Committee on Agriculture, *Hearings on S.2439*, June 11, 1937, 75th Congress, 1st sess., pp. 24, 25.

75. Varden Fuller, "Political Pressures and Income Distribution," pp. 255, 256.

CHAPTER TWELVE

1. Burns, *Roosevelt*, pp. 319–339.

2. Leuchtenburg, *FDR and the New Deal*, pp. 244–251.

3. "Spend or Starve," *The Nation*, April 16, 1938, pp. 428, 429.

4. Bruce Bliven, "Shall They Starve? *New Republic*, April 13, 1938, p. 299.

5. Samuel Lubell and Walter Everett, "The Breakdown of Relief," *The Nation*, August 20, 1938, p. 171.

6. Bliven, "Shall They Starve," p. 300.
7. Harold L. Ickes, *The Secret Diary of Harold L. Ickes, The Inside Struggle, 1936–1939* (New York: Simon and Schuster, 1954), p. 501.
8. Henry Morgenthau, Jr., transcript of a meeting with staff regarding the relief situation, May 12, 1938, Morgenthau Diaries, book 124, pp. 362–363, Roosevelt Library.
9. Transcript of telephone conversation between Henry Morgenthau, Jr., and Surgeon General Thomas Parran, May 16, 1938, Morgenthau Diaries, book 125, p. 35.
10. Transcript of staff meeting, May 12, 1938, Morgenthau Diaries, book 124, pp. 369, 381.
11. Transcript of staff meeting, May 13, 1938, Morgenthau Diaries, book 124, p. 401.
12. Transcript of staff meeting, May 12, 1938, Morgenthau Diaries, book 124, pp. 366, 367.
13. Jacob Fisher, *The Response of Social Work to the Depression* (Cambridge: Schenkman, 1980), pp. 176–180.
14. *New York Times*, May 20, 1938.
15. George Haas to Henry Morgenthau, Jr., Memorandum on a Meeting at the White House, May 31, 1938, Morgenthau Diaries, book 126, pp. 320, 321.
16. *Ibid.*
17. Transcript of staff meeting, May 13, 1938, Morgenthau Diaries, book 124, pp. 401, 402.
18. Transcript of phone conversation between Henry Morgenthau, Jr., and Eleanor Roosevelt, May 23, 1938, Morgenthau Diaries, book 125, pp. 466, 467.
19. Transcript of staff meeting, May 12, 1938, Morgenthau Diaries, book 124, p. 367.
20. Years later, this same confusion over the use of Section 32 was to resurface in another controversy over food for the hungry. On July 1, 1967, in the midst of the nation's rediscovery of hunger, Secretary of Agriculture Orville Freeman returned $200 million of unspent Section 32 funds to the treasury. Asked by Senator Javits how he could return so much money to the treasury while there were hungry people in need of food, the secretary explained, according to Nick Kotz, "that he could only use these Section 32 funds to buy perishable commodities such as beef, pork, citrus fruits, or vegetables when market prices fell below 90 percent of parity." Later, however, Kotz reported, Agriculture Undersecretary John Schnittker clarified that virtually any crops could have been bought legally with the Section 32 funds. "Surplus foods are what the lawyers say they are," food program administrator Rodney Leonard later admitted. "We begin buying off commodities from whatever commodity group has enough muscle to get included." Kotz, *Let Them Eat Promises*, p. 71.
21. Transcript of staff meeting, May 25, 1938, Morgenthau Diaries, book 126, pp. 172–173.
22. *New York Times*, May 19, 1938.

23. Miss Lonigan to Secretary Morgenthau, Memorandum, May 25, 1938, Morgenthau Diaries, book 126, pp. 126, 127.
24. Transcript of staff meeting, May 25, 1938, Morgenthau Diaries, book 126, p. 174.
25. James E. Brickett to J. Tapp, May 24, 1938, memorandum, Morgenthau Diaries, book 126, p. 35.
26. FSCC, *Report, Fiscal Year 1938*, p. 11.
27. Transcript of staff meeting, November 15, 1938, Morgenthau Diaries, book 151, pp. 16-E, 16-F.
28. Transcript of staff meeting, May 13, 1938, Morgenthau Diaries, book 124, p. 411.
29. Roosevelt, Second Inaugural Address, January 20, 1937, *Public Papers and Addresses*, p. 4.
30. Benedict, *Farm Problem*, pp. 286–289, 312–313. For an account of the Agriculture Department's role in stimulating the establishment of school lunch programs, see Gordon W. Gunderson, *The National School Lunch Program: Background and Development* (Washington: U.S. Government Printing Office, 1971). See also, Gladys L. Baker et al., *Century of Service*, pp. 185–186.
31. Benedict, *Farm Problem*, pp. 289–294; U.S. Agricultural Adjustment Administration, *Report of the Administrative Official in Charge of Surplus Removal and Marketing Agreement Programs, 1940* (Washington: U.S. Government Printing Office, 1941), pp. 10–13; and U.S. Agricultural Adjustment Administration, Report of the Administrator of Surplus Marketing Administration, 1941 (Washington: U.S. Government Printing Office, 1942), pp. 15–19.
32. See Howard, *WPA and Federal Relief*, pp. 557–558, 569, 573, 574 for discussions of the failure of wartime employment to eliminate unemployment. See Donald E. Montgomery, "Third of Nation Can't Afford Full Food Rations," *PM Daily Picture Magazine*, January 12, 1943, for a discussion of the termination of the Food Stamp Program.
33. In fact, the surplus purchase and distribution functions of the corporation had been transferred in a reorganization plan effective June 30, 1940, to the Department of Agriculture's Surplus Marketing Administration that combined the functions of the FSCC and those of the Division of Marketing and Marketing Agreements. The corporation continued to exist as a legal entity until 1942 and was used briefly for other purposes, notably the purchase of naval stores. For a discussion of the termination of statewide distribution projects and the shift to local option and control, see Howard Thorkelson, "Federal Food Programs and Hunger," in Jeremy Larner and Irving Howe, eds., *Poverty: Views from the Left* (New York: William Morrow, 1968), p. 187.
34. *Agricultural Statistics*, 1973, Table 797, Food and Nutrition Service Programs, (Washington, D.C.: Government Printing Office, 1974), p. 568; Maurice MacDonald, *Food, Stamps, and Income Maintenance* (New York: Academic Press, 1977), p. 5; Kotz, *Let Them Eat Promises*, pp. 50, 51.

35. MacDonald, *Food, Stamps*, pp. 5–7; Benedict, *Farm Problem*, pp. 289, 290.
36. Lowi, *End of Liberalism*, pp. 102–115.
37. Randall B. Ripley, "Legislative Bargaining and the Food Stamp Act, 1964," in Frederic N. Cleveland, et al., *Congress and Urban Problems, A Casebook on the Legislative Process* (Washington: Brookings Institution, 1969), pp. 279–288.
38. Ripley, "Legislative Bargaining," pp. 288–291; MacDonald, *Food, Stamps*, pp. 6–7.
39. Ripley, "Legislative Bargaining," pp. 291–300.
40. *Ibid.*, p. 294.
41. *Ibid.*, pp. 300–310.
42. Kotz, *Let Them Eat Promises*, p. 56.
43. George McGovern in foreword to Nick Kotz, *Let Them Eat Promises*, p. vii.
44. Robert F. Kennedy, excerpts from remarks at Valparaiso University, April 29, 1968, reprinted as an introductory comment in the Citizens Board of Inquiry into Hunger and Malnutrition in the United States, *Hunger USA* (Boston: Beacon Press, 1968), p. 7.
45. *Ibid.*
46. Senate Committee on Nutrition and Human Needs, *Hearings, Part 1: Problems and Prospects*, 90th Cong., 2d sess., December 1968, p. 9.
47. Senate Select Committee on Nutrition and Human Needs, *Hearings, Part 2: USDA. HEW and OEO Officials*, 90th Cong., 2d sess., January 1969, pp. 225–226.
48. George McGovern in Kotz, *Let Them Eat Promises*, p. viii.
49. For critiques of federal domestic food assistance in the late 1960s and early 1970s, see Citizens Board, *Hunger USA* and Citizens Board, *Hunger USA Revisited* (Atlanta: Southern Regional Council, 1973); *Hearings* of the Senate Select Committee on Nutrition and Human Needs; and Kotz, *Let Them Eat Promises*.
50. See Kotz, *Let Them Eat Promises*, p. 56.
51. For a summary of the reforms achieved in the 1967–1977 decade, see Nick Kotz, *Hunger in America: The Federal Response* (New York: Field Foundation, 1979).
52. Winifred Bell, *Contemporary Social Welfare* (New York: Macmillan, 1983), pp. 168, 169.
53. Berry, "Consumers and the Hunger Lobby," p. 68.

INDEX